THE BLOODY BRIDGE

And other Papers

Relating to the Insurrection of 1641

(SIR PHELIM O'NEILL'S REBELLION).

BY

THOMAS FITZPATRICK, LL.D.

KENNIKAT PRESS SCHOLARLY REPRINTS

Ralph Adams Brown, Senior Editor

Series In

IRISH HISTORY AND CULTURE

Under the General Editorial Supervision of

Gilbert A. Cahill

Professor of History, State University of New York

THE BLOODY BRIDGE

And other Papers

Relating to the Insurrection of 1641

(SIR PHELIM O'NEILL'S REBELLION).

BY

THOMAS FITZPATRICK, LL.D.

KENNIKAT PRESS
Port Washington, N. Y./London

THE BLOODY BRIDGE

First published in 1903
Reissued in 1970 by Kennikat Press
Library of Congress Catalog Card No: 71-102602
SBN 8046-0779-6

Manufactured by Taylor Publishing Company   Dallas, Texas

KENNIKAT SERIES IN IRISH HISTORY AND CULTURE

CONTENTS.

V.—THE IMITATION.

VI.—ACCEPTABLE SERVICE.

INTRODUCTION.

ALTHOUGH full or regular narrative is not attempted in the present work, I trust that something has been done towards elucidating the history of a period "about which men wrote as desperately as they fought."

In answer to those who may be disposed to ask why such a publication should now be attempted, I wish to say here that the following papers have no other object than to lay bare the groundless nature of the charges which for centuries, and down even to the present hour, have been employed to create disunion, and foster animosities among different sections of the inhabitants of Ireland.

There was, perhaps, no national movement known to history which could more readily have been composed than the Irish Insurrection of 1641—Rebellion, except in the technical sense, it was not. And never was the action of an entire people so elaborately, so disingenuously, misrepresented. It was, perhaps, of the fitness of things, that the subjects who had themselves taken up arms against their legitimate Sovereign should the most affect wonder, or indignation, that, at the same time, the Catholic people of Ireland should find any cause for complaint.

That a people so treated before, and especially during, the Civil War, should be wholly crimeless, were contrary to all experience of Mankind. The Insurrection of 1641 did not differ so much from the great movements for redress of long-standing grievances as to be altogether blameless. There were many crimes committed which must be deplored and condemned.

On the other hand, the alleged "Massacre"—the Massacre of Milton, Temple, Borlase, May, Rushworth, Cox, Harris, Carlyle, and Froude—is a stupendous falsehood, even on the showing of the very documents upon which the charge is, ignorantly or malignantly, based, namely, the Depositions preserved in Trinity College, Dublin.

Of these Depositions I have a good deal more to say than counts to their credit, or to the credit of those who were concerned in getting them up. But this I say here, as the result of my own examination of the MSS. —

That while the Depositions were intended to blacken to the utmost the Irish Catholics of the time—indeed of all time—the fact (heretofore not sufficiently, if at all, recognised) is, that so far from affording proof or indication of general massacre, either attempted or intended, the volumes contain ample evidence—all the more cogent because incidental and involuntary, if not reluctant—of the baselessness and malignity of such imputations.

It is hardly possible for any one who has got more than a child's idea of evidence, to go any considerable way into these documents without perceiving the vile purpose to which they were directed. And yet the standard writers who profess to base their allegations of massacre and cruelties on the " sworn evidence taken by Royal Commissioners, appointed under the Broad Seal of Ireland," have not scrupled to make the most unfair and misleading use of the supposed testimony.

Of this unjustifiable use of the Depositions some striking instances will be found in the following articles. Starting with the assumption that the " Irish Rebellion of 1641 " was simply the outcome of the depravity, or rather the religion, of the people who, at the sacrifice of worldly advantages, had clung to the Faith of their Fathers, and in no manner connected with the government or misgovernment of the country, many writers of eminence, in the most shameless manner, suppress leading facts, and distort others, to make the history of Ireland conform to their favourite ideal. So much has it become the settled practice—a thing apparently more of instinct than of reason—on the part of the many who feel impelled to parade their ignorance of Irish history or their fanatical attitude towards the religion of the great majority of the Irish people, that it may now seem an unwarrantable proceeding to attempt the *dis*proof of calumnies so long standing and so deep seated, by drawing upon what has come to be regarded as the particular repertory of the horror-mongers. Yet, I am persuaded that sufficient refutation of the Temple-Froude school of writers—and they are unfortunately the guiding lights of the many—may be found in the very documents which they claim as their own.

To make clear how unwarrantable has been the practices of the writers of "the things called histories," * I begin with a full examination of the alleged sources of Walter Harris's *View of the Ancient and Present State of the County Down* (1744). The author alleges, in general terms, the authority of the T.C.D. depositions for the accounts of massacre and cruelties which make so imposing a figure in his book. The result of my examination I give in detail.

In the first and title paper of the series, I examine, in the light of the later as well as the earlier depositions, the alleged cold-blooded massacre of THE BLOODY BRIDGE (or "The Ballagh"), near Newcastle, in the County Down. Harris, using only the hearsay statements taken by the Parsons-Borlase Commissioners, and ignoring the fuller investigation before the Commonwealth Commissioners sitting at Carrickfergus, in the Spring of 1653, has given a distorted and exaggerated account of an incident which the later evidence shows to have been, at the worst, but an act of wild retaliation, the number executed not exceeding one-fifth of what Harris, following Borlase, suggests. The story, as told by Harris, has been adopted by Dr. Reid, the Rev. George Hill,† Dr. Knox, and others of less note.

I have collected all the depositions and examinations touching upon the subject, and I have given everything which I believe to be any way pertinent to the inquiry, the greater part now printed for the first time. It is perfectly clear from all the circumstances that the prisoners were taken to Newcastle to be exchanged for Irish prisoners in the hands of the Scottish commanders of Down; and that some eight or ten were put to death in return for the hanging of the Irish prisoners. Yet Harris, and his followers, will have it that the prisoners, who had been over two months in the hands of the Insurgent leaders at Newry, were conveyed all the way, and by a needlessly circuitous route, to Newcastle, only to be slaughtered in cold blood.

* Edmund Burke.

† To those who are familiar with the late Rev. George Hill's invaluable researches, it may seem that I have been unduly severe in my strictures (in art. iv. especially). My remarks apply to Mr. Hill only as he has allowed himself, in his annotations to the *Montgomery MSS.*, to be misled by Harris. In his really great book, *The Macdonnells of Antrim*, which he worked up from his own investigations, he has shown the breadth of view, the enlightenment, and impartiality, of the scholar and the historian. Had he only made full investigation for himself of the grounds on which Harris has preferred such charges, it is more than likely he would never have allowed his name to be associated with much that he has taken on trust from that reputed authority (*v. infra*, note, p. xxiv).

There is not even a hint given by this historian that any
cruelty was practised upon "the Rebels." Yet Harris had
before him Mr. High Sheriff Hill's boastful account of the
execution " by martial law of above three score notorious
Rebels " (*v.* p. 135) and of other "acceptable services." It
hardly came within the province of the chroniclers of that
period to take any notice of the wholesale butchery of the
Irish, except when the "service" was worthy of particular
record in favour of the perpetrators. There are, indeed,
some obscure, almost enigmatical, allusions in the *Montgomery Manuscripts* to practices which, had the writer been
more explicit, would, doubtless, have thrown light upon the
tragedies of " The Ballagh " and Ballee (p. 98).

In the second paper—" The Surprisal of the Newry"—
ample proof is adduced of a serious misapplication of the
Depositions.   Dr. Reid states that, on the capture of the
town by the Rebels, fifteen of the townspeople were hanged
(*v.* extract on p. 26).   Harris dilates on the sufferings of
the Protestant inhabitants, but mentions no execution or
murder at or within the town.   Dr. Knox repeats the
charge of murder in this aggravated form :—" Sir Con
Magennis attacked and took the castle and town, destroyed
the church,* and put many of the inhabitants to the
sword." Reid makes parenthetic allusion to the Depositions
as his authority.   I am unable to find anything in the
collection to favour Reid's view.   Not one of the
dozen or more Newry deponents appears to have heard of
that hanging, or putting to the sword, of townspeople
there, during the twenty-seven weeks of Insurgent occupation, excepting the two cases related at length (pp. 30-32).
If Reid and Knox may be supposed to allude to the
Ballaghonery tragedy, they must make the same occurrence
count twice—first in October, and again in the following
January.   Moreover, Reid fixed the number put to death at
" The Ballagh" as " thirteen," not " fifteen." The matter
is an instance of the free hand which historians exercise
when dealing with the supposed events of the period.†

---

* No authority for this. Dr. Knox mixes up here what is said to have
happened at Armagh in the following May.

† In the Contents (p. xiv.) to vol. i., Miss Hickson's *Ireland in the 17th
Century, or The Irish Massacres of 1641-2,* we find " Massacres at Newry, pp.
294-313." On p. 294 (Joanna Constable) we read : "About the time that the
Newry was taken and won again from the rebels, they, ranging up and down
like merciless wolves, did most barbarously drown at one time in the Blackwater," etc., but nothing is said about anything occurring at or near Newry.

I am satisfied there was no massacre in or near Newry before the beginning of May, 1642, when the Scots army converted the town and neighbourhood into a " Covenant shambles."

How the " relieving " forces signalised their advance to " The Newry," their triumph there, as well as the return march of the main body through Iveagh and Kinelarty, is shown by the extracts from Pike, Turner, and the " General-Major " (Monroe) himself. One further incident of the occupation I add here :—

Near Newry, we read of Monroe and his soldiers " killing in one day 700 country people—men, women, and children—who were driving away their cattle ; " while the parties he sent into Westmeath and Longford " burned the country, and put to the sword all the country people that they met."*

The contemporary account of the slaughter of the 700 in the mountains between Newry and Dundalk is to be found in the T.C.D. MS., F. 3, 11, Paper No. 23. Having failed to take Charlemont Castle, the army marched to Newry.

The next day another party was sent into the mountains, and a place appointed for them to meet the maine bodie, which marched another way into the mountains passable for the cannon. Att night they mett, and the partie brought in manie cowes, and killed about 40 men or more, and *manie women* and *children* (in all some say 500, some say 700). Of the Scottish souldiers few were lost ; divers or those who came without command in hope of gaine, and are here called plunderers, An Ill race of people and verie hurtfull to an armie, were lost. The Rebells made no fight at all. They had not anie Powder in yᵗ place. Yet they did endeavour to drive back their cowes.

This occurred on the Louth side of Newry, for it is mentioned that the Rebels were driven towards the garrison of Dundalk.

It is shown, in like manner *from the Depositions*, that the alleged " massacre " of 1,200 at Glenwood (parish of Donaghmore), of over 1,000 by Bryan O'Neill, and of

On p. 313 Elizabeth Croker's deposition mentions only the " 15," who, according to her account, were hanged at Newcastle, on the opposite side of the county. This deponent makes complaint of robbery, but does not appear to be aware of any murder in Newry. The only relevant reference to Newry, within the twenty pages indicated, appears to be (p. 300) Mrs. Jane Beare's allegation that her husband and two of her children were murdered between Newry and Dundalk on the way to Dublin ; but how that occurred we are not told. Thomas Richardson (p. 312) has much to say about pillage, nothing about " massacre."

* Lecky, *Hist. of Ireland*, i. 86 ; Carte, *Life of Ormonde*, i. 311.

numerous companies said to be drowned "at the bridge of the Scarvagh," are wild myths, and that other much-advertised instances of "St. Bartholomew in Ireland " are either baseless or are exaggerated and distorted to false-hood. With the exception of Harris (v. art. iv., pp. 92-94), the "historians" and compilers of massacres give the Donaghmore case a wide berth. Yet, it is just as good, and as well sworn, as most of the matter on which they found their indictment of the Irish people and their "faith" (v. p. 150). Those truth-loving people who put their trust in the Depositions ought not to be allowed to dispose of the Glenwood (Donaghmore) case by the facile process of ignoring so monstrous an outcome of testimony "solemnly deposed" by the Rev. Dr. Maxwell, of Tynan (afterwards Bishop of Kilmore). The stereotyped defence that the rebels themselves (not one of them named) are responsible for the charge, I can describe only as fraud upon fraud.

Two papers (Nos. vii. and viii., pp. 163-242) are more particularly devoted to the consideration of the Depositions. As the result of my own examination of the T.C.D. manuscripts, I take up a somewhat independent position. I find myself in accord neither with those who appear to accept the Depositions as so many chapters of Holy Writ, nor with those who will put aside the entire collection as all through unworthy of credit. Both parties, I find, err in treating the papers as *of one character throughout*—either all good, or all worthless. There are depositions and depositions. Never did "witnesses" receive more latitude or more encouragement to indulge to the utmost in story-telling, fiction, calumny, and in downright lying and perjury without fear of frown from human authority. In such circumstances it were altogether childish to doubt that masses of fiction and falsehood have been put on record as testimony "duly sworn" and "solemnly deposed." Yet there are depositions which may be accepted as trust-worthy, so far as the deponent confines himself to what was within his own personal knowledge and experience. But such depositions are not for an Irish "St. Bartholomew."

The Depositions will, I think, be found to be of every degree of merit from worthlessness upward, or, to put it in another form, from fairly trustworthy relation downwards— the "downward" being the general tendency, certainly of those that figure in "Massacre" collections. In many cases a single deposition may be found, in respect of both merit and demerit, as a sort of epitome of the entire lot. In one part of the statement the deponent, with all appearance of candour, relates of what came under his own observation, and then takes excursions through all the wilds and labyrinths of hearsay.

It is altogether needless—in fact, altogether wrong—to charge deponents with the general faults or shortcomings of the Depositions. The weakness or worthlessness of the testimony is due not so much to lack of veracity on the part of examinants, as to the eagerness with which the Commissioners receive "all manner of idle, silly tales about what this body heard another body say,"* to discredit the older inhabitants. Neither were the Commissioners so remiss in receiving without check or question such stuff as came their way. The business of those appointed by Parsons and Borlase was *not* to investigate, but to pile up charges against "the rebels." By the terms of their commission they were debarred (supposing them so inclined) from taking the slightest notice of any crimes or cruelties practised upon the Catholic people of Ireland, who were all indiscriminately dubbed "rebels." With such objects in view, veracity would be assumed as long as the evidence was sufficiently sensational. What more effective machinery—what more promising project—could the art of man devise for misrepresenting and calumniating a despised and hated nation? The Commissioners were in race and religion hostile, and had a special interest in bringing home guilt of the blackest dye against the accused. The "witnesses" were impelled by passion or prejudice on their own part, and by direct incentive or compulsion on the part of the examiners, to make the worst of anything they knew, or ever heard, against the rebels. In short—

The Campaign of Oaths was organised and carried out in the same spirit as the Campaigns of Fire and Sword conducted by Coote, Cole, Saint Leger, Monroe, and others of that race of Attila in Ireland.

The later Commissions, issued under the Commonwealth, though leavened with the old spirit, had more the character of inquiry, the object being to collect evidence for prosecution of prisoners; they took note of some

* Warner.

murders committed by those who were exempted from indictment by the Parsons-Borlase Commissioners. The special feature of the later is that they serve to reflect the infamy of the earlier proceedings.

Much of the "evidence" upon which the "Irish St. Bartholomew" is supposed to rest is simply no evidence at all, so far as that charge is concerned. But it has some significance in a different way; it is good evidence for one thing, and one thing only—the unscrupulous, vindictive, and exterminating policy of the party then in power in Ireland.

It is simply deplorable that, at this time of day, any writer of eminence should think it not beneath him to urge these Depositions as "the eternal witness" of the blood of thousands "barbarously and satanically" shed by the Irish in 1641-42. As the late Mr. John P. Prendergast aptly said of Froude's claim: "The Depositions may more truly be called the eternal witness of British brutality and malignity." And certainly no sane person, who really wished to promote good-will among all classes of his Majesty's subjects, could (except perhaps in ignorance) urge such palpable calumnies against "an integral part of the Empire." For it is to be borne in mind that Froude urges the "eternal witness"—as Temple, Jones, and their following urged it—against a Nation and against a Creed; not simply against those who may have been guilty or suspected of crime.

Take any published collection of Depositions got up on the "Massacre" ideal, and how much of it is evidence? How much of it will bear the slightest cross-examination? Very little will stand this simple test: How could the deponent *swear* so and so? Warner's phrase, "Idle, silly tales," is the correct description of the bulk of the recitals on which Froude and his friends rely.

Dr. Ferdinand Warner (1703-1768) was among the first, if not himself the first, to appreciate the radical faults and innate absurdities which give character to the Depositions generally. His views on the question are all the more valuable that, towards the Catholic religion, he was anything but tolerant, as he shows for himself, in the preface to his *History of the Irish Rebellion of 1641*. He pointed out the vicious and calumnious character of the allegations. Unfortunately, however, he gave so much prominence to the discovery he had made (v., art. vii.,

p. 171) that his more important strictures have been
almost lost sight of in the controversy he originated.

Notwithstanding that Sir John Gilbert considered it
worth while to defend Warner against Reid's criticism,
I must regard the whole discussion as a trumpery matter,
and altogether beside the real question. Concerning the
statements taken by the Commissioners, or other officials,
acting under Government authority, it is, in most cases,
of more relevance to ask, whether the matter is such as the
deponent *could* swear with due regard to the sanctity of an
oath. To my mind, the circumstance that a particular
statement is made upon oath may but accentuate its
worthlessness, as bringing out in deeper hues the un-
scrupulousness of those more immediately concerned in the
inquiry. And such, indeed, is the character of most of
the sworn statements paraded by the " Massacre " people.
Why, the parties who cite such sworn stuff could swear to
the truth of the allegations with as much regard to the
obligations of an oath as most of the deponents on their
lists. Couldn't any one nowadays *who puts trust in the
evidence* also declare that he or she has been credibly
informed and " is verily persuaded," say, of the truth of
Dr. Maxwell's big " massacres ? " (*v.* p. 178.)

Of the latitude accorded to deponents, abundant
illustrations will be cited in the course of this work. Nor
are these in any way exceptional. One has only to look
into any collection of the Depositions already in print to
see how widely these Depositions, as a rule, differ from
evidence. Story-tellers are many, but witnesses few.

This fatal distemper was noticed in a tract, or dialogue,
printed at Kilkenny, on the publication of Dean Jones's
Remonstrance, 1642, (which contains about 80 of the depositions then taken). A manuscript copy of the Kilkenny
tract, with marginal annotations (the whole in the handwriting of Dr. Henry Jones), is preserved in the T.C.D.
MS. F., 3. 11, paper No. 5. The Commissioners are taxed
with " taking hearsay for positive truth." Against which
Jones notes :—

Neither do we take hearesay for positive truth, *but leave it to the
reader to consider of it, as it was presented ; neither are all hearesays
to be cast off, especially being delivered by credible persons and upon
oath.*

Plausible and ingenious as is the Dean's explanation, it
really amounts to this : " We take all who can allege crime

or cruelty against rebels as credible persons. And hearsay may happen to be true "—as a blind man may hit a
mark. The credibility of the person who recites a hearsay
story is no guarantee of the truth of the matter. He may
declare truly that he heard so and so. The story may be
altogether fiction, or it may have gone through many
versions ere it reached him ; and at every turn it gathered
something. Just apply the principle laid down by
Jones to Archdeacon (afterwards Bishop) Maxwell's big
"massacres." Apply it to what Coote swore at Lord
Maguire's trial (*v.* p. 69 *note*; also p. 210).

If the reader wishes to know who were "the rebels" that
"confessed" such astounding massacres to Dr. Robert
Maxwell, he can't find them now—Dr. Jones and his
colleagues took good care of that. Or, again, if we wish
to inquire into the reality of that "ffranciscan" (pp. 179-
185) who is credited with inspiring Dr. Henry Jones's own
masterpiece of deception, we are left altogether in the dark.
From beginning to end, we haven't got a single name of
those "heads of the Romish Clergie and other laymen of
their faction" who are supposed to have planned all the
horrors of the rebellion, at Multifarnham, or "wheresoever."
It is only given us to know that "A man and many others
agitated," etc.

The Dean's plausible explanation is, I submit, at bottom
a confession of fraudulent assent on the part of the Commissioners, and also on the part of those by whose authority
they acted, to fiction, forgery, perjury, as well as the
ravings of fantatics and romancers. When an examinant
poses as "credibly informed," there is an urgent
necessity to look into the sources of his information, and
where that facility is denied (and, as a rule, it is denied us)
the statement is absolutely worthless as evidence against
the accused ; but it may be worth something as against the
accusers, including the Commissioners themselves. In a
few cases, names of second-hand informants are given ; but
we hear no more of these, and are left to speculate in vain,
as to how *they* may have got their information. Take, as
a weighty example, the Lough Kernan case (pp. 87-90).
Mr. Peter Hill is the sole authority for that alleged tragedy ;
and he was not there or thereabout at the time, or at any
time, so far as his deposition shows. He indulges in the
most excruciating detail, alleging as his informant one
Bellow or (Bedloe), who is never again heard of, except he

be one of the gang who long afterwards created such panic in England.　As I point out in art. iv, this Lough Kernan affair appears to have been passed over in later inquiries. I can find only one reference to it, independent of Mr. Peter Hill's story.　Mr. Dunphine, the Minister of Donaghmore, just mentions the matter as a thing he has heard of (p. 90).

It must strike every person who understands anything about evidence that, not unusally, the wrong party is called to give testimony.　It is not the man, or the woman, who has any independent knowledge of the matter, but the man or the woman who is "credibly informed" or who has heard it from "the rebels themselves" (whoever *they* may have been).　And even when the admission is not so made, it will be clear enough that the deponent travels far beyond the limits of experience and personal knowledge.　It is idle to attempt to vindicate the deponent's *veracity* in such cases; the story may be independent of *his* veracity.　There are, indeed, direct statements touching upon isolated occurrences; but these go only a very short way in establishing a "St. Bartholomew."

There can be no better test of the general character of the depositions—no clearer illustration of the morality of that "inquiry," than Dr. Maxwell (p. 178) has furnished in the big "massacres" of which he is the sole "witness." There are over a hundred and twenty depositions in the County Down volume.　I have transcribed over eighty of these, and have looked into all; but I cannot find that any County Down man or woman knew or heard anything of the Glenwood (Donaghmore) massacre of "1,200 helpless Protestants."　Mr. Dunphine, Minister of the Parish, says not a word about it; nor is there the faintest indication that he, or anyone else, was asked a word about it, by the Commissioners, when examined at Carrickfergus in 1653. Yet was the "evidence" of the deposition good enough to fling at Sir Phelim O'Neill in the dock, while the deponent himself (then Bishop of Kilmore) was kept out of sight.　More wonderful still, if such could be, Bishop * Henry Jones (as he then was, although to suit the times, he had put aside the dignity), was certainly in Dublin at the time, and he was not put forward; nor were *his* depositions alluded to, although the files of those papers had

* See *note*, p. 173, also p. 235.

been ransacked for matter to prove the "plotting" and the "generality" of the rebellion. Dr. Jones's "ffranciscan" revelation ought to have been worth a cartload of ordinary depositions. But when it might have been put in evidence it was not produced, nor was the deponent himself, although he took credit for holding in his hands all the threads of the conspiracy from the beginning. *His* story was not for the open court. Besides, there was a second version of the story (*v.*, pp. 195-6.)

It was no secret to Dr. Henry Jones and his colleagues, that the wildest statement possible to put on paper would find ready acceptance in England; that in such a time of panic, there was not the least danger or likelihood of the matter "duly sworn" being closely scanned or criticised by anyone who was opposed to the rebels; and that, to inflame the passions of the superior race, the hearsay horrors would be quite as effective as if the allegations were proved by eye-witnesses—with some people it is so, even to the present hour.

Had the Commissioners, and their employers entertained any honest, straightforward purpose—had they been actuated by any but the most sinister motives—they could not have stopped short, as in most cases they did, with taking sensational relations of massacres and cruelties on mere hearsay, but would have inquired into the *bona-fides* of the relation. It is manifest that they regarded such recitals as more "credible" when not closely looked into; that it would only spoil a good story to seek for the grounds of the relation. And Dr. Maxwell's astounding fables regarding the two counties of Down and Antrim were not, so far as I have been able to ascertain, followed up by any further inquiry in the matters alleged.

The working rule of the Commissioners evidently was, that all who left the country owing to "the rebellion," all who died of the pestilence or otherwise, and all who were killed in fight or conflict, "with many others," should be returned as "murdered and massacred;" and among the "massacred Protestants" it was permissible to include the much greater numbers of rebels who died from similar causes. Had Temple been put in the witness-box, and left to the care of a good cross-examiner, I think it likely enough he would have been obliged to admit that, when he spoke of "300,000, murdered and driven from their homes" in the space of two years, he had in his mind's eye all manner of sufferers, Irish as well as English and Scotch. And when Dr. Jones says (*v.* p. 182), " In some places they are generally *put to the sword* and other miserable ends," the statement is so cunningly contrived as to convey to perhaps 999 out of the thousand, that the Protestants in some localities were all *massacred*, while leaving him an opening to point out, if hard pressed, that "put to the sword," means also "killed in battle," and that " they " includes all who so fell.

It has been assumed—quite too readily, I submit—that it was in the nature of the case that the returns should be so mixed up. And, at this point, Froude and Lecky touch skirts. It was inevitable, according to Mr. Froude, that the " murdered " were confounded with the enormous multitudes that perished in the civil war. Why " inevitable?" Alluding to the Jones Remonstrance (1642), Mr. Lecky says :*

Several depositions contain only hearsay evidence, flying rumours caught up and repeated by ignorant and panic-stricken fugitives. It is very difficult to distinguish in them the cases of those who perished in fight, and it must also be remembered that, during the latter part of the time, the English had been waging what was little less than a war of extermination.

And this characterization applies, not only to the eighty selections made by Dr. Jones for use in England, but generally to the entire mass of sworn allegations against " the rebels." The lack of discrimination, to which both these distinguished writers direct attention, was not due to any necessity in the nature of the case, or to any remissness on the part of either Commissioners or deponents ; it was of the end and aim, the very essence, of that wondrous "inquiry," an inquiry from which Froude's " agonized curiosity " was so much and so conspicuously absent.

In the course of the civil war the insurgents were by far the greatest sufferers. Yet it sometimes happened that they inflicted decisive defeat on their opponents. In art. viii., pp. 221-2, I show how two defeats—one at Garvagh, the other at Ballymoney—suffered by the British of Cole- raine, have, in Dr. Robert Maxwell's sworn recital, been transmuted into " massacres." It is possible that this reverend deponent may have heard, or overheard, while a

* *History of Ireland in 18th Century*, i. 66.

prisoner at Kinard, some boastful accounts of these battles, and of the numbers lost by the enemy. To put down these statements as "confessions" of massacre was easy enough, and regular enough, according to the settled practice of the Commissioners. As I point out (p. 222) such engagements receive no attention in the Depositions. We find there nothing but savage and insatiable fury on one side, and on the other side nothing but meek martyrdom.

The portion of Ulster charged with most of the murders and cruelties—Armagh and adjoining counties—was overrun, time after time, by British forces. One finds little or no trace of these hostile operations in the voluminous statements taken upon oath, except in the prodigious tale of massacres and cruelties. That there were many massacres and outrages committed by the Government forces and their allies is clear enough from such accounts of these expeditions as have been preserved—most of them still in manuscript; and we are not to suppose that the writers of dispatches and diaries thought it necessary to notice all the "services" rendered by the troops in the way of hanging, cutting, drowning, shooting, burning, on their marches through the country. That such "services" were simply the order of the day, was no more than "the State" authorised and commanded; and it would be the most extraordinary thing in the experience of mankind if there were no wild acts of retaliation on the part of those in revolt.

The writers who lay down that the "British sometimes *imitated* the rebels" assume the very antithesis of the real history. Do the worst that they could, the forces and the Loyalists could allege ample warrant from the Lords Justices and Council.

There are in the Depositions many piteous stories of drownings in the Bann and Blackwater rivers, the victims being in all cases Protestants. There is not, so far as I have observed, the most remote allusion to any drowning of rebels in the Bann or the Blackwater. In the T.C.D. MS. volume lettered F. 3. 11, which I have cited above (p. xvii), under No. 23, I find the following:

Upon the 9 of this month, 300 Musquetiers and 40 horse, commanded by Capt. Rawdon, Lighted upon some of the Rebells yt were returned into the woods and boggs of Killulta and Killmore to avoyde the Scottish Armye, and killed divers of them, *drove some of them into Lough Neagh*, where they *were drowned*, and the rest fledde over the Band.

The rebels returning to Killulta and Clanbrassell (the district about Lurgan), Captain Rawdon, with 400 foot and 90 horse, marched to the Bann side and cleared the woods. The fugitives were once more driven over the river. The account adds that the rebels " have acquainted themselves and their cattle so with taking the river that they do it as readily as ducks."

The next day some horsemen were sent back with order to fire the Cabbins alongst the woods in their way to the Lurgan. After they made great haste to overtake the Rebells who fledde towards Charlemont, and, to make speede, left theire carriages, catle, mantles, children, and what else troubled them. There was standing corne in diverse places by the wayside, which saved manie of them. The horse pursued them to the Blackwater side, *where manie of them were drowned, manie were killed in theire way*, and much more execuçon had been done, if the horse had not beene tyred : there was not 12 y^t could come up with Captain Rawdon to the end of the chase.

But, some one may object, this is not sworn—the narrative is not a deposition. It is not. Had it passed through the hands of Dean Jones and his colleagues " under the Broad Seal of Ireland," the drowning and slaughtering of rebels would have been held to be irrelevant, and would not have been taken down.

I have (in art. iii., pp. 83-6) cited several sworn statements relating to the insurgent taking of Downpatrick and the siege of Cromwell Castle beside the town ; and I pointed out that the non-combatants said to have been murdered may have been killed by the defenders of the castle. While a siege of some duration is admitted, no mention is made of any casualty of war—a few " murders," and that's all.

We have a similar representation of what took place at Lurgan. Carte* charges the Irish with violating the terms of capitulation to the extent of committing slaughter of the unresisting. However, one deponent, of the many who were examined at Carrickfergus, incidentally refers to the circumstance that five or six townsmen were killed *in a skirmish* when the rebels came to the town. Carte mentions also the " stout defence" of the castle by the owner, Sir William Bromley (or Brownlow), during " a fortnight's siege." But, with the exception of the one incidental reference, there is not a word in the Depositions about casualities—nothing but " murders." This case I hope to take an early opportunity of more fully investigating.

* *Life of Ormonde*, i. 188.

The alleged massacre at Portnaw, a ford on the lower Bann, near the town of Kilrea, is also an *alias* for a British disaster.

A defeat which the forces under Colonel Archibald Stewart, who was guarding the ford, sustained in January, 1642, at the hands of the afterwards celebrated Alaster M'Donnell, is distorted into a massacre. Several writers, even down to Froude, quoting each other in succession, or relying on the veracious depositions in Trinity College, represent Alaster M'Donnell as initiating the war by an act of treachery and murder at Portnaw. The learned Presbyterian minister, the Rev. George Hill, in his *MacDonnells of Antrim*, places the affair in its true light, and faithfully testifies that young M'Donnell was a formidable antagonist on a fair field ; but he was not a treacherous foe like so many of his opponents.*

Archibald Stewart's move to get a hold on the ford was a good one, had he not fallen a prey to the false security that comes of contempt for the foe.   Had he succeeded, he could have broken the communication between the insurgents of Antrim and those of Derry.   He might also have crushed M'Donnell's smaller company.

After carefully calculating the chances, MacDonnell attacked Stewart early in the morning of the second of January, and when daylight appeared he had scattered the enemy in all directions, leaving several dead in their encampment, and some even in their beds. If Stewart placed no sentinels on the watch, or if his men were asleep when they ought to have been standing to arms, any blame in the affair attaches to him and certainly not to MacDonnell who thus inflicted on him such a signal defeat. (Hill, *Macdonnells*,† p. 63).

History of Down and Connor, by the Rev. James O'Laverty, P.P., M.R.I.A., vol. iv., p. 80.

† In his views of the objects and ways of the insurgents, the learned and impartial author of *The Macdonnells* differs, almost by the breadth of the sky, from his friend, the Rev. Dr. Reid. In a note, p. 62, Mr. Hill, referring to the *History of the Presbyterian Church in Ireland*, i. 300, says :—"Dr. Reid dignifies this young (Alaster) MacDonnell, who never had been previously heard of beyond his own little world of Colonsay, by calling him ' an influential Romanist.'   He was, in fact, a juvenile outcast from his own land on account of his religion, although the son of an ancient house."   In note to p. 83, Mr. Hill has the following :—" *Colkitto.*—Perhaps no other historical Celt has been so often misnamed, as Alaster or Alexander Macdonnell.   He is almost invariably called Collkittagh, or Colkitto, which is exactly a combination of his father's Christian name and nickname.   Dr. Reid (i. 340) styles him ' the noted Collkittagh,' although he had previously explained, at p. 300, that Alaster Macdonnell was the son of Collkittagh.   Spalding, who might have guarded himself against any inaccuracy on this point, actually writes the name *MacColl MacKittish*, whilst English writers have occasionally transformed Alaster into *Colonel Kitto*.   Burton, one of the latest and most pretentious of Scottish historians, actually speaks of this commander as *Macdonald of Colkitto*, thus mistaking the latter word for the name of a residence.   See Burton's *History of Scotland*, vol. vii., p. 189."

Of course, it was a wicked and cruel massacre when " the British " were the sufferers, and had themselves to blame. But it would have been a brilliant and praiseworthy piece of strategy on Stewart's part, had the rebels been caught as their opponents were.

It would therefore appear that the forces of Stewart, like those of Arabi Pacha at Tel-el-Kebir, in the recent Egyptian war, neglected to keep sentinels, but partial historians describe McDonnell's success on the 2nd of January, 1642, as " the Murder of Portnaw," while for the success of his night attack on the 13th of September, 1882, England heaps honour after honour on Sir Garnet Wolsley.—(O'Laverty, *Down and Connor*, iv., 81-2.)

The commonly received British accounts of that period (and not of that period alone) appear to have been dictated in the spirit of Sir Andrew Aguecheek's challenge :

I will waylay thee going home ; where if it be thy chance to kill me—Thou killest me like a rogue and a villain.—*Twelfth Night*, act iii., sc. 4.

Aguecheek's " good and valiant " purpose peers through all the official accounts of the Civil War in Ireland. I have noted some apt illustration in " Urban Vigors : his Account of the Rebells' proceedings in Munster," a letter of 24 pp. foolscap, dated 16th July, 1642, addressed to Dr. Henry Jones (T.C.D., MS., F. 3. 11., No. 21). The writer was chaplain to Lord Broghill's forces, a militant parson, who rode in the forays and pursuits, and gleefully descants on the " services " performed by his party. He opens with the following :—

The Rebells entered into the province of Munster committing a great spoyle on the march. Sir William Saintleger, Knight, Lord President of the said Province, with 200 horse, ffryday the third of December, killed 200 of them between Clonmell and Waterford, *besides a great number that were drowned* ; many prisoners were then taken whereof *40 of the ringleaders were hanged* at the Citty of Waterford, the Munday following.

It does not appear that any particular charge was preferred against those upon whom such terrible execution was done. There is no allegation of murder, cruelty, or any crime except " spoyle."

He makes frequent complaint that the rebels will not give the chance of cutting them down in the open, but, like the Boers in the recent war, were mean enough to take advantage of the physical features of the country.

Wee continued in the field at Kildorrery two days and two nights, expecting their coming, according to promise and their many threatenings. But they did not dare to come to us or fight us there ; for wee had a dainty champion country, which doth much antipathize their cowardly notions. They fight and deal altogether upon advantages ; they will have woods and boggs to second them, or they will not fight, can they any way shun it.

Shabby fellows ! Yet between the lines one may read that the rebels were not the only parties who would "fight only on advantages," and who preferred to choose their ground.

This pregnant sentence relates to what was done in Lismore when the insurgent party withdrew :—

The next day wee did make them sensible of their errors in the town that did consort themselves with them.

It was not necessary, writing to Dr. Henry Jones, to be more explicit. The full meaning unquestionably is, that the townspeople who, whether willingly or not, harboured, aided, or in any way consorted with the rebels, were, in the usual course, hanged and otherwise subjected to exemplary punishment. We meet with announcements of this kind which, for contemptuous brevity and fearful suggestiveness, may compare with Cæsar's despatch (*v.* conclusion of Major Burley's deposition in art. ix., p. 247). Another instance from Mr. Urban Vigors :—

Our scouts took that night a gentleman and his man which were riding to Dungarvan, *but hanging prevented them.*

The "Wee" of this rev. narrator is much in evidence when "services" in the way of "executions" and "burnings" are to be recorded.

Thursday morning being the fourth day of March, our army, between eight and nyne of the clock, came close before the Towne of Dungarvan. Wee took it within three hours' fight, and burned most of the houses, which were Theatched, and burned likewise a stately stone House, well slatted, of Mr. Hoare's, adjoining to the Towne. There were divers gentlemen that escaped over the Strand a-horseback, the water being then fordable, for it was the beginning of the floud. My Lord President, perceiving it, caused a squadron of the best shott to make to the strand with all haste, which killed many of the Rebells notwithstanding many escaped. Whereuppon, my Lord caused a party of horse of every Troupe to be chosen out, to ride to the other side of the River, and *burne the Towne* upon that side *and kill as many as came over.* Wee were forty horse upon that service. Captayne George Walsh, who is now in this citty, was with us, and behaved himself valiantly, and did good service to my own knowledge, for I was an eye-witness unto it. Wee burned the Towne on that side, according to our directions. There were killed by our party of horse neere fifty, and I think there were killed *and hanged*, the like number on the other side ; and in the Towne were many killed *which were thrown into the sea.* There is not any one man, I dare say, can tell certaynly how many were killed *and drowned.* Some say 200, some 300, and some 400. But I am of the opinion that 200 were the most that were slayne. . . Those in the Castle stood out and shott at us ; they killed four of our men, and hurted three or four more. That was all the lost and hurt on our side.

How altered the tone of the next extract ! It was, of course, very naughty of the Condons to meddle with troops that were rendering such glorious " services " in their midst :

The Cundanes doe much mischief neere ffermoy and Castlelyons. They killed at one time three and twenty of the Earle of Barrimore's Troopes that Roade to Coole, an English plantation, about a mile from the Towne, to fetch Corne. It was a most Barbarous Cruell Murder. *I trust the All-seeing eye of the Almighty will not suffer it to goe long unpunished.*

Mr. Urban Vigors furnishes some capital illustrations of the force and truth of Mr. Lecky's observation :—

A ruling caste never admits any parity or comparison between the slaughter of its own members and the slaughter of a subject race. What is called in the one case murder is called in the other an execution,* and a few deaths on one side make a greater impression than many thousands on the other.

It was so in Ireland for centuries before, and for centuries after, the outbreak of 1641. When issuing their exterminating ukase of 8 February, 1641-2, the Lords Justices and Council could really plead the *custom* of that Board in all precedent commotions. There was no principle better understood, none more indubitabtly sanctioned by the invariable practice of five hundred years, than that it was no murder to kill an Irish enemy, and no robbery to plunder him of land and chattels. And, therefore, it is that, in the so-called Government inquiry of the earlier years of the Civil War, no notice whatever was taken of any manner of outrage committed against those indiscriminately described as " Rebells."

The writers, therefore, who persist in parading the Depositions as the true history of the Ireland of that time

* Or " service ; " " acceptable service," as Mr. Peter Hill, High Sheriff of the County Down, calls it, in his deposition. (*v.* p. 135.)

can be excused only on the supposition that they know not what they do. The Depositions were never intended to give the history of the rebellion, but to furnish material to suit the policy of the grabbers and speculators then at the head of affairs, who were, indeed, the only real enemies the King had in Ireland.

It is well established that the recorded statements often differed materially from the oral statements of the examinants, both omissions and modifications being extensively practised, not only by the clerical commissioners, but by high judicial functionaries as well.

In the preface (p. xxvi.-xxviii.) to the second volume of Sir John Gilbert's *History of the Irish Confederation*, there are some striking instances of such tampering with examinations (T.C.D. MS., F. 3, 9).

Among some extant memoranda prepared by Lord Netherville for his defence are the following :—

"That some of the examinations taken against him were extorted by menace and threatening with the rack, and such like punishments.

"I say that Cornelius Moran and Richard Streete were threatened by Sir Robert Meredith with the rack, and other menaces, upon their several examinations against me.

"That his [Netherville's] own examination was much enforced *by leaving out* all that might lawfully mitigate or excuse our offence.

"I say that I confess to have spoken to my father ; which was entered by Sir Robert Meredith. I also said that the occasion and effect of my speech was that he should come and submit unto his Majesty's mercie as the best and safest way ; but that *he* [Meredith] *refused to enter.*"

In the second volume of the Thorpe Tracts* (Irish History) there is given a case in point, which, for more than one reason, I reprint in full :—

The examination of James Peisley, late of Dublin, in the Kingdome of Ireland,

"Saith that about the moneth of March, 1641-[2], it was his fortunes to be present when Mackmaghon was Wracked, and his examination taken by Sir Charles Coote, senior, in the presence of Sir Francis Willoughby, Sir Arthur Lester, the Constable of the Castle, and some others. The said Mackmohan (*sic*) confessed that the Originall of the Rebellion was brought over to them by their committee who were employed by the Irish Parliament to his Majestie for redresse of their grievances in that kingdome, and that they, having often solicited his Majestie for that purpose, was answered, That he was willing to grant them their desire, and that he did confesse they were his good subjects, but that he was so oppressed by his Parliament in England that he knew not how to releeve them ; wishing he knew how to be revenged on them,

* National Library, Kildare Street, Dublin.

or words to that purpose ; Which occasioned Sir Charles Coote to take
him up, calling him Rogue and Raskall, for offering to lay such a
charge upon the King, whom (*sic*), he said, would assist them in all
things honest and just, but not give them commission to cut our
throats. *This narration was not incerted in the examination* read
to Mackmaghon after Sir Charles Coote had finished it.

The principle established by the practice of the Council
Board, and no less by the High Court Judges and officials,
would not be lost on the despoiled clergymen who were com-
missioned to receive complaints against *rebels*—whether the
complaints were true or false did not concern the inquisitors,
so long as the accused were held up to odium. The
Commissioners had it in their power (and may well have
considered it within their duty), by skilful omission and
translation, to make the deponent's statement more
damaging than he intended or fully understood. In going
through these papers I have often admired the art with
which weak points are got out of sight by an instantaneous
shifting of scene and action. Where there is seeming
negligence or obscurity, there is some artful illusion to lead
the reader to suppose himself in the midst of horrors of
which the deponent, after all, only heard, perhaps only
dreamed.

And the deponents have not—taken at the worst—
merited so much blame as the writers who have drawn
pictures by piecing together the wildest things taken at
the examinations, and, so far from sifting the evidence,
have thrown into it immeasurably more malice than was due
to it. I am sure that many deponents have invented, com-
pounded, or otherwise wrested statements far from the
straight path. But I don't believe that even the most
skilful or audacious prevaricator among them can be
charged with more misleading suppression, more ingenious
perversion, than is charged—and justly charged—against
Froude's account of the rebels of 1641. In his version of
the mysterious meeting at Multifarnham, Froude foists in
a statement of a very serious nature, for which there is
absolutely no foundation in Dr. Henry Jones's own statement. "*According to the priests, heretics were entitled to no
mercy !*" We need not wonder that deponents who had
suffered by the tumults should draw on the imagination
when a writer of eminence could, towards the close of the
nineteenth century, so coolly advance a charge for which
he had no authority in the deposition before him while he

wrote.   Nor is this a slip or an isolated misrepresentation.
Clogy's Life of Bishop Bedell he ignores, for reasons which
may be inferred from the following :—

> The narrative of Clogy is one of the most important documents
> relating to the insurrection of 1641.   It has been again and again
> quoted, and as it furnished the chief materials for *The Life of Bedell*
> by Burnet, it was familiar to all students before the original manuscript
> was printed in 1862.   It proves conclusively that the rebellion had not
> the ferocious character which many writers, and pre-eminently Mr.
> Froude, have assigned to it.   Mr. Froude has taken no notice of it,
> and it is not even mentioned in his history.   In the same way, while
> admitting in general terms, that the leading Catholic nobles "had no
> sympathy with murder and pillage," he has suppressed every particular
> instance of humanity on the part of the rebels—all the evidence which
> shows that over the greater part of Ireland, and in some instances even
> in Ulster, they acted with remarkable humanity and self-restraint.   He
> has suppressed all evidence of the savage spirit in which the soldiers
> carried on the struggle, though the horrors committed from the very
> first, undoubtedly, contributed largely to give a character of general
> ferocity to the contest.   He has suppressed all the reasons stated in
> the text which throw a great doubt upon the depositions in Trinity
> College, and upon the veracity of Temple.   He has reduced to the
> smallest possible proportions the intolerable provocations which produced
> the rebellion, asserting as we have seen, in one place, that the rebellion
> was merely a consequence of the indulgence of the Protestants.   His
> narrative consists chiefly of a collection of the most hideous crimes
> narrated by Temple—most of them on Temple's own showing, resting
> upon the loosest hearsay evidence—and these crimes are represented
> as if they were at once unquestionable, unprovoked and unparalleled. *

It is hardly possible to imagine a heavier indictment
against a historian than the foregoing.   Without Temple's
excuse for such excesses, Froude makes himself responsible
for Temple's calumnies, when he could easily have shown
the true nature of the foundation on which they rest.
The Parsons-Borlase and later Commissioners might feel

---

* Lecky, *Ireland in 18th Century*, i,, 99.

Mr. Lecky has much just appreciation of the " reasons which throw great
doubt upon the depositions and upon the veracity of Temple."   Yet, strangely
enough, he devotes, in his first chapter, many pages to the recital of cases from
Jones's Remonstrance, a production which, if possible, is even beneath Temple's
in respect of veracity.   It is hardly correct to speak of it as a report : it was
simply a sensational pamphlet got up for circulation in England when Jones
was sent to London to raise funds in aid of dispossessed ministers.   All the
objections applying to Temple's history apply to the Jones Remonstrance, I
should say, with greater force ; and in the matter of veracity, in such a case,
Jones is no more to be trusted than Temple.   Mr. Lecky properly takes Froude
to task for saying that the Irish Catholics rebelled because they had too much
liberty.   That absurdity did not originate with Froude, but with Jones.   In
the first page of the Remonstrance, Jon mentions the " surfeit of freedom " as
one of the chief causes of the re.   'lion (i p. 117 note ; also p. 185).

confident that their work would serve its purpose, when, almost two and a half centuries later on, a great historian "and many others" (as the Depositions say) could turn a blind eye towards every shortcoming in the pretended evidence.

In the course of this work I have used a variety of depositions, although but a small portion of what I have marked for comment. I think it well to submit here the examination of Anthony Stratford (whose statement of losses will be found at the end of Art. ix., p. 268) which, as a piece of "evidence" might have taken the attention of even Froude.

In the statement of losses he says he was prisoner among the rebels for nine months; in the later one (from which I now make extracts) he mentions ten months. The manner of his escape is stated in connection with his account of losses (p. 268.)

And further saith that in Dungannon, in the county of Tirone, or nere thereabouts, the rebells murthered *three hundred and sixteen* Protest[s.] And between Charlemont and Dungannon, above fowre hundred, there were murthered and drowned at and in the river by Benburb, the Blackwater, between the counties of Armagh and Tirone, two hundred and six protest[s.] And Patrick McCrew, of Dungannon aforesaid, murthered thirty-one in one morning. And two young rebells [* viz., John Begg, Bryan Harney] murthered, in the same county of Tirone, *one hundred and forty* [* poore women and children that could make noe resistance]. And the wiffe of Bryan Kelly, of Loghgall, in the County of Armagh (one of the rebell Captaines) did with her own handes murther *fforty-five*. And this depon[t] further saith that one Thomas King, sometyme Sergeant to the late Lord Caulfield's company, with this depon[st] comãnds (he being inforced to serve the Rebells, and was one of their provost Martialls), Gave the depon[t] a list of every howseholders name so murthered ; *wch list the depon[t] durst not keepe.*

At Portadown there were drowned at seuerall tymes about *three hundred and eight*, who were sent away by about forty, or such like numbers [at once] with convoys, and there drowned. There was a lough nere Loughgall afores[d.] where were drowned *above two hundred*, of which *this aeponent was informed* by severall persons, and particularly by the wiffe of Doctor Hodges, and twoe of her sonnes who were prisoners, and designed for the like end. But by God's mercie, that gave them favour in the eyes of some of the Rebells, they escaped. and the said Mrs. Hodges and her sonns gave the deponent a List of the names of many of those that were soe drowned, *wch the depon[t] durst not keepe.*

And saith that the said Dr Hodges was employed by Sr Phelim ôNeile to make gunpowder, but he, failing of his undertaking, was

---

* Interlined in a blacker ink.

first half-hanged, then cutt down, and kept prisoner three months, and then murthered *with forty-four more*, within a quarter of a myle of Charlemont aforesaid, they being by Turlogh oge ôNeile, brother to Sir Phelim, sent [towards] Dungannon, prisoners, and in the way thither murthered ; *this deponent was shown the pitt where they were all cast in.*

Att a mill pond in the parrish of Killaman, in the county of Tirone, there were drowned in one day *three-hundred.* And in the same parrish there were murthered of English *one thousand twoe hundred* as this deponent was informed by Mr. Burge, the late minister of the said parrish who certified the same under his hand *wch note the deponent durst not keepe.* The said Mr. Burge was murthered nere in the first breaking out of the Rebellion. But the particular tymes this deponent cannot now remember, neither the persons by whom they were committed.

This depon^t was *credibly informed* by the said Sergeant and others of his this deponent's servants (whoe kept company with the Rebells and saw the same), That many yong children were cutt into quarters and gobetts (*sic*) by the Rebells. And that 18 *Scottish infants* were hanged on a clothier's tenter-hooks, And that they murthered a yong fatt Scotchman and made candles of his grease. *They* took an[other] Scotchman and ripped up his belly that they might come to his small gutts, The one end whereof they tied to a tree, and made him goe round untill they had drawn them all out of his body ; they then saying, That they would try whether a dogg's or a Scotchman's gutts were the longer !

Deposed, Martij 9°, 1643 before us. ANTH STRATFORDE
HEN : JONES
HEN : BRERETON

It is not expressly stated, either at beginning or end (except so far as may be implied in the term "deposed",) whether this wonderful production was "duly sworn." Nor does it matter. The piece has as many repellent points as a hedgehog. It is guaranteed safe owing to the inimitable complexity of absurdities. This is one of Dr. Henry Jones's own taking, if not very much of his own making. It was, perhaps, necessary to give the counterblast to the statement in the earlier deposition (taken 7th February, 1642-3, by Messrs. Adams and Aldrich : *v.* p. 268), which was, perhaps, rather favourable to the rebels. The earlier statement is evidence ; and the more sensational story is nothing of the kind. There is, however, much evidence of Dr. Jones's conjuring hand. Who could possibly doubt that the forty-five prisoners were murdered, when Captain Anthony Stratford, *was shown the pit* into which they were cast ! He ought to have seen something more particular. But "agonized curiosity"* did not lead the Commissioners

* Froude (*v.* extract on p. 64).

so far. The places mentioned as the scenes of murder—
Charlemont, Dungannon, Blackwater, Loughgall—all
figure in the contemporary accounts of military operations
against the insurgents. But Captain Stratford had, for the
time, forgotten all about those things: he can remember
only "murders." He seems, at first sight, to do better
than some deponents, as he gives names of informants.
But, then, the "credible" informants drop into the limbo
of forgetfulness: we hear no more of them. That mill
pond at Killaman was a dreadful place. "Agonized
curiosity" did not lead Jones or Brereton to call for the
grounds of the statement. The story was, perhaps, better
without that. And there were twelve hundred, besides
these three hundred, "murdered" in Killaman, apparently
at the very outbreak, as witness the unseen certificate of
the dead minister of the parish. One who wished to make
sure of his ground, might like to hear something direct
from some of those servants who had been "among the
rebels." They, too, are kept out of reach of the inquisitive.
And the documentary evidence is, of course, none the
worse, that the documents themselves were never seen
except by the man who destroyed them—because *he durst
not keep them.*

That was necessary—for the deponent's own safety?

If any one so objects, I beg to direct his attention to the
following from Archdeacon Robert Maxwell's deposition
(*v.* also extract in note, p. 177) :

> And saith he might add to these many thousands more but *the
> Diary which he the deponent wrote amongst the Rebells* being burnt,
> with his House, Books, and all his Papers, he referreth himself to the
> number in gross which the Rebells themselves have upon inquiry
> found out and acknowledged, which, notwithstanding will come short
> of all that have been murthered in Ireland, *there being above one
> hundred fifty-four thousand* now wanting of the British within the very
> province of Ulster !

Dr. Maxwell, prisoner in Sir Phelim's own house, can
write and keep his diary without fear or molestation from
rebels. And the gallant captain, through fear, is impelled
to destroy three documents which ought to have been of great
importance to the inquiry.

Again, how artfully he brings in the rebels as his authorities!
One might think that, while making oath, he had got before
him, if not his own diary, the next best thing, certified
copies of returns prepared by order of Sir Phelim and his

advisers. Now, it is certain that he had never seen any such returns, and that the entries in his own diary were but travestied versions of the chaff of the guard-room, and that in his deposition he was giving a new and still more imaginative version, trusting, at the best, to "the near guess of memory." The chief interest, however, lies in the difference between the two deponents in respect of retaining documents.

Froude and some other authors of note, rather resolutely misrepresent the attitude of our national writers, particularly the late Sir Charles Gavan Duffy and the late Mr. John P. Prendergast,* as if these had denied that the rebels were guilty of killing any but in fair fight. It were going very far indeed to attribute such a condition of sinlessness to any popular uprising in the history of mankind. Both Duffy and Prendergast fully admit that, in the course of the Civil War, there were many guilty acts on the part of the insurgents. Both held, and held properly—just as Mr. Lecky holds—that there was no massacre at the beginning ; none at any time, such as the Temple-Froude historians recount; and the blood so shed at any time by the insurgents was a consequence of the war of extermination waged against them. Mr. Lecky, perhaps, goes beyond Duffy and Prendergast in his views of the rebellion in Ulster—views which I must regard as being much in excess of the facts. All three will, however, be found to agree that many grave " considerations restrict the pretended massacre to narrow limits, and are sufficient to show that it has been exaggerated in popular histories almost beyond any other tragedy on record."† Mr. Lecky aptly remarks that " these exaggerations were connected with the title-deeds of property." John Mitchel put the matter with still more force when he said, " There was Money in the Massacre."‡ The more the Irish were aspersed the better would be the pay when it came to a settlement.

* In an article to the *Nation* (Dublin) soon after the appearance of Froude's *English in Ireland* (1872), Mr. Prendergast relates a rather humorous anecdote of his own experience. On his first appearance in the hall of the Four Courts, Dublin, after the publication of his *Cromwellian Settlement in Ireland*, he was accosted by a distinguished Q.C. " Why, Prendergast," said his learned friend, " I hear you deny *The Rebellion* of 1641." Mr. Froude and that gentleman were evidently of one mind. That the Rebellion and the " Massacre " are synonymous terms, had, and held, possession of both the learned Q.C. and the accomplished book-wright.

† Lecky, i. 59.

‡ Review of Froude, reprinted in *Nation* (Dublin) of 11th January, 1873.

There is one short sentence* in which Sir Gavan Duffy
appears to hold that not more than one was murdered by
the rebels for at least a week after the rising ; but it is only
by separating it from the context that the statement can
be made to bear any such interpretation as some have
insisted upon.   Mr. Lecky says that " the first intelligence
of the outbreak appears to have been given by Lord
Chichester, who wrote to the King from Belfast, on October
the 24th, announcing the capture of Charlemont, Dungannon, Tanderagee, Newry, and that " they have slain
only one man."   The letter, dated 23 October, from Bishop
Henry Lesly to Lord Montgomery of Ards (*v.* p. 71 *note*),
appears to have been the origin of the statement which
Duffy has adopted.

In art. ix., p. 261, I show how pillage must have led to
conflicts in which lives would be lost even from the start,
and private revenge would in some cases add to the number
of victims.   All that fell in battle opposing the rebels, all
that died of wounds in that way received, all that died of
exposure and pestilence, as well as all who escaped from
the country, " with many others," are spoken of in the
Depositions as " murdered."   I have the strongest conviction
that when the contemporary accounts of operations against
the rebels are fully examined it will be found that every
serious case of " alleged massacre," not coming under any
of the foregoing heads, was really an insurgent victory
(like Garvagh), an act of retaliation (like " The Bloody
Bridge,") or an absolute myth (like Donaghmore, County
Down).   And no less confident am I that it will be found
quite impossible to show that, on the side of the
insurgents, there was any such deliberate massacre as
those of Island Magee and Ballydavy.   On the other
hand, the Orders in Council and instructions issued to
commanders, together with such accounts as were written
by military men, show, in the clearest manner, that
the slaughter of the Irish, men, women, and children,
" by all ways and means," was authorised, commended,
and required by " the State."   I would add that the
accounts of outrage and cruelty which, in the Depositions,
are, on the strength of " credible information," or
" common report," urged against the rebels, represent
more truly the performances of those who were arrayed

* See *note* p. 71.

on the side of the Government.* Many horrible and
nameless crimes are charged in those wondrous Depositions, such as were never before, and never since, imputed
to the Irish people, whatever their faults otherwise may be.
Had the "credible information" been searched into, many
horrible things charged against the Irish of that time might
turn out to have been inflicted upon them. This, at any
rate, I maintain—that if any deponents were disposed to
charge "the Rebells" with the crimes and outrages perpetrated by the British soldiery and their following, every
facility was afforded them by the earlier Commissioners, and
no inconvenient questions asked. This conclusion I have not
come to hastily, but after a lengthened, and (I may add)
laborious examination of the Depositions in T.C.D.†

From the beginning of the rising, it was loudly proclaimed that the Rebellion—and, of course, the "Massacre"
—was mainly or altogether the work of the priests. It is
so averred by Dr. Jones and his colleagues in the opening
of their Remonstrance to the English Parliament and
people (v. p. 185). And isn't the matter "solemnly
deposed" and "duly sworn"? (v. p. 215.) That there
were some priests then, as at any other time, who acted
with but little discretion, is likely enough. And it is in these,
or, perhaps, in the rarer case of the man who may disgrace
his calling, that the maligners of the Irish Nation and of
the Catholic Religion seek for representatives of the order.
Mr. Lecky's remarks on this subject appear to me just and
clear-sighted :

It was inevitable that they [Catholic clergy] should throw themselves
vehemently into the contest, for their religion was in imminent danger
of annihilation, and the Lords Justices gave express orders that all
priests who fell into the hands of the soldiers should be put to death
(*Borlase*, 264, 265). It was equally inevitable that in the Puritan
accounts of the Rebellion, and in the report of a Commission,
consisting exclusively of Protestant clergymen, everything should be
done to magnify the part played by the Catholic priests. But on the
whole I think a candid reader will wonder rather that it was not larger,‡

* "In 1641 the name of Irishman was so odious the Protestants were almost
in as great danger of being killed by the newly-arrived troops as the mere
Irish."—Prendergast in *Nation*, 16th November, 1872. In same contribution :
"Mr. Froude's hatred amounts to madness. It has not only extinguished all
his humanity (if he ever had any), but has obscured his reason."

† "The 17th century was the period of our most thriving Protestant trade in
swearing."—John Mitchel in *Nation* (Dublin) of 11th January, 1873. (Reprinted article.)

‡ See art. vii., p. 189.

and will be struck with the small amount of real religious fanaticism displayed by the Irish in the contest. Carte asserts that not more than two or three priests appear to have known of the conspiracy from the first ; and the respect and admiration which the saintly character of Bedell extorted from the rebels in the heart of Ulster, and in the fiercest period of the rebellion, is quite incompatible with the theory of a religious war.—*Ireland in 18th Century*, i. 96-7.

Mr. John P. Prendergast, a still greater authority on such questions, says* :

> That Mr. Froude will find plenty of charges against priests of having committed atrocities in the rebellion of 1641 I know. I have read more of their crimes in this rebellion or war than most men, far more than Mr. Froude ever has read, or will read. *I am not of their religion ;* but this I can say, that *I have never,* to my recollection, *found any of these charges substantiated.* The more horrid the details of imputed crime the more quickly is the judgment made captive through the imagination, though the opposite ought to be the course. Yet, often have I found some terrible imputation against priests end in an act of benevolence carefully screened by their adversaries behind a mass of horrid imputed details that are left embedded, as it were, in the memory, the good deed so hid as to be forgotten. Let any one in search of instances read the lately published *Life of Bishop Bedell*, by Alexander Clogy, the Bishop's son-in-law.

Mr. Froude, it appears, knew nothing, or affected to know nothing, of that work (*v.* p. xxx., above.)

I have endeavoured to make my own position clear in respect of the religious aspect of that much-maligned movement, and to avoid imitating those narrow-minded fanatical enthusiasts who, like Archdeacon Maxwell, can see nothing on the side of the rebels but " a friar or a devil, or both " (*v.* p. 43). Writers of this class have unfortunately got the start of those more worthy of attention. Yet it were a great blunder, if nothing worse, on the part of an Irish Catholic to follow their unworthy example, or to "imitate" those who preach that the Catholic *faith* is to blame for all the wrong imputed to the insurgents.

Catholics are well aware that the crimes and cruelties— the " services " of contemporary anti-Irish writers—did not begin with the Puritans, or with the Puritan period. The Puritans might—supposing them to know so much Anglo-Irish history—have pleaded ample precedent for

* In a letter, dated " Sandymount (Co. Dublin), 17th November, 1872," to the *Freeman's Journal* (19th November), reprinted in *Nation* of 23rd November, 1872.

all the burnings and slaughterings. Yes, indeed, they might have gone back to that period of English rule in Ireland when religious differences had not begun, and even then have found that the practice of civilising by fire and sword, by indiscriminate slaughterings, had been followed for centuries before the Reformers were born. It ought not, at this time of day, to be necessary to mention that in Catholic Ireland the honour roll of Protestants who have earned the confidence of the big majority is a lengthy one ; but there is a set of peculiarly " enlightened " people who have never yet come to the knowledge of such toleration on the part of Irish " Romanists." And they are lovers of truth ! A strange sort of "truth" which would seek to keep up the distrust and animosities of ages long gone by !

The rising in Ulster bears the blame of the ten or twelve years' war that ensued. In any case Ireland was certain to be drawn into the conflict between the king and his rebellious Parliament. That both parties in England would have sought support in Ireland admits of no doubt. The king would find willing support from the Catholics of the Pale, and probably from most of the Protestant settlers in Munster. The old Irish of Ulster had no reason to be enthusiastic in the cause of any Stuart, but they could have been ranged on the king's side against the Puritans. The flame of civil war was, therefore, bound to extend to Ireland. What the issue would have been it is needless to speculate; but the course of such a conflict could be no other than bloody, and the struggle might have lasted much longer, as parties opposing each other in 1641 would, in the supposed case, have opposed the Parliament. Much prominence, in the Depositions, is given to the intention on the part of the insurgents to fight for the king in England when they had gained their purpose at home. To all " Papist-hating men " that would seem a particularly wicked and " rebellious " design. Yet if it had happened, in any other part of the habitable globe, that people in revolt were disposed, or determined, to fight in the cause of their king, there were little difficulty about finding something rather incongruous in speaking of such subjects as " rebels."

Had Charles come to Ireland in person, he could have altered the whole course of the war in that country, and perhaps in England. That might or might not have been a good event for English liberty ; but it would have saved an infinity of misery and much bloodshed if the king had cleared "the Castle" of the clique who were gambling in the proceeds of rebellion, to the ruin of king and country. That Charles should be able to see and judge for himself was not consistent with the projects of those then in power, and they succeeded in persuading him that the air of Whitehall was better for his Majesty's health.

The Lords Justices and Council, "veneered with sanctimonious theory," and affluent of pharisaical cant, had their own game to play, and their master stroke was to make the king himself a party to the so-called massacre, and so to rule him out of taking any action but such as might be dictated by the Parliament of England at the instance of "the State" in Ireland. In one respect the then rulers of Ireland cannot be said to have caused the outbreak, inasmuch as the causes extended far back in the history of Government administration; but they certainly did much more to make the "rebellion" what it was than Sir Phelim O'Neill and his colleagues ever could have done, even though they had tried.

The "cruelties and barbarities" of the Irish have been harped upon with amazing intrepidity, or amazing ignorance, even to the present day (*v.* p. 131). Yet such humanity as was shown or practised in the course of the war was wholly on the side of the insurgents, while the opposing forces maintained a uniform course of practices at variance with the law of nature.

From the accounts left by commanders and others acting on the part of "the State," in the form of despatches and diaries, the inference is clear and inevitable, that, under pretence of "cutting off rebels" the slaughter of unresisting country people, men, women, and children, was perpetrated by the fanatical soldiery to an extent too horrible to realise. Those who have taken up the parrot-cry of the ages of persecution and wrong-doing, would do well to act on Petty's suggestion, and "review the grounds of their opinion." If for "Irish Massacre" they will read "Massacre of the Irish," then indeed they may rest assured that they read history, and not, as heretofore, rhetorical rant and imposture.

It requires no very special gifts to write high-sounding denunciations of the Insurrection of 1641. All such movements stand condemned when they fail.

> Treason doth never prosper : What's the reason ?
> Were it to prosper, none dare call it treason.

There were faults enough both in the design and in the execution. But there was no time, during the progress of the Civil War, at which it would not have been possible for the Government of the day to have peace with honour (*v.*, pp. 295-6). The party in power preferred confiscation to peace : and the bloodshed went on. When *did* it cease? To have the feud, in some form, continued for ages yet to come, would still seem to be the object of those who fancy they find sufficient warrant in the Depositions. " The eternal witness!" Yes, the eternal witness of the iniquitous policy that brought about all the troubles which harass the Governments of more recent times.

THOMAS FITZPATRICK.

DUBLIN, 30*th April*, 1903.

∗ In printing the numerous extracts from the Depositions and other T.C.D. MSS., an endeavour has been made to keep to the original forms and orthography.

[Matter interlined on the MSS. has, in this work, been placed within square brackets.]

THE BLOODY BRIDGE.

———❖———

TOURISTS and others who have taken the very enjoyable coach-drive between Newcastle (County Down) and Warrenpoint, by way of Kilkeel, are familiar with the Bloody Bridge, and have heard that it is so called on account of a shocking massacre perpetrated there by the Irish during the Insurrection of 1641, commonly called Sir Phelim O'Neill's Rebellion. As the road from Kilkeel approaches the base of Slieve Donard it crosses a gorge cut by the rivulet which collects the rainfall on the south and south-east sides of the big mountain. The road formerly crossed the ravine a few perches higher up, where the old-fashioned bridge still stands, and is pointed out as the scene of a horrible tragedy, the victims being, it is alleged, some prisoners taken at Newry when that town was surprised by the Magennises and their allies, on that fateful Saturday, the 23rd October, 1641. On the map in Dr. Knox's *History of County Down* the stream is marked as the 'Bloody Bridge River.'

The blood-curdling story finds place in several works, but we owe it, in the current form, to Walter Harris, who in 1744, published anonymously a history of the County under the title of *A View of the Ancient and Present State of the County Down,* and more recent writers copy from him as sufficient authority for the period in question. What amount of credibility is due to Harris, on this and kindred topics, I hope to bring out in the course of this article. A contemporary of his own—Charles O'Conor of Belanagare—alludes to Mr. Walter Harris as " a gentleman unversed in the philosophy of history, and flagrantly abusive, but fit enough for his office of a compiler." Harris's indefatigable industry in the work of collecting and copying materials for history is evidenced by the great collection of his MSS. preserved in the National Library, Kildare Street, Dublin ; but the laborious collector showed little capacity for turning his stores to proper account. His so-called *History of Down* shows not only that he was

A

incapable of writing in a spirit of fairness, but that, when in connection with the troubles of the 17th century, he found anything which might be turned to the disadvantage of the majority of his countrymen, or against their religion, he clutched at it with eagerness and without the slightest pretence to investigation, even while the absurdity ought to have been palpable enough to stare him in the face while he wrote. In the work just mentioned, he has shown to a hardly-credible extent, a disposition to put the worst possible construction upon occurrences which appeared to fall in with his views ; and he has, in the most barefaced manner, suppressed everything which might lead people to conclusions at variance with his own. All this might pass without notice if writers of more recent date had not copied his narrative, seeming to take it that his name is sufficient warranty for what they relate on his authority. The following is his account of the incident with which we are at present more particularly concerned :

Before the rebellion of 1641, Newry was in a flourishing condition ; but it was then destroyed by the Irish, who exercised numberless cruelties on the Protestant inhabitants. It was surprised by Sir Con Magennis at the first breaking out of that infamous rebellion, and continued *ten weeks in his possession*, when it was retaken by the Lord Conway. During this period the Protestant townsmen suffered the common calamities of war in a high measure, such as ransackings, plunderings, imprisonment, misery, hunger and cold, by which many perished. But these were only slender misfortunes if compared to the sufferings of others. For in January that year [following the old style], Mr. Tudge, Minister of Newry, and Chaplain to Sir Arthur Tirringham, Lieutenant Hugh Trevor and his wife, Mr. Weston and others to the number of twenty-four, some say fifty [*and Reid* says thirteen*] were made prisoners by Sir Con Magennis, and sent from Newry to Carlingford, in order to be embarked for Dublin *as he pretended*. But waiting for a wind, Michael Garvey, then sub-sheriff of the County Down, came with a warrant from Sir Con, empowering him to carry them over to Green Castle at the mouth of Carlingford Bay, and from thence to convey them (*as he pretended*) to Down, in order to exchange them for some Irish prisoners. But no sooner were they brought to Newcastle, about nine miles short of Down than Sir Con met them, and the next day caused them to be sent back from thence a few miles into a wood called the Pass of Bealachneir, *alias* Ballyonery,† where they were most barbarously cut, slashed and

* *History of the Presbyterians in Ireland*, 2nd Edition, 1876, Vol. I., pp. 331-2.

† *Ballaghonery* is the modern name of the townland. From the Golf Links, and the great Railway Hotel, at the northern end of Newcastle, Co. Down, there is a magnificent view of Slieve Donard, towering high over the village at the opposite or southern extremity. The mountain appears to rise out of the sea, which has cut a line of cliffs along the base ; and just

hacked, and at length hanged by George Russell of Rathmullen, and divers of his assistants, instigated and commanded by Sir Con: Two of the examinants in proof [*Mark the proof !*] of this inhuman action add further that Sir Con, falling sick, and lying on his death-bed, conceited that Mr. Tudge would require his blood at his hands, and was still in his sight, and often willed his friends to take away Mr. Tudge, as if he had seen him ; for that he thought he was come to fetch him away ; and he left directions with his friends, that no more Protestants should be slain but in battle, dying in that raving condition. They add that the Viscountess of Iveagh was so cruel against the English and Scottish Protestants of Newry, that she often expressed her resentment against the soldiers for not putting them all to death (!)   Many other inhuman barbarities were committed on the English inhabitants of this place.—HARRIS'S *History of Down*, pp. 92–93.

The two examinants who were so well acquainted with what passed in Sir Con's death-chamber, were two women, Mrs. Elizabeth Price and Mrs. Elizabeth Crooker, both of " the Newry," who give the story as " of common report," a circumstance which, although of some importance, disappears from the narrative as told by Harris.   One of these gossiping witnesses, Mrs. Elizabeth Price, is the only authority that I can discover—and Harris mentions none —for the following, which is connected with the same place, and which he sets down to all appearance with as much confidence as if he were citing Holy Writ :

Before we leave Newcastle, we must not omit an instance of great barbarity committed here in the rebellion of 1641, when an Englishman, a Scotchman, and a Welshman were imprisoned in the stocks, and obliged by their merciless enemies to sit on raw hides without breeches, and kept in that condition so long, till their joints rotted, and the foot of one of them when they were hanged, fell off by the ankle.—*Id.* p. 81.

It would, indeed, be a pity to omit that story which, of itself, is sufficient to show the character of the would-be historian who adopts it, and which, in its way, is so capital an illustration of the matter, at that time got up for consumption in England, to excite and keep alive animosity against Charles I., as well as against " the bloody Papists." It is but fair to add that the writers who usually adopt

above these cliffs, like a notch in the slope, is the coach road to Kilkeel, Greencastle, Rostrevor, and Warrenpoint.   This road, when clear of the base of the great mountain, crosses the glen and stream still pointed out as the scene of the ' massacre.'   The passage by the side of the mountain is called by the country people " The Ballagh " (*bealach*, a mountain pass).   To the English settlers about Downpatrick it was known as the Pass of Dundrum. As seen from the old De Courcy Castle above Dundrum the Pass seems quite near, although it is at least four miles distant.

Harris's statements and conclusions shrink from having anything to do with this ridiculous concoction of some disordered or ill-contriving brain—not necessarily Mrs. Eliza Price's.

The affair of "the Bloody Bridge," or Ballaghonery Pass, is not, in my opinion, quite so baseless as the story of the unfortunate three left to rot, as alleged, on raw hides. But as told by Harris, the narrative is distorted, the number of victims exaggerated, and the purpose entirely misrepresented. The general drift of his recital is that the prisoners were brought all the way from Newry—and by a strangely circuitous route—to Newcastle, and from Newcastle some three miles back along the way by which they came, and all this that, in the end, they might be murdered! The repeated use of the phrase "as he pretended" I once thought was an interpolation of Harris's own. I find, however, that the words were used by one of the examinants, as will appear further on. The adoption of such an expression shows how little our great authority was disposed to question or examine his materials before thrusting them on the public. What need was there for any "pretending"? The prisoners were in Sir Con's power. And if it had been his object to put them to death what could he gain by dragging them so far to kill them in the end? If he wanted a quiet place wherein to perpetrate a crime he could find it among the mountains and woods close to Newry and all around it, without going to the enormous trouble of dragging them over thirty miles to have their blood shed near his own door. The route from Newry to Newcastle* either by way of Hilltown and Bryansford, or by the modern coach route through Mourne, was in the hands of the Irish party. Why then send the prisoners to Carlingford on the Leinster side of the Bay, which had then to be crossed to reach Green Castle on the County Down side, where the old fortress of the De Burgos still frowns upon the channel leading up to Greenore? There was a more direct route through Mourne without having to cross any water other than a mountain stream. On their way to Newcastle, then, the prisoners had to pass the very spot which tradition points out as the scene of the massacre. They had to proceed three miles further to reach Sir Con's Castle (which stood at the mouth of the Shimna, on the spot occupied by the "Annesley Arms" Hotel of more recent times). From the

* The town of Newcastle, under the shadow of Slieve Donard, on the shore of Dundrum Bay, was so named from the castle there erected, or perhaps re-erected, in 1588, by Felix Magennis, which was, in 1641, the residence of Sir Con Magennis.

Castle they are dragged back along their line of march, and there, if we accept Harris's story, they were all put to death, with the accompaniment of cruelties as revolting as needless.

Such is the story held out for our acceptance, and as such it has been accepted and passed on by writers of considerable repute, who have been content to take Harris as Harris takes the most absurd depositions—namely, without analysis or question ; and it has been quoted, or substantially adopted by more recent authors—the Rev. Dr. Reid in his *History of the Presbyterians in Ireland*, the Rev. George Hill in his ample and, in general, very interesting notes to the *Montgomery Manuscripts* and, of course, by many of less note. Yet it must be evident to anyone after a moment's thought, that, as we have it here, there are chasms in the relation, even if we take it that the statements are all correct—and, for the most part, they are anything but correct, as I hope to show. It is important to bear in mind, that while we are invited to accept the account given by Harris, there is ample testimony to show that at the same time there were prisoners of note detained unhurt in the Castle of Newry, in the Castle of the Shimna, and in several houses in the country near Newcastle. We have the depositions of several of these prisoners, and with a rare exception —Mrs. Eliza Crooker is one—they have nothing to allege against their jailors beyond detention. Why a selection should be made for massacre—" massacre " is the term with which our authors familiarise us—is left to each one's fancy to solve for himself. But the real crux is, why all the rounds should be gone before the poor prisoners could be put to death. That we have not yet the entire case before us is, I think, clear enough. We have just enough to excite our horror—to excite, let us say, a storm of indignation against a certain creed, a certain nation ; and, that effected, further details would be superfluous.

Until I had an opportunity of examining the original depositions, I was puzzled to account for Harris's blundering statement, namely, that Newry " continued ten weeks in Sir Con's possession, when it was retaken by the Lord Conway." Now Newry was surprised and taken on the very day of the " rising "—the 23rd October, 1641. Counting ten weeks from this date brings us to the 1st of January only. The laxity of the original writers in respect of dates was noticed by Dr. Warner, well nigh a century and a half since, and this laxity or negligence—sometimes wilful I fear —is often a source of perplexity to the inquirer. But in the case of Lord Conway's expedition to Newry there is no occasion for uncertainty as to dates ; for, from the day of the muster at Drumbo Hill, near Belfast, we have a record from day to day in the accounts left by Monroe, Sir James Turner, and Roger Pike. From these accounts it appears that Newry was not reached till the 1st of May. So that the Town and Castle were in the hands of Sir Con Magennis and his party *for twenty-seven weeks*, instead of *ten weeks*, as stated in the extract above cited Could a person of Harris's research be ignorant of the accounts mentioned ? Not very likely. But it is rather likely that he would pay little attention to them owing to the circumstance that they unreservedly—those of Turner and Pike especially— admit that many things were perpetrated by these forces contrary to the laws of religion and humanity, as well as the laws of war ; whereas he—like many who went before him, and many who have followed him—would have his readers believe that the crime was wholly on the side of the Rebels, the wicked and " bloody " Papists. However that may be, I find now that our trusted authority stultified himself by his implicit faith in Mrs. Eliza Price's deposition, in which (after mentioning how she was "deprived, robbed, or otherwise dispoyled ") she

saith that the names of those that soe robbed and dispoyled them she knoweth not, but is assured it was [by*] the tennants and souldjers of Sir Con McGennis, Knight, which Sir Con was the first that took the Newry, and *kept itt tenn weekes;* and in that tyme he suffered those [Rebells] of the name of the Russells and the Magennises his souldjers, to kill Mr. Tudge, minister of the Newry , and chaplayne to Sir Arthur Tirringham [nere Newcastle], and Lieutenant Trevor and his wiffe, one Mr. Weston, and others to the [number] of 24 Protestants more, the deponent's neighbours, *as the Rebells themselves confesse :* And as this deponent did know, for shee saw their clothes brought back, and worne after they were put to death ; and the Rebells tould her the reason why the said Mr. Tudge was putt to death was because he was a [protestant] minister, and because some of the Papist preistes were putt to death in England : Howbeit, *this deponent hath beene tould and heard it seriously reported* by the Rebells, That the said Sir Con Magennis on his death [bedd] was so much affrighted with the apprehension and remorse, that the said Mr. Tudge so slaine was [still] in his presence, that he left directions that noe more Protestants from that tyme should be slaine but what should be killed in Battayle. And after his death the [said Sir Con] Magennis his brother would have observed his direĉon. But . . . (*a couple of lines mutilated and illegible owing to the bottom of page being worn and broken*) . . . and the mother of the said Lord Ivagh were very earnest to have

* The words within the square brackets are *interlined* on the original depo-sition in T.C.D. Library. I have observed that, in many instances, these interlineations are not in the same ink as the body of the deposition.

all the rest of the protestants putt to death. *But the said [Sir Con's] brother prevented their soe bloudie intensions.*

An extract from this deponent's statement is given in Sir John Temple's *History of the Rebellion* (first published in 1646), and had previously appeared in certain pamphlets issued by authority of the Irish Government. The omissions in the printed copies are of some consequence :

Elizabeth Price [*Peirce* in the original MS. deposition], wife of Michael Price of the Newry, deposeth :
That Sir Con MaGennis suffered his souldiers the Rebels to kill Master Turge * (*sic*) Minister of the Newry, and several other Protestants ; and he the said Sir Conn MacGennis on his death bed was so much affrighted with apprehension that the said Master Turge so slaine was still in his presence, as that he commanded no Protestants from that time should be slaine but what should be killed in battle ; and after his death, Sir Conn MacGennis his brother would have observed his directions but one John MacGennis, the young Lord of *Evah*, and Monk Creely, were earnest to have all the rest of the Protestants put to death !—TEMPLE'S *Hist. Irish Rebellion,* p. 124.

The point at which Temple's extract breaks off is worthy of attention. He expunges all expressions indicating that the evidence is mere hearsay. The name of the "young Lord of Evah," was not John, but Arthur, the third Viscount Magennis of Iveagh.

Harris, while, in the account cited above, making use not only of the matter but the particular terms and expressions of the Depositions preserved in Trinity College, Dublin, makes no direct reference to any one deposition in particular. But in a footnote to page 92 (under "Newry") he gives this general intimation :

Original depositions of the inhuman barbarities of the Irish in the Rebellion of 1641 are extant in MS. in 33 vols., folio, in the Library of the College of Dublin, taken by virtue of a Royal Commission † which would afford useful and plentiful materials for compiling a Matryrology of Protestants at that period. There has been often occasion to quote these documents in this Survey ; and, therefore, whenever any of these cruelties are mentioned *let the reader once for all conclude that they are cited from the said collection.*

---

* Tudge is the form in the original statement : it is written more distinctly than proper names usually are in the same papers. This extract is also to be found in Rushworth, but in the opening lines the name thrice appears as Sir *John MaGennis*—a misprint, no doubt.

† The earlier depositions were taken under commissions issued by Parsons and Borlase as Lords Justices ; the latter under commissions issued in the name of the Commonwealth of England.

There is a "general warrant" for the authenticity of his statements! And, should anyone feel disposed to cavil at the security, why he can (after some preliminary trouble) look up the old crabbed and worn MSS.—which he will find altogether a delightful task!

In the Appendix to Borlase's *History of the Execrable Irish Rebellion of* 1641 (London : 1680, folio) there is a summary of murders, etc., committed *by the Irish Rebels* (those committed by others don't count) : which summary I find is a reprint of a pamphlet of somewhat earlier date (1679), and which gives as the authorities for the Ballagh-onery (Bloody Bridge) massacre the depositions of Eliza Peirce, Peter Hill, Esq., Capt. Henry Smith, and Arthur Magenniss. Eliza Peirce's evidence is given above, and it may be interesting to see what the others have to say.

Peter Hill's deposition runs to fourteen or fifteen closely-written folio pages. He was, at the beginning of those troubles, High Sheriff of the County Down, and says that "he knows the county well." This is what he says about the Bloody Bridge affair ; and it is interesting to note how the number of victims varies :

That about January, 1641 [O. S., of course], *about seventeen* Protestants, vizt. :—Lieutenant Hugh Trevor and his wife, Mr. Tudge, Minister of the Newry, and the rest *whose names he remembereth not*, having bin prisoners at the Newry with Sir Conn Magennis; the gran Rebell, were by the said Sir Conn's direcons sent from the Newry down to Carlingford to be embarked for Dublin, and there [they] staying for wynd, one Michaell Garvey, then sub-sheriff of the said county of Downe came with a warrant from the said Sir Conn to carry them on to Greene Castle and so to have them conveyed [*as he pretended*]* to Downe to be exchanged for some prisoners of the Irish.† But noe sooner were they brought to Newcastle, which is within 8 myles of Downe, But the said Sir Conn met them there, and the next day he cawsed them to be sent thence about a myl and a half into a wood called the Pass of Ballyonery, where and when they were all most miserably and barbarously hackt, slasht, cutt in pieces and murthered by George Russell of Rathmullan ‡ and divers his assistants instigated and commanded by the said Sir Conn Magennis, *as this deponent hath very credibly heard. (Jur :* 11 Maii, 1645.)

Some may say that Harris sticks very well to his text. We shall see. And one would almost fancy, so circumstantial and so confident is Mr. Peter Hill, that he had been looking on while the alleged butchery was in progress.

* Interlined.

† "As was pretended" struck out.

‡ In this allegation Mr. Peter Hill is not borne out by other deponents, as will appear in due course.

The little admission at the end, however, puts a somewhat
different complexion on the narration.   Mr. Hill being
used to legal documents affects the jargon and tautology
of the law.   As an instance, and in an earlier portion of
the same deposition, giving an account of his quarrel with
Sir James Montgomery, he tells how " this deponent was
expulsed and driven out of the said County of Down ; soe
as he was forced to fly to Dublin, for succour, relief, and
safety of his life." In somewhat similar strain we have that
harrowing account of the murders—an account which
loses nothing in the carriage through the pages of Harris.
Captain Henry Smith (" late of Loghedyne, in the County
of Downe "), in a long and rather interesting deposition,
tells us that

> This deponent hath formerly in his Ma'ys service broken a legge,
> was upon the xxiii. of October [most treacherously] taken prisoner
> by the Rebells . . .   and was kept with his wiffe and children
> and servants in prison for 27 weeks together. *   . . And *during
> the time of the deponent's imprisonment*, the Rebells pretending
> they would ease the towne of some of the English prisoners, culled
> out about 50 of them, and told them they should be sent to Downe
> in company of other prisoners : but thereupon they being carried
> to Conn·Magennis his house, there or nere the same, they were
> cruelly massacred and murthered, and there they stript (*sic*) and
> hung up stark naked (*a bit here torn out of the side of the paper*) Mr.
> Richard Tudge, the Minister of the Newry.   (*Jurat*, 11 June,
> 1642.)

The deponent was, at the same time, in prison, almost
thirty miles from the scene of the alleged outrage. Curiously
enough he does not seem to know anything of the fate of
the other prisoners—not even of Lieutenant Trevor's death,
although they, deponent and Trevor, lived in almost the
same locality, namely, in the neighbourhood of Loughbrickland.
Arthur Magneisse (or Magennis) belonged to the
Kilwarlin branch of that ancient and once powerful County
Down family.   It appears from his own statement that he
was a Protestant, and was accordingly treated as an alien,
seeing that

> he lost by the Rebells in corn, cowes, horses and maires to the
> value of £125 and upwards.   And in household stuff, apparrell,
> linens, woollens, &c., to the value of three score and ten pounds,
> at least. . . .
> And further sayth, That *he heard it credibly reported* that Lief-
> tenant Trevor, his wiffe, and one Mr. Tudge, clk., and divers others
> *to the number of ffifteen* or more, were putt to death by one Hugh

* *i.e., From the breaking out of the Rebellion till the Relief of Newry.*

Maginn and others in the county of Down. And he [deponent] hath bin detayned in prison or hould by Sir Conn Magennis in his liffe-tym, and by means of one Richard Stanihurst, Lifetenant-Coll then, and after their decease by Daniell Oge Magneiss, *as this deponent was credibly informed.* (*Jurat,* ix Junii 1642.)

Such is the testimony of the four witnesses cited by Borlase—or rather by the pamphleteer whose work Borlase reprints. And to what does it all amount ? Mere rumour, if we except Eliza Price's strange statement about the clothes worn by the victims on their last journey in life. It is rather strange that these authors pass by Eliza Crooker, who was in a position to give one item which makes a very near approach to direct evidence. Her story is a bit wild and incoherent ; but the matter just alluded to receives some confirmation from later depositions. She deposeth upon oath :

That att or about the beginning of the Rebellion she was stripped and had taken from her in leather and other household goods and clothes to the value of Ten pounds and upwards by the Rebells there, and that she herself and her son were taken by the Rebells and carried out to be drowned, and by the extreamity of the weather were cast upon a rock where she and her childe lay there almost naked and starved, and cominge agayne into the Newry, afterwards when there with divers others [shee] and divers others (*sic*) *were carried to Newcastle to be hanged.* And there were some 15 of [them] hanged, and *the rest of us were turned away and came to the Newry agayne* where we were kept prisoners by the space of seaven weeks, induringe much misery and hunger and cold [and there they] soe remayned untill the Lord Connoway came and took the Newry.

Mrs. Eliza Crooker, on her own showing, had some miraculous escapes. But her allegation as to the liberation of some of the prisoners is borne out by later testimony which we may regard as independent, at all events of any influence on her part. And one may surmise that it was on account of this very allegation that her evidence was not cited by Borlase or his friends. She undertakes to give details of Mr. Tudge's murder which—like her account of Sir Con's death-bed remorse—she could give only on hear-say :

And further saith, that the said Colonell Magennis and his souldiers hanged to death one Mr. Tudge a protestant minister of the Newry : and he holding upp his handes, and praying to God [a little before] they hanged him : some of the Rebells cutt and slashed him over the handes with swords. And not long after, the said Colonell Magennis falling sick and lying upon his death bed, complayned there that Mr. Tudge, whom he had hanged, would require his blood at his handes : and was still in his sight there before him. And often wished his friends to take away the said Mr. Tudge [as if he had seen him] for he was comen thither to fetch and take him, the said Colonell Magennis away, for putting him to death, with many other grievous expressions to that purpose, which contynued by the said Colonell Magennis untill he dyed ; and especially hee forewarned his friends to take heede from thenceforth whom they killed : ffor still the said Mr. Tudge's blood was upon him. (*Jurat*, 10 Martii, 1642.)

There is—as we might expect—a close agreement between this, Mrs. Eliza Crooker's account of what passed in Sir Con's last moments, and that told on the same subject by her neighbour Mrs. Eliza Price. If good for anything, this story of the woman goes to show that Sir Con was not disposed to shed blood. Even yet there is a hiatus—or more than one—in the treatment of the case ; and it is rather interesting to note how long "the missing link" is kept out of sight, even when the testimony appears to accumulate.

We can trace, with some degree of confidence—perhaps with certainty—the movements of the prisoners. In the Thorpe collection of pamphlets (National Library, Dublin) Vol II., there is printed a portion of the evidence of one Roger Holland of Glaslough, in the County of Armagh : it is one of a great number of extracts from the depositions, attached to the Remonstrance addressed to the English Parliament, with the recommendation of the Irish Lords Justices (Parsons and Borlase). The date of the Remonstrance, or of the accompanying letter of the Lords Justices, is 7 March, 1641–[2].

And further saith, That at Carlingford, when the said Roger was there three or four days, Sir Conn Magenis sent his warrant to send away all such prisoners as came from Newry, to Greencastle ; which warrant was directed to one Jo. Babe, Provost Marshal, directed by Sir Con Magenis : which Provost Marshal according to his direction sent them away : which prisoners were sent for the releasing of some prisoners that were taken at Downpatrick : but no sooner came the aforesaid prisoners on to Greencastle but they were all cut off. And the next day following the said Sir Con Magenis sent a convoy with all such prisoners as were there left ; what became of these this examinant cannot tell.

Another sojourner at Carlingford, John Wisdome of Armagh, in his deposition, made the 8th of February, 1641–2, gives a bit of independent testimony as to the passage of prisoners from Carlingford to Greencastle, the return of some of the same party to Carlingford, and their joining the deponent and friends from Carlingford to Dublin. The following is found on the second page (the rest of which is blank) of Wisdome's deposition :

Whilst I was in Carlingford staying for a wind, I sawe 3 boates laden with English (wch. were turned out of the Newry), sent

from Carlingford to Greene Castle ; as the Irish reported, they were
to be convoyed to the County of Downe to redeeme some rebells
yt ye Scotts had taken prisoners. One boate load of the 3 came
back againe, and part came away with us. As for the rest, I know
not what became of them ; it is reported that those that were to
Green Castle were put to death.

The statement, attributed to Mr. Roger Holland, Glasslough, grows a bit muddled towards the end. To say that
" they were *all* cut off " and that those who were left were
sent on, under convoy, looks like an Irish bull. But it is—as
most of the stupid things are—anti-Irish. The deposition
shows, however, that the prisoners, in the first instance,
were sent from Newry to Carlingford. While differing
from the account accepted by Harris as to the part enacted
by Michael Garvey, the sub-sheriff of County Down, this
deposition tallies with the explanation of Colonel Donnell
(or Daniel) Magennis, uncle to the young Viscount Iveagh,
when before the Commission at Carrickfergus, on the 9th
of June, 1653 :

And sayth that Lieut. Hugh Treavor, and others [then]
prisoners at the Newry, were sent from the Newry to Carlingford,
by Michael Garvey as their conductor, and there delivered them
(*sic*) safe to one John Babe *to be shipt from thence into England ;*
but what became of them after being in Carlingford, this examinat
knoweth not, only heard that Lieut. Trevor was murdered, but by
whom, or how soon after, he knoweth not.

It is evident that the County Monaghan man confounded
Greencastle and Newcastle, two places fifteen Irish miles
apart. John Wisdome appears to make the same mistake.
The following record of the arrival of the prisoners at
Greencastle turns up among the County Antrim depo-
sitions :

The examination of James Warren, Gent. of ye Newry, of the
age of 47 years, taken at Carrickfergus, June 3, 1653 :
Who being duly sworne and examind, saith yt in ye
beginninge of the Rebellion he was at Green Castle,
and yt it was first taken by Donnell M'Cowley; *
and afterwards it was comanded by Art ro Magenis, and his wiffe,
Rose M'Cartan (now living towards ye Route) at which time Lieut.
Trevor, his wiffe and family with severall other Brittish came to
Greene Castle prisoners, and was put into ye church, and kept by
a guard, but who brought them, this examt. knowes not; neither
can tell who sent them to Downe-Patrick, nor who carried them,
but remembers yt one (*blank*) Russell, a browne-haired man, and
one Merriman, a yellow-haired man, betwixt 30 and 40 yeares of

---

* The name may be M'Creely (for Creely). M'Cowley seems to me very
strange. It is very difficult in some cases to make out the correct form of the
proper names.

age, as this deponent believeth, and yt Russell was younger, yet that Russell, this deponent is not certain [off] ; and hears yt ye sd. Lieut. Trevor and ye rest were pittifully used and killd, but by whome this examt. did not heare ; and further saith not, saveing yt he heard yt Donnell oge McEnos, now in prison was [after yt] Governor of Newry, and himself and other prisoners at Greene Castle when they heard of him were afraid, for yt they heard he was a sharp man.* JAMES WARREN.

Attested and sworne before
GEO. RAWDON,
RICH. BICKERSTAFFE.

At least two witnesses saw the prisoners on the way from Greencastle to Newcastle :

Patrick Doran, of Ballyran, in Mourne, taken on the 8th day of June, 1653 :

Who being duly sworne and examined sayth, That about Christmas next after the Rebellion of Ireland, Lieut. Huge Trevor, John Weston, Mr. Tutch, a minister, and divers others, were sent from Newry with a convoie towards Newcastle ; which convoie, namely George Merriman, Art O'Neile, brother to Mr. Bryan O'Neile, and Nicholas Russell, sonne to John McGeorge als. ffitz-george [Russell] of Killough in ye sd. county, brought the said Trevor, Weston, and Tutch to this deponent's house, beeinge in their way, where they, with the rest under that convoie, stayd about ye space of two hours, and from thence to Edmond M'Bryan Doran's house, where they contynued that night :

The said Edmund Doran, examined on the same day, being duly sworn, saith :

Yt. at ye begining of this Rebellion he lived in Mourne, and kept entertainment for travellers, and about the begining of this Xmas, 1641, Lieut. Trevor, beinge prisoner, was brought to this deponent's house, by one George Merriman, now livinge nere Dundrum, and Art O'Neile, and one Russell of Killough's sonn, and more he remembereth not ; and there were prisoners with ye sd. Lieut. Trevor his wiffe and two children, with one Mr. Toutch, and one Mr. Weston, all wch. staid all night wth. this examt., and ye next morninge went away towards Newcastle, but what became of them this examt. doth not know, but heard they were all murthered, but by whom this examt. did not heare [sauvinge one Con Maginis], and further saith not.

It will appear that this examinant was misinformed when told that *all* the prisoners were " murthered."

There was, at the time, detained as prisoner, in a house near Newcastle, a Mr. Dunfin (or Dunphine), Minister of

---

* It does not appear that Warren and his fellow-prisoners had any complaint to make about their own treatment as prisoners. This deposition has all appearance of being made in truth and with judgment, containing none of the wild reckless statements so common in the earlier depositions.

Donaghmore, near Newry. On the 26th of May, 1653,
this gentleman was examined at Carrickfergus, before
Messrs. Traill and Bickerstaffe, Commissioners on behalf
of the Commonwealth, "concerning the things transacted
to his knowledge and heare-say in the County of Downe,
and thereabouts the first half yeare of the Rebellion, during
which time he, the said Mr. Dunfin, with his wife, were
prisoners with the Rebells, having first robbed (*sic*) them
of all their goods."

Imprimis, being sworne, he saith, concerning the murder of
Lieut. Trevor, he this deponent was then lying sick in one Pierce
Mc....* house [who was bound for his forthcoming] within two
miles of the place where .... murder was comĩtted, and that one
Edm. ... . oge M'Hugh M'Phelim Magenisse came to .... sd. house
the evening before the murder was comĩtted ; and because he came
from Newcastle where Sir Con Magenisse was, who was then
comãnder in chefe of the Irish in those parts, this deponent asked
what news he had ; and he replied that he had non strange, but
that he left Lieut. Trevor, and the rest of the prisoners that were
with him, at Newcastle, amongst whom he said he saw Frank
Symonds, the deponent's parish clarke, and when this deponent
asked him what did he think Sir Con would do with his prisoners,
he answered he did not know, but he believed he would send them
back to the Newry ; and then the said Edmond oge Magenisse
went (as they said) to his own house. But the next morning there
came one Patrick Roe O'Gormley to the said house, where this
deponent lay, and drew out his skeen, and was glorying that he
killed Lieut. Trevor and his wife with that [same] knife ; and what
further past concerning that particular murther, or who were
there besides, this deponent knoweth not, but only that he heard
that one Con McArt Magenisse, nephew to the said Edmund oge
Magenisse, was either there or at least knows who were there, and
therefor his testimony, if he could be found, would give a great
deal of light on this particular.

It is rather remarkable, while in th earlier depositions
Mr. Tudge figures as the principal victim, in those taken
ten or eleven years later, little notice is taken of the clergyman, and the lieutenant comes to the front ! Indeed it is
very remarkable that the deponent just cited does not
mention his brother clergyman, and near neighbour.

Hugh Maginn, while denying his own part in the execution, makes some significant admissions. In a second
examination Maginn admits he was at Newcastle the day
the prisoners were carried under guard to the Pass.

The Examinacõn of Hugh Maginn of Dromara, in County
Down, taken this 1st Jan. 1652 [-3] :
Who being accused for having a hand in ye murdering of Lieut.
Trevor and severall other persons in the Pass neere Dundrum, at

---

* The deposition torn at margin, and some words missing.

ye beginning of ye Rebellion, denyeth that he had any hand in it, neither was he present or knew of it till it was done, but sayth that he heard one Donell M'Kendrigan and Patrick O'Gormely and Bryan M'Rory and Torlagh M'Murphy, being Collo M'Murphy's brother sone (*sic*), and Aghalee McArt M'Hugh M'Phillip Maginis, and divers others that he cannot now remember, confest they were at ye Action, and he saw him yt was chiefe in ye said murder, and had comand of the rest, dealing the said cloathes, whoe is called Con. M'Art M'Hugh M'Phillip Magennis, whom he saw lastly at Dromore.

Pat O'Sheale and Teige oge O'Sheale can testifie in this matter. *Jur.*: GEO. RAWDON.

Teige O'Sheale, of Mourne, examined on oath, 8th June, 1653,

Who saith that he lived in Ardaghy (parish of Kilcoo), at the beginning of the Rebellion being within four miles of Newcastle but saith that he did not remove from his own house, lest his cattle and corne should be taken away. . . . Saith he heard yt one Lieut. Hugh Trevor with his wife and children, and one John Weston, were prisoners at Newcastle aforesaid, and were from thence to be convoyed to one William Kellye's house, and by one Don. Magin, Hugh Magin, Donell McKengrian, Bryan McGrory, and others whose names he remembers not, [by order of Sir Con Magennis then governor there,] and from the said Wm. McKellye's (*sic*.) house they were to be guarded to Lisnegarvy (*sic*) to release the son of the said Wm. Kellye. . . . Saith that on their way to Mr. Kellye's house aforesaid, heard [by a common report yt.] they were all slaine by the said Don. Magin, Hugh Magin Donell MacKengrian, etc.

Pat O'Sheale gives a similar account, with the addition or variation that the men who were to convoy the prisoners to Wm. Kellye's house " excused themselves saying, they had to go to other places of greater concernment .. .. soe they did not goe."

We have an important statement from another prisoner, Edward Sanders, a soldier of Sir Arthur Tirringham's company, who was made a prisoner when Newry was surprised, and who being carried with the Irish army as far as Lisnegarvey (Lisburn) was at length lodged in Sir Con's house at Newcastle. His deposition, taken 3 May, 1653, sets out that he was born " aged 34 years or thereabouts "; so that he was about 22 years of age at the time the rebellion broke out, and when he became a prisoner in the hands of " the Rebells " :

Sayth that he being prisoner at Newcastell, in the County of Downe, at the beginning of this Rebellion, saw the undernamed persons two or three hours before they were put to death. And being demanded what the Executioners' names were yt put them to death, sayth that he remembers the names onely of two of them,

to wit, Con O'Donelly, and Donelly O'Gorman ; his cause of knowledge is that he saw the sd. pties. after the execučon bringing
sd. people's clothes into the said Castell, whose shirts were bloody,
and yt. he knew one suite of the sd. clothes wch. was worne by
Mr. Tutch, Minister of the Newry ; and also sayth that he was informed by some of Sir Conn Magennis's servants, then in the said
Castell, that the said persons undernamed were put to death by
the orders of the sd. Sir Conn Magennis : and further sayth not.

It is stated at top (fol. 59) that deponent was duly
sworne, but no name of magistrate or commissioner appears.
In the place where the *jurat* and names of presiding
commissioners would appear, we have the list of persons
" undernamed " by the deponent : namely,

> LT. TREAVOR, his wife, *and maid*
> MR. TUTCH, Minister of the Newry
> MR. WESTON
> SAMUELL HANLON
> CLEMENT* STURGEON
> NICHOLAS FOSTER
> FFRANCIS SIMONS
> THOMAS GASKYN.

—Ten persons in all, counting " the maid " mentioned by
no one else—at all events, not mentioned by the son of the
murdered lieutenant, whose deposition is as follows
(fol. 86) :

The examination of Lieutenant Tho. Treavor, of Morne, in
County Downe, aged fourty years or thereabouts, taken 12
May, 1653 :

Who [being duly sworne], saith that he with his ffather, Lt.
Hugh Treavor, lived in Lisnekeade † in the said County of Downe,
at the beginning of the Rebellion, and about three days after his
said ffather was taken out of his house by one Art Maginis, Conn
McBrin, Denis McHullogan, and others, whose names he cannot
remember, being their following, and from thence brought him
prisoner to the Newry, as they alleged, by orders from Sir Con
Maginis, then Governor [thereof], and there he taried untill the
latter end of December, at the end of which time he was brought
out from thence, and carried to Carlingford, and from thence to
Lecale, where [this examinant's said father with others] were to
be exchanged for severall prisoners of the Irish party, then in restraint in Lecale [aforesaid]. But at their being brought thither
Edm. oge McHugh M'Phill Maginis, Hugh Magin, Con Maginis,‡

---

* *James* Sturgeon is the name, as it appears in other depositions.

†Lisnageade, between Scarva and Loughbrickland, still in possession of the
Trevor family.

‡ Mentioned by Mr. Dunphine as the nephew of Edmund Oge Magennis—
not *Sir* Con.

M'Art Groome Maginis, with others whose names he knows not, in whose custody the sd. Lt. Treavor with the rest (vizt., Charles Haughton, Mr. Touch, Minister of Newry, John Weston, Margett Trevor, mother to this examinat, and severall others to about the number of twenty) were (*sic*) hearing yt *ye sd. prisoners belonging to the Irish party were hanged by the English, in Lecale aforesaid,* they [were bringing] the said Lieut. Trevor with the rest back againe, whereupon [in] their way, ye said Edm. oge M'Hugh M'Phil Maginis, passing through ye woods (*as this examinat hath heard*), was lifting up his hand to every tree demanding [of the rest], whether it was high enough or not ; wch. this examinat doth believe that question was propounded in regard that *Lieut. Trevor, this examinat's father, was Provost Marshall before the Rebellion, and had hanged the said Edm. oge M'Hugh M'Phil Maginis his brother :* and Hugh Magin answered that he would have his owne trout (*sic*) ; upon which he did fall upon the said John Weston, and was slashing upon him with his sword untill he broke it, and afterwards gott another sword from one of their party to kill him downe-right, saying that he should not call him to Asizes or Sesions for it ; and in the meantime the said Con M'Art Groome Maginis answered that he would not be more backwarder than any of the rest, and so fell upon the sd. Lieut. Trevor untill he killed him, and the rest of the Irish party upon the English untill they murdered them all. And this examinat saith, that at this time when the sd. murder was comited he was a Lieutenant under the comand of Coll. Chichester, and that he heard the whole relation of the murder comitted upon his sd. ffather, Lieut. Trevor and the rest by the sd. Edm. oge M'Hugh M'Phil Maginis and others from Captain Clarke. And further saith not.

Taken before us.　　　　　　　　　　　THO : TREVOR.
　GEO. RAWDON,
　JA: TRAILL.

The details of the murder are given at second-hand. The really important matter—so carefully kept out of sight by our " historians "—is that the prisoners were put to death in retaliation for the hanging of those of the Irish party for whom they were to be exchanged. Private revenge may have actuated some individual actors in the tragedy, but retaliation was the object : a dreadful business surely, but still distinguishable from the cold-blooded massacre which Harris and his followers so love to dilate upon, with the object of placing in the dock not simply the perpetrators of the crime, but the Irish nation and the Catholic religion for all time.

It may be noted in passing, that Lieut. Thomas Trevor says nothing about the "maid " or the " children " mentioned by other deponents. His statement was taken seven years after the first appearance of Sir John Temple's book—pamphlet, it may be called, differing in no way from the

many blood-curdling brochures of the period but in bulk,
and perhaps in virulence.   But Harris had gone through
all the depositions—there can be no doubt of that—yet he
takes good care to make no allusion to any crime or cruelty
which would rest at the door of any but the Irish Papists.
Yet even Harris, writing in the time of George the Second,
when to blacken the Papists—to at least affect a horror
for their " bloody principles "—was almost a mark of good
taste, may be more easily excused than the nineteenth
century authors who have taken him upon trust.

There are several other depositions bearing on the
execution, which were taken at Carrickfergus in May and
June, 1653, but they add little to what has been cited
already.   Two of these, however, are worth quoting at
length.   On folio 99.

The Examination of Edward Cleark, of Drumlee,* in the county
of Down, gent., adged twenty years or thereabouts, taken before us,
at Carrickfergus, the 8th of June, 1653 :
    This Examinatt duely sworne sayeth, that about Christmas, in
1641, he heard that Lyet. Hugh Trevor, Mr. Tuich, Mr. John
Weston, with severall other prisoners, were conveyed from Newry
through Mourne to Newcastle; this examinatt heeringe his brother
Thomas Clerk, who was in a friend's house be name Edmond oge
Magneise, was sent alsoe to that said Newcastle, went Imediately
thither, and remaining there all night, could not meet his brother
there, but the next morning did see the said Lyet. Trevor, Mr. Tuich,
Mr. John Weston, and other prisoners brought out of a barne neere
Newcastle, by one Hugh M'Ginn, Conn Magnoiss, Conn O'Donell,
with several others their companye, and conveyed them (sic) a
mile from the Castle *where they devided the said prisoners in [two]
halves (sic)*, the said Hugh M'Ginn tooke away the said Lyet.
Trevor, Mr. Tuich, Mr. John Weston, *with the number of six more*,
and marched towards the Pace of Dundrum;† further sayeth that
hee sawe them strip off the sd. prisoners, and did alsoe see them
streevinge (sic) about the said John Weston's scarlett cloak ; further
sayeth that hee saw Con O'Donell and the rest of his comrads
dreevinge ffrancis Symons, James Sturgeon, with others, beinge
his owne neighbours, upp Armerside towards Dundrum Pace ;
further sayeth, that one Rowry O'Morgan came to the examinatt, and
desired him to come along with him, and would bring [him] where
his brother Thomas Clerk was at Edmond oge Magneise's house, and
afterwards as the examinatt and Rowry O'Morgan were mairching
hard by the said Pass of Dundrum, heard a crye, and inquired of
the said Rowry what crye it might bee, the said Rowry answered

---

* Drumlee, in the parish of Drumgooland, about five miles from Rathfriland
and four from Castlewellan, in the County Down, a townland of about
540 acres.   There is also a Drumlee in Antrim, Tyrone, and Donegal
Counties.

    Pass of Dundrum—' The Ballagh ' or pass between Slieve Donard and the
sea.

and said that it was the prisoners hee sawe a-conveying that were a-killing and a-hanging by those that did convey them ; further sayeth not.

Acknowledged [and sworn]* before us
RICH. PRICE;
OWEN WYNN.

EDWARD > CLEARK;
his mark.

Mrs. Eliza Crooker's statement as to the liberation of some prisoners here finds confirmation from an eye-witness who had no other part in the affray. From the statements of others it is to be inferred that the number of prisoners taken to Newcastle did not much exceed twenty, or did *not* exceed that number. According to the last " examinatt " *nine was the number led to execution*, and this agrees with Edward Sanders' list, excluding the " maid " about whom Lieut. Thomas Trevor appears to know nothing. It is deplorable to think that even so many innocent persons were doomed to a violent death, by way of retaliation or otherwise. But the affair, bad as it is, falls far short of the unprovoked enormity put forth by Harris and his faithful followers.

Edward Clarke's brother, an officer, was at the time a prisoner in the house of Edmond Oge Magennis. He does not mention the liberation of any prisoners ; but he was not looking on. His account of the murders is gathered from what he heard in Edmund Oge Magennis's house.

The Examination of Captain Thomas Clarke before Captain Richard Prior, Griffin Howard, and Roger Lyndon, Esquires, the 12th of May, 1653 (fol. 117) :

Who being sworne and duly examined sayth, that at the beginning of the Rebellion, Lieut. Huge Trevor, John Weston, ffrancis Symonds, James Sturgeon, Mr. Tutch, minister, and divers others, were taken from their respective dwellings, and carried to the Newry, to Sir Conn MacGennis, who caused them to be sent from thence to Newcastle neare Dundrum, there to be kept till such prisoners of the Irish party taken in Lecaill by Sir James Montgomery would be exchanged for theis. Butt before that theis came to Newcastle *those Irish prisoners were hanged*, as reported. Whereupon Conn McArt Magenis, Hugh McGinn, and severall others now not alive, havinge the chardge of the said Lieut. Trevor, Weston, and the rest sent from Newry, tooke them away out of Newcastle, and caryed them two myles of to a wood at ye Passe of Dundrum and there murdered all the sayd prisoners, wch. murder on Lieut. Trevor and Weston was as followeth, *as this deponent credibly heard*, hee then a prisoner within 5 myles of Dundrum, in the hands of Edmund Oge Magennis and his souldjers : hee sayth (as informed) that Hugh M'Ginn, being of those that carryed the sayd prisoners

---

* The words 'and sworn' interlined, and in a different ink.

to the passe, tooke John Weston by the collar. ' This man ' (said hee) shall be my share of the trouts ; and presently drewe his sword and struck the said Weston on the head, wth. wch. stroak his sword brake, who thereupon called to his cozen, Art Ballagh O'Rory then standing by, for his rapier, and, taking it into his hand, runn the said Weston twice or thrice thorow the body, saying, ' That will make an end of him, that he shall never write a mittimus to send mee to Downe Jaoyle againe.' And sayth that about a ffortnight after, hee this deponent saw the sayd Art O'Rory were some of the said Weston's cloathes. And demanding of the sayd Rowry why he did not save the sayd Weston, hee answered that hee could not save him out of [Hugh Magin's] hands from being kild. And sayth yt. ye. sayd. Rowry confessed to him that Lieut. Hugh Trevor was kild there ye same tyme, and yt. Conn Maginis* before-named gave him the first blow on his head with his swoord. And sayth all this was alsoe told him by divers of those who said they were present at ye murder, and sawe some of them were Lieut. Trevor's cloathes ; who came that night from the murder to the said Edmund Magenis's house, where this deponent was prisoner. And more sayth not.

Jurat   THO: CLERKE.
RICH: PRICE, ROGER LYNDON, GRIFFIN HOWARD.

Those who will insist on the Ballaghonery executions, deplorable as they were, as evidence to show the intention, if not the perpetration, of an Irish " St. Bartholomew," ought not to overlook the proof of the contrary incidentally —and more convincingly because unintentionally—brought out in statements of deponents who were in no sympathy with " the Rebells." The last deponent was a prisoner in the house of a man suspected, not without reasonable grounds, of being implicated in the murder of Lieutenant Hugh Trevor and his companions in misfortune—a house frequented by those who certainly had a hand in the deed. Yet no attempt is made to molest him by the men whose hands were, we may say, red with the blood of the murdered prisoners. We have seen that it was the same with the Rev. Mr. Dunphine, with Edward Sanders, and with the prisoners elsewhere detained, especially those in the Castle of Newry. If any there are who hold, with our " historians," that Lieutenant Trevor and the others were brought so far simply to be murdered, it is because such persons start, as from an axiom or primary fact, with the assumption that "Papistry and blood " are necessarily associated, and because, like Mr. Walter Harris, they contrive to put out of sight every circumstance not in harmony with the said assumption.

I do not pretend to justify Sir Con's action in this matter. It is hardly necessary to inquire whether he actually gave

*Not *Sir* Con Maginnis.

orders for the execution. We may assume that nothing of
the kind would have been attempted without his assent
express or implied. I unhesitatingly condemn every such
deed of retaliation, however common, in that age, although
I am not sure that something of the kind might not, even
at the present day, be enacted by a superior nation, on
similar provocation. But it is only fair to say that the
execution of these prisoners is altogether exceptional in Sir
Con's career as an insurrectionary leader. On the 25th
October, 1641—that is, two days after he had surprised
"the Newry," and possessed himself of the military stores
there collected, he wrote to the opposing commanders in
the County Down.

" Wee desyre noe blood to be shede, but if you mean to shede our
blood be sure wee wilbe as ready as you for the purpose: This
being all in hast, I rest your assured frend, as I am still,

CONNE MAGNEISE:

Two days later, or on 27th October, the Lords Justices
and Council in Dublin sent Commissions to the Viscounts
of Clandeboye and Ardes to raise the Scots in the northern
parts ; and also wrote to Sir William and Sir Robert
Stewart, with other gentlemen of quality in the North,
giving them power to "prosecute the rebels with fire and
sword." We may imagine how discriminating commanders
armed with such powers would be at such a time—how
cautious and careful the men in their service would be to
avoid hurt or offence to the innocent and defenceless !
Further treatment of this aspect of the subject I must
for the present forbear.

John Babe, mentioned in the deposition of Roger
Holland, was arrested on the double charge—or rather on
the suspicion—of murder and of having been concerned
in a plot for the betrayal of the King's Castle at Carlingford
into the hands of the insurgents at the very outbreak. On
the 18th of June, 1652, being then a prisoner, Babe was
examined at Carrickfergus, and the portion of his statement
I give here shows, or helps to show, why the prisoners
were sent from Newry to Carlingford, why they were sent
from thence to Greencastle, and how many were executed.
This Babe appears to have been a shadowy sort of character,
of no settled principle, and I should not mind his evidence
except where it is corroborated by deponents with whom
there is no suspicion such as rests upon himself. I pass
over the depositions bearing upon his own case, merely

remarking here that, in connection with the warrant, he gives names that no one else gives. Babe was then Marshall or Provost of Carlingford.

And he further saith that there being certain Protestants . . . had quarter given them by ye Rebells, and sent to this examinant to be transported by sea to some of the English quarters, and that before they could . . . conveyed, one Michael Garvey, then provost of ye Newry, where now he liveth, came with a warrant to this examinant from Munke Kryly and Ever McEnos, who acted under Sir Phelim O'Neile to take away *eight of the* . . . *Protestants* from this examinant to be sent, as he, the said Michael Garvey reported, to Downpatrick in ye county of Down, there to be exchanged for prisoners, but by the waye att a place nere Dundrum, the said *eight prisoners were murthered* by one Edmund McEnos and his party of Rebells, as this examinat was tould ('by Michael Garvey' *struck out*.) . . . The names of some of these eight were Lt. Hugh Trevor, Mr. Tudge, minister of ye Newry, the rest of their names he cannot remember. And further sayeth not.

(The Deposition is 'duly sworn,' and signed by 'Rob. Meredith, Hen. Jones, R. A. Hunt, and Edw. Byers.')

" Eight " was, very likely, the number which Babe heard of the " murdered," and that would fix itself in his mind longer that the mere number sent by him from Carlingford to Greencastle. The closeness to the number of the slaughtered as fixed by Edward Sanders and Captain Thomas Clarke, is rather remarkable.

To those who may incline to the " pretence" idea, it may be of some interest to know something more of " Roger Holland of Glaslough, in the County of Monaghan, gentleman," and how he happened to be at Carlingford when the order came for sending a number of the Newry prisoners over the bay to the County Down. The said Roger deposes to losses, owing to the rebellion, amounting to £1,102, a large sum for those times.

He further deposeth that after he was robbed as aforesaid, he was detained in prison with his wife and children, one fortnight in Glaslough, and afterwards they were removed prisoners to Armagh, by Turlogh Oge O'Neil's comand, where he remained prisoner untill the 14th of December, at wch. time he was dismissed by the consent of the said Turlogh Oge O'Neile and others of the Irish comanders, and with great perill of his liffe by God's mercie came to. Dublin the xxviiith of December following.

He was one of a number of prisoners sent from Carlingford by water to Dublin. Their boat was driven into Skerries in the County Dublin. Of his experiences there, he gives a lively and on the whole rather pleasing account:

And when he [*and others*] arrived at Skerries fryer Malone his company shott one shott at the vessell, and asked whether we had a passe or not. Wee told them [wee] had. Whereto they replied that if we had not wee should all suffer, but, so soone as we showed them our passe, they made much of us and told us we should take noe hurt, *wch. they performed.* The next day (being Xmas day) about 2 of the clock in the afternoon (wee going to one Mr. Cardiff's house) the said frere allighted from his horse, and saluted us poore prisoners, upon wch. meeting wee applied ourselves to him, and showed him our miseries, and he told us that we should take no harme as long as [wee] were with him and that he would convey us saffe and sound, *wch. he did perform accordingly.* The next day after he made us stay at his owne howse, and made us very welcome.

It is clear enough from the incidental testimony of Roger Holland, Glasslough, and John Wisdome, Armagh, that the Newry prisoners were taken to Carlingford for the purpose of being sent by water to a place of refuge ; and Wisdome deposes that some of them who had returned from Greencastle, accompanied his party to Dublin. However, while waiting for a favourable wind, or perhaps for the arrival of a vessel, stirring events were in progress in East Down. " The Scots," under Sir James Montgomery, having possessed themselves of Dundrum Castle and Downpatrick, were raiding the Irish districts of Iveagh and Kinelarty. Sir James had succeeded so far as to attack Sir Con Magennis's own strong house " The New Castle," " with a brass field-piece and some falconets of his own, the like whereof the enemy had not ; he so warmly plyed it, that the besieged conditioned to give it up if not relieved by their friends in three days."* The expected relief having arrived, the besiegers retreated to Dundrum ; where the insurgents followed but were prevented by the rising tide from making an attack. The author of the *Montgomery Manuscripts* hints at some sharp practices towards the Irish by the Dundrum garrison. Had he been more explicit as to the exploits of his father Sir James's followers, we should, in all probability, have had less difficulty in finding the explanation of the Bloody Bridge tragedy.

THE MAGENNIS VISCOUNTY.

I. Sir Arthur Magennis, of Rathfriland, in the County Down having been knighted, 1 Nov., 1604, by the Lord Deputy, and having released, before 1613, all his territorial claim to the district of Iveagh, received several extensive " grants " (of his tribal lands), and was created, 18th July, 1623, VISCOUNT MAGENNIS OF IVEAGH, in the

* *The Montgomery Manuscripts*, p. 310.

County of Down. He married, before 1599, Sarah, daughter of Hugh O'Neill, Earl of Tyrone, by his second wife Judith, dau. of Manus O'Donnell. This Arthur, first Viscount Magennis, died 7th May, 1629, and was buried at Drumballyroney, near Rathfriland. (The name of this burial place is incorrectly given as Drumbalong in the Peerages. O'Hart gives the correct form.) He was succeeded by his son,

II. Hugh, the 2nd Viscount Magennis, *b.* in 1599. He *m.* Mary dau. of Sir John Bellew of Castletown. He *d.* April 1630 ; *s.* by his son.

III. Arthur, the 3rd Viscount Magennis. He was excepted from pardon in Cromwell's Act of 1652 ; was one of the Catholic nobility who " remonstrated " in 1663, and appears to have been restored, at least to title. He died, without issue, and was buried, 1 May, 1683, at St. Catherine's Dublin ; *s.* by his brother,

IV. Hugh, the 4th Viscount Magennis, who died without issue and was buried 5 Dec., 1684, in St. Catherine's, aforesaid ; *s.* by his brother.

V. Bryan, the 5th Viscount Magennis (1684 to 1691), who, in 1689, sat in the " Patriot Parliament " held by James II. in Dublin ; for whom he raised a regiment of dragoons, and one of infantry, and by whom he was nominated Lord Lieutenant of County Down. By his attainder in 1691, the peerage became forfeited. He entered the Austrian Service with a battalion of 500 men, whom he landed from Cork at Hamburgh, in June, 1692. He died, without issue, in 1693.

In the *Cokayne Peerage*, iv., 324, is the following note :

" This title seems to have been assumed by various parties even as late as 1783, in which year was hung for murder, Daniel Magennis, M.D., whose nephew thus styled himself (See N & Q, 7th Series, xi., 398). It is stated in Burke's Extinct Peerage (edit. 1883, p. 611) that Magennis, styling himself Viscount Iveagh, was Colonel of the Irish Brigade in Spain, at or shortly before the breaking out of the great French Revolution. Documents signed by him as Viscount Iveagh are in existence."

Sir Arthur, the first Viscount Magennis (*Art Ruadh*) had issue, Hugh Oge (the second Viscount Magennis), 2 SIR CON (of Newcastle), 3 Arthur, 4 Rory, 5 Daniel or Donnell, and three daughters, Rose, Evelin, and Eliza. Sir Con married a daughter of Ever Magennis of Castlewellan.

In King James's Parliament, sitting in Dublin, 7th May to 18th July, 1689, the County of Down was represented by Murtagh Magennis, of Greencastle, Esq., and Ever Magennis, of Castle wellan, Esq. ; the borough of Killyleagh, by Bernard Magennis, of Ballygorrianbeg, Esq.

II.

THE SURPRISAL OF THE NEWRY.

HAD every part of the programme sketched for themselves by the " contrivers " and " authors "· of the insurrection of 1641 been carried out as promptly and as effectively as the capture of " The Newry " (as it was then usual to term the place), there is hardly room to doubt that success would have wiped out the " foul dishonouring word," Rebellion.

The event, as regards this town, was indeed a complete " surprisal." The secret must have been well known to many in the town and throughout the country, yet, no whisper of what was in the air appears to have reached the governor or any of the garrison, or of the " loyalist " inhabitants. Nor was the case of Newry in this respect singular ; for, with one conspicuous exception, the knowledge of the conspiracy was wondrously preserved from coming the way of the betrayer, although it must, for some time previous to the outbreak, have been entrusted to many thousands of persons in every condition of life. Indeed, in this circumstance, as in a good many others, the uprising of that time stands apart from all other commotions recorded in the history of Ireland. The historian, Dr. Reid, very forcibly and—except in one particular from which, further on, I mark my dissent— accurately relates what occurred on the day of outbreak, Saturday, the 23rd of October, 1641 :

Sir Phelim O'Neill of Kinard or Caledon, in the County of Tyrone, engaged to commence the insurrection in Ulster, on the same Saturday by the seizure of its chief places of strength. He was especially charged with the capture of Derry ; his relation Sir Henry O'Neill was to be urged to surprise Carrickfergus ; and Sir Con Magennis, his brother-in law to seize Newry. The Protestants were to be taken and imprisoned with as little violence as possible ; and agreeably to the King's commission, the Scots were to remain unmolested.*—*Reid, i.,* 308–9.

* *History of the Presbyterians in Ireland,* by the Rev. James Seaton Reid, D.D.; 2nd Edition, 3 vols., Belfast, 1867.

And a little further on :

On the same eventful day, Sir Con Magennis, at the head of the Magennises and the M'Cartans, led on by a Father Crelly, surprised the town and Castle of Newry. The governor, Sir Arthur Tirringham, very narrowly escaped, but the entire garrison were captured and disarmed, *and fifteen of the townspeople hanged.** (MS. Depositions in Trinity Coll., Dublin.) The rebels found in the Castle a considerable supply of arms, and, what was still more seasonable, a large quantity of gunpowder.—*Id.* i., 312–13.

The allusion to the king touches upon a controversial point about which Dr. Reid held a very decided opinion— an opinion which has not commanded, and is not likely to command, general acceptance. Exception may also be taken to the alleged intended imprisonment of the Protestants, but these are trifles compared with the imputed execution of fifteen inhabitants of the town, for which he advances no specific authority. The parenthetic reference to the immense collection of depositions in the Library of Trinity College, Dublin, is on a par with the recommendation to search the haystack for the needle. To many, I am sure, the search for the needle would be child's play compared with the herculean labour of wading through the thirty-two or three folio volumes of musty, faded, and for the most part, barely legible, manuscripts. I have devoted some labour and attention to these documents, more especially those relating to the province of Ulster, and among the many wild allegations I have found nothing to support, or even to countenance, the charge which Dr. Reid puts forth in so unqualified a manner. I don't say that he has invented the story : I am sure he was incapable of such a fraud. But he has evidently taken the thing upon trust from some one who, like himself, had no specific authority,—no particular knowledge of the source (if any) of the allegation. Reid's own acquaintance with the T. C. D. depositions was but slight. He tells us he had looked at them to see whether Dr. Warner was justified in saying that most of them were but parole evidence, the words " duly sworne " being struck out. Further on I advance some statements from the depositions to show that the charge is unfounded, and that, so far

---

* Dr. Knox repeats this baseless charge : " On the brea king out of the rebellion in 1641 Sir Con Magennis attacked and took the castle and town (Newry), destroyed the church, *and put many of the inhabitants to the sword."* (*History of Down*, p. 453.) I should like to know what authority there is for either the " destruction " or the " slaughter." I am satisfied there was no such massacre in Newry till Conway and Monro retook the town six months later on. Carte says nothing about such atrocities on the taking of Newry.

as we have any evidence bearing on the matter, we may feel quite sure that nothing of the kind occurred at any time during the seven months of occupation by the insurgent Irish party. I can find no certain allegation of more than two executions within the six months of Rebel occupation ; one of these, if not both, would perhaps come within the purview of the modern military law ; and one of the executed was not an inhabitant of Newry. This will, however, be taken up in due course.

The official accounts of the capture make no allusion to murders or hangings. In their report to the English Parliament the Lords Justices (Parsons and Borlase), writing on 25th October—two days after the outbreak—say :

On Sunday morning, at 3 of the clock, we had intelligence from Sir Arthur Tirringham, that the Irish in the town had that day also broken up the King's store at the Newry, and where the store of arms hath lain ever since the peace, and where they found four score and ten barrels of powder, and armed themselves, and put them under the command of Sir Conn MacGennis, Knt., and one Creely, a monk, and plundered the English there, and disarmed the garrison. *And this, though too much, is all that we yet hear is done by them.*

Nor does it appear that the Lords Justices had anything worse to report from the same quarter, during the ensuing six months. The execution of the prisoners at Ballaghonery Pass,* near Newcastle, Co. Down, is of course inseparable from the history of the insurgent occupation of Newry ; but it is certainly not square dealing to make the same incident count twice—first, on the 23rd of October, and again in the following January; and "fifteen" happened to be the number mentioned in Mrs. Elizabeth Crooker's deposition, as hanged at Newcastle.

The loss of so important a centre and of so large a quantity of arms and ammunition, was a serious matter for the Government of the country. Almost immediately after, they made an attempt to rouse the Ulster Scots to the rescue of "The Newry," sending out several commissions on or about the 27th October. Regarding the recapture of Newry, they must have very much over-rated the response to this appeal, as would appear from a letter of the Lords Justices, dated 5th November, 1641, addressed to the Earl of Clanrickard, the one Catholic nobleman, who all through the long conflict, was never under suspicion of trifling with his allegiance :

* Frequently alluded to as the " Pass of Dundrum," although three miles farther from Dundrum than Newcastle.

We have intelligence that 5,000 Scots are risen in arms against the rebels, and these Scots lie now at Newry, *where they have slain many of the rebels*, and dispersed them from thence saving a few environed in a Castle, which cannot hold out against the Scots.

This announcement was premature. It is not easy to account for such a despatch except on the old hypothesis that the wish was father to the thought. Almost six months had yet to elapse before the Scots and their allies appeared in force before Newry under the command of Lord Conway and General Monro. From the 23rd of October, 1641, till the 1st or 2nd of May, 1642—a period of twenty-seven weeks—Newry remained in the hands of Sir Con Magennis and his kindred. Had they been disposed to such deeds of blood and cruelty towards the Protestants as some authors either artfully insinuate or openly maintain, there was ample opportunity of putting to death every Protestant and Englishman within the Lordship of Newry and the Barony of Iveagh.

I have, in another paper, pointed out a blunder into which Harris has been drawn by one of the deponents— Mrs. Eliza Price—who avers that Newry was *ten weeks* in Sir Con's possession, while he had, if capable of exercising any reasoning power, ample material for fixing the true time, which is almost thrice ten weeks :—

During this period [he writes], the Protestant townsmen suffered the common calamities of war in a high measure such as ransackings, plunderings, imprisonments, misery, hunger, and cold, by which many perished.

The inhabitants, doubtless, suffered the common calamities of war, in having a hostile garrison quartered upon them, and that is no small misfortune at any time. But that there were murders of Protestant or English townsmen, Harris does not say ; and he says enough to show that, if he knew of anything of the kind, he was not the man to pass it over in silence. The " ransackings " were, indeed, the order of the day. At the very time while Newry was in the hands of the rebels, Sir James Montgomery, the Royalist Commander, had quartered himself in the neighbourhood of Downpatrick and Dundrum, where he " subsisted his men by the grain which the enemy had deserted on his first appearance ; *and by the help of the grain of substantial British inhabitants* living next the Ards, and by preys of cattle taken from the Irish beyond Dundrum. Thus "—continues his son, Mr. William Montgomery of Rosemount, author of the *Montgomery Manuscripts*—" he *protected* Lacahill Lecale), for divers months against all the great body of the Irish dwelling on Mr. Bagnell's and the McGennis's estates, and those in Kinnelarty and Iveagh Baronys." *Thus* did Sir James "protect" the lesser English Pale of East Down, the barony of Lecale! There need be no quarrel about the "pillaging." There was plenty of that. And as Dr. Reid and others would say, the British were not slow to "imitate" —if they did not actually lead—the Irish when they could in safety lay their hands on the goods and chattels of the rebels, and, failing these, on the goods of any others as occasion might offer. There was imprisonment also for as many of the Protestant English settlers as it was deemed necessary to keep neutral—a great hardship certainly to those who were imprisoned, but more a question of policy than of cruelty on the part of those who, for the time, had got the upper hand.

The great difficulty of dealing with the allegation of general massacre—or intended massacre—arises from the utter absurdity of the charge. One cannot help feeling that in noticing the thing at all he must, by the very fact of so doing, recognise in some degree the legitimacy of the question. That there are instances of murder or cruelty on the part of particular individuals is, however deplorable, quite another matter. We need not wonder that writers who lean to, or virtually adopt, "the massacre" as their corner-stone, are silent about the letter written at Newry by Sir Con Magennis on the 25th October, 1641—the very day on which the Lords Justices were reporting to the English Parliament the outbreak of the insurrection.

CON MAGENNIS TO COMMANDERS IN THE COUNTY OF DOWN :

DEERE FRIENDS,—My love to you all, although you thincke it as yet otherwise, truie it is I have broken Sir Edwarde Treuere's letter, fearinge that anything should be written against us, wee are for our lives and liberties as you may understand out of that letter, wee desyre noe blood to be shede, but if you mean to shede our blood, be sure wee wilbe as ready as you for the purposse. This being all in hast I rest,—Your assured friend as I am still,

CONNE MAGNEISE.

Newry, 25th October, 1641.

Endorsed : For my loveinge and worthy frends Captain Veaughan, Marcus Trevor, and all other Commanders of Downe these be [delivered].

— GILBERT, *Affairs of Ireland in* 1641, i., 364 (on the opposite page a fac-simile of the original in the Public Record Office of Ireland.)

That letter is scarcely the production of a blood-thirsty rebel. A gentleman of ancient and honoured lineage—

a lineage which was " noble " centuries before James I. conferred a peerage on their house, the very idea of conflict with the English gentry, with whom he had lived on terms of amity and good neighbourhood, was hateful to him, and he would gladly, could the means be found, have accepted a pacific settlement of the matter. The shedding of blood he evidently contemplated with aversion. Yet, if there was nothing else for him, he would not shrink from the terrible alternative. The letter appears to have been written by way of explanation or apology for intercepting and opening a letter addressed to Sir Edward Trevor, then a prisoner in the Castle of Newry. Marcus Trevor was the son of Sir Edward.*

The letter addressed to Sir Edward Trevor but intercepted, I have no doubt whatever, is the same that was sent by Captain Patrick Trevor commanding at Dundalk to Sir Edward Trevor, the bearer of which—named O'Rowney, who ought to be an Irishman—was hanged by order of a court-martial, as was stated by Colonel Donnell (or Daniel), Magennis (younger brother to Sir Con), before the committee of the High Court of Justice, sitting at Carrickfergus, 9th June, 1653 :

As he remembers, long before Christmas next after the Rebellion began, in Anno 1641, there came a messenger called Bryan O'Rowney, from Capt. Patrick Trevor and Sir Henry Touchbourne to Sir Edward Trevor and to Marcus Trevor. In which letters it was desired by them that the English forces in Vlster should bee of good couradge, and march away to Drogheda, where Sir Henry Touchbourne was governor ; that they and this party should joyne together to suppress [and root out] the Irish Rebells ; which letters being taken from the said O'Rowney, after perusal at a counsell of warr held there by the sayd Turlogh Roe O'Neile, then called Governor of Vlster, and ye rest of ye company before set down ; the sayd Ever (Magennis) and this examinant were sent with those letters to Sir Edward Treavor to reade them . . . And sayth that the next day after, by the sayd counsell of warr, the said Bryan O'Rowney was directed to bee hanged, and was accordingly executed, albeit yt this examinant did sollicit earnestly for his life.

It was a bad business for poor Bryan O'Rowney (or Rooney) ; but, at the present day, would anyone fare better if caught " within the lines " bearing letters from the enemy to prisoners ?   A man named King, it also appears, had a narrow escape from the rope for being in some way connected with the same transaction.

* Sir Edward Trevor, in his will made in 1641, styles himself ' a prisoner in Newry, but late of Rostrevor'—anciently Castle Roe or Rory, from the Magennis family.—*Knox, Hist. of Down*, p. 663.

When he made the statement from which the extract is taken, Colonel Donnell Magennis was himself a prisoner at Carrickfergus ; and according to the evidence of others, founded upon common report, the Colonel had a more responsible part in the execution, but all are agreed as to the other circumstances :

The examination of Patrick King, of ye Newry, taken 4th June, 1653, at Carrickfergus :

Who being duly examined and sworne, saith, yt at ye begining of ye wars he lived in ye Newry, and that Captain Patterick Trevor, having employed a messenger called Bryan O'Rooine (*sic*) from Drogheda to Sir Art (*sic*) Trevor and others with letters, was taken by the Irish Guards in ye Newry, and caried with his letters before Coll. Plunkett, Tirlogh O'Neill, brother to Sir Phelim O'Neile, and Hugh boy M'Conell (*sic*) and other Irish gent. then there, amongst whom was Donnell Magennis now in prison. Who having taken the letters from ye said O'Rooine, caused him to be examined, and pretending him to be a spy, caused him to be hanged. And as for Lieut. Trevor, and a man yt was a Dyer he cannot say anything.

William Hall of the Newry, examined 28th May, 1653, upon oath, saith :

Yt. he never heard of any murders comitted in ye Newry at ye beginning of ye Rebellion, except one Will, a dyer, who was hanged there, as this examinant was informed by many, for attempting to run away to Dundalk in regard his house was pulled down by the Irish, but doth believe he was hanged by orders of Donell oge Maginis, because he was Governor there that time.

Patt Babe of the Newry, merchant, examined upon oath, 27th May, 1653, saith :

Yt. he heard not of any murdered in ye Newry, at ye beginning of ye Rebellion, only one William, a dyer, and a Protestant [as he heard credibly], was hanged at ye Gallowes of ye Newry, about Aprill, 1642, for attempting to run away to Dundalk, as he was credibly informed and believes it was by order of ye Governor, for yt none els durst doe it ; and being demanded who it was that had comand at ye time, saith to the best of his knowledge, it was Donell Oge Maginis, now prisoner in Carrickfergus, and Hugh Maginis, Captain of ye castle in his absence

John Butterfield of Newry, examined on oath, 27th May, 1653, saith :

Yt. he heard not of any murders in ye Newry at ye beginning of ye Rebellion except one William (*blank*), a dier, who was hanged at ye gallowes of ye Newry, for attempting to run away to Dundalk in regard his house was puld down by ye Irish, as this examt. was informed by severall in ye Newry, and doth believe he was hanged by ye orders of Donell Oge Maginis, being that he was Governor there at that time.

Michael Garvey, examined upon oath on the same day (27th of May, 1653), deposed to the execution of O'Rowney, but fixes the occurrence "in or about January, 1641-[2]" —an error in dating, but in no way wonderful, at the end of nearly twelve years.

Not one of these deponents—although clear enough about the unlucky postman and the nameless "dyer"— has any knowledge of "the hanging of fifteen townsmen," in the beginning of the rebellion or at any time while the Irish party were in possession. And what may be even more significant, no question relating to such allegation appears to have been put by the Commissioners to any of the deponents. We may take it that, had there been any such execution, it would not have been so passed over, seeing that the hanging of the humble "dyer" receives so much attention. There is, indeed, something left unexplained in the dyer's death. That he was executed by order of the authorities for the time being is well brought out ; and there must have been more in the case than the deponents have cleared up. There is no reason to suppose that the man was put to death merely for attempting to run away, at a time when, if we may credit another deponent, the Protestant residents were ordered to leave the town.

Temple and Dr. Borlase make much of the alleged cruel treatment and murder of a Scotchman and his wife in Newry, during the insurgent occupation, and they parade one Owen Frankland, of Dublin, as witness. This Frankland appears to have been a resident in Newry prior to the outbreak, and to have been somewhat of a money-lender. He makes a joint deposition with Christian Stanhawe (County Armagh, fol. 75, *et seq*) :

Being sworn and examined, Saith, that when the Rebellion began hee, this deponent, was with the said Christian Stanhawe at Clonbelew aforesaid, being sent for thither by her husband to receive of him 40 li and over wch. he owed this deponent, and sayth that he was forced to stay there till January last. : : .

And this deponent further saith, that when the Rebellion began, this deponent had owing unto him in some parts of the Kingdom severall sums of money, whereof, by the Rebellion, he is quite de deprived and spoyled, amounting in all to 550 li at leaste ! . . .

And further sayth that Michael Garvey of the Newry told this deponent and many more that there was a Scotchman, a taylor, that the Rebells drove out of the town of Newry and knockt him on the heade, stript him, and digged a little place, and covered him with turfe. But the poor man, recovering, came [back] naked into the Towne : whereupon the Rebells carryed him and his wife out of the town, and cutt him all to pieces, and with skeans ript. : . .

(*Jurat*, 23 July, 1642.)

He gives revolting details of the butchery of the woman alleging a third death in consequence—all this on the authority of "Michael Garvey of the Newry." Now, Michael Garvey was examined at Carrickfergus, 27th May, 1653 (fol. 188). He told what he knew of Rooney's death. But of the infinitely more heinous crime charged by Temple and Borlase against the Irish of Newry he said nothing, *and was asked nothing*, so far as the examination shows. To parade "Owen Frankland, gent," as a witness to the fact, was gross fraud on the part of those writers ; and it is but one of a multitude of frauds perpetrated by the same "honourable persons," and condoned by their followers. Frankland relates the following on his own authority, apparently, he being then a prisoner :

And a little before Christmas one Mr. Acklan son to ("the" *erased*) a Bp. * and his man being brought to the Newry, and Counsell of Warr sitting upon him, they presently condempned and half hanged his man, then cutt him down, and the next day hanged him outright ; and his Master *being hoodwinked*, was thence carried away to Downpatrick to be prisoner : further, the said Mr. Acklan *levied some men against the Rebells*, which the Rebells meeting withall, killed the most part of them.

So far as I have been able to inquire, Mr. Owen Frankland has this story all to himself, although many natives of Newry were examined at Carrickfergus in 1653.

In addition to the prisoners belonging to the town, it would appear that there was an attempt to secure the persons of all influential parties in the rural district, who would be likely, if left in the enjoyment of liberty, to oppose the Irish movement. Most of the prisoners so secured were brought to Newry, but they were not all kept there. Some were detained in Narrow Water † Castle, some in Green Castle, and in Carlingford Castle, as well as in the Castle of Newry ; and, as it also appears, a good many were billeted in country houses, the owners being held responsible for the "forthcoming" of their wards. We have an interesting account of one such case ; and there are incidental references to other prisoners so detained in country houses ; and they were, I have no doubt, in some respects more fortunate than those immured within the strong walls of the old fortresses. The minister of Donaghmore, a parish situated a few miles from Newry on the way towards Loughbrickland,

* Bishop Echlin, of Down, d. 1635 ; succeeded by Henry Leslie. If there is anything in Frankland's story he places last, what undoubtedly came first, in order of time.

† Probably some were in Narrowwater ; in the other castles, certainly.

the Rev. Patrick Dunphine in his lengthy deposition (fol. 153), made at Carrickfergus on the 26th of May, 1653, says :

> Concerning passages at the Newry, he knows nothing, being there two or three nights only ; but heard that one Con (*sic*) O'Rowney who came from Capt. Patrick Trevor to Sir Edward with letters was hanged, but by whom, or at whose direction, those that lived there then, as Mr. Garvey, Patrick Babe, and others that were moderat and favourable to the Protestants [there] can better tell.

Both men so mentioned by Mr. Dunphine were examined and their statements, so far as they bear on this matter, are given above. Evidently Mr. Dunphine, whose parish lay so near to Newry, had never heard of the " hanging," of which Dr. Reid appears to have so little doubt. Unlike most deponents, the minister of Donaghmore is careful, all through his deposition, to distinguish clearly what comes within his own knowledge and experience from what comes to him through common report and hearsay ; and, unlike some of his colleagues, he has the sense to discover, and the honesty to admit, that there were influential Catholics who were " moderate and favourable to the Protestants." Michael Garvey, who held the rather important position of sub-sheriff, must have been personally known to the deponent ; and his testimony is all the more valuable that Mr. Dunphine was himself a sufferer under " the common calamities of the war." How he became a prisoner in the hands of " the rebells " is thus related by himself :

> Concerning the first coming of the Irish to [Dromore], Sir Con Mageniss sent one Patrick O'Shiel, who is yet living, with a warrant for this deponent the night before they went to Dromore, who brought this deponent from his own house at Donaghmore, near the Newry, to Rathfreylan,* where Sir Con then was, with the whole country about him, and said in the hearing of this deponent that he would goe that night with his army to Dromore to take it or to burn it, and desired this deponent to goe home till he came back, and that he should heare further from him.

Rather civil on the part of the rebel captain. Instead of loading his captive with chains and casting him into a dungeon, he advises him to go home to await further orders. Mr. Dunphine does not think it necessary to say anything of his final arrest. Incidentally he intimates that he was taken to Newry, where he was detained for no more than two or three nights, and, as appears from

---

* In those times the head quarters of the Magennis sept. The Viscount Magennis of Iveagh lived in the Castle, from which the Castle Hill, just outside the Town, was named. The Castle was partly demolished by Mr. Hawkins after the " Settlement."

another portion of his narrative, he was then taken to the neighbourhood of Sir Con's own house at Newcastle, and lodged with a Magennis, whose name turns up in connection with the tragedy of Ballaghonery. But of his own treatment, while so detained, Mr. Dunphine has no complaint.

Since allusion has been made to the expedition against Dromore it may be in place to note briefly what followed. The governor of Dromore, Colonel Matthews, made a promising attempt to defend his town, and succeeded in repulsing a party of the invaders. In the meantime the inhabitants, including the Protestant bishop (Dr. Theophilus Buckworth), had provided for their own safety by a stampede from the place ; the town was left in the hands of the rebels—as it is the custom to call them—and Sir Con made good one part of his avowal made, before leaving Rathfriland, to take or burn the town. Harris says that the Town, including the Cathedral Church, was burned. But when the army in command of Lord Conway and General Monro was advancing to the relief of Newry in the closing days of April, 1642, they found the church alone standing. Doubtless it must have been injured by the fire that consumed all around it ; but it does not appear that any deliberate attempt was made to destroy the Cathedral. The firing of the Town looks like vandalism ; but it probably occurred when the place had to be abandoned by the insurgents.

Without mentioning any authority, Dr. Reid says (i. 322) : " Sir Con Magennis immediately took possession of Dromore *and treated with wanton and unprovoked cruelty* the few Protestants who had ventured to remain."*
" Giles Barrett of Dromore, gent, in the County of Down," had not heard of these " wanton and unprovoked cruelties " when he made his deposition two years after the taking of that Town. Being " sworn and examined " he proves to losses in " goodes, chattells, beasts, cattle, horses, sheepe, corne, hay, fewell, household goodes, apparrell, debts, and other his means of the value, and to his losse, of one thousand and six pounds."

* In recording these events Dr. Reid usually follows Carte, sometimes adopting his words and expressions. In this case he improves on his information. Carte says : " Soon after he (Colonel Matthews) left the town, Sir Con Magennis entered it, and used the few inhabitants that adventured to stay behind *very cruelly* " (*Life of Ormonde*, i., 187). Carte mentions no instance of cruelty—a very unsatisfactory way of writing history. Dr. Reid's paraphrase is worse still. He expands the term "cruelly" into the more damaging phrase, "with wanton and unprovoked cruelty," a proceeding which is certainly not justifiable.

And saith that the Rebels that soe robbed and dispoyled him were those of the septs and (*sic*) Magennis and the O'Neilles [and their companions] as this deponent hath bin credibly tould by his owne wiffe, and that the said Rebels then or soon after, burned all *or the most part* of the said towne of Drumore (he, this deponent being then in England).   GILES BARRETT.

Jur : 3rd Nov., 1643.
      HEN. BRERETON,
      EDW. PIGOTT.

It is not too much to assume that had any cruelties such as Dr. Reid speaks of, been practised, Mr. Giles Barrett would have heard of them from his " owne wiffe," and could hardly have forgotten the matter when testifying to the burning of *most* of the town.

Sir Con must have felt unequal to the task of garrisoning and retaining the town—that is, if the burning was intentional, and not accidental. At any rate he returned to Newry where he was joined by Sir Phelim O'Neill and Rory, the brother of Lord Maguire of Enniskillen, two leaders that have, rightly or wrongly, been held up to much odium by some writers who command perhaps more attention than they merit by their treatment of Irish questions. At Newry, on 4th November, Sir Phelim and Rory Maguire, it is said, issued a manifesto, to which was appended the alleged royal commission which has occasioned so much controversy, with the result that the question of authenticity remains much as it was. In my opinion, both parties to the controversy have been on the wrong track. My present object, however, is not to discuss the merits of Sir Phelim's commission, but to examine the allegations put forth by Harris,* and repeated again and again by subsequent writers, who accept that author's statements almost as they would, perhaps, accept Euclid's axioms.

It is significant that while every deponent makes complaint of robbery and spoil, there is no mention made of any murders such as Reid would certify. Indeed, some deponents, residents in the town, confine themselves to a detail of their own losses. For instance, the very first one in the volume containing the papers relating to County Downe, is as follows :

Christopher Crow, weaver, saith, that about the time of the beginning of this Rebellion, this deponent was robbed and spoiled by the Rebells of all his goods and chattells hereunder mentioned, vizt., cowes and heifers worth xx ^{li}, two mares and a coult worth

* Harris is not indeed so responsible for the allegation of massacre in Newry by the Irish.

ii ^{li}, swine and sheepe worth ii ^{li}, xvii s, corne and hay worth xviii ^{li}; provisions and household stuffe worth xxxv ^{li}.; wch. goodes were taken away at severall times by these Rebells who came into the Newry with Sir Con Magennis, amongst whom the deponent knew Patrick Creely, of the Newry, mercht., James Drumgoole, fo the same, mercht., who tould the deponent that they had warrant from the Governor of the Newry, meaning Sir Conn Magennis, to take up the deponent's goodes for the sd. Governor's use. This deponent had alsoe the lease of a house in the Newry, wh. [house] ˙cost the deponent xxx ^{li} in buildinge, wh. lease is for 3 lives 2 whereof are yet in being, the proffitt of which house it being worth iiii ^{li} per an., the deponent is like to lose until better times of settlement in this kingdome ; soe that the deponent valueth his losses by this rebellion to amount unto an hundred and fowerteene pounds ster.

Signed *pro dic.* IIII CHRISTOPHER.

Jur. 24 *ffebr.*, 1641, *coram nobis.*

(marks by four upright bars):

WILL. HITCHCOCK.

ROGER PUTTOCK.

The values—which we may assume, touch the high-water line—are interesting at the present day.

The second depositions in the book is also a history of losses " by occasion of the Rebellion," and is also interesting from other points of view : *

Christopher Jesson, late of the Newry, ropemaker, being sworne upon the Evanglists, Saith upon his oath, that he was in the citty of Dublin in October last, and he returned homewards on the 22nd of the same month, and on the 23rd of the same month, on his way neere Dondalke, he met Mr. Thomas Croke, Ensign to Sr. Arthur Tirringham, who tould him yt ye Newry was the night before taken by Sir Conn Magennis and other the Rebells of his company, and that all the Protestant houses were ransacked, and their goodes taken away and possessed by ye sd. Rebells. And this deponent coming to Dondalke, sent imediately one Thomas Smith, a boy of about xi years of age, to his this deponent's wife to know whether this deponent might safely returne to his house in ye Newry aforesd., wch. boy brought this answer to the deponent : that the deponent's house was ransacked by ye Rebells, and all his goodes taken away, and that ye deponent might not returne home without perill to his life. And this deponent further saith, that at the time of his going from ye Newry to Dublin [which] was about ye middle of ye said month of October, the deponent wa possessed of the goodes undermentioned to the value undermentioned,

---

* At the risk of being a little tedious I give these two depositions in full. They have never, I think, been printed before, nor, so far as I know, been even mentioned in print. There is a prevalent notion that the depositions all tell tales of blood and massacre. There are a great many, such as these, which have not a word about any crime but that of pillage.

all wch, goodes he left in and about his sd. house, vizt. : beastes and cattle worth ix [li], household stuffe, provision, apparell, and ware belonging to his roper's trade worth at least one hundred and one pounds ten shillings, timber worth ix [li] xiii [s], vi [d], in ready money xxiv li, one lease of a house in ye Newry for 14 years to come, or thereabout, worth forty-six shillings and eight pence a yeare, one lease of a [nother] house for 14 years to come, or thereabout, worth 12s. a yeare, one other [lease of a] house and two parcels of land in Newry for some ten years to come, worth, besides the chiefe rent, clearly 5 [li] per annum, the proffitt of all which leases the deponent is like to loose by occasion of this present rebellion ; and this deponent hath alsoe bestowed in building and repairing of ye sd. houses, lx [li].   And this deponent further saith that there were severall debts due to ye deponent by severall persons whereof [as this deponent is informed and believes] some are now in rebellion, and the rest, by reason of ye Rebellion, disabled to make satisfaction, amounting to ye sum of forty pounds, ster.   And this deponent alsoe left at ye house of Mr. Vesey of Dondalke one horse worth five pounds, which horse this depont. is informed was taken away by ye Rebells, but by whome, in certaine, depont. cannot tell.   Soe that this deponent's whole losses by ye present Rebellion doe amount to the sum of ccxlviii li, ix s. viiid., ster., at the least.

Jur. 25 ffebr., 1641,   The mark of the sd.
WILLIAM HITCHCOCK,   CHRISTOPHER JESSON,
ROGER PUTTOCK.   (his mark, a rude form of the initials " C. I.").

In these two depositions there is not a word about murder or any cruelty beyond that involved in the seizure of goods and chattels.   Jesson's wife, quite naturally, felt alarmed for his safety.   She had probably heard of arrests, and rumours of slaughter may have already been in circulation ; but nothing of the kind in Newry.   The lad of eleven years makes his way to Newry and back again to Dundalk without mishap ; nor does he return with any worse news than Jesson had already heard, except that his wife is apprehensive, and wishes him to hold back for the present.   How the wife herself fares we are not told, but it is reasonable to think that if she had been subjected to any personal hardship some notice of the matter would have been taken in the deposition.*

* In the Antrim volume of depositions is the following :—The examination of Henry Allen, of Ballenderry, merchant, taken at Carrickfergus, the 3rd day of June 1653—Who, being duly sworne and examined, saith, yt at ye beginning of ye rebellion he was a constable in Newry, and so continued a certain time after, in wch. time, about January, 1641, as this examinant heard say, there was one Bryan O'Rooney, yt was hanged for carrying letters to Sir Edward Trevor and others, but who comanded him to be hanged, or who did hang him, this exam. knoweth not nor did heare ; and also that there was a dyer hanged, but by whom or by what comands his examt. knoweth not.

The constable, Allen, relates what he heard of Lieut. Trevor, but of the " fifteen hanged " (according to Dr. Reid) he has evidently never heard, although he was a constable on duty in Newry at the very time when such execution should have occurred. And this deponent was the one to give evidence as to other cruel practices alleged by Mr. Walter Harris, if any such did occur. But no question touching upon anything of the kind was, it appears, put to him by the Committee.

Thomas Richardson, late of ye Newry, saylor, and an English Protestant, sworne and examined, sayth, That since ye begining of ye present Rebellion, vizt. : about ye xxiii of [October] last, in ye yere, 1641, this deponent by the Rebells hereafter mentioned was expelled from and dispoyled of his howses and farmes in Newry aforesd., to his damage of xxx i^r. ster. ; and was by ye same Rebells then robbed of x ^{li} in ready money, of beastes and cattle worth xvii ^{li} x ^{s} , of a fishing boate and nette worth xxxi ^{li} ster. In household goodes and barreld fish, worth lxiii ^{il} ; In all one hundreth and fiftie one pounds x ^{s}

This deponent goes into a rather lengthy recital of the principal actors among "the Rebells," relating some extravagant sayings rather than doings :

Alsoe James Weldon, of ye Newry, gent, Captain of ye Rebells whoe said that the Protestants were all blynd ; ffor that for thousands of yeres the papiste religion (which was true) had contynued. And that it was in their (the papistes') power to bring the Protestants to God, but they (meaning the Papistes) durst not trust them, and that the papistes wold take Tredarth (sic) and Dublin, and there establish a lawe ; and that thoes pties. following were alsoe in ye present rebellion.

And, amongst them,

John Bath, of ye Newry, whoe was purveyor for ye Rebells (and the man that rebelliously took and carried away Sir Arthur Hill's cowes.)

In the list of leaders among " the Rebells," are many names which are still prominent among the townsmen of Newry, such as White, Weldon, Drumgoole, Dowdall, Hanlon, Murphy, O'Hagan, Creely (or Crilly), Garvey, Fleming, etc., and of course, in all these statements, the Magennises come out large.

This deponent, (Thomas Richardson), adds a truly distressful account of his own further experience, which, for the credit of humanity, we may hope is exaggerated :

And further sayth, that after this deponent was pillaged and robbed of his goodes, and after that he and his wife had gathered or [recovered] some poore clothes, as other poore English had done ye Rebells made a proclamation for all English to depart or suffer perpetuall imprisonment or death. Whereupon ye deponent and his wife and 5 smalle children goeing away, were stript of all their clothes and meanes [left] and flying away for safftie naked in ye frost, one poore daughter of his, seeing him and his (*sic*) mother greeve for their generall misery., in way of comforting said, she was not cold, nor would crye, although presently after * she died by that cold and want.

This proclamation is not mentioned by any other deponent. It is not unlikely that some were exposed to such ill-treatment, perhaps, owing to unpopularity ; and unpopularity does not always come of desert. The two sensational deponents, Elizabeth ʃCrooker and Eliza Price (or Peirce), have some dreadful things to relate, but they cannot be taken as corroborating the allegation of general expulsion.

Elizabeth, ye wiffe of Michaell Peirce, late of ye Newry, in ye County of Downe, sworne, deposeth and saith, That since ye begining of ye present Rebellion, and by meanes thereof, her sd. husband and shee were deprived, robbed, or otherwise dispoyled of their meanes, goodes, and of all els worth one hundreth and nynetie pounds, and of deedes, evidence, and writing manifesting their estate to landes [and tenements] in England neerly 60 ᴵᴵ. per an : The wch. she feareth wilbe lost from her and her children for want of the said deedes, evidence, and writing . . . And sayeth, that her husband about the xvth of December last dyed of a sickness which she thinketh was procured by greefe and occasion of the Rebellion : and by a blow he had from a Scott, that since the Scottes recovered the Newry, hindered him in the 'xecution of his place.

The deponent has nothing to say about "the hanging," on the surprisal of the town, "of fifteen townspeople," nor does she allude to any bad treatment, beyond " the spoyle," on the part of " the Rebells " ; and it was from one of the " relief " party that her husband, it appears, received his death blow. The greater part of her deposition relates to what took place, not in Newry, but at or near Newcastle on the opposite side of the county, in January following ; and she winds up with this enormity :

And many of the men and women [of the best ranke and quality among the Rebells] did confidently averr, That they and the other Irish soe much hated the English, and their very fashions in clothes, that [they resolved] after the Irish hadd gotten the victory, all the women in Ireland should, as formerly, goe [only] in smocks, mantles, and broages, as well ladyes as others ; and the English fashions to be quite abolished.

Jur : 10 Jan : 1642–[3].

* *Struck out ;* ' as this deponent is verely persuaded.'

Mrs. Elizabeth Crooker has many extraordinary experiences, and has heard of many harsh things done, or
intended to be done in Newry and elsewhere, but she has not
heard of any bad effects from the cruelty with which she
credits the Viscountess Iveagh.

And saith that the Viscountesse Ivaghe *was so cruell* agt. the
English and Scottish that *she was very angrie* with the souljers
because they did not put them all to death.

Mrs. Elizabeth Price had heard of the same "cruelty,"
but she adds that "Sir Con's brother prevented the bloudie
intentions." It is no way wonderful that the two Eliza's
living in the same town had got the same story. Had there
been such thing as cross-examination at the taking of these
depositions, Mrs. Price, or Mrs. Crooker, would perhaps
have been asked to say how she came to know so much
of Lady Iveagh's mind and dispositions, for on that point
as on many others we have no more than "the talk of the
women." It is, however, satisfactory to know that, if the
noble lady had any such wicked propensity,—and there is
really no evidence of it—she was not permitted to have
her own way.

The Lady Iveagh here alluded to, is, I have no doubt,
the relict of the second Viscount (Hugh, who died in 1630,
at the early age of 31, having been born in 1599), and
mother of Arthur, the third Viscount who, at the time when
the rebellion broke out, could be little more than a mere boy.
The young Viscount could hardly have exercised much
influence either on the outbreak or on any of the events of
those years. He was present at the siege of Downpatrick—
or rather, of Lord Cromwell's * strong house (which stood
on the rising grounds adjoining the town)—in the spring
of 1642, but he could have taken little part either in the
siege or in what followed, although his presence on the
occasion has been noticed by several deponents. Ill-founded
as the notion would appear to be, it was not confined to
the women deponents. Captain Henry Smith of Loghedyne
in the County of Down, gives a pretty long enumeration
of the rebels whom, during his twenty-seven weeks' imprisonment, he had observed to be prominent or active
in the movement and among them,

Ever Magennis† father-in-law to Sir Con Magennis, (*blank*),
M'Cartan, Esq., of the County of Downe, the young Lord of Iveagh,

* The Cromwells of Ardglass, Viscounts of Lecale, were descended from
Thomas Cromwell, Earl of Essex, and therefore nearly related to the Protector.
† Of Castlewellan.

a young, but a desperate and cruel rebell, and *his mother,* the sister of Sir Christopher Bedloe* *a cruel and forward rebell alsoe.*

But, all the time, we hear of no overt acts, to bear out the character for cruelty, on the part of either mother or son   The charges, so put forth, were of course sufficient to secure from the government of that day, the outlawry of the young Lord of Iveagh ; but that he could not have been guilty of cruelty or murder, or in way responsible for the hardships of which, no doubt, some had reason to complain, is amply sustained by his restoration to title under Charles the Second, a " favour " not likely to be bestowed upon him if not held to be "an innocent Papist." The boy Viscount might mingle in the stir, but the authority and the responsibility remained with his uncles, Sir Con, Daniel (or Donnell), and Rory, and not one of them showed any real competence for military command. To Donnell even hostile witnesses allow the credit of preventing murder, and that is no ordinary tribute, coming from such sources. As governor of the Castle, in the absence of Sir Con, he appears to have been actuated by motives of humanity : none of the prisoners in his charge made any complaint of harshness, and it is almost certain that had there been any grounds for such complaint it would be forthcoming. But all the while "the Colonnell," as he was called, was not a man of military genius. Had there been among them even one capable commander, Newry would not have been retaken so easily as the event proved.

John Parry, gentleman, of Armagh, one of the more important witnesses at Sir Ph' lim O'Neill's trial, in his lengthy and somewhat sensational deposition (sworn 31 May, 1642), relates certain passages which he heard from one William Taafe in the house of Michael Harrison at Curren, County Tyrone :

Likewise the said Taafe, speaking of the young Lord of Evagh, said that he could Love him but that his face Looked English-like.

This was of course seized upon to show how intense was the animosity of " the Rebells," against the English, and everything that was English if only in semblance.

The part assigned to " Monk Creely," both in the official despatches and in the " depositions " is explicable only on the hypothesis so much in vogue then and since, namely, that no plot against the state could be either con- cocted or carried to effect without the aid of a priest, a friar, or—better still—a Jesuit. If Monk Creely showed

* Bellew.

himself at all among the insurgents we can understand
how the circumstance would be laid hold on—how it would
be turned and magnified till " Monk Creely " would become
the director-general of the business, having principal
charge of the engines of torture, and these, of course would
all be of his own contriving. The Rev. Dr. Maxwell,
Rector of Tynan, and subsequently Bishop of Kilmore,
whose voluminous deposition has been, among writers
of a class, regarded as a text book on the horrors of the
Rebellion of 1641, assures us with much gravity, " so that
a man can see noe part in this tragedie wherein there is not
a devil or a friar or both ! " And had the rev. deponent
been asked to indicate which he considered the more productive of evil, he would very likely, and without hesitation
aver that the " fryer " being the more visible was the
more active member of the firm.

In the sixth volume of the very interesting collection
of pamphlets known as the Thorpe collection * is one
" licenced on 23rd December, 1678," which bears the following sensational but highly suggestive title : " An Account
of the Bloody Massacre in Ireland, Acted by the Instigation
of the Jesuits, Priests, and Friars, who were promoters of
these horrible Murthers, prodigious Cruelties, barbarous
Villanies, and inhuman Practices executed by the Irish
Papists upon the English Protestants, in the year 1642."

It was therefore necessary to give a post of honour—
not, by any means a sinecure—in the surprisal of Newry
to a Friar ; and, the Friar being in it, there must, in consequence, be a large output in the shape of hangings, and
other inhuman practices !

I have already made some allusion to the names of those
who took a part more or less forward in the insurrection.
Of the Newry names a good many are not of Irish origin,
some being decidedly English. It is the same generally
over the county, the south and east in particular. In the
long list of outlawry contained in the deposition of Peter
Hill of Downpatrick, Esquire, High Sheriff of the County
Down, much prominence is given to the descendants of
the early English adventurers in Down—the Russells,
Fitzsimons, Audleys, Savages, etc.—whose ancestors came
with John De Courcy to make settlements for themselves
in the rich claylands of Lecale,—a district which in a short
time they organized into another English Pale. Mr.
Peter Hill would make one of the Russells responsible
for the tragedy of the " Bloody Bridge," but although

* In the National Library, Kildare Street, Dublin.

Walter Harris follows on the same lines, the depositions of all who had some means of knowing the circumstances, are wholly inconsistent with such allegation. That the old English of Lecale and Ardes were, however, actively concerned in the Irish movement is beyond doubt. And the circumstance is not a little remarkable, when we consider how short a period had elapsed since they regarded themselves as a people altogether distinct from, and altogether superior to, the old Irish around them. Campion, writing in 1571, mentions the Russells, Savages, Fitzsimons, Audleys, etc., as English gentry. The waves of more recent colonization, of Elizabeth's and James's reigns, effected a great change, bringing home to the "gentry" that isolation would no longer avail, and that in the hungry eyes of the new-comers they were but Irish Papists, and subject to all the disabilities of the "mere Irish," such as the Magennises, M'Cartans, and O'Neills. The writers, who will maintain that the Rebellion of 1641 was without cause, must put out of sight that it was not without sufficient reason that hereditary foes, the old gentry of the Pale and the older gentry of the hills, joined hands under a common standard.

With the fall of "the Newry," the other strong places on the shores of Carlingford Bay—the castles of Carlingford, Narrow Water, and Green Castle—came into the hands of the insurgents. The recapture of these places by the British—the English and Scotch forces combined—at Maytide, 1642, I treat of in another paper. But by way of relieving the sombre character of what is already set out, I take leave to add some sketches and incidents from the career of the man to whom we owe no inconsiderable part of our knowledge of that expedition for the "relief" of "the Newry," and of what happened in and about the town during the two years ensuing. These incidents are associated with an interesting little Romance of the Scotch occupation of the town which lasted till about the close of 1643, when, by arrangement with Ormond, the place was given over to an "English" garrison, Royalist, at least in name.

I shall have occasion when I come to the "relief" to make some use of Sir James Turner's Memoirs (printed at Edinburgh, 1829.) There is a blunt honesty in the homely record of this Scotch soldier such as one seeks for in vain in most works written at the time. He was, if of any particular principle in politics, a royalist; but, rather than be left out in the cold, he had no objection to take part with those who were not among the King's friends.

" I had a principle," he says, " not yet having studied a better
one, that I wronged not my conscience in doing anything
commanded to do by those whom I served."

Sir James served his apprenticeship in the horrors,
if not the art, of war, in Germany, on the side of the King
of Sweden, Gustavus Adolphus. One scene of slaughter
which he witnessed he thus describes :

We layd siege to the strong towne of Hammelln which held
out with the destruction of multitudes of our men till the 28th of
June, and till the two Earls, Merod and Grunsfield, both Imperial
Generals, came with an army of 20,000 men to relieve it. We broke
up and met them foure English miles from hence, and fought them.
This was a battell wherein so much blood was shed, as was enough
to flesh such novices as I was. We gained the victorie, which
was a great one to be gained with so little losse on our side. Neer
nine thousand of the Imperialists were killd in the place, three
thousand taken, with eighteene canon, and above eightie standards
and collors. The Towne yeelded thereafter on articles. After the
battell *I saw a great manie kild in cold blood by the Finns who pro-
fesse to give no quarter.* . . . I had often heard at School
Dulce bellum inexpertis.

One other picture of the horrors of war I cannot forbear
transcribing :

In the year 1637, I went with some commanded men with Lieut.
Generall King into the land of Hessen to assist the Landgrave
to beate some Imperiall regiments out of his territories, who, indeed,
were making havocke of all among his poor subjects. Upon our
approach they retird ; bot thogh we were tuo to one against them,
and that Bigod, who commanded them made a stand at Eshvegen,
yet did we retire in great haste though in good enough order back
to Cassels, the Landgrave's residence and capital citie, and left
the poor country to the mercie of an enraged enemie, who had
order by fire and sword to force the Landgrave to accept of *the
Peace of Prague.* Neither did Bigod spare to burn three faire
Tounes, Eshvegen, Olendorpe, and Vitsenhausen, before our eyes.
A mournfull sight it was to see the whole people folow us, and
climb the two hie rocks which flanked us. Old and young left
their houses, by the losse of them and their goods to save their lives.
Aged men and women, many above four score, most lame or blind,
supported by their sonnes, daughters, and grandchildren, who
themselves carried their little ones on their backes, was a ruthfull
object of pitie to any tender-hearted Christian, and did show us
with what dreadfull countenance that bloudie monster of warre
can appear in the world. Neither did our feare (which often masks
itself with reason of state, as then it did) permit us to make anie
stay at Cassels, bot pousd (*sic.*) us with some haste to Westphalia.

These incidents are by no means irrelevant to our
theme ; and, as will be seen again, the man, who had grown
familiar with " the dreadful countenance of the bloody

monster " while in Germany, condemns in the strongest
language the cruelty and slaughter practised against the
Irish by his companions in arms.

Turner had not been long in Germany when he had
almost fallen victim to the charms of a youthful widow :

> In the beginning of the year, 1634, our English and Scotch
> regiments came to be quartered at Oldendorpe, neere to which
> the battell [of Hammelln] was fought. I was lodged in a widow's,
> whose daughter, a young widow, had been married, to a ritt-master
> of the Emperor's. She was very handsome, witty, and discreet ;
> of her, thogh my former toyle might have banished all love thoughts
> out of my mind, I became perfitlie enamoured. Heere we stayd
> six weeks, in which time she taught me the Hie Dutch, to read
> and write it, which before I could not learne bot verie rudlie
> from the sojors.

Turner did not after all, find his fate in Germany,
but in Ireland while he was stationed at Newry as an officer
of the Scotch Garrison under Lord Sinclair :

> Thus was I at toyle and trouble enough for the space of tuo
> years in Ireland, having got no more in the employment than what
> maintained me.   Yet I had a purchase in it that I value more
> than anie worldlie riches, that was of my deare wife Mary White,
> with whom I was first acquainted, and then enamoured, at the
> Neurie. She was comd of very good parents ; her father being
> the second son of a knight, and her mother of ane other good familie
> of the Whites. She was thought by others, much more by me,
> to be of a good beautie. For the qualities of her mind I have had
> such experience as they have rendered me happie amidst all the
> afflictions hath befallen me since. I did not then marry her, because
> at that time she was tenacious of the Roman Catholick persuasion,
> which was very hatefull to our leading men of Scotland ; neither,
> indeed, in the condition where in I was then could I maintain her
> in any good fashion

Did Mary grow less " tenacious " of the " persuasion "
of her family ?   There is a suspicious note in the little phrase
" at that time." Besides, further on, he tells us that for
him she abandoned *all* that was dearest to her. Years
of strife and trouble passed, and Sir James was drawing
closer to the King. In the summer of 1646, Charles threw
himself into the arms of the Scots at Newark only to
find himself, not merely a prisoner, but a chattel, in their
hands. It was then that Sir James decided on making
Mary his wife, without further delay, although his pros-
pects were just then gloomy enough :

> When I perceavd things in this troublesome condition, not
> knowing what might be the issue, whether I might not be necessitated
> to fly beyond seas (for the Committee and Generall entertained

very ill thoughts of me), and not daring to go to Ireland least they sould think I went about more serious affairs, I sent and desired her who was to be my wife, to be at the trouble to come to England to me; which she willingly did. This both *shew* her affection to me, and the trust she reposed in mine; leaving her parents, her friends, country *and all that was deare to her*, upon my word.

The incident which he next sets forth, without the least affectation or reserve, is characteristic of the man :

And, indeed, she found me but in bad condition, and it was well it was no worse; for having drunke at one time too much at parting with a great person, riding home I met one Colonell Wren, between whom and me there was some animositie. He was afoot, and I lighted from my horse; drinke prevailing over my reason, I forced him to draw his sword, which was too great handfulls longer than mine. This I perceiving, gripd his sword with my left hand, and thrust at him with my right; bot he stepping back avoyded it and drew his sword away, which left so deep a wound betweene my thumb and foremost finger, that I had almost lost the use of both unles I had been well cured. Ane other hurt I got in the left arme. The passengers parted us; bot I could never find him out after to be revenged on him, though I sought him farre and neere. This was one effect of drinke, which, beside the sinne against God, hath brought me many inconveniences. This was the first time ever my blood was drawne, thogh I have hazarded it and my life very often, not onlie in battells, skirmishes, rencounters, sieges, sallies, and other public duties of service, bot also in severall private duells. I was not well recovered when she I lovd best came to England. Shortlie after, we were married at Hexame, in presence of an honourable companie, on 10th of November, 1646. Many sad storms and blasts of adversitie hath she patientlie stood out with me since, and both of us have reason to blesse God who hath graciouslie deliverd us out of them all.

Of his two years of " toyle and trouble " at the Newry, he gives some lively sketches. He accompanied the " relieving " forces in their destructive march through Iveagh and Kinelarty, " to bring up from Craigfergus as many of the regiment as were comd from Scotland." This reinforcement to the garrison of Newry he brought by water from Carrickfergus to Carlingford. Their life at " the Newry " was not a happy one.

We complained, as we had good reason, to be left in a place which *our owne people had made destitute* of all things. . . .Pitifull quarters we had, and when the rest of the regiment came over which that summer they did, we found we had not houses for the half of them; for we were necessitated to take down a great many houses to make the circumference of our walls the lesse. Our owne preservation taught us to worke allmost day and night, till we had finished the irregular fortifications begunne by the rebels. This great fatigue and toyle, a very spare dyet, lying on the ground like sheepe, constant watching, Sir Phelemy being for the most part allways within a day's march of us, all these, I say, added to the change of the aire, made most, or rather indeed, all our officers and sojors fall sicke of Irish agues, flixes, and other diseases of which very many dyed. Those who recovered, being inured to hardship and well trained, became excellent sojors and good firemen . . . Not one officer or sojor escaped sickness, except the Lieut-Colonell. About Januare, 1643, I fell grievouslie sicke of an Irish ague, which brought me to deaths doore, but it pleased God, I recovered.

Of their privations, and how they obtained supplies, he says :

My Lord Sinclaire stayd with his regiment, in great scarcitie at the Neurie, till the next year, 1643, and then fell dangerouslie sicke ; being recovered, he returned to Scotland. In the time of his stay we fingered bot little moneys, and meale so sparinglie as seldom we could allow our sojors above a pound a day ; for this reason, whenever we had intelligence where the rebells were with their cows, either my Lieut.-Colonell or I sought them out with a partie of three or four hundreth foot and some horse; in most of which little expeditions we were successful, bringing in store of cows, with the flesh and milk whereof we much refreshed the decayed bodies and fainting spirits of not onlie our sojors, bot many of our officers also. Some losse of men sometimes we suffered, but seldome ; many prisoners we tooke, on whom, if we did not set them at liberty, we *bestowed* some maintenance, *bot made them worke at our fortifications.*

This generosity towards rebels was certainly worth recording. And at the same time, and in the same place, every poor Irishman who had a cow was sure to be a rebel— or to be treated as one. I wonder did these foraging parties draw no blood while out among the hills around " the Newry." I am afraid they did ; but blood was too much of an every-day experience to think about in those years. And notwithstanding their industrious pillaging, the garrison's supplies remained at a low ebb.

About Lambes in this year 1642, came Generall Leven over to Ireland. . . . Great matters were expected from so famous a captain as Leven was, but he did not answere expectation. One cavalcad he made in which I joynd with him, with 300 men, in which I could not see what he intended, or what he purposed to himselfe. Sure I am he returned to Craigfergus without doing anything. And the same game he playd over again at his second march, except that he visited the Neurie, for which we were but little obliged to him, being forcd thereby to part with our hay, wine, beere, and breade, of which we were not very well stord.

He has some sly hits at this " Old Lesley," Earl of Leven, who at eighty years of age had still " so good a memory that he was never known to forget himself." One little brush, Turner had with Owen Roe O'Neill, but Owen was not yet in form to show what he could do :

In May, if I remember right, of the year 1643, Monro tooke the fielde with 1,800 foote and two or three troops of horse. When he came to Kirriotter (Poyntzpass), seven miles from the Neurie, he wrote to my Lord Sinclare to send him 300 musketeers, and either his brother or me with them.

Next day Sir James Turner and his musketeers joined Major-General Monro at Armagh, as arranged at Poyntzpass:

We marched from Armagh foure miles into the baronie of Loughgall, a very close country, full of hedges and ditches. I told the Major-Generall that undoubtedlie we wold find O'Neale before us, and therefor desird that no horse soud be permitted to goe before me, in regard they could do no service in that country bot be an hindrance to the foot. Yet Major Ballantine wold needs march before me ; bot at a place called Anachshamrie, which was Generall O'Neal's owne house, he was shamefully chasd back upon me, two of his horsemen being killd, three hurt, and the rest exceedinglie terrified. The roadway being none of the broadest, and ditches on everie side, I was more troubled with these horsemen than I was by the Irish. . . . I then made a stand, and lyned the hedges on all sides of me, constantlie fireing from them, and advancing still on the hieway, thogh verie leisurlie. The body of Monro's foote were a great deal farther behinde me than either I thoght, or O'Neale fancyed, otherwise, I suppose he wold have left his post advantageous as it was, and advanced on me, being five to one against me. The dispute continued very hot about an houre, and then Major Borthwick, since a Colonell, and Captaine Drummond, since a Lieut.-Generall, came up with a great pace to my releefe. . . . O'Neale perceaving his men beganne to looke over theire shoulders, resolved rather to retire than flie ; and so he did to Charlemont. Thither did also runne the most parte of the countrey people, with neere 3,000 cowes, all which we had got if we had pursued our victorie. Owen's house was immediately plundered and burnt and so were many other fine houses in the right pleasant country.

In this skufle I lost thretteene sojors and a sergeant, all killd on the place, and aboute eighteene I had wounded ; neither myself nor any other officer being hurt. The Irish confessd to have lost about three score.

The Scotch forces in Ulster held aloof from the Cessation of 1643. Turner and his comrades had, however, got enough of " the Newry," and they set about arranging a truce with the Irish in a fashion which shows how much the Scotch Royalists and the Irish Rebels had in common :

Towards the end of this yeare, 1643, our garrison at the Neurie fell in extreme want of all manner of provision, both for back and bellie. For this reason, by Monro's toleration, I had a meeting with an Irish Colonell, one Thurlo O'Neale sent by Sir Philemy. We met at Kirriotter, each of us tuenty horse, and after ane houre's discourse, *and the drinking of some health's in Scotch aquavitie and Irish uskiba,* we concluded a cessation of arms with them for our owne garrison. Bot this did not supply our wants ; for no monie came to the armie, either from England or Scotland, and very little meale came from Craigfergus to us. Where for my Lieut.-Colonell, and I resolved that I sould go speedilie to Scotland and procure ane order to the regiment to march to the Ards and Clandeboy, and that immediately after I was gone and that a ship with some meale which we hourly expected, was arrived, he sould ship in his ammunition, baggage and sick men, and then march straight to the Clandeboy. The Neurie was to be presentlie delivered to the English, for I had gone to Dundalg (*sic.*), and agreed with my Lord Moore. This was presentlie put in execution.

III.

WAVES OF BLOOD.

PART FIRST.

THE pamphleteers and historians, so-called, of the time, have racked their brains in the endeavour to portray the " Irish Rebellion of 1641" as the greatest and most gratuitous iniquity in the records of mankind, and they have stretched their endeavour to the very utmost extravagance and hyperbole. The spirit and the political outlook of the age, in some measure, excuse the rancour of those writers. But no such excuse can be made on behalf of many modern authors, some of them claiming to be of the front rank, who, instead of approaching the subject in judgment and moderation, would fain 'outvie the seventeenth century horror-mongers, and, in their eagerness to imitate, betray a sort of "admiring despair."

In the tracts and pamphlets preserved in libraries there is a plentiful supply of the "shockers" of those days, but the gem of them, I venture to say, is the speech delivered by Colonel Audley Mervyn to the English House of Commons, on the 4th of June, 1642. Much use has been made of that speech by writers who aim at keeping up the Empire by decrying an "integral part" of it; but they one and all do the gallant and honourable gentleman the injustice of ignoring the very passage which, if he had said not another word, ought to have been enough to immortalize him :

But now, Master Speaker, the thunder roars from the rebell's cannons, the lightning flashes from their fire-works, *the waves of innocent bloud crouds** up in heaps !*

And a little further on :
Though the poyson of this rebellion was diffused through the veines of the whole kingdom, yet it broke the skin with its playgue token in the Co. of Tyrone and Fermanagh first.

* *Sic*, as in Gilbert, *Affairs in Ireland in 1641*, i., 465.

The Colonel's history, like his metaphors, is of his own making.   There was a rather noticeable " eruption " at Newry as early as " the poyson " anywhere " broke the skin " ; but the orator was thinking of the county with which he was himself more immediately connected. There was nowhere much " thunder " roaring from the rebel's cannons, for the very good reason that they had no cannons to speak of. Nevertheless, the Colonel's "roaring " was heard over all England, and he found enough of imitators to keep it up.   But who among them all, from that day to this, ever reached the sublime of horror with anything to equal " the waves of blood "* that " crowd up in heaps."

Yet some of them have done not badly. Less grotesque, perhaps, but hardly less extravagant, is Burnet in his Life of Bishop Bedell of Kilmore :

> But here I must open one of the bloodiest scenes that the sun ever shone upon, and represent a nation *all covered with blood* that was in full peace, under no fears or apprehensions, enjoying great plenty, and under an easy yoke, under no oppression in civil matters, nor persecution on account of religion.
>
> BURNET : LIFE OF BEDELL, *p.* 136.

All covered with blood ! Now the very county in which Bishop Bedell lived may be cited in contradiction of such a charge, if anything so ridiculously absurd admits of contradiction.   All are agreed that the County Cavan, owing to the humanity and influence of Philip O'Reilly, one of the " authors " of the rebellion, was singularly free, or almost free, of the stain of murder.   The Rev. Richard Parsons, Vicar of Drung, in the diocese of Kilmore, in his deposition, taken 24 February, 1644 (o. s.), was able to tell the Commissioners a good deal about many murders committed in other parts of Ireland—" generally in all the province of Ulster *except in the County of Cavan,* where they spared more lives than were spared in the other counties."

The account which Burnet gives of the rebels' behaviour towards the subject of his biography is, of itself, a sufficient answer to his wild statement about " blood."   From the outbreak of 23rd October till the 18th of December following Dr. Bedell was permitted to remain in his own palace, and to make it a sanctuary for many refugees.   He was then taken with his two sons and son-in-law to Clough-Oughter Castle.   It was, no doubt, a hard trial to the good

---

* I am afraid Dr. Reid has been doing a bit of quiet plagiarism when at the close of his VIth chapter he mentions the rebellion which broke forth, ' and deluged the country with *seas of blood.*'

old man to be taken at mid-winter from his own
home, and quartered in the comfortless, and scarcely
habitable old castle, closely surrounded by the water
of the lake. But no harshness, beyond detention, was
offered or intended. After about three weeks' confine-
ment they were released in exchange for four Irish prisoners
taken in a sally by Sir James Craig, Sir Francis Hamilton
and Sir Arthur Forbes. But the Bishop, then over 70
years of age, was released only to die.* His remains were
followed to the grave by the " rebel " soldiery, who manifested their regard for the noble and saintly qualities of the
deceased, as if he had been of their own flock.

And then, what a paradise was Ireland previous to that
Rebellion ! The reign of Saturn must have been a sad time
compared to that which Ireland enjoyed under Elizabeth, and
James, and Charles ! Only the wretched people could never
be made to understand how supremely happy they were
under the rule of Mountjoy and Carew, Chichester,
Wentworth, Parsons and Borlase ! The Irish people would
not put up with contentment and plenty. They would
arise as one man—the high, the low, the rich, the poor—
the English Lords of the Pale and the Milesian peasants of
the bogs and the mountains—all would rebel, for no other
reason than that they would have it so ! If you doubt this,
ask Gilbert of Sarum, and he will assure you that such is
the fact. And some who claim a higher status as historians,
or as philosophers, will second the same gossiping Gilbert
of Sarum when he postulates an order of events in Ireland
which may become possible when the streams, of their own
accord and of their own free choice, run up instead of down
the hill—but not till then.

Sir Richard Cox† makes a desperate attempt to keep
pace with Bishop Burnet ; but he very soon gets out of
breath :

—One of the bloodiest scenes that ever was seen in the world.

Sir Richard's effort is but feeble after all. However
he tries to make up for that in what follows :

For on Saturday, 23rd October, 1641, (being a day dedicated
to St. Ignatius (*a fit patron for such a villany !*) broke out a most
desperate and formidable rebellion, an universal defection and

---

* He took ill on 31st January, of ague, having been released on 7th January.
He died on the 7th February.

† *Hibernia Anglicana* (1690)—' Reign of Charles I.,' p. 72. The allusion
to St. Ignatius occurs in the letter of 25th October, 1641, sent by the Lords
Justices into England.

general revolt; wherein not only all the *mere Irish* but almost all
the old English that adhered to the Church of Rome were openly
or secretly involved.

The allusion to St. Ignatius, shows the historian ! Cox,
is not alone in imputing " *universal* defection " to the people
of Ireland at this time.   The curious thing is that not one
of them appears to be in the least degree sensible of the
incongruity of representing a happy and prosperous people
as rising in general revolt.   History will be searched in vain
for an instance of a people rising in their might against
authority unless they have had some sufficient cause.
There might in any conceivable community be a section—
a weak minority—ready for any enterprise that promised
reward, or even for mere change, when there was little
promise of improvement.   But that a whole nation, or any
considerable majority of the people, including those of
position and means, should, *without very grave cause,* agree
to accept the risks and penalties of civil war—which in any
event would mean death to many, with at least temporary
ruin to all—would imply an order of events such as the
world *never* did, and never can witness.

I dare say it was the frequent use of the term " universal "
by the seventeenth century writers that suggested Mrs.
Catherine Macaulay's historical " screamer " :

A universal massacre ensued ; nor age nor sex, nor infancy were
spared ; all conditions were involved in the general ruin,* etc.

A charge so recklessly made and so overwrought, it
would not be worth while to notice, were it not that a more
recent writer of considerable eminence—Dr. James Seaton
Reid, in his " History of the Presbyterians in Ireland "—
has thought fit to quote the passage at length, and has
endorsed it with expressions of admiration.   Better might
have been expected from a nineteenth century writer who
held the position of Professor of Ecclesiastical and Civil
History in the University of Glasgow, than to cite such a
rant as sober history.

I had intended to make some extracts from Sir John
Temple and his more voluminous follower, Dr. Borlase, but
I find that their choice bits are really of volume length ; or
their ideas have been appropriated by later authors, just
as the same ideas were gleaned from the current pamphlets
of a troublous time.   Indeed, Borlase prints some of those
pamphlets entire in his numerous Appendices, or incor-
porates them with his text.   The pamphleteers not only led

---

* Hume has the same ' universal massacre, nor age, nor sex,' etc.

their own age, but, through the adaptations called histories, have led, in no small degree, every subsequent age down to our own.* And very extraordinary things most of those pamphlets are—extraordinary in many aspects, but chiefly for recklessness and ignorance—the writers, in some instances, treating of Irish affairs as vaguely as if Ireland were a region in Cathay, or were situate among the South Sea Islands. Here is an excerpt from one, of the date, " Dec. 1641 " :

Still bloody news from Ireland. . . . Their cruelty hath had effect so farre that they have taken Tambit, burned Armagh, and Toyhull, surprised the castle of my Lord Blayg, affronted my Lord Moore, and slew 300 of souldiers, still affirming that their holy Father the Pope assisted them. Which being effected, they retired to the utmost end of Ireland. . . .

Their treachery also bends (*sic*) to the Counties of Cayneth, Comming, and the County of Carring, where they get great abundance of meate, and ammunition, which in part doth maintain their rebellious hearts against the Protestants, and destroy them in such cruel and bloody manner.†

The readers who found that on their breakfast tables might pray, " Now good digestion wait on appetite ! " The geographical nomenclature is a curiosity. And, indeed, every particular in the record shows ignorance of the country and misconception as to what was going on in Ireland.

More wonderful still is the ignorance or the audacity of the writer who describes with the aid of a woodcut, the siege of a walled town called Athigh, and gives details of an alleged conspiracy at *Rockoll*, within six miles of Dublin, no such place having ever existed. It is clear enough now that the thing is a concoction on the part of some garret-writer, who knew nothing clearly about Ireland, but who, all the while, knew what would take in England. He understood that there was a demand for " murders " and atrocities, and he supplied the " news " accordingly. The " vaulting " of the Hill of *Rockoll*, over which the King's forces must pass " coming out of England," required such a volcanic charge as a hundred Popish Priests, Friars and Jesuits, *in addition* to a hundred barrels of gunpowder ! I transcribe this extraordinary tract as a supplement to this paper.

---

* Among these tracts and pamphlets are many things of great value to the historian ; but there is a lot of ignorance and extravagance in most of the accounts of Ireland, then got up for circulation in England.

† Another extract from same tract is given at close of the Appendix to this paper.

Indeed so little was then known about Ireland by the reading public of England (and, we may add, Scotland) that a pamphleteer might indulge in any sort of romance or imposture which would not clash with the popular prejudices and superstitions. It is not to be wondered at that the astrologer, as well as the politician and the newsmonger, found in the Irish Rebellion a field for enterprise. In the fourth volume of the Thorpe Collection is a pamphlet bearing on the title page : " *Bellum Hybernicale,* or Ireland's Woe Astrologically Demonstrated," with diagrams and intricate calculations, running to 36 pages ; " by Captain Geo. Wharton, Student in Astronomy. Printed in the year 1647."

That sort of thing is harmless. Unfortunately, as much cannot be said for the great bulk of the pamphlets relating to Ireland. We have heard in recent times a good deal about " incitement to crime." The phrase is but a halting description of the following, which is one of many of the same tenor :

A briefe Declaration of the barbarous and inhuman dealings of the Northerne Irish Rebels and many others in several counties uprising against the English that dwelt both lovingly and securely among them, by G.S., Minister of the Word in Ireland.

On back of the title page :

As Popery and Treachery goe hand in hand while Popery is kept under ; so Popery and Tyranny are inseparable companions when Popery gets the upper hand.

On pp. 13 and 14, this " Minister of the Word " thus holds forth :

God hath promised his Church (Rev. 17, 14), that they who begin to make warre with the Lambe shall be overcome by the Lambe. Then reward them even as they have rewarded us, (Rev. 18, 6), give them double according to their Workes, and in the Cuppe that they have filled to us, fill them double. Reward them (we pray), as Jehu did Baals priests. Or deal with them as Samuel dealt with Agag :   *Hew these trayterous Agags in pieces, before the Lord !* Severity is but justice when Lenity puts all in hazard.
[Published by direction of the State in Ireland.]

That this address was not lost upon the forces sent to Ireland we may rest assured. And it is to be noted that the pamphlet was written for and published by the State, that is the Lords Justices and Council in Dublin Castle.

Nalson (" Trial of Charles I." Intro. xxix) cites another " Minister of the Word " who holds forth in similar strain. The time is a little further on, but the charitable spirit of the preacher is by no means exceptional : " Cut down the Malignants with the sword of Justice, root them out and consume them with fire that no root may spring again."— (*Walker's Sermon*, Jan. 29, 1644.) If such was his exhortation as to the treatment of Protestant Royalists in England, what might be good enough for Popish " rebels " in Ireland ? In the way of comment, Nalson adds : " If the Devil himself had filled the pulpit, that old Walker . . . could not certainly in fewer words have expressed more comprehensive cruelty, or a more barbarous thirst after human blood."

It is a relief to turn from such productions to the work of Dr. Ferdinand Warner, *The History of the Irish Rebellion* (1768) * Dr. Warner was about the first Protestant writer who had the independence and honesty of purpose to examine the subject, declining to be led implicitly by the writers of the previous century.   That he did not come out clear of the old prejudices is no discredit to him, while it is very much to his credit that he succeeded in shaking off so many of them.   Of his predecessors he thus speaks in the preface to his *Irish Rebellion :*

Although the business of the Massacre hath made as much noise, and been as much the subject of dispute and crimination as any point in history in the world, it hath never yet been fully or fairly represented. Indeed, to say the truth, it hath not been in the power of many writers to do this ; and of the few that could do it, not one hath been so inclined. The original Protestant Irish writers of this period are Sir John Temple and Dr. Borlase : the first who was Master of the Rolls and a Privy Councillor hath confined himself entirely to the Massacre and Rebellion in the early part of it ; and the sense of what he suffered by the insurrection, together with his attachment to the Ministry, led him to aggravate the crimes and cruelties of the Irish : the other was the son of Sir John Borlase, one of the Lords Justices at the time, and seems to have been an officer in the Civil War; who hath made great use of Temple's History, and, as far as he liked it, of Lord Clarendon's vindication of the Marquis of Ormond. If both these authors are to be read with great suspicions of partiality—as they certainly are—except in the copies of the original papers, and the facts which tally with them, Sir Richard Cox, who hath done little more than transcribe the accounts which they have given, is entitled to less merit, and yet open to the same suspicions.

The Catholic writers of the period he regards as erring in exaggeration on the other side.

Mr Carte treats professedly of this whole rebellion, in his Life of the Duke of Ormonde, and is by much the most copious and best

* This is the date of the 2nd edition.

writer upon it : but there are so many flagrant instances of his
partiality for the King, and of his prejudice against the Irish
Ministers at the breaking out of the insurrection, that he is never
to be read, where the ill conduct of the first is palliated, or the other
censured, without the utmost caution. In the business of Lord
Glamorgan particularly, he is extremely culpable ; and, contrary
to the evidence that was before him, throws all the blame of that
transaction from the King upon his Lordship.

Sir John Temple is, however, the author who is most
cited by those who dilate upon the " Massacre." Harris
assures us Sir John was a man of honour, who, being at
head-quarters, had exceptional opportunities of making
himself acquainted with all that was passing ; and Froude
gives expression to similar views. He was an honourable
man ! " So were they all, all honourable men." But the
point of honour in the same circle was to hesitate at nothing
which might serve to bring odium on " the rebels," that is,
upon all who were politically opposed to " the Castle "—
not, by any means, opposed to " the King " ; and to suppress
everything which might tell against the Government, or
in favour of the Irish Catholics. It was, as Carte says, a
principle with these men that the crimes of the Irish could
never be too much exaggerated. On this principle of honour,
Temple's History was got up. And as for his opportunities,
he, as a prominent member of Council, was as deeply
implicated as Parsons and Borlase in the " mismanagement "
—not to use any stronger term—which made the revolt
general, with a view to extensive confiscation. His work,
which has been always, by the party to which he belonged,
regarded as a sort of Koran—a something dictated by an
archangel—is thus described by Charles O'Conor of Belanagare, in the notes to his friend Dr. Curry's *View of the
Civil Wars in Ireland* :

Sir John Temple published his history in the year 1646, by
the direction of the parliament party, which then prevailed, and
to which, though long before in actual rebellion, he was always
attached. The falsehoods it contains are so glaring and numerous,
that even the Government, in 1674, seems to have been offended
at, and himself ashamed of, the republication of it. This we gather
from a letter of Capel, Earl of Essex, then Lord Lieutenant of Ireland,
to Mr. Secretary Coventry in these words : " I am to acknowledge
yours of the 22nd December, in which you mention a book that
was newly published, concerning the cruelties committed in Ireland,
at the beginning of the late war. Upon further enquiry, I find
Sir J. Temple, Master of the Rolls here (Ireland), author of that
book, was this last year, sent to by several stationers of London
to have his consent to the printing thereof, but he assures me that
he utterly denied it, and whoever printed it did it without his
knowledge ? "

That is rather an unkind cut at a book which has become
the guiding light to so many later historians ; and the
blow comes unwittingly from the " honourable " author
himself. In fact, the so-called history is but a political
pamphlet of more than usual length and more than
usual virulence, got up in a time of turbulence to meet
the exigencies of the party (including the author) then
in power at the Castle, the party who, nominally in the
King's commission and service, were using the King's
name to further the cause of his majesty's most deadly
enemies in England. But a condemnation, if possible still
more emphatic, appeared in 1812, when an edition of
Temple's work was brought out as a means of helping
that anti-Emancipation craze which Sydney Smith denom-
inated " Percivalism." This issue bears on the title-page
the following significant notice : *Now reprinted for the
Perusal of all Protestants, as a most effective Warning-Piece
to keep them upon their guard against the Encroachments
of Popery!*

The No-Popery Percivalists of those days well understood the purpose for which the book was, in the first
instance, got up ; and in selecting it for their purpose they
showed themselves wise in their generation. I don't blame
the bigots of Percival's following who were openly and
honestly hostile to the Catholic claims ; but I do blame
writers of later date who would repudiate any supposed
connection with that school, while at the same time following
stealthily in their footsteps, and virtually adopting the
same tactics under the thin disguise of simulated zeal for
moderation and fair play.

Although Dr. Borlase is as virulent as Temple, his
bulky and somewhat chaotic history has some merits. He
can now and then admit that the crime and cruelty were
not all on one side ; and that the rebels were not destitute
of pluck. As an officer who had been much in action
during the Civil War, his narrative, though often obscured
by the elaborately involved construction of his sentences,
is not without interest ; and he has collected a great number
of documents relating to the period of which he writes.
But he is the faithful disciple of Temple and Colonel Mervyn :
his cardinal point is that the " massacre " is, and must be,
measured by the hundred thousand.   An enthusiastic
loyalist after the Restoration, he was busy enough in the
interests of the Parliament while loyalty was losing ground,
but all the time the Irish are *the* Rebels, even those who
lost everything in the cause of the misguided King.   As
a specimen of Borlase's style, as well as of his attitude

towards the Irish, I submit the following taken from page 304 of the original folio of 1680 :

And certainly whatsoever conspired to compleat so execrable a design as the murther of the King, nothing contributed more than the Irish deluding his sacred Majesty so long with their promises of a Competent Army, whereby he relying on them (too confidently assured of their Ability and Power to perform it), deferred those agreements which else he might have seasonably composed at home.

And could there ever be an equaller Distribution of God's Vengeance than that they by a parallel Court should suffer the loss of their Estates, Lives, and Fortunes ? Which though unusual was the only Expedient.

Further up on the same page he notes, following the Bishop of Derry, that Militiere's attempt* to saddle the death of the King on the Protestants "only radicated deeper in his religion ; that those intended for his evil proved his good."

How deeply Charles II. had been "radicated" in that religion was shown five years later on when a Popish confessor attended him on his death-bed.

. But among Sir John Temple's followers and admirers Walter Harris is, perhaps, the one who most resembles the master. As an antiquarian Harris takes a deservedly high place ; but it would have been well for his reputation as an historian that he had never undertaken to write his *View of the Ancient and Present State of the County Down* (1744), or, that having undertaken it, he had tried to make an honest use of his materials. His treatment of certain portions of the subject would pass ; but he has made an altogether erroneous or misleading sketch of the Civil War in relation to that county. With this matter I deal particularly in other papers, for the present merely directing attention to a passage which shows only too clearly the spirit in which he wrote the greater part of this book—the book which, unfortunately, is looked upon as an authority by some more recent and more popular authors. Referring to the Charter School, then established at Killough in East Down, he says :

The design of the Charter Scheme is now so well understood by the good effects of it in several counties of the kingdom, that we may soon expect to see it universally received. All Protestant gentlemen condemn the superstitions and idolatrous worship of the Church of Rome ; *they abhor and detest her bloody and des-*

---

* Very audacious of Militiere to attempt such a thing, when the "Romanists" of Ireland were so deeply implicated in the "murther" of the King !

tructive doctrines and principles; they eagerly wish to see their lands tenanted, planted, and improved by a race of honest and industrious Protestants, that they and their posterity may continue to live in peace and quiet, *free from the danger of any future insurrections and rebellions;* and the wit of man could not suggest a more effective or rational scheme *for making this a Protestant nation.* As penal and coercive laws, which in their nature are odious in respect to religion, can have but little influence on the minds of people especially the lower sort, who have nothing to lose, yet it is not strange that so many sit coldly down as unconcerned spectators, and take no share in the glorious design of securing the rising generation of Papists to the interests of that Protestant State, which their Popish forefathers have more than once brought into very great danger, and caused much blood to be shed in defence of it.*—*Harris's Down.* pp. 17, 18.

What a pity that the author did not live to witness the Battle of Ballynahinch, and so to realise the worth of his assumed connection between Protestantism and Peace! His appreciation of the Penal Laws is the only topic in the foregoing which merits approval. The Charter Scheme hardly ever came into real life. But the point in which Harris shows his hand is the contention that blood and rebellion are of the essence of what he denominates Popery ; to wit, the religion of at least three-fourths of his countrymen. We cannot, indeed, wonder that an author, holding the views set forth in this extract, should, like the gallant Colonel, find that " the waves of blood crowd up in heaps " when he comes to deal with the events of 1641 and subsequent years. Yet the direct influence of Walter Harris at the present day is trifling in comparison with that exercised

* Mr. Walter Harris, it would appear from his collections, contemplated authorship on a monumental scale, but it would also appear that he received not from his contemporaries the necessary encouragement. In the Appendix to the 8th Report of the Historical MSS. Commission, Part I., Sir John Gilbert gives the following lively communication, written by Charles O'Conor of Belanagare to his friend, Dr. Curry, Dublin. The date is 5th October, 1757 : " I met a bookseller also whose chief business it was to hawk about your friend Harris's ' Life of K. William,' his ' Bishop's ' ' Down,' ' Hibernica,' and the Answer to the ' Dialogue.' ' What success had you, friend, on circuit ? ' ' None at all,' said he, ' and may G—— d——Harris and all his works ! I bought them dog cheap from Flyn, and yet what I sold would hardly answer the expense of my horse and drams.' ' How have you sold this book (" Fiction Unmasked ") ? ' ' You are welcome to one, sir, for ninepence.' ' What ! surely you must have had profit on it at so high a price ? ' ' Yes, sir ; I bought two dozen at 6s. 6d., but having sold but a few, I am likely to be a loser, if Flyn does not take them back.' ' Well, sir, to encourage you, here is ninepence.' Thus, sir, you have my adventure with this hawker. One Mr. Irwin had the curiosity to dip into the book I bought. Next day he came to me, highly vexed at the author's malice and scurrility. ' Is it not a shame,' said he, ' that the gentleman [Dr. Curry] concerned did not reply ? ' I told him it did not become a gentleman of a public profession to enter deeply into a party controversy."

by writers who have found in his pages, ready made, the sort of thing which, perhaps, they wished to find —the writers who, at all events, accept his conclusions as amply sustained by his reputation as an antiquarian. Harris is the great authority with the Rev. Dr. Seaton Reid ; he has misled so able and fair-ninded an author as the Rev. George Hill. Dr. Reid is a great favourite with James Anthony Froude. Dr. Knox, the more recent historian of County Down, alludes to the scenes of murder "as depicted in the pages of Froude." Thus it goes on very much as in the nursery drama : " The cat at the rat, the rat at the rope," etc. About that same Froude I must have a word. First let me refer to one or two things put forth by the sage—or, ought it to be Savage ?—of Chelsea. Savage he certainly shows himself to be when he has occasion to speak of Ireland. Then it is that he wishes to show how he, too, can wield " the hammer of Thor." (I refer, of course, to his notes in " Letters and Speeches of Oliver Cromwell.")

Nov. 1 (1641). News came to London, to the re-assembled Parliament that an Irish Rebellion, *already grown to be an Irish Massacre*, had broken out.

Now it was pointed out by Dr. Warner three-quarters of a century before Carlyle penned this note, that the news received in London on that date justified no such description of the insurrection in Ireland. The Earl of Leicester, who, although he was then Lord Lieutenant of Ireland, had never been in that country, made, in his statement to the English Parliament, a gratuitous addition to the information which he had just received from the Lords Justices (Parsons and Borlase,) in Dublin ; his Excellency availed himself of the privilege of an absentee to blacken, as much as in him lay, the people of the country in which he ought to be a resident, if he would discharge the duties of his office.*

* 'Unless on the hypothesis that there is a separate scheme of divine and human law, and a separate law of nature, applicable to Ireland, it is difficult to account for the contradictory judgment which a man ordinarily so wise and just as Mr. Carlyle applies to nearly identical circumstances in Ireland and France. In Ireland the agricultural population, driven wild by pillage and oppression, rose and repossessed themselves of lands recently taken from them, and in the process committed and endured cruel excesses : in France the agricultural population, also long oppressed and pillaged, rose and burned the chaâteaux of the noblesse who had possessed them for centuries, killed the owners wherever they could find them, and when their partizans were in prison, rose in conjunction with a city mob and murdered them in cold blood. Of the Irish transaction Mr. Carlyle has written a vehement and unmeasured condemnation. Of the French massacre he says, "Horrible in lands that had known equal justice. Not so unnatural in lands that had never known it."'— Sir C. Gavan Duffy's *Young Ireland* (1880) p. 107. *Note.*

Nov. 22. The Irish Rebellion blazing up more and more into *an
Irish Massacre* to the terror and horror of all anti-Papist men.
(i. 95.)

Strenuous efforts were made to create such impressions
in England. But the Lords Justices—who were, of all men,
the least likely to screen the Irish or to minimise the gravity
of the situation, had not yet discovered anything like
" massacre " on such a scale as this, would imply. When
they issued their first Commission of Inquiry (23rd December,
1641) to collect evidence of robberies committed by the
rebels, nothing was said about murder or massacre. On
the 18th of January, 1641-2, a further Commission was
issued to the same parties extending their powers to take
notice of murders committed *by the rebels.* Had there been
such *massacre,* how very strange that it was only at the
end of three months the Lords Justices and Council in
Dublin thought it worth while, or thought it their duty,
to institute inquiry into the matter, more especially as they
were about to appoint eight Commissioners—all clergymen
—to collect information *regarding the pillage and " spoil "*
committed since the 23rd October, 1641. The news, therefore, to which Carlyle directs attention, although in a high
degree sensational, is not well founded, but he doesn't
mind that. Then, again :

Ireland, ever since the Irish Rebellion broke out *and changed itself
into an Irish massacre,* in the end of 1641, has been a scene of
distracted controversies, plunderings, excommunications, treacheries,
conflagrations, of universal misery *and blood* and bluster, *such
as the world before or since has never seen.* The history of it does not
form itself into a picture ; but remains only a huge blot, an indiscriminate blackness [Why not *redness* ?] . . . There are parties
on the back of parties ; at war with the world and with each
other.

The " indiscriminate blackness " is rather in the philos-
opher himself. Parties and divisions indeed arose especially
after Ormond began to practise on the Confederation. Nor
was Ireland so singular even then. Were there no parties
within parties in England ? Just suppose a writer to
approach that subject in the spirit in which the great Sage
deals with Ireland ! And about *Tam* Carlyle's own little
country—no divisions, no party conflicts there ! Ay, are
there. But the Sage can with more composure allude to
those conflicts :

The factions and distractions of Scotland, its Kirk Committees
and State Committees and poor Covenanted King and Courtiers,
are many.

And to

— that sea of confusions in which the poor Scotch people have involved themselves by soldering Christ's Crown to Charles Stuart's.

Sea of confusions! Yet poor Ireland must be held up to ridicule and scorn for its parties at the same time! Party and faction in England or Scotland can be dealt with as things no way extraordinary. But for Ireland the "indiscriminate" is good enough : it has been the way so long that it must, after all, be the right way! "The waves of blood" must, at all hazards, be kept well to the front.

Froude, more polished and more sophistical, manages with much art and dexterity to produce the same effect, while keeping up a show of judicial fairness. And this is the way *he* tells us that "the waves of blood crowd up in heaps"; for all his "balancing" on the narrow "edge" leaves that impression in the end :

We are now upon the edge of the gravest event in Irish history, the turning-point on which all later controversies between England and Ireland hinge. The facts, real or alleged, are all before us ; for the excitement created was so terrible that the most minute ; particulars were searched into with agonized curiosity. Thirty three volumes of depositions are preserved in the Library of Trinity College, which tell the tale with perfect distinctness ; and as the witnesses relate one consistent story, they are dismissed by those who are offended by their testimony as imaginary beings, forgers, liars, calumniators. The eagerness to discredit the charge is a tacit confession how tremendous the guilt, if it can be proved ; the most certain facts can be made doubtful if they are stoutly and repeatedly denied ; * and not evidence, but sympathy or inclination determines the historical beliefs of most of us. Those who choose to think that the massacre of 1641 was a dream will not change their opinion. Those who see in that massacre the explanation and the defence of the subsequent treatment of Ireland, however unwilling to revive the memories of scenes which rivalled in carnage the horrors of St. Bartholomew are compelled to repeat the evidence once held to be unanswerable.

It would not, I fancy, be easy to find outside the same work a passage of the same length which exhibits more dexterous turning and "posturing" : it surpasses the performance of the acrobat balancing and wheeling on the wire, while all the time flaunting in our faces a red rag on the end of his balancing-pole. Of ordinary readers, few, if any, will gather from the passage that there can be the least doubt about the evidence *once* held to be unanswerable.

---

* And the wildest extravagance of allegation and assertion may obtain a large amount of credence if Titus Oates will swear to the truth and accuracy thereof, or James Anthony Froude will write it up.

What are the points most prominent in the extract? Massacre—massacre—carnage—St. Bartholomew! And —why not St. Brice or Mullaghmast as well? There are little artful reservations slipped in to save the credit of the historian, but they are so modest and retiring that they almost evade notice ; and all the rest is flaring crimson.

I deal elsewhere with the depositions, merely remarking for the present that Froude's certificate is rather absolute for one who had not examined the originals.* And his assumption of the importance of these documents in relation to the government of Ireland in subsequent ages is, to say the least of it, a bit chimerical. Supposing that the depositions *were* legal evidence—and they are anything but that—they could bring home guilt only to the authors and perpetrators of the crimes. The facts—" real or alleged " —prove nothing against those unborn at the time, and to carry the punishment down the stream of ages is nothing the better of the wildly improbable tales contained in those thirty-three folio volumes. Mr. Froude tells us† that he had intended to examine the depositions, but distrusted himself as he had distrusted Mr. Prendergast. " My sympathies," he says, " are on the side of England." Well, Mr. Prendergast was a Protestant of English or Anglo-Norman descent. And why should not an Englishman of culture and ability be capable of extending his sympathies to Ireland, at least so far as to admit that the people of Ireland are of the same human race as are the English ; that human nature in Ireland is not so widely different from human nature even in the country of " the predominant partner " ; and if there are differences in modes of life, in habits, etc., perhaps it will be found that the history of seven centuries may, in some measure, be responsible.

I leave for the present our author's acrobatic performance to glance at the views of some writers who have, in dealing with the period of the alleged massacre, shown themselves more capable of acting rationally, if less brilliant, than Carlyle and Froude, contenting themselves with plain common sense and common justice, in lieu of the genius that leads astray—the possessor, most of all.

I have already made use of Dr. Warner, and I wish to produce another extract from the same writer :

* So he tells us in the preface which he wrote for Miss Hickson's work, which is of more recent date than his " English in Ireland."

† In the preface to Miss Hickson's " Ireland in the 17th Century." I shall show in another paper that the depositions are not all of this character ; but it is on " the wildly extravagant tales " that the St. Bartholomew people mainly rely.

E

As to the murders that were committed in the first week of the rebellion, if we say with the Protestant writers, that there were great numbers, we shall speak, by all that I have seen, without authority; and if we affirm with the Popish writers that there were not above seventeen persons killed at the beginning of this insurrection, we shall conclude against evidence and probability. But throughout this whole affair, not a single writer that I have seen observes dates with any accuracy (p. 71).

I believe it will be found that the complaint as to negligence in the matter of dates applies generally to writers of that time : those, at any rate, who treat of Ireland.

Now the Rebellion was only a week old when, if we follow Carlyle, it had grown into " an Irish Massacre." Dr. Warner was not above some of the prejudices of his time ; but for one who wrote in the middle of the eighteenth century, he must be credited with having made an honest attempt to find out for himself where the truth lay. A contemporary of his, Edmund Burke, held more decided views on the subject, and these will appear further on.*

In 1831 there appeared in "Constable's Miscellany," Edinburgh, two handy volumes, " The Civil Wars of Ireland, by W. C. Taylor, Trinity College, Dublin," a work which ought not to be lost to the present and coming generations, for—in reference to the period in question—it contains an amount of really valuable matter such as seldom can be met with in volumes so unpretentious. Take the following as to the origin of the Civil War of 1641 and subsequent years :

There has been no little confusion introduced into former histories of this eventful period by the authors having neglected to distinguish between the *causes* and the *occasions* of the war. Most writers have argued that there could have been little cause of complaint against the government when the tranquillity of the country had remained undisturbed for nearly half a century ; forgetting that every insurrection which tyranny has provoked broke out only when circumstances seemed favourable to the hopes of redress. The materials of a conflagration may be for years accumulating, but the presence of a torch is necessary to the bursting forth of the flame.

Then as to the Causes :

The plantation of Ulster, and the menace of similar spoliation in Connaught, completely and justly alienated the minds of the native Irish from the Government. They believed that a determi-

---

* I am aware that some flimsy attempts have been made to discredit Edmund Burke's views on the matter as one who "gave up to party, etc." He knew the history of Ireland under the penal laws, and his knowledge was not for party use.

nation had been taken to strip them of all their property, by a mixture of violence and chicanery ; and the conduct of the King and his ministers proved that they were not mistaken. In fact, the Royalists and the Parliamentarians in England distinctly avowed their fixed resolution to colonize Ireland with *good* subjects ; and, opposed as they were in everything else, Charles and the Commons showed wondrous unanimity in devising plans for fresh confiscations. The virulent declarations of the English Parliament against Popery were justly alarming to the Irish Catholics ; and the shameful execution, or rather judicial murder of several priests in London, for the offence of saying Mass, showed that the persecution threatened would not long be confined to pecuniary penalties and disqualifications. The sin of tolerating Popery was a favourite theme with the Irish clergy of the Established and Scottish Church. Similar denunciations had been made even in the Irish Parliament, and were only suppressed when the aid of the Recusants was required to complete the ruin of Strafford.

The character of Parsons was a third cause of the rancorous hostility to Government which was generally prevalent among the Irish. The appointment of such a man to the office of Lord Justice, was felt to be a direct sanction of the principles on which he acted. The tragedy of the O'Byrnes was too enormous and too recent to be forgotten. There was every reason to expect that spoliation and not protection would be the chief object of an administration at the head of which was a wicked and unprincipled adventurer.

And as to the Occasion :

The successful resistance of the Scots was the occasion of which the Irish Lords determined to avail themselves.

. . . The flame of rebellion easily spreads from one country to another. We have ourselves witnessed countless examples of the contagion of revolution. It is no wonder that the Irish, who had suffered under severe wrongs, and had far greater grievances to redress, should have resolved to emulate the successful revolt of their brethren in Scotland.

Very different, indeed, is the theory of Temple and his followers : the Irish had no real grievance to complain of : they rebelled just because they were thirsty for blood ! Froude does not, indeed, go the length of saying that the insurrection was without cause. He says :

That a rebellion should have broken out at that particular time, was in itself so natural, that a looker-on might have predicted it with certainty.

But with his usual adroitness he would have us believe that the main cause lay in the habits of the people.

Mr. W. C. Taylor rightly contends that massacre, such as the horror-mongers assume—massacre general, wholesale and unsparing, of the British and Protestant residents in

Ireland—never was intended, and never even at the worst was attempted.

' The Irish massacre in 1641,' has been a phrase so often repeated even in books of education * that one can scarcely conceal his surprise that the tale is as apocryphal as the wildest fiction of romance. No mention is made of these extensive murders in any of the proclamations issued by the Lords Justices even so late as 23rd December [*i.e.*, two months after the outbreak] ; and truly the character of Parsons does not induce us to believe that he would have suppressed anything likely to make his adversaries odious. The protestation of the Irish Parliament is equally silent on the subject, nor does any State-paper of the local government afford the slightest ground for the charge. Stories of massacre and horrid cruelty were indeed studiously circulated in England, because it was the interest of the patriot [Puritan] party in Parliament to propogate such delusions. They increased the popular hatred of Popery, and rendered the King's suspected attachment to that religion more generally odious ; and they afforded a pretence for assembling an army on whose officers and soldiers the Parliament could rely. When, at a later period, it became necessary to excuse the monstrous iniquity of the Act of Settlement, advantage was taken of the general belief in this unfounded calumny to justify an instance of royal ingratitude and shameless injustice not to be paralleled even in the dark annals of the Stuarts.

Nor does he confine his strictures to those who appear to feel under some obligation to justify or excuse " the monstrous iniquity " of the Act of Settlement of Charles II., and of the many monstrous Acts which were passed in subsequent reigns as corollaries to that iniquitous and shameless piece of party legislation.

The accounts published by the Catholics on the Continent are full of misrepresentations almost equally glaring. . . . There were doubtless many disgraceful atrocities *on both sides ;* but are they not inseparable from civil war ? These crimes were owing to the wickedness of particular men. We wish neither to palliate nor disguise them ; but they were disapproved of by the leaders on both sides ; and it is fair to add that *all atrocities were not only discouraged, but punished by the Catholic nobility and gentry.* It is equally wicked and foolish to make these sad events the subject of charge against sects and parties at the present day. This was a war for property rather than religion. The Northern Irish wished to recover their estates. Parsons and his supporters desired to enrich themselves by new confiscations. Both employed the sacred name of the deity to cover their real designs ; but assuredly religious principle had little influence on either. The present generation is not answerable for the crimes and follies of those which have preceded. The errors of our ancestors are recorded for our instruction that they should be avoided and not imitated.—*Civil Wars in Ireland*, i. 274.

* " School histories, in particular," he might have added.

Yet the very thing that our great writers of the Temple-Froude School insist on is that the Irish people of to-day and of every day since the 23rd October, 1641, are to be held responsible for, and to suffer the penalties of whatever crimes or misdeeds stained the " rising " of that time. Else, what is the meaning of saying, as Froude says, that " the eagerness to repel the charge is a tacit confession how tremendous is the guilt *if it can be proved !* What charge ? The charge made by that " honourable person," Sir John Temple ? Why, Froude himself feels called upon to discredit that, although he can, all the time, contrive to flaunt the bloody rag.

Sir John Temple considered that 150,000 perished in two months and 300,000 in two years. At the trial of Lord Maguire the figures were sworn at 152,000. Such guesses, for they could have been little more, prove only that in the presence of occurrences exceptionally horrible, the balance of reason was over-turned. Clarendon, on cooler reflection, reduced the number to 40,000. Sir Wm. Petty, followed by Carte, to 37,000. *Even these figures will seem too large,* [*] when it is remembered how appalling is the impression created by the slaughter in cold blood of innocent unresisting people, how little rage and terror can be depended on for cool observation, and how inevitably the murdered were confounded afterwards with the enormous multitudes which indisputably perished in the civil war which followed.

All this is by no means easy to reconcile with what he writes, some pages earlier, about " the depositions" " which tell the tale with perfect distinctness," and the " witnesses " who " tell one consistent story." That, after all, is but the story of people whose " reason was overturned." Are we to take it also that Sir John Temple's reason was over-turned ? In a way it was ; but only as the reason of occupants of the judicial bench in Ireland has, in too many instances, been " overturned," from that day to this : his sense of justice was overturned, even to the disregard of decency. The " charge "—the charge of massacre by the hundred thousand—is " founded" on " sworn " testimony ;

---

[*] Although only a fourth part of what was sworn to ! Yet we are to take " the faithful relation of Sir John Temple " as the correct history of the insurrection ! In the speech which Cooke intended to deliver, had Charles I. consented to plead before the High Commission Court, is the following :— ' But concerning Ireland, where there were no less than 150,000 men, women, and children most barbarously and satanically murdered at the first four months of the Rebellion *as appeared by substantial proof* at the King's Bench, at the trial of Maguire ; if the King had a hand or but a little finger in that massacre, every man will say, Let him die the death !'—*State Trials*, iv., 1035. It was Sir Charles Coote who swore to the 150,000 at Lord Maguire's trial ; on what grounds will, I trust, appear when I come to deal more particularly with the depositions.

and has been as good as sworn to by Temple himself, and by many of even higher repute as authors ; yes, and as good as sworn to by Froude also in that curiously balanced paragraph, the first I have quoted from him. Hasn't it become the settled practice to write about " the massacre " as if the hundreds of thousands slaughtered in cold blood were beyond all dispute ? And then, when it comes to a question of figures, Temple must be thrown over, and his hundreds of thousands must give place to tens of thousands —an estimate which has really no better authority, both alike being founded upon *evidence once held to be unanswerable*, and even now *assumed* to be so. The confidence with which " these hundreds of thousands " of martyrs have been paraded, in defiance of common sense, rises to an article of faith—with many writers the strongest point in their creed. Mrs. Lucy Hutchinson, pious little soul, can assure us in this strain :

> While the King was in Scotland, that cursed rebellion in Ireland broke out wherein above 200,000 were massacred in two months' space, being surprised and inhumanely butchered *and* tormented ; and, besides the slain, abundance of poor families stripped and sent naked away out of all their possessions.

An extraordinary thing that of the English in Ireland in 1641 there could be such " abundance " of families to send away, after more than 200,000 had been " massacred inhumanely butchered *and tormented* " !

Mr. C. H. Firth, in a note to this passage, says :

> Mrs. Hutchinson here seems to take May as her authority, who states that ' the persons of above 200,000 men, women, and children were murdered, many of them with exquisite and unheard-of tortures within the space of one month.' May himself relies chiefly on ' the faithful relation of Sir John Temple.' Clarendon, Rushworth and Whitelock give equally high figures. Mr. Gardiner estimates the number of persons slain in cold blood of the outbreak of the rebellion at 4,000, and thinks that about double that number may have perished from ill-treatment.

Such, indeed, was the estimate of Dr. Warner (in 1768) and of Mr. W.C. Taylor (in 1831), writers, who, while revolting from " the faithful relation of Sir John Temple," yet inclined to rather exaggerated views of the blood shed in some quarters, particularly under Sir Phelim O'Neill. The late Mr. Gardiner does not commit himself to even so high an estimate as 4,000 ; he gives that as the utmost possible. His treatment of the subject creditably contrasts with the posturing of Froude or the rude insolence of Carlyle :

> Of the number of persons murdered at the beginning of the outbreak it is impossible to speak with even approximate certainty

Clarendon speaks of 40,000, and wilder estimates still give 200,000 or 300,000. *Even the smallest number is ridiculously impossible.* The estimated numbers of the Scots in Ulster were 100,000, and of the English only 20,000. For the time the Scots were spared. In Fermanagh, where the victims fared most badly, a Puritan officer boasted, not long afterwards, that he had rescued 6,000. Thousands of robbed and plundered fugitives escaped with their lives to find shelter in Dublin. On the whole it would be safe to conjecture that the number of those slain in cold blood at the beginning of the rebellion could hardly, by any possibility, have much exceeded four thousand, whilst about twice that number may have perished from ill-treatment. Before long the tale of war would resound through England in a wildly exaggerated form.

And the circumstances of the alleged cruelties are as wildly and ridiculously exaggerated as the numbers of murders in cold blood. That at least twice as many perished from the hardships to which they were exposed in being deprived of their means, and imprisoned or thrust out in the winter season, as were put to death by foul means, I have no doubt whatever. That there were murders—too many, if any—is what every one who has considered the period admits and deplores.* But that—excluding ·the

---

* I am aware that by a strained interpretation some have been made to say that "not one Protestant was put to death but in fair fight." Sir Charles Gavan Duffy has been taken to task for the following :—' Though there were dreadful excesses committed by both parties in the end, it is certain, beyond all controversy, that the first aim of the Irish was to regain their own without any sacrifice of life. On the night of the rising and during the six days that followed, *only one man was killed* ; a fact which stamps with complete certainty the original purpose. When blood is shed it is like kindling the prairie ; no one can any longer pretend to limit the devastation. But there were some signal instances of moderation.'—*New Ireland,* 2nd Edition, p. 104.
    There must have been at the very start conflicts in which lives would be lost, contrary to the original purpose. Except in that one clause, which is by no means essential to his contention, Sir Gavan gives a correct view of the origin and progress of the insurrection. A letter written to Lord Montgomery of Ards by Bishop Lesley of Down may be the origin of the allegation that no more than one person was killed at the outbreak ;
' Right Honorable,
                Ther is newly come into Lesnegarvy a trowper post who assures us that this last night Charlymount was taken, and Dungannon by Sir Phelome O'Neale, with a huge multitude of Irish souldiers, and that this day they are advanced as farre as Tonregee. Captayne St. John fled, *his trumpeter slayne,* and all the country fleeing before them. This night we are putting ourselves all in arms. I pray your Lordship to think of some course to be taken for making head against them, and let my Lord of Claneboyes know so much. I am likewise sending poast to my Lord Chichester. So in great haste I recommend your Lordship to God's grace, and rest
                    ' Your Lordship's most affectionate servant
' Lisnegarvy, 23 Octob. 1641.   ' HEN : DUNENSIS.'
    ' To the Right Honourable my very good Lord, the Lord Viscount Montgomery of Ards.
    Gilbert, *Affairs in Ireland in 1641,* ii., 362.

mythical hecatombs for which no evidence can be adduced such as will bear examination—the number of murders done in cold blood could have reached even so high a figure as 4,000 I more than doubt. I have given a good deal of attention, and such thought as I am capable of, to the matter ; and my conclusion is that if we divide by 100 the numbers given in " the faithful relation " of Sir John Temple we shall still be on the upper limit or above it—much above it, I should say.

Mr. Lecky's conclusions on the subject have drawn eulogistic remarks from the late Dr. Gardiner, and that is no ordinary certificate of merit. Referring to the association for the relief of the disabilities of the Catholics of Ireland formed early in the latter half of the eighteenth century by Dr. Curry, Charles O'Conor of Belanagare, and some prominent co-religionists, Mr. Lecky takes occasion to make some well-considered and, I think, just remarks on this question.*

'" The notion that this rebellion began with unprovoked, deliberate, and general massacre of the unarmed and unsuspecting Protestant population, not less extensive than the massacre of St. Bartholomew, had passed; on the authority of Clarendon and Milton, into the popular belief, had been lately adopted by Hume with his usual carelessness, and in its most exaggerated form, had been spread over the Continent, and has been frequently repeated to our own day. To the few persons who have examined with any care the original evidence on the subject, its falsehood will appear sufficiently glaring ; and it may be mentioned that Burke, who was well versed in Irish history, could scarcely speak with patience on the subject. The collection of purely Protestant evidence which was brought together by Curry,† at least shook the popular tradition.

Mr. Lecky has the following note to the foregoing passage (" Ireland in the Eighteenth Century," ii., 184).

' Indeed I *have* my opinion on that part of history, which I have often delivered to you —to everyone I have conversed with on the subject : and which I mean still to deliver whenever the occasion calls for it, which is that the Irish rebellion of 1641 was not only (as our silly things called " histories " call it), not utterly *unprovoked*, but that no history I have ever read furnishes an instance of any that was so *provoked ;* and that in almost all parts of it, it

* " Ireland in the Eighteenth Century," ii., 184. In the opening chapter of vol. i. he deals with the subject more at large, and with rare judgment and acumen.

† Froude speaks of Curry as a violent Nationalist. The idea of a violent Irish Nationalist in the middle of the 18th century ! Dr. Reid would have said ' Romanist.' And he was a courageous ' Romanist' who would venture to raise his voice at all, at a time when Catholics were known to the law only as subjects for punishment.

has been extremely and most absurdly misrepresented '—*Burke's Correspondence* i. 337.* On the utter falseness of the common story about the rebellion in Ulster having broken out with a general massacre, see the recent and very decisive testimony of Mr. Gardiner, *Fall of the Monarchy of Charles I.*, ii., 313.—[The passage referred to is that quoted above.]

I shall add only one further extract taken from a work †
published in 1819, conveying similar judicious views on
the alleged cruelties of the rebels of 1641 :

> The accounts given of the cruelties perpetrated by the contending parties during this dreadful Civil War should be received with great caution. They were written at a time of violent national agitation, when a spirit of anti-christian animosity was vividly diffused over the whole country. The depositions inserted in Sir John Temple's work are filled with incredible tales of shrieking and clamorous spectres crying aloud for revenge ! Oaths of this nature prove nothing, but that the deponents were under the influence of strong passions and disordered imaginations. On such testimony who can rely ?

Too many have relied on such testimony, and Froude
at least affects reliance upon the same. That such leaders
of thought should place all the enormities against the Irish
side shows how trustworthy they are. It is a trick of theirs
to represent the question as—" St. Bartholomew " or " a
dream " ; and to insinuate, if not more openly affirm, that
there is no escape from the choice. Mr. Evelyn Philip
Shirley in his bulky but interesting " History of the County
Monaghan " and others, chime in with Froude in misrepresenting the attitude of the late Mr. John P. Prendergast
on this question. The author of the " Cromwellian Settlement of Ireland " is very far from maintaining that the
Insurrection of 1641 was free of murder or crime ; for that
would be to maintain that there was no Civil War. He
says, and says aptly :

> The truth seems to be that the English were to the full as bloody as the Irish.

His great research and cool investigation enabled him
to make sad havoc among the favourite theories of over two

* To put Burke's opinion aside we have been reminded that he kept the
estate which had come to his family in a way that was good only by the Penal
Laws. How does that affect the value of the opinion he gives regarding the
insurrection of 1641 ? If there is any effect it must be in favour of the opinion
which he so forcibly expressed. Had he held with Temple and his ' faithful '
followers, every one could say, Burke thought so and so, because he owed an
estate to that rebellion and what followed.

† *Historical Memorials of the City of Armagh*, by Dr. James Stuart, recently
republished and, in part, re-written, by Fr. Coleman, Dundalk. The extract
is from the original work, p. 273.

centuries ; and for that reason he incurs the penalty of misrepresentation on the part of those who had the spoils of war, and of those " goody " friends who see in the Confiscation and penal enactments of subsequent times the righteous treatment of a nation of exceptionally wicked people, and who must needs think *these Galileans were sinners above all the men of Galilee because they suffered such things.*

APPENDIX TO III.

[FROM THE THORPE TRACTS*]

VOL I.

TREASON IN IRELAND for the blowing up of the King's
English Forces with 100 Barrells of Gunpowder, with
the names of the Chief Agents ; and the maner of the
Discovery, December 10. With a plot discovered at
Athigh. Sent into England by Mr. *Hierome,* Minister
of God's Word at *Athigh* in Ireland. London : Printed
for Salomon Johnson, 1641.

About the space of six miles from Dublin in Ireland, there is
a town inhabited with Irish called *Rockoll,* in which town is no
more English inhabited (*sic*), save onely two, William Clarke is the
name of one, the other is a widdow, both Innekeepers in *Rockoll.*
About a mile from the said *Rockoll* dwelleth one *Patrick Lock,*
at the foote of the hill called the hill of *Rockoll.* The said *Patrick
Locke* is a great Papist, and a man of great meanes in those parts,
having a very great estate, who had vaulted his house round about :
in which Vaults he hath kept foure severall smiths and Forges,
working upon provision of warre ever since the first Treaty with
the English and Scots, that is for the space of these two years.

He hath also since the first intent of rising of the Rebels in
Ireland he hath entertained four score men, who by the Rebels
have been set on work, to vault the said hill *Rockoll* round about.

The Vault is so farre finished that there is entertained in a Vault,
wherein they have undermined the hill great store of Rebels ; to
the number of about 500, as is credibly reported : whereof one
hundred are Popish Priests, Friers, and Jesuits.

The passage over this hill is a great rode through which they pass
from Dublin to the chiefest part of the Countrey towards Munster,
and other places where the Rebels for the most part lie, and the
Countrey is most oppressed : so that when the Kings Majesties
Army hath been come into Ireland from England to relieve the
Protestants against the Rebels : this hill was the direct and readie
Rode for them to pass over in the Vault whereof, which they had
digged for that purpose. They have been preparing powder in
readinesse as they could plot it ; expecting thereby to blow up the
Hill therewith, when the Army marched over it.

There was one of the Rebels called *William Rafter,* that was
taken by Colonell *Carot Topey,* who discovered this plot, and con-

* Original Tracts illustrative of Irish History, collected by Thomas Thorpe.
Bookseller, London, 10 vols., small 4to (1629-1758), and 2 vols., folio, 1693-
1758) ; in the National Library, Kildare Street, Dublin.

fessed that the said hill was all undermined, and that there was 100 barrels of powder in the Vault, and their purpose was, that if they could take *Athigh* and the Castle, then they knew that when the King's Forces came to Dublin they would immediately move that way, because by that place they should be much strengthened, and to come to them the way doth lie directly over the said Hill, *Rockoll,* and with the said powder in the hill, they had determined to blow them up as they passed by.

And he discovered, moreover, that M. *Ochashen* of *Azabe* in the Queen's County, about 20 miles from *Athigh,* and 8 miles from the Fort of Leise, together with Sir *Florence Fitch-Patricke* of Castle Town, should have come by night with 5000 armed men to the Fort of Leise, and lie as souldiers that were to ward, the Papists within had agreed, and were appointed, to let in a certaine Company of the Rebels appointed for that purpose to burn and batter down the Town.

Hereupon Captain Picket went forth to meet that company with 500 men who fell upon them, and slew 3 or 400 of the Rebels, and the rest fled into the woods.

Himself sustained the losse of 60 men, slaine and dangerously hurt.

The said Rebels did rove extraordinarie up and down in Ireland, on Thursday, the 3 of December, 1641, and did them much hurt in divers places of the Countrey. They came to the town of *Rockoll* spoken of before, on the same day. The Rebels had a paire of Bag-Pipes which played before them as they marched, which played exceeding loud, which the towne hearing, rose to meet them, and at the towns end saluted them, and made them great entertainment, and joined themselves with them by an oath.

Afterwards they went to the aforesaid English inhabitants, William Clarke, and there they slew him, his wife, children, and family, 7 persons in number, of whom they left not one alive, but cruelly murthered them. From thence they marched to the *Nassey,* that is about 5 miles, a Town of Irish inhabitants, also they did go to the house of an *English man,* called *Henry Orell,* where they slew his wife . . . her daughter in the most barbarous manner that ever was known, and . . . and mangled her body in pieces without pitie or Christianity.

From thence they marched next day towards *Athigh,* which is 10 miles from the *Nassey,* towards which place, having marched about a mile from the *Nassey* aforesaid, they came to the Town of *Puckingell,* a Town inhabited of English, where they fell upon the inhabitants thereof, and slew them in a cruell manner, without mercie to the number of above 20 families, men, women and children. One woman, above the rest, they hanged at her own door with her children, by the haire of the head, and afterwards burned up the whole Town with fire.

Having made that place desolate, they marched the next day forward as before, and having marched some three miles further, they came to an *English* man's house, where first they slew the man at the doore, and afterwards they entered the house where they found the woman and her maide a-brewing; for it was an Ale house where they brewed their own drink The maid they took, and . . . and when . . . they threw her into the boyling Caldron, or panne of wort, that was then over the fire ; and her Mistris they slew and cut off her head ; and afterwards fired the house.

Then they came on toward the Town of *Athigh* with an intent to surprize the Towne and Castle ; but God prevented their intentions by one Master *Carot Topey*, an English Colonell· under the States there appointed by the Lords Justices and Counsell over 500 foote and 100 horse, who with his Regiment fell upon them and slew 300 of the Rebells, and put the rest to flight.

The most part of the Rebells that fled, ranne over the Bogges and tooke the Woods.

This Regiment of Rebells are about 2,000 strong. Their chiefe Commanders, are—

> PATRICK ONELL.
> TEAGE OKELL.
> CHARLES ROWE.
> WILLIAM RAFTER, taken prisoner.

Colonell Topey lost in this Skirmish fifty-five men, that is fifty foote, and five horse.

A Defcription of *Athigh*.

[On the eighth and last page of the original tract, is a very well executed woodcut, representing an imaginary *Athigh* as besieged by the rebels, who are blazing upon it from eight cannon. Our view is reproduced from the copy in the National Library, Kildare Street, Dublin, by kind permission of the Librarian, Mr. T. W. Lyster, M.A.]

Another pamphlet says :

Once they flew back to the West part, but that was but to increase their forces, which did appeare by their over running of the South West county of Tyrone, the Kingdome of Ireland from the County of Monahan, which they beate down and put to destruction according as they did Bel Tarbit . . . . With two thousand men they beat down Dundalke, also they beat down almost to the same number in the County of Warthedefloure, the men and women there in a most cruell manner they slew, their Tangeshire (*sic*) when of this opinion that the dogs should eate the flesh of *Ahab*, which they slew righteous *Naboth*, notwithstanding the confidence they put in their holy Father, the Pope.

IV

WAVES OF BLOOD.

Part Second.

THAT very learned antiquarian, the late Bishop Reeves, describes the "Montgomery Manuscripts" as "a work in which truth and pedantry are strangely blended."

The "pedantry" is evident enough in the quaint style which affects forms and turns of expression, somewhat archaic for the days of William the Dutchman ; and the "truth " is, at all events, not below the level of the historical work of the time. The author, James Montgomery of Rosemount, Esquire, belonged to the house of Viscount Montgomery of the Ardes in County Down. The work was intended to set forth the family history during the seventeenth century, but there are chasms, more particularly in reference to the period of which full and faithful record are especially desirable ; that is, during the period of the Civil War. The account of Sir James Montgomery—who, as Royalist commander in County Down, showed much activity—is but a fragment of what, as appears from certain references in the text, was written on the subject ; and the life of the second Viscount is wholly missing, or was missing when the volume was printed in 1869.

Sir James Montgomery "eminent in peace and war," second son of the first Viscount Montgomery of Ardes, was born in the year 1600, that is, before the family came from their native Scotland to take up the inheritance of the O'Neills of North Down. As a member of the Irish Parliament in 1640,—and taking a prominent part in reference to the Remonstrance of grievances under the government of Strafford—Sir James was one of the three Ulster members appointed on the committee to present the Remonstrance to the King. "Though charged by the deputy* on their allegiance, not to leave Dublin, they

* Christopher Wandesforde, Master of the Rolls.

set out privately, on the 12th November. On their arrival
in London, they found the oppressor of their country, once
so formidable, stripped of his power, impeached by the
Commons of England, and imprisoned under the charge
of high treason." *

It is, however, of Sir James, "eminent in war" that
I am to speak, or rather to let his son and heir of Rosemount
speak (chap 18) :

> Sir James armed . . . and went into the barrony of Lecahill,†
> about the beginning of December, 1641, and subsisted his men
> by the grain which the enemy had deserted on his first appearance
> (which was wonderful soon); and by the help of the grain of sub-
> stantial British inhabitants living next the Ardes, and by preys
> of Cattle taken from the Irish beyond Dundrum. Thus he pro-
> tected Lecahill for divers months against all the great body of the
> Irish dwelling on Mr. Bagnal's and the M'Gennises estates, and
> those in Kinelarty and Iveagh Barronys, who were assisted by
> their neighbours, in the Fews, and other places, in the County of
> Armagh, Sir James being desired to return thither, ‡ as he did,
> on the 20th of April, 1642.

The dates mentioned in foregoing will be of importance
presently. The next extract from same chapter brings
up the main question to be discussed in the present
paper :

> Here I must not omit to mention the keenness and spight with
> which his men had fought (I may say without fear or witt), especially
> the troopers, for they were *men that escaped on horseback with
> sword in hand and had seen* (as most of the foot also had escaped
> and beheld) their houses burned ; *their wifes and children murdered.*
> So they were like robbed bears and tygers, *and could not be satisfied
> with all the revenge they took,* for they spared not the enemy nor
> themselves.   It was a commanders labour to restraine their charging
> till the due time ; and then their enraged and implacable fury was
> unresistable, for they whetted one another's malice when they
> went to fight, saying : *Let us take amends for the murders and
> mischiefs those cowardly dogs and their friends have done to us and
> ours !*

There's a good deal in that "spight," and a lot implied
in that "malice," and the cry "to take amends"—a good
deal which, had the biographer chosen to be more explicit,
would probably have thrown much l ght on the alleged
increase in cruelty on the part of the rebels, as time wore

---

* Reid i., 278 (Ed. of 1867).

† Lecale.

‡ *Thither—i.e.,* to the Ardes.   Rosemount is near Grey-abbey.

on, and as they witnessed more and more of the " spight "
against themselves *and their friends*. There is certainly
matter for speculation here, but I pass on to what admits
of closer examination.*

One absurdity lies on the very front of the author's
statement. What a picture of a military hero—galloping
off, brandishing his sword, to observe, from a safe distance,
his house in flames, his wife and children murdered at
the door ! Mr. William Montgomery of Rosemount, like
many who had preceded him, and not a few who came after
him, in his eagerness to paint the rebels as demons at
large, takes leave of common sense, and loses all sense of
the ridiculous. A commander having any claim to
" eminence in war " would have shot such poltroons, had
they come his way ; and Sir James was not destitut: of
soldierly qualities. It is possible that some of those who
fled from Dromore, when Sir Con Magennis came against
the town, may have enlisted in the Ardes troops under
Sir James Montgomery and his brother the Viscount ;
but although Sir Con's followers are charged with burning
the deserted town, there is no imputation of murder being
committed there or thereabouts. By putting together
what actually occurred at Dromore with what *is alleged*
to have happened elsewhere, our author was able to produce
what was intended to be a picture but comes out a grot sque
caricature.

The Rev. George Hill, editor of the *Montgomery MSS.*,
prints a letter written by the Viscount which shows that

* Yet it appears from the depositions of Mr. Peter Hill, of Downpatrick, and
Captain Valentine Payne, of Strangford, that Sir James Montgomery was by
some regarded as too favourable to the rebels. Captain Payne (*Down* depositions, fol. 19), deposes : ' And this deponent doth afyrme that the said Sir
James during his abode in Downe, protected dyvers rebells, and many that are
gone into Rebellion since, and are now in Rebellion. . . . And this
deponent likewise affirmeth that, of late, the said Sir James hath protected one
George Russell of Rathmullan his wife, his son and children, who was a
cruell murtherer and one of the cheefe drawers forth of the inhabitants of
Lecale unto Rebellion.'

Mr. Peter Hill, whose account of ' The Ballagh ' Harris adopts almost word
for word, makes George Russell, of Rathmullan, the principal executioner.
The deponents who had a better right to know give no countenance to Hill's
hearsay statement, as will be seen from the evidence I have collected in the
first paper of this series.

' George Russell, of Rathmullan, was a member of the General Assembly of
the Confederated Catholics who sat at Kilkenny between 1641 and 1650. In
1650 he took the field, and died at the battle of Skerfolas. Then the lands of
Tyrella were confiscated, and the Russells of Rathmullan passed away.'—*Life
of Lord Russell of Killowen*, by Barry O'Brien, p. 15.

That the officer who protected the wife and children of such ' a rebel ' should
be accused to the State is significant.

the "tygers" could sometimes run away from the "cowardly dogs." The letter is dated "Mount Alexander the last day of December, 1641."

. . . Heer I lye with a matter of eighte companies of foote and three troupes of horse. At Killyleagh there is the Lord Clandeboyes, whoe, to speak truely, is extreame weake, onlye he has a strong hous. Upon Wensday last, Major Barclay, Capt. Inglis, and Mr. Elliott went abroade with ellevin or twelve score men, as the report comes to me, whereof there was seven score musquetiers and the rest pikemen, some fyve or six miles of Killyleagh. They mett with a party of the rebels, whose custome is *to fall one with a great shout or cry*, whereupon *the most part of the soldiers* that wer with Barclay and Inglis *fled, before ever the rebels charged them* ; soe as these two or three gentlemen, with the most part of all the men together with their arms were losed. . . . That night I sent out my Lewtenant Colonell and Major Crawford, with a party of 300 foot and 80 horses, whoe marched all night, and in the dawning came to the Leigure [Lagan?] where the rebels lay that ar on this syde of the countrey, whoe we did not think to have seen so strong as indeed they were. But praised be God ! they returned home yester night with the losse of only two or three foote soldiers and four or fyve wounded, whoe, I hope will not be the worse. They brought with them a prey from the rebels of a matter of twelve or thirteen score cows, and had the cutting off of about fifty of the rebells, who were upwards of 1,000 men. . . . My brother, Sir James, lyes at Downpatrick with a matter of six or seaven companys of his own and a troupe of horse. . . . The people that are fled of the Countys of Armagh, Fermanagh, Tyrone, Monoghan, and those of this county itself, from the Newry all the way to this place, ar *soe burdensome that in trueth we much fear ther will be scarsety* . . .

MONTGOMERY.

Among other points of interest, this letter shows that a good many, after all, escaped the *universal* slaughter !

I have now to direct attention to the annotation of Rev. George Hill, on the "tyger" passage, above cited from p. 317, *Mont. MSS.* :

Murdered.—These recruits of which Sir James Montgomery's force was largely composed, had made their escape to the Ards from other districts in Down where atrocious massacres had been perpetrated by the rebels. At Downpatrick, Killyleagh, Newcastle, Donaghmore, Newry, Lough Keran (near Tullylish), and Poytzpass, the most revolting cruelties had been perpetrated under the immediate sanction of Bryan O'Neill, Lady Iveagh, and other influential Irish. (HARRIS's *State of the County Down*, pp. 35, 76, 81, 84, 85, 92, 106.)

The Lough Keran massacre was perpetrated by means peculiarly horrible. The tragic details are *in part* preserved in the deposition of Peter Hill, Esq., taken in the year 1645. [Then follows the extract as printed by Harris, with which I deal further on.]

The massacre at Downpatrick is detailed *in part* in the following deposition of Lieut. Edward Davies here printed for the first time, and interesting as preserving the names of several Irish leaders of the district:

' Saith, that he was in the Lord Cromwell's house in Downpatrick, when it was beseidged by the Lord Maginis Viscount Evagh, and Col. Con Oge O'Neill, the 9th of ffebry., in the year 1641.* And that about six weeks after Lieut. Col. Alexander Hamilton, whoe commanded the said Lord Cromwell's house, did capitulate with the aforesaid lord Maginis and Colonel O'Neill. [The articles of capitulation are set forth.] . . . And this deponent further saith, that the same day their armey marched into Lecale and to Downe that their were *several* ould decreppit men, and women in Downe that lived upon the almes of others, and others that were house-keepers that stayed in the towne, *many* of which were most bloodeyly murthered at theire entereing into Downe, but *by whom, or by whose command this examinatt doth not know*. . . .

In part! An inch is part of a league. I submit the lieutenant's evidence—if evidence it can be called—does not advance the charge to the extent of an inch to a league. The deponent does not even tell us what means he had of knowing whether such meaningless " murders " were at all committed. There were, we may be sure, rumours of bloody deeds, on the coming in of " the rebels." Part of the town was burned, whether by accident or design ; and fatalities are likely enough. But how vague is this informant! He can give no idea of the number killed— of the manner of killing—or of the murderers! But he knows it must have been the Irish who committed the murders because he knows of no others to blame. Yet, some of the " murders " he mentions may have been due to stray shots from his own party, the defenders of Cromwell Castle, which castle overlooked the town. He mentions no casualities on the side of the besieged—nothing but *murders*. Had the deponent been cross-examined, we had found, in all likelihood, that the men he mentions were killed in defence of the castle, and the non-combatants—cripples and housekeepers—by his own fire. One case he mentions is a good deal like that of Bryan O'Rooney who was hanged at Newry for attempting to convey dispatches to the enemy.

Allsoe this examt. saith that there was one Rorey O'Donlahan that was formerly a servant to this examt., and he was sent from Mrs. West of Ballydogan to this examt, with a letter, and was taken by the party *and hanged*.

No mention is made of the time at which this occurred. We are told only that O'Donlahan (who can hardly have

* Old style,

been English), was hanged for carrying a letter to his own master. The incident would not have looked so like a murder had the deponent added that he was then besieged in the Castle, and the messenger was caught attempting to pass through the lines of the besieging forces.

There are, however, other depositions relating to the surrender in which " murders " are mentioned, but nothing to justify the allegation of slaughter such as is imputed. One deponent heard of murders but did not see any corpses. The following is more definite in some particulars, but keeps to the principle that all who died during the siege were murdered.

Examination of John Smith, of Downpatrick, taken at Carrickfergus, 10th day of June, 1653, in behalf of the Commonwealth :

Who being deposed upon his oath, saith, That about the nynth of ffebruary, 1641 (o.s.), he being in the house of the Lord Cromwell, Viscount of Lecale, in Downpatrick, after the Rebellion began, and the said house was besieged, Neil Roe O'Kelly and his forces entered the town, at which time one Philip Currie, a servant of the deponent's was murthered in the town. And further sayth, that about two or three days after the Lord Magennis, Viscount of Iveagh, and much about the same time Patrick M'Cartan of Loughin Island and Owen M'Cartan, his brother, came into the said town with forces. And further sayth, that George Russell of Rathmullan, Esqre., with his forces were there upon the delivery and yielding up the said house, and received half of the armes* in the house pretending to defend the Barony of Lecale against all that should oppose the Irish. And that during the continuance of the said Lord Magennis, Patrick M'Cartan, Owen, his brother, and Russell, their being in town, Katherine Gradell, wife of Richard Gradell, was murthered, and Abraham Hampton and Dorothy, his wife, Ellen Erwyn, an old blind woman, Anne Botte, wife of William Mathew *and several others were likewise murthered.* And further sayth, that Daniel Magennis, now in prison, was then there in comand, and hostage for performance of the articles concluded upon for surrendering the said house. And further sayth, that, upon surrendering the house, there were then there, and thereupon sent, Patrick Russell, of Comonstowne, and James boy Russell, his brother. And this deponent further sayth not.   Jo: SMITH.

(No name of Justice or Commissioner appears.)

There is still a vague element in the reckoning. We may take it that every sudden death, from whatsoever cause, would be set down as a murder, and charged against " the rebels." One matter lightly touched upon in the deposition is important. Colonel Daniel (or Donnell) Magennis,

---

* In accordance with the articles of surrender.

younger brother of Sir Con, and uncle of the young
Viscount Magennis, was given up by the Irish party
as a hostage for the due performance of the articles
of surrender, and as such was sent to Lòrd Clanneboye's
castle at Killyleagh. The Colonel's own statement
taken by Roger Lyndon and John Reding, acting
on behalf of the Commonwealth at Carrickfergus, on
the 9th day of June, 1653, contains the following at
the close :

> And sayth, that within a week after the town was taken, the
> said Lieut. Generall Bryan O'Neile, and this examinant came to
> Downpatterick, they found the said Lieut. Magennis and Con O'Neile,
> with Phillemy M'Toole, and other commanders, under Con Og
> O'Neile, and being there two or three days faceing thersaid Lord
> Cromwell's house * and endeavouring the gaining thereof from
> Lieut.-Coll. Hamilton and Lieut. Thomas Abraham, and having
> laid seidg soe close against that house, and parleying with the said
> Lieut.-Coll. Hamliton, the said Hamilton writt to my Lord
> Clanneboyes that he would not deliver up the house, on any tearmes,
> unless that this examt. (whom hee heard was then in towne),
> would be sent as pledg for the performance of the conditions that
> should bee agreed upon ; whereupon this examt. was sent to
> Killyleagh as pledg till the conditions were performed, and house
> delivered up to Con Og and the rest, which done this examt.
> was released from Killyleagh.

Had anything occurred at Downpatrick to warrant the
imputation of "massacre" even to the extent suggested
in the depositions of Lieut. Davies and John Smith, aforesaid, it is not likely that Colonel Daniel Magennis would
have been allowed so readily to depart out of the "strong
house" of the Hamilton's at Killyleagh.

Dr. Reid, the historian, and Mr. Hill, the antiquary, in
company with a good many others, have allowed themselves
to be deluded by Harris to an extent that cannot altogether
be excused by their dependence on that writer's research
and ability. Had Mr. Hill paid any attention to dates, he
could hardly have so strangely committed himself as he
has done in the place from which I have quoted. Let us
keep in view that Sir James Montgomery's "army" was
ready to take the field early in December, 1641—they
must have been ready somewhat earlier, for Sir James was
then encamped in the barony of Lecale, and in the neighbourhood of Downpatrick. Now, we have seen that the reputed "massacre" in that town occurred—so far as anything

---

* Cromwell Castle stood on the rising grounds just outside the town of
Downpatrick.

of the kind did occur—in February 1641–2.* The New-castle affair is placed in January, 1641–2. The Lough Kernan (not " Keran ") tragedy is fixed by the principal, indeed the only " witness," in March, 1642. At Newry or Poyntzpass ("Scarvagh Bridge," in the earlier authorities), there is no reason to think that anything of the kind occurred at any time. I have shown in the paper devoted to " The Surprisal of the Newry," that the allegation of massacre there by the rebels is not only unsupported by any evidence, but is utterly at variance with all the depositions I have, after much search, been able to discover. I hope to show that there is nothing in the Scarvagh or Poyntzpass " slaughter " but an echo of the Lough Kernan case of the same neighbourhood ; and that *the Donaghmore allegation is a pure myth.* Again, the purport of William Montgomery's remarks is that the " massacres " were of *the inhabitants* of the respective localities. Now what happened at Newcastle (" Bloody Bridge ") ? No one I think will attach any credence to Mrs. Eliza Price's nursery horror of " an Englishman, a Scotchman, and a Welshman," rotted on raw hides, although Harris vouches for it. The parties put to death at the bridge in Ballaghonery were prisoners brought from Newry, and the number there executed did not exceed one-fifth of that suggested by the same writer, following Borlase and the earlier pamphleteer: " some say 50." And on similar cause, the like execution (although " worked off " in more regular form) might occur in any war even at the present time. The slaughters fixed at all the other places were, to follow the story, not of the inhabitants, but of refugees from Armagh. Besides, the same story will in all cases have it, that " men, women, and children " were remorselessly done to death ; whereas, Mr. William Montgomery's and Rev. George Hill's story will have it, that *the men* took very good care of themselves, leaving the women and children to their fate ! Such stories are not merely incompatible : each loses itself in a fog of absurdity ; and, in that way, commonly eludes analysis. The fact is that the stories I refer to were never intended to be analysed or examined : *they were to be swallowed* whole

---

* Not earlier than February. The statement of Lieutenant Davis is some-what vague as to the time of surrender. But where was Sir James Mont-gomery while Downpatrick was at the mercy of the rebels ? His son, the anthor of the *Montgomery MSS.*, relates that Sir James was encamped near Downpatrick early in December, 1641, and remained there, or thereabouts, till the beginning of April following ; but we hear nothing of him at the very time when there was work for him at Downpatrick. The deposition of Captain Payne of Strangford (already cited) charges Sir James with playing into he hands of the rebels. Mr. Peter Hill will follow in similar strain.

upon trust, and the intention has been realized to an extent
as extraordinary as unmerited.

In the long list of tragedies which Hill gives from Harris's
Down, not more than two are deserving of notice : I allude
to the Newcastle (" Bloody Bridge ") and Lough Kernan
cases. The former I have already dealt with at length,
and I now proceed to the results of my inquiries regarding
the latter.

And first as to the name and location. Although printed
as Logh-Keran in almost every work that notices the tragedy,
the name of the lake—or rather of the townland in which
it is situated—is Kernan, and as such it is written distinctly
enough in one part of Mr. Peter Hill's deposition : it is
situated in the parish of Tullylish. The boundary of the
townland may be said to be about two miles from Gilford
and about the same distance from Banbridge, on one hand
and Scarva on the other. The Great Northern branch
line of railway nearly bounds the townland on the side
towards Gilford. Tracing the line from Banbridge, it
runs close to the River Bann as far as the bleaching village of
Laurencetown (formerly Hallsmill), and then breaks off,
leaving the river on the right, curving more and more to
the left till it joins at Scarva the main line between Dublin
and Belfast. The course of the railway between Laurencetown and Scarva is marked out by a trough-like valley ;
in which, about two miles from Laurencetown and three
from Scarva, is a small deep lake or tarn called Drumarn
This little lake receives the outflow of Lough Kernan,
which lies just out of view, not quite half a mile to the south.
Although so near, it is situated at a considerably higher
level on a sort of plateau with a rim of green hills. This
Lough Kernan,* is a pretty and prettily situated lake,
nothing about it to suggest crime or tragedy.†

While I have but little doubt as to the commission of
some such crime, I have very grave doubt as to the magnitude and even more serious doubt as to the circumstances
by which additional horror is given to the atrocity. The
whole story may be said to rest on the statement of Mr.
Peter Hill of Downpatrick, High Sheriff for the County
Down in 1641 and subsequent years. This gentleman's

---

* Area about 90 acres (*Harris*).

† There is, however, such a tradition in that neighbourhood. I remember
well, one fine summer's evening, in the year 1872, meeting on the shore of the
lake an intelligent old farmer named McInerney, who lived within a stone's
cast of the water. He told me how " Phellimy O'Neale drownded the people
in that lough the time of the Wars of Ireland." I regret that I did not then
make a note of what he further said : but his statement leaves no doubt as to
the tradition of a tragedy having been enacted there.

evidence would appear to derive great weight from his official position and social standing. Of that, however, I shall have something to say. His is one of the longest among the depositions, running to about fifteen pages, folio, closely written, with some interlining and alterations especially in the portions dealing with " the murthers and cruelties comitted by the cruell Irish Rebells of the County of Downe." It is worth noting that his account of the Lough Kernan tragedy is not continuous, occurring in two places separated by three paragraphs dealing with matters having no connection with that story, except that they show the bias of the deponent.

And further sayth, that about the beginning of March, 1641 (o. s.) about [ffowr score]* men, women, and children of English and Scottish were sent by direction of Sir Phelim ôNeile from the County of Armagh downe to Claneboys, in the County of Downe, *where* they were mett by one Capt. Phelim M'Art M'Brian, and his company of Rebells (most of his owne Sept), which said Captain Phelim and his company carried and forced all these Protests. from *thence* into a lough called Lough Kearnan in the same county, In which Lough, he and his said company forced [them upon the ice]† and drowned them all, both men, women, and children, spareing none of them at all.

That is the account as first given by Mr. Peter Hill. It will be observed that there is something perplexing in his use of the adverbs of place which I have marked, both pointing to the assumption that this Lough Kernan must be quite near to Clandeboye, the country adjoining Strangford Lough,—the territory then belonging to the Montgomerys and Hamiltons ; whereas the places are hardly less than 30 miles apart. Kernan was indeed quite out of the direct road. Harris appears to have been sensible of the difficulty implied in Mr. Peter Hill's hazy geography : he explains—or suggests on the authority of Temple and a deponent named William Clarke, of the Co. Armagh, tanner,—that the refugees from that county were taken across at Scarva because the bridge at Portadown was broken. It is true that then the valley extending from Portadown to Newry, between the two counties, was one unbroken line of morass passable at only three or four points—hence, Scarvagh Pass, Poyntz Pass, and "Tuscan Pass " (*Harris.*) At any rate, Kernan being so near to Scarva, to people living at any distance, whatever extraordinary thing happened at the less known would be connected with the better known place. But we must not lose sight

* Interlined.　' One hundred and forty Protests,' scored out.
† This interlineation is in a paler ink than the text.

of Mr Peter Hill. In the concluding paragraph of his
deposition (sworn 29th May, 1645, before Dr. Henry Jones
and Mr Henry Brereton), he gives a new and still more
sensational version of the story. This paragraph is
written in a different ink, pale and indistinct, so that some
words can hardly be deciphered.*

This deponent further saith, That *he hath been credibly informed* by one Christopher Bellow (whom he hath great cause to
beleeve) that whereas the said Phelim M'Art McBrenn (*sic*), and his
wicked company had brought the fourescore English and Scottes,
that came out of the County of Armagh upon the aforesd. lough,
called Lough Kearne,† And whereas they found it so frozen with
ice that they could not be drowned nere the sides thereof, then
they forced them as far as they could on the ice, But not dareing
to drive or pursue them farr for feare to breake the ice under their
owne fete, and soe to be drowned themselves, They those wicked
and merciles Irish [then] tooke the sucking children from their
parents, and those that carried them, and; with all the strength
they could, threw them as far as they were able towards the place
where the ice was weake and thinn : Whereupon those parents,
nurses, and friendes, striving to fetch off the children, went soe
farr that they burst and brake through the ice. and then and there
both they and the children perished together by drowning, all save
one man (that escaped from them wounded) (*sic*), and a woman,
whose names he cannot express.‡

No wonder that the Rev. George Hill was shocked
by "the tragic details" as printed by Harris from Mr.
Peter Hill's *sworn* statement. But Harris withholds the

* Between his two statements relating to Lough-Kernan, Mr. Peter Hill
has the following :—" Hee further saith that since the Rebellion began, but
especially for a year and above now last past, it hath been a very comon and
ordinary thing for the Irish to murther and devoure and eate the persons of
such English as they could light upon, and when they could light upon none
of them, then to kill, devoure and eat one another."
    Then he tells us how he had himself condemned to death an Irishwoman
" because *he was credibly informed* that such a lyke fatt woman had killed and
devoured divers others !" Next, he tells us how three troops of the Lord
Conway's going out to forage, were suddenly surprised by the Irish near Lisnegarvy (Lisburn) :—" Which three troops were then and there murthered, and
afterwards their flesh eaten and devoured by divers barbarous Irish women that
lay in the wood. And the very bones of these men were afterwards fownd in the
woods cleene pickt, and the flesh (first [as was conceived] boyled) eaten quite off
the same." All of which is sworn as " evidence," and having so delivered
himself, he resumes the Lough-Kernan story, also on the basis of belief in what
he had heard from others.

† *Sic* in this place.

‡ I find the following note made while the original lay open before me :—
' The signatures, *jurat*, and date—all at end—are in same ink as the body of
the deposition (leaving out the last par. Bellow's story is in some parts almost
illegible owing to the paleness of the ink). The concluding words: " whose
names he cannot express," and some interlining appear to have been added by
a different hand.'

vital circumstance that *all this earnest swearing is but hearsay*. Mr. Peter Hill was not the man who ought to give that information—evidence it is not. He forgets the names of the man and woman who escaped. Why didn't he put down the names as he has noted the names of some hundreds of *rebels*? We should all have had greater cause to believe Mr. Christopher Bellow had he been produced in court and called upon to shew what ".great cause" *he* had to certify such a story. This is not alleged to have occurred in a desert island, but in one of the most fruitful and populous districts in the County Down, and there ought to have been little difficulty in finding those who could testify to the fact or to the circumstances more immediately connected with it. In this, as in scores of cases connected with the same inquiry (save the mark!) the wrong party is in the box. The " witness " that comes forward is not the one who knows where the truth lies, but the one who can tell the most exciting tale. I have not come to this conclusion hastily, and I have in this and other papers produced many striking illustrations of the enormous part played by *hearsay*, and even by mere imagination, in piling up calumny against the Irish. Mr Peter Hill told a good story for the English market ; and there is no indication that the Commissioners, or any one else, troubled him with inconvenient questions.

And here I must note another circumstance of much significance. While the Newcastle (" Bloody Bridge ") case was followed up with persistence and success by the Committee of the High Court sitting at Carrickfergus, quite a crowd of examinants being produced in that matter, comparatively little notice was taken of what is alleged to be the much greater " massacre " of Lough Kernan. Mr. Dunphine, the Minister of Donoughmore, it appears, was asked to state what he knew about the matter, and he simply answered :

> Concerning the people that were drowned at Logh Kyrnan, this deponent knows nothing, but that he heard it was acted by the M'Bryns in general, and that Edmond M'Art M'Bryn, if he may be found, may be of greater use to cleare that particular.

An honest deponent, undoubtedly. He could have given " evidence " as well as Mr. Peter Hill, but he would not be guilty of such imposture. Lisnageade, a seat of the Trevors, adjoins Kernan, or comes pretty close to it. Lieut. Thomas Trevor, the son of the " murdered " Hugh Trevor, made two depositions at Carrickfergus, and never referred to anything dreadful or otherwise in his own neighbourhood.

To my mind, at least, these are strong presumptions that
the Lough-Kernan " massacre "—if any such thing occurred
there—has been prodigiously exaggerated.

I do not call the Scarva " massacre " an invention,
but a mere " double," although it is mentioned by more
deponents than the Lough Kernan case ; but, as I have
already pointed out, it is the Lough Kernan affair all the
while.* Capt. Henry Smith, who was a prisoner in Newry
from the outbreak till the beginning of May, 1642, gives
the following bit of evidence :

> And saith, that *he hath been credibly informed by general report,*
> that at the Bridge of the Skarrow (*sic*), in the County of Downe,
> the Rebells drowned about cxx men, women and children, English
> and Scottes, *besides many others they drowned in severall other places.*

Valuable evidence ! In Borlase, App. p. 109, is the
following :

> At Servagh-bridge 100 drowned, more 80, more 60, more 50,
> more 60, 27 men murthered.

And Capt. Henry Smith is mentioned as the authority.
But not many then suspected that the 'witness' was immured
in another part of the country while all this was going on !

The notion seems to have been that Scarva is on the
River Bann, the nearest point on which (at Gilford), is
three miles distant. I have often wondered where at
Scarva, " the bridge " could then be. There is no stream
or river there. There is a railway bridge, and a canal
bridge very close to it. But there was no canal for a
hundred years after " the massacre " (which so many have
written about). There is also a little trench separating
the counties of Down and Armagh, but it is, I believe,
of more modern date ; and at any rate no crowd of people
could have been drowned there. I dare say, it was from
a knowledge of these circumstances, that the Rev. George
Hill changes the scene three miles further south to Poyntzpass, near which there is a lake. And, truly, he might
make " a massacre " at every village in Down and Armagh
as well as at either Scarva or Poyntzpass. What was then

---

* In Sir Gerard Lowther's judgment against Sir Phelim (High Court of
Justice, 5th March, 1652-3), which Miss Hickson prints from the Stearne MSS.
in T.C.D. (F. 4, 16), the following appears :—" 8. You yourself confessed, as
is testified, that you killed 680 at *Scarvagh*, that you left neither man, woman,
nor child in the barony of *(illegible)*, and left none at all in the plantations
about you." (*Ireland in 17th Century*, ii., 185.) The name Scarvagh must be
a misprint for GARVAGH, which is distinct in the original MS. notes. As Miss H.
remarks, these notes are very difficult to decipher, but I have no doubt about
this name.

required at Scarva was not a bridge but some kind of cause-
way across the morass. "The bridge" at Scarva is a reflection of the "the bridge" at Portadown. In fact, the
deponents not only multiply tragedies at the same place,
but turn up the same "massacre" at several places. The
following is a good (but not exceptional) illustration of
this mixing up, and dealing out all around, as it is also a
capital specimen of *fearless swearing* :

> Margaret Bromley of Ballymore, al* Tonoragge (Tanderagee),
> in the county of Armagh, widow, sworne :
> . . . And this deponent further saith that four score and
> some Protestant men, women and children were all drowned at
> one tyme by Toole M'Cann, of Portadowne and his companions.
> And the Rebells afores[d] gathered out of severall parishes within
> the county of Armagh, w[ch] they drowned at Scarvagh bridge,
> vizt. : one hundred at one tyme, four score at another time, three
> score at another time, and fiftie at another time. And there were
> divers other persons killed and drowned by the Rebells at other
> tymes and places whose names she is not able to express. And at
> the last tyme of her knowledge of their most excessive cruelty,
> the Rebells gathered together three score and odd Protest[ts]
> pretending they would sent them to Clanyboyes, to the Lord
> Hamilton : but [in] the stead thereof, they most miserably drowned
> them at Scarvagh Bridge, afores[d].

Here we have all the stories of Portadown and Lough
Kernan boldly transferred to Scarva. I don't at present
discuss the Portadown "massacres," but I have no doubt
that the multiplication of these is due to hearsay evidence,
the story of the same event assuming new forms as it comes
back from different quarters.

But all these are outdone by what I must call *the
Donaghmore myth* ; of which we will first hear the Rev.
George Hill's great authority, Mr. Walter Harris, to see
how history is writ :

> DONAGHMORE, a parish church, stands eastward of the Tuscan
> Pass, near three miles, and is about midway between Loughbricklan
> and Newry. . . . This parish, which bounds the Lordship of Newry,
> will ever be infamous for the merciless butchery of a great number
> of *Irish* Protestants in 1641. The Papists had not long broke out
> into Rebellion in the neighbouring counties before their companions
> in blood gathered together in this parish, at Glyn or Glynwood,
> an ancient manor of the family of Magennis, now (1744), of William
> Innys, a minor, west of this church ; where in the covert of the
> thicket, *like ravenous wolves, they flew upon their prey and massacred
> upwards of twelve hundred defenceless naked Protestants.* This
> with other instances of inhuman barbarities, which multitudes
> suffered in divers parts of the kingdom, drew from the pen of *an*

*honourable historian,** then in a high station in Ireland, the following reflection (Temple's *History of the Irish Rebellion*, p. 100) : ' If we look,' says he, ' into the sufferings of the first Christians under the Tyranny and cruel Persecutions of the heathen Emperors, we shall not certainly find any one kingdom, though of a far larger extent than Ireland, where more Christians suffered, or more unparalleled cruelties were acted within the space of the first two months after the breaking out of this rebellion.' Part of these were the unhappy sufferers at Glynwood, whose persecutors hoped to leave neither the name nor posterity of a Protestant behind them. But their hopes, God be praised ! are fully blasted ; for Protestants in this single parish are estimated at more than one thousand, and the Papists, not eight hundred ; and *to forward the conversion of the latter*, a private gentleman of this parish has bestowed a house and some acres of land upon a Protestant schoolmaster, to encourage him to teach the poor children the principles of the Protestant religion.— Harris's *Down*, 85–6.

Now, what grounds existed for this dreadful charge to which are tacked on so much commentary, so many pious homilies ? Harris does not, in this case, call in the services of Mr. Peter Hill. The High Sheriff of Down, who takes care to inform us that " he knows the county well "—who knows all about Newcastle (" Bloody Bridge ") all about Lough Kernan,—who, moreover, is able to assure us that some companies of the Lord Conway's were *boiled and eaten* in the woods near Lisagarvey—this same well-informed person cannot tell a word about Glynwood (or Donaghmore), although we have heard of a butchery there exceeding the tot up of all those about which he makes so much ado ! His silence here is eloquent.

But there is silence more eloquent still. Mr. Dunphine, the deponent above mentioned, was Minister of this very parish of Donaghmore near Newry. In his deposition, attested and sworn before Messrs. Traill and Bickerstaffe, on the 26th of May, 1653, he tells *what he knows* about the Newcastle affair, and *what he has heard* about Lisnagarvey, Downpatrick, Newry, Mourne, Dromere, and Lough Kernan ; *but has not a word to say about his own parish.* Now, had twelve hundred—or one hundred—or only twelve — been murdered there, or thereabouts, could the clergyman of the parish have so ignored the matter ? Utterly inconceivable !

I submit, therefore, that the alleged " massacre " at Glynwood or Donaghmore is an absolute myth.

Did Harris invent the story ? No ; he has still the infallible authority, " the depositions," to fall back upon,

---

* The introduction of Temple's remark would seem to imply that *he*, too, is committed to this story. The responsibility rests with Harris himself.

although in this case he has to go some distance—into another county—before he can find what he wants.   He finds it in the depositions of Dr. Robert Maxwell, Vicar of Tynan, and afterwards Bedell's successor in the see of Kilmore.   This deposition, running to fifteen folio pages, closely written in the original, taken 22nd August, 1642, was printed very soon after, and is to be found in the Appendix to Borlase : *

> In the Glenwood, towards Dromore, there were slaughtered (*as the Rebells tould the deponent*), upwards of 1,200 in all, who were all killed in their flight to the Countie of Downe.

Such is the "text" of the sermon we have just heard. The rebels *tould* so to Dr. Maxwell while he was a prisoner in their hands at Kynard.   And who were the rebels that told him the story ?   We are left to guess ; and we can hardly guess amiss if we take it that they were the soldiers of his guard, who amused themselves by telling him many horrible tales—the only cruelty they seem to have practised on him.   Dr. Robert Maxwell is also the authority for various other " massacres," which no one living at or near the supposed scenes of atrocity would ever have known anything about but for his diligence in noting what " the rebels did confess unto him.   He " deposes " that the rebels did so confess unto him that Col. Brian O'Neile killed about 1000 Protestants in this county of Down *besides* 300 killed at Killyleagh.†   He testifies to murders in Antrim, in Armagh and Tyrone, his " cause of knowledge" being that the rebels did so and so confess to him ; and he is particular to urge his advantages as to the accuracy of his figures relating to Portadown tragedies, which he gives "by their own report," without naming any informant.
    And this is evidence !
    The Rev. George Hill's first reference to Harris is, p. 35, as follows :

> In the Rebellion of 1641, the Protestants in and about Down suffered grievously.   The historians of that calamitious time inform us that *numbers* were put to cruel deaths ; and, *by the confession of even some of the Rebels*, it appears that the inhuman butcher, Col. Brian O'Neal embrued his hands in the blood of about one thousand of those unhappy sufferers !

By the confession of *some* of those rebels who, *in another county*, where whiling away the time telling stories to

---

* Temple prints only a portion, and does not give this extract.
† *Borlase,* App. p. 113.

their prisoner, *it appears,* etc. But in what other way does it appear ? Can no one, rebel or loyalist, who lived near the scene give evidence to the same effect ? In what part or parts of the County Down were these massacres perpetrated ? No one there ever heard of such fiendish slaughter until the historians—among whom we may reckon the Rev. Dr. Maxwell of Tynan—made the discovery. These big " massacres " are always most felt in the distance. The excerpt from Harris thus ends :

At present the country about Downpatrick is for the most part Protestant ; yet some remains of Popery still continue, and will probably always do so *as long as St. Patrick's wells,* before mentioned, *are held in such high veneration* by the credulous vulgar !

The reference, Harris, p. 76, is to Killyleagh :

This place suffered grievously by the Papists in the calamitous year of 1641, who not content with the cruel deaths of *numbers* of Protestants at Down and Castle Island *pursued their thirst of blood,* and inhumanly butchered 300 of them who fled thither for refuge. The scene is happily changed, the Protestant religion flourishes, and the Linen manufacture accompanies it ; the fine thread here is in demand.

The transition is a bit remarkable— from blood to fine thread ! The use of the word " numbers " here and in other extracts is worth noting, the term conveying, or being intended to convey, something of the force of " myriads." In much the same sense, or with much the same intenion, " several," " divers," " others " are used. Vague terms, opprobrious epithets, generally in the super-lative degree—not the superlative of eminence, but the superlative of detraction— show up in profusion, the un-failing resource of the horror-mongers, among whom Mr. Walter Harris takes a front seat. This, as already noted, is one of Dr. Maxwell's " massacres," one of those which " the rebels did *confess* to this deponent." Had anything of the kind occurred—had even one-tenth of 300 been murdered—some Killyleagh man, or some man of that neighbourhood ought to have come forward to depose to the fact. Lord Clanneboye who lived in Killyleagh, or some among the Hamiltons, ought to have risen to the duty of giving evidence instead of leaving the matter to the Blackwater incumbent. Dr. Maxwell well deserved to be made a bishop, he had proved so excellent a " confessor," excellent in all respects but one—he would tell. And he did tell many things that no one else would tell or could tell. Some deponents did indeed mention a few names of

persons killed in the neighbourhood of Killyleagh in the
first rising. It is highly probable that conflicts would
occur there and eleswhere, and some deaths would result.
That is bad enough. But the slaughter of 300 at Killyleagh—as described by Dr. Maxwell and Walter Harris—
may be relegated to the category of myths.

Castle Island, mentioned in the last extract from Harris,
is a townland in the parish of Saul, barony of Lower Lecale
in the neighbourhood of Downpatrick — a small place
containing only about 112 ac., but in 1851 the population
was given as 179. The massacre here amounted to
"numbers"; which may mean, units, tens, hundreds, or
thousands, according to the views or zeal of the interpreter.
Wishing to find out, if possible, what grounds existed
for the charge of massacre, I turned to Borlase, App.,
p. 113, who gives "William Gore,* Co. Down,"† as the
authority. I have transcribed his deposition (*primo
Julij*, 1643), but it is mainly taken up with a detail of
the losses he sustained, amounting to "ffive hundred
poundes ster. at the least, by the handes and means
of "—(a long list of "Rebells" follows) :

> ⸸ And further sayth, that the Rebells Kellyes, aforenamed, and
> others of their Confederates, in the beginning of the Rebellion, when
> they Robbed the protest^{ts} in yt p^t. of the countrie, murthered
> in the island called Castle Island one Robert West and Adam
> Gradwell, *severall* [English] Protest^{ts} . . . And the Rebells also
> murthered near Downpatrick, one Robert Holmes another English
> protest^t. And also murthered by hanging, and other deaths
> at Downe *a great number* of other protestants whose names he
> cannot express.

Not unlikely most of the "several" and of the "great
number" never had a name. This is all the witness for
the prosecution can say about the "massacre" at Castle
Island : two names ; then, *as many as you like*. As he
moves away from the scene, he appears better informed.
He knows more about Downpatrick than about Castle
Island, and more about Portadown and the County Armagh
than about his own Down. But that is nothing
unusual.

Had hundreds, or even tens, of Protestants been
murdered at Downpatrick, or Killyleagh or Castle Island,
who had a better right to know than Peter Hill of Downpatrick, in the County of Down, Esquire ? Yet, this active

* He signs 'Willm Gower.'
† "Ballentogher, in the County of Down," on deposition.

representative of his sacred Majesty who knows so much about the county and has shown so much interest in the few who fell at Bloody Bridge, or the alleged four score who perished in Lough-Kernan, takes no interest at all in the trifle of 300 " butchered " (we are assured) at Killyleagh, the " numbers " butchered in his own town, and in the townland of Castle Island ; hasn't a word to say about one of them ; nor even about (Col.) Brian O'Neill's 1,000 victims !

Had the "confessions" in that far-off place not been made, or had Dr. Maxwell's " deposition " been lost, or had it been estimated at its worth, what evidence would remain of " St. Bartholon.ew " at Downpatrick, Killyleagh, or indeed any other place in the same county ? At those two places some deaths are mentioned ; and we can hardly say that they were murders without knowing more of the circumstances.   But, to avoid conflict on a side issue, let us assume that all who are named were murdered ; so far from establishing the charges preferred by Harris, they prove that no such extensive massacres or cruelties took place.   The local deponents show no disposition to minimise matters ; and when such deponents, after mentioning *two* names, can give no further particulars than the vague and worthless assurance that " several others were murthered," we may take it that the " several other " cases were not worth investigating.   Yet, it is on such foundations, such wild vague or exaggerated statements, that the dealers in blood and cruelty build all their tall castles of horror.

The allegations of wholesale massacre at Downpatrick, Killyleagh, and Castle Island are amply disproved by the very documents which are audaciously, or ignorantly, held forth in support of the charge.   So recent a writer as Dr. Knox (*History of County Down*, 1875, p. 412) says :

In 1641, the town (Downpatrick), was attacked by Col. Bryan O'Neill, who burnt a magnificent castle that had been erected by Lord O'Keha (Okeham ?) *and commited great slaughter on the Protestants who had fled thither for refuge.* A narrative of the massacre there, as well as of that at Killyleagh, where many had repaired for safety, and *the sworn testimony by which it was supported*, may be referred to in Sir John Temple's history of the Rebellion.

Now the " sworn testimony "—and take it as stands— gives no support to these statements regarding " slaughter " at any of the places named.

The " inhuman butcher," Brian O'Neill, who is so held responsible for the slaughter in cold blood of so many above a thousand in this County of Down, makes much

G

less figure in the depositions of those who ought to know
as much about the matter as Dr. Maxwell or any who
did confess unto him than his brother Art O'Neill. This
Art or Arthur O'Neill stands charged with a very wicked
performance at Ballee church in Lecale. The charge
is more serious than anything that appears to have happened
in Downpatrick, Killyleagh, or Castle Island, and is more
clearly brought home in the examinations. Yet, strange
to say, it is not mentioned by Harris (unless he identifies
it with what is alleged to have occurred at some place
already named), and he could have founded on it as great
a " carnage " as any connected with that part of the county.
The statements are not tested by cross-examination, but
they are the averments of parties who were in a position
to know, and unless there has been a conspiracy of collusion
(an hypothesis that finds no favour with me), the matter
seems not to admit of doubt. It is not improbable that
the crime was in return for some manifestation of the
" spight " about which Montgomery of Rosemount is so
jubilant ; yet it was none the less a crime, a wicked and
detestable crime. The charge, as alleged against Art
O'Neill, is fully set forth in the following deposition, which
I give at length so that a better judgment may be formed
of the merits of the complaint :

The examination of Thomas Allen, of Ile-Lecale, aged 25 years,
taken before us the 18th of May, 1653 :
Who being duly sworne and examined Saith that hee hath
known Art O'Neile, brother to Sir Bryan O'Neile since about the
first of January next after the beginning of the wars of rebellion.
And saith that the said Art, in that month of January taking
upon him the comand of four score men, or thereabouts came to
the Church of Ballee, in Lecale, within three miles of Downpatrick,
and coming with his said partie to a house near the Church, a man,
called John Millar was then and there killed by them, whose corps
this dept. saw the doggs eat. And presently after the man
was soe murdered, the said Art and companie came to the
church door, where this deponent, six men, three women,
and two little boys were, and cast stones at the church
doore to break it open. Then one Charles Kinning,
one of those in the church, called and said, Who is there ?
(it being about midnight), whoe had noe answer made him. But
saith that suddenly after, the said partie without placed straw
to the church doore and put it afire. And then the said Art called
to the said William (*sic*) Kinning, You have done me once a pleasure,
and I will doe you another now : Yield the church and I will save
your lives. How shall I know that you will save our lives ? Whereupon the said Art said : Here is my hand. How can I get your hand
through the fire ?   Here it is, said he, through this hole, that
not a drop of your blood shall be spillt.   On which tearmes the

fire being removed, hee the said Art and his companie entered into the church, in the presence of this deponent, leaving two of his men at the church-doore that none should goe out of the church. And saith that the said Art, notwithstanding his promise, did com̃and some of his men then in the church, to tie Kinning and all the rest of the said persons formerly with him in the church, except the three women, this deponent, and the two children, theire armes behind them with some Lynnen yearne, they found in the church and they being soe pinioned, hee caused them to bee bound, two and two together, and from thence tooke them away about a mile and a half, and caused them to be murdered, as this deponent afterwards heard. And saith that the said Art when he left the church, hee tould Kinning that Strangford was gon, and Downe was gon, and that Ballychinder * was on fire, and therefore give me your moneys and I will warrant you. And further saith not

THOMAS ALLEN.

Sworne before us, 19th of May, aforesaid.

ROGER LYNDON.
GRIFFIN HOWARD.

The story so told is highly dramatic, but not free ot difficulty and inconsistency. It is, however, in the main, corroborated by other deponents. And it is not the sort of story in favour with the horror-mongers who must needs have man, woman and child butchered without distinction. The time corresponds with that of the Newcastle (" Bloody Bridge ") tragedy, and was likely enough due to some similar provocation. Yet was it, all the same, a great crime. There were three Kinnings in the Church. And William Kinning,† an elderly man, suffering from disease, was liberated. Had it been a " thirst for blood," seven individuals would not have been spared.

William Carshan (or Carson) deposed to meeting William Kinning the elder, next day in Down, and hearing from him the story much as Allen tells it ; but no allusion to money. Carshan and others afterwards found the bodies and had them interred. Carshan was bound in the sum of £50 to the Commonwealth of England to appear on four days' notice to give evidence before the high Court of Justice *re* the foregoing charge.

John Kinning, son of William Kinning, senior, deposes to meeting with his father in Downpatrick, and learning from him that the other men, five in number, were put to death ; namely, Charles Kinning, William Kinning, junior, John Carshan, Thomas M'Burney, and William Maxwell. This John Kinning assisted at the interment of the murdered men. There are other depositions. One

---

* Ballykinlar.   † Or Cuming.

document has a pathetic interest, and for that reason, as well as for its corroborating Allen's testimony, I make no apology for printing it :

Wee whose names are here underwritten doe by these presents humbly certifie to all whom it may concern that widow Cuminge, *alias* Marion Tate, did declare before us at Downe, the 16th of May, 1653, and thereupon take a book in her hand, and took her volontarie oath :
.That she was in the church of Baly,* when Art ôNeile, brother to Mr. Bryan ôNeile, cam thither to the said church in a murtheringe way.   And murthered one John Miller in his house within a pistoll shot of the church afore the the said Neile and his confederats cam to the sd. church.   William Cumings, (elder), Charles Cumings, William Cumings (younger), John Carson, Thomas M'Burney and William Maxwell, being then in the church aforesaid, a purpose to save their lives from the inhuman masaker of the Rebels.   And that Art O'Neile cam to the church doore and flung stones at it.   And seeing he could not prevaile with stones, caused (*sic*) sett fier to the doore of the church, and in the midst of that hott dispute, the aforesd. Art O'Neile called uppon William Cuminge (elder) and sd. that the sd. Cuminge had don him a curtesie before, and that hee the sd. Neale would doe the lyke to him now.   Whereupon Cuminge answered and said, What curtesie is it that you will doe to mee ?   then Neile said, that if hee would come out of ,the church hee would save all their lives and that one drop of their blood should not be drawen.   Whereupon the said Neile and Cumings joyned hands through the doore, but as soon as the said Neile got into the Church hee caused take (*sic*) the men aforementioned and flightered (*sic*) their hands behinde their baks, and tyed them two and two together, and caried them away and was murthered (*sic*) the neixt day afterwards.   And the said widow Cuminge that if she were able to goe to Carikfergus either on futt or horseback shee would com and depose the same before the Lord President of the high court of Justice.

All this wee humbly certifie, and shal bee redie to depose the same whensoever occation shall serve, witness our hands this 16th of May, 1653.

his
JOHN KINNIN, WILLIAM + CARSON,
mark
his
WILLIAM + CHAMBERS.
mark

On the turn-over of the same sheet ·

The within named John Kinning, William Carshan, and William Chambers, subscribers to the within certificatt, cam before us this 19th day of May, 1653, And deposed to the truth of said within certificatt of Declaracion of the within-named Widow Kinning, as within sett downe

JA. TRAILL, ROGER LYNDON.

* Ballee.

The next deposition shows that in May, 1653, when the Committee collecting evidence for the High Court of Justice was in session at Carrickfergus, Art O'Neill was still at large. Brian O'Neill had been arrested about the end of March preceding, not, so far as appears, for the "thousand murders" but as accessory after the fact to the murders laid to the charge of his brother Art.

Andrew Daniel, of Ballincross, late of Ballyhornan*. . . taken

* *Ballyhornan*, a village (and townland, area, 330 acres) on the east coast of the County Down, opposite Gun's Island, a short distance from the entrance to Strangford Lough, "At Ballyhornan coals are occasionally discharged, and small quantities of grain shipped. There is a small boat-harbour at Sheepland, the property of Colonel Magennis, who is descended from the territorial lords of Iveagh " (Knox, *Hist. of Down*, p. 453).

The Rev. George Hill has the following note to p. 367, *Montgomery MSS*: —" *Ballyhornan.*—A Col. Bryan O'Neill was traditionally known as the *Butcher* because of his atrocities, perpetrated at several places throughout the County of Down during the massacres of 1641 (See Harris's *State of the County Down*, p. 35). He is not, however, to be confounded with another Bryan O'Neill, whose extensive family estates had been almost wholly swept away by confiscations from time to time, and who was compelled to go abroad in early life as a soldier of fortune. The latter served for a time in Holland under the Prince of Orange, and afterwards in the army of Charles I., being probably induced to do so by his kinsman, Daniel O'Neill. For his bravery at the battle of Edgehill, Charles conferred on this Col. Bryan O'Neill an English baronetcy by the title of Sir Bryan O'Neill of Upper Clannaboy. His first wife was Jane Finch, a lady of the Nottingham family, by whom he had one son, Sir Bryan, the second baronet, who became Baron of the Exchequer in 1687."

I am afraid the Rev. George Hill has once more been put on the wrong track by his trusty guide, Harris. It were idle to attempt the identification of the Bryan O'Neill who committed 'the thousand murders in the County Down,' for the simple reason that the story has no foundation in fact. In 1657, Mr. Bryan O'Neill, of Ballyhornan, had a contest at law with William Montgomery, of Rosemount, about the possession of lands—clear evidence that *he* was not concerned in such horrible murders. Bryan O'Neill, 'the inhuman butcher,' is not a historical character.

In Col. Donnell Magennis's examination at Carrickfergus (9th June, 1653) is this passage:—" The sayd examt. being demanded, Whether hee was at the burning of Downepatrick, or where hee was then, hee sayth hee was there a week before it was burnt in company of his brother-in-law, Lieut.-Generall *Bryan O'Neile*, who that yeare came from beyond seas, with Coll. Plunkett, Hugh M'Phellemy Byrne, Con Og O'Neile, and others whom he remembers not."

And on same day Patrick M'Cartan, of Loughinisland, deposed, regarding the siege of Down :—" Sayth that those that [were the chief men] there were the Lord of Iveagh, Donell M'Birne Magneise (now in prison), *Bryan M'Hugh boy O'Neile*, and Con O'Neile, and severall others."

The Rev. William Fitzgerald, of Armagh, in his examination (4th June, 1642) before Sir Robert Meredith, of the Court of Exchequer, says :—" The Cathedral Church of Ardmagh, the verie same daie being fired and burnt to the ground, all by the comand of the said Sir Phelim O'Neile, *as this examt. hath been informed*, who att his departure there left Collonell *Brian M'Hugh boy O'Neile* att Ardmagh to see execution done to such rebellious wicked designs, wch said Bryan (as this examt. hath been informed by severall of the Irish) within short time after fell sick of an ague, grew frantick, and in this raving manner cried out allwaies to kill the English churles and Scottes *in which woful case he shortly ended his miserable life*."

18th May, 1653. Who being duly sworne and examined, Saith that he hath known Art O'Neile brother to Sr Bryan O'Neile of Ballyhornan in the said countie 18 years. And saith that the said Art *alias* Arthur lived in a poor widdowes house in Ballyhornan, called Mary nee Quilan *alias* fitzWilliams, from Christmas last till about the beginning of March last where [then] said Sr Bryan was apprehended and brought thence. And saith that he saw the sd. Arthur O Neile in Sr Bryan's house 2 severall times, when Sir Bryan was absent. And saith that sundry times he saw the said Arthur's boy bring meat and drink from his brother Sr Bryan's house to the said widdow's house, where Art O Neile lodged. But whether Sr Bryan was at these times at home hee this deponent knows not. And saith that he saw a peice of cloath that was bought in the said Ballyhornan from Margaret O'Raverty, and carried into Sr Bryan's house, whereof a suit of clothes was made by two taylors in the house, And sent to the sd. Art, which this deponent saw on his back. And saith that the sd. Sr. Bryan allowed unto this deponent and three others joint tennants the money which they paid unto the woman for the said cloathes as part of moneys due by them unto the said Sr Bryan

ANDW. DONNELL.

Sworne before us the 19th *(sic)* of May, abovesayd.
ROGER LYNDON.
GRIFFIN HOWARD.

If the man who was charged with the murder of five or six men endeavoured to keep out of the way, the alleged " butcher " of a thousand and more made no attempt to evade the authorities, as the following will show :

Captain Jacob Knowles, of Downpatrick, being duly sworne and examined (19th May, 1653) Saith, that hee having a warrant for the apprehending of Art O Neile, and severall others, for murder, did make search for the said Art O'Neile, about the 26th of December last, at Ballyhornan, and could not find him ; but coming out of that towne, where hee mett with a boy of Mr. Bryan O Neile's, and asked him if he knew where Art O Neile was ; hee answered, that hee did lye in the said towne, and had beene six weekes sick, and that hee was gone abroad that same day, and that the Lady O'Neile had sent him a *(illegible)*, and that he was gon towards Mr. Simon Jordan's house, a mile from the said place ; whereupon this deponent went thither, but could not find him [there]. About three or four days after, this deponent being in Downpatrick, he mett with the said Mr. Bryan O'Neile, and hee [asked] this deponent what order hee had for his brother ; this deponent made answer that he had an order, and thereupon showed him, the said Bryan O'Neile, the said order. And the said Mr. Bryan O'Neile said that his brother would cleare himself. And more saith not.

JACOB KNOLLEYS.

Sworne before us the sayd day.
ROGER LYNDON.
GRIFFIN HOWARD.

The further history of this case cannot be traced in the depositions; there are others, but they merely repeat what is so far related. I have thought it advisable to go so fully into the matter and to give the foregoing statements at length—they are interesting in more than one respect. In my view they are highly important, inasmuch as they serve to show that where a crime was known to be committed by any " rebel " leader, or any " rebel " of name, the matter was followed up with determination and energy by the tribunals of the Commonwealth ; and, to speak the truth about the same tribunals, they did not, like the Commissions of Parsons and Borlase, limit their sphere of action to one class of evil doers. I have made allusion to some parity between this tragedy of Ballee and that of the " Bloody Bridge " ; there is another of greater consequence. In both cases, the depositions are numerous, showing that the authorities of the time were satisfied that they had in those places matters requiring close investigation. Why should they be less active in respect of the much greater "massacres" and " slaughters " and " carnages " alleged to have occurred in other portions of the same county ? The inference must occur to every one who thinks of the matter at all. The prodigious " massacres ", the inhuman hecatombs, were not for investigation. It were as idle as to investigate Burnet's extravagance about " a country all covered with blood," or to undertake the physical dissection of a trope. " Such assertions," says Dr. Lingard, " appear to me rhetorical flourishes, rather than historical statements." But the mischief is, and all along has been, that the writers of the "things called histories " * will insist on putting forth these monstrous " flourishes " as solid facts, deprecating, at least in their own practice, any test or analysis, such as even common sense might furnish. If such statements related to any other country than Ireland, they would have met with but sorry reception in these countries.

That there were, among the Irish, individuals guilty of crimes or cruelties is not denied, nor does any one defend such deeds. The perpetrators were well deserving of the utmost penalty of the law. But it is quite another thing to attempt to found upon these isolated cases of murder and cruelty such charges as were urged by interested parties in the seventeenth century and maintained by some even to the present. The myths of Donaghmore, Scarva, and Poyntzpass are disgraceful only to those who

* Burke.

have sought to raise the wild fictions to the dignity of history. As regards the County Down I have to submit that, while, among those said to be in rebellion, deeds disgraceful enough were committed, there was far more slaughter and cruelty practised against them,—of course under the sanction of " the State,"—of which the " historians " take little or no notice.

V.

THE IMITATION.

WARNER, Taylor, Stuart, and others who have taken the more rational view of the Civil War of 1641 and following years, charge the earlier writers on the Irish side with exaggeration almost as extravagant as that which they blame in Temple and his followers. The charge, however, as regards the Irish Catholic writers refers more particularly to their accounts of the Island Magee massacre. The number —3,000—said to have been butchered on that occasion is quite impossible in a place of so limited area. But, as the Rev. James O'Laverty, M.R.I.A., remarks,* the population would then be much swollen by refugees from the other portions of the county. The butchery, at the very lowest estimate, was deliberate and done in cold blood. Yet I cannot help thinking that, in some respects, too much has been made of this Irish Glencoe. I refer not to the exaggeration. There has been a good deal of controversy as to the particular time at which this undoubted massacre took place, and, in my opinion, quite too great importance has been attached to that question, as I hope to show by and by. Another mistake, I am convinced, has been made in speaking and writing of the Island Magee tragedy as if it were the only one of the kind—the only deliberate massacre of defenceless, unresisting people committed by those who took the side of "law and order."

Yet, in or about the month of January, 1641-2, there was, on the opposite side of Belfast Lough, another "Island Magee" of which little or nothing has been said, either because it did not happen to become so much known to the earlier writers of the Irish party, or that at such a time it did not attract particular notice ; and, of course, Harris is silent about it. The Rev. George Hill incidentally notices the matter by printing the following deposition in his note to page 318, *Montgomery MSS.*

---

* *History of Down and Connor,* iii, 128. A similar remark occurs in Dr. Curry's *Review of the Civil Wars in Ireland.*

The examination of Katharine Gilmore of Ballenahince, taken 4th May, 1653 :

Saith, yt 8 days before Candlemas next, after ye Rebellion, shee then living in ye townfand of Ballydavy, in ye Barrony of Castlereagh, altogether with tenn familyes more, of all wch. 11 familyes there were (of men, women, and children) killed to her own knowledge, seaventy and three by a great company of people (being) to her estimacon in number about 200, who were brought thither by one Andrew Hamilton of the fforte, James Johnson the elder, and James Johnson the younger, both of Ballydavy, John Crafford of Crafford's Burne ; and further she saith that James Johnson the elder, killed one Henry O Gilmore, brother to the examinat, in her own sight, and likewise she sawe the sd. James wth. his swoord slashing att one Edmond Neeson, who was killed but shee knoweth not whether* hee made an end of him or not, for on the receipt of the first blow, the sd. Neeson rann to the lower end of the house, among the rest of his neighbours, the cause of her knowledge is that a short space before, the said Andrew Hamilton had putt her out of the doore of the house in consideracon of her† after which shee saith that by reason there were many of Hamilton's company about the doore, she lay her down in a ditch which was right before the doore where she was unespied of any as she supposeth, the night being very darke, rayny and windie, and 4 or 5 lights in the house ; the wch. lights the said Hamilton or his men caused the examinat's mother to make for them a little before supper tyme, of which lights they carried some to every house to give them light to compasse their designe.

The Examt. further saith, she saw one Abraham Adam kill James O Gilmore, her owne husband, and Daniell Crone O Gilmore, and Thurlagh O Gilmore ; shee further saith, that at her going forth of the house, a sister of hers tooke houlde of her for to go out with her, and the sd. Abraham Adam strock of her sd. sister's arme from the elbowe, with a broade swoord, the sister's name was Owna OGilmore.—[T. C. D. Depositions, *Down*, fol. 38.]‡

One might, perhaps, doubt this story in its more heinous particulars, were it not more than confirmed by several other depositions ; for this is one of the cases which appear to have been taken up in earnest by the High Court of Justice Commissioners sitting at Carrickfergus. The following is deserving of notice and attention, as it goes to the root of the matter, and as the deponent cannot be suspected of any active sympathy with the " rebels." This rather startling statement is taken from folio 155 of the County Down depositions in T.C.D.

---

* The word in the original appears to be ' or ' instead of ' not whether.'

† Left blank in Mr. Hill's printed copy. The missing word is ' Brackan ' (in the MS. deposition).—the term meaning wrap or plaid, See note p. 107.

‡ *Sic* as in *Montgomery MSS.* The folio number is 159.

The Examination of James Gourdon, taken the 3rd of May, 1653 .
Who being duly sworne and examined sayth that about
Christmas next after the Rebellion, this examt. liveing in the
towne of Bangor in the Clanneboys, his mother told him that there
were some of the town, two or three tymes looking for him, this
examt. to speake with him, and that she heard it was *to goe out
with them to kill the Irish that lived neere and about the towne;* therefore she advised this examt. to put himselfe out of the way, and
not to have any hand in the busines ; whereupon this examt.
tooke his bed clothes and went and stayed and lodged in his mault
kilne, a pretty distance from the sayd towne of Bangor.

And this Examt. further sayth, that within a night or two
after, most of the towne of Bangor and the parish together made
a compact wth. those of Ballydavy about Holliwood (as this
examt. was informed) *to fall out in two partyes in the night upon
the neighbouring Irish to kill and plunder them.* And this examt.
further sayth, that accordingly they went forth in the night and
killed of men, women and children (poor labouring people and their
familyes) a great number. His cause of knowledge is, for that
the next morning after the sayd murder was comitted, he saw those
of the towne of Bangor that had beene acters in it come in with bloody,
brakans* and other goods, cattle, and household stuffe ; his further
cause of knowledge is that there was a collection made through
the whole towne of Bangor for burying those were killed,
whereof this examt. payd a part, but cannot now remember how
much.

And further sayth, that the names of those, he this examt.
knew and saw (so come in) from killing the sayd Irish as aforesayd
(*illegible*), James M'Cullie, who, he undestands is dead, William
Martin, he heares gone for England or Scotland, James Martyn,
he heares being in Munster, James Madder, John M'Cullie, Abraham
ffrizell [about Downe] William Knowes, and more remembers
not that are living. And further sayth not.

Jur : GEO. RAWDOW.   JAMES GOURDONı

(Deponent bound in xxᴵᴵ to give in evidence.)

There may have been more people butchered in Island
Magee, but in some respects the Ballydavy massacre seems
more base. The deponent, Gordon, shews how elaborately
the " business " was planned. There is no allegation that
the raid was in any way provoked by the people of Ballydavy.
The reception of the murderers was friendly, for they were
entertained at such supper as the poor people had for
themselves. This may be inferred from what Catherine
O'Gilmore says about the lights ; but the matter of entertainment is put more clearly by another O'Gilmore who
escaped the fate of his friends.

---

* *Bracken.* Here means a kind of tartan or plaid. (*Breac* spotted,
chequered)—*Murray's Eng. Dicty.*

The examination of Owen O'Gilmore* . . . of the age of thirty years :

Saith yt at ye begining of ye Rebellion, in ye month of January, 1641 (o.s.), he lived at Ballydavie in the parish of Holliwood, in ye countie of Downe, and hearing yt ye Scots were gathering together, there came a partie of them to ye sd. Ballydavie, and wisht the Irishmen there living to gett themselves into [Bryan Boy's] house, and it being not able to hould them, they went into two houses, where *that party of Scotch men did abyde with them and supt with the sd. Irish, and were very merry till about midnight,* and then yt party ffell upon ye sd. Irish, and stript them and a little aforeday fell a-killing of ye sd. Irish, after yt Andrew Hamilton, now of Crawfordsburne in Bangor† parish [came to them] who was to bring order for that work, and came and shott off his pistoll before Bryan Boy's doore, whereupon ye sd. Scots party fell upon killinge ye sd. Irish, and so killed of men, women and children, three score and odd, and ye names of ye persons yt this examt. remembers yt were at [ye place yt night] were ye sd. Andrew Hamilton, John Crawford, Jam: Johnson, senr., and Jam: Johnson, junr., Captain Will Hamilton, Robt. Morris, John Watt and Gabriell Adam, and did see ye sd. Watt and Morris‡ kill sev'n of ye sd. persons.

Also this examt. saith, yt he, escapeinge this danger by hydeing himself in ye kilne, did so soone as he could escape thence towards one Hen: M'Williams M'Gilmore's house to secure himself, and as this examt. came nere the sd. house, he heard the Scotchmen aboute the sd. house, and so durst not go thither, but perceived yt ye sd. persons were the two James Johnsons, aforesd., and the said Watt and, others not known to this examt. ; but this examt. heard ye sd. James Johnson, junr., say to ye sd. Gilmore, Open the door, but ye sd. Gilmore denyed, and then ye sd. Johnson said, You know me, to wch. Gilmore said, yt he did, but for all yt must not open ye door ; then ye sd. Johnson desired ye sd. Gilmore to light some straw, ye wch. Gilmore did, whereby ye sd. Johnson put in his pistoll and shott and kild ye sd. Gilmore, whereupon they broke open ye doore, and went in and kild one of ye children of ye sd. Gilmore and did wound ye sd. Gilmore's wiffe and one child more, and left them for dead, but ye sd. wiffe recovered, and tould this examt. the foresd. relation.

Also this examt. saith, yt he went from thence for his security to a lame man's house, called old Gildy OGilmore, and went in and lay down in the straw, where shortly ye sd. party of Scotchmen came, but none went in there ; ye sd. Watt and ould James Johnson went about the house, and finding a hole, said, They are all escaped hence, and also did bid ye sd. Watt not to kill ye sd. old Gildy ; and ye sd. Watt had a pitch-fork in his hands, and ye plades about him was ye sd. M'William M'Gilmore his wife's ; ye sd. Watt, finding this examt. said, What are you ? and for that this examt. was in

---

* Down Depositions, folio 157.

† ' Bangnell ' is the form in the MS.   But Crawfordsburn is in *Bangor* parish.—(*Census Index of Townlands.*)

‡ In a supplement to her deposition, Katherine O'Gilmore gives the names of seven others of the invading party, and *six* of the seven are marked as since dead.

feare, and did speak ye Scotch speech, said yt he came from Kille-
leagh, and his name was Shirley ; so that party went away.

Also this examt. saith, yt ye fourth day after ye sd. murder
this examt. being at Kirkdonnell, heard yt ye constable one Robert
Jackson of Hollywood, did bring with him one Thomas O'Gilmore,
uncle to this examt. ; whom ye sd. Jackson brought to ye sd. place
with his hands bound behynd his back with match, ye sd. Jackson
brought ye sd. prisoner before Capt. Alex Hamilton, who did com̄and
ye sd. constable to cary ye sd. prisoner to Bangnell to ye . . . . and
ye sd. Capt. would not receave him at all ; so ye sd. constable took ye
sd. prisoner back, and this examt., thinking yt they would
cary him to Bangnell (sic), accordingly did follow them ; but as ye
constable [and another man] went up ye mountaine betwixt ye sd.
Kirkdonnell and Hollywood, *this examt. did see ye sd. Jackson,*
constable, kill ye sd. prisoner, Tho : O'Gilmore with a sword, and
this examt. did goe to him after yt ye sd. constable was gone
away, and perceaved severall wounds yt ye Tho : had, both cutts
and stabbs.

Taken before us,
    JA : TRAILL.
    RICH : BICKERSTAFFE.

           his
OWEN + GILMORE.
    mark

We have no clearer or no more circumstantial narratives
of a " massacre " than those relating to the Ballydavy affair ;
in no case are the details more specific, or the leading
members of the gang more certainly identified. I shall have
to consider other instances of the same truculence in quarters
where we should least expect it, the sufferers being not of
the foreign element. And once more I must call attention
to the care with which this Ballydavy atrocity has been
investigated by the Committee of the High Court of Justice,
and that we have nothing of the kind in the alleged matter
of the " thousand and more slaughtered in cold blood by the
inhuman butcher, Colonel Brian O'Neill," or by anyone
else—the very charge which, if at all presumable, would
have called for the labours of a Commission of Inquiry to
itself. And it is almost certain that outrages not recorded
were committed against the Irish living in the Scottish
portions of Down from the very beginning of the movement,
and that these helped to spread the flame of " rebellion."
It could hardly be otherwise owing to the incitements held
out by " the State," that is, by Parsons, Borlase and their
colleagues at " the Castle." The cool business-like way in
which the murderers of the Ballydavy people went to work
points to the conclusion that theirs was not an extraordinary
performance and that the design did not originate with the
perpetrators of that shocking crime. It will be remembered
that one of the very first moves of " the State " was to get
the Scots to rise in Ulster, and the Commissions sent down

to Ulster—to several gentlemen of the County Down—virtually authorised any extent of extermination by fire and sword against "rebels and their sympathisers, aiders, and abettors." The incitement was of a very general character; and although not expressly or avowedly covering such as the Ballydavy case, the operation of that call to arms would not be restricted to military rule. Doubt on this matter is precluded by the terms of the commissions of inquiry issued on 23rd December, 1641, and two later dates, to Dean Jones and his colleagues; in which they are authorized to inquire into crimes committed by "the rebels" *only*; so that the Ballydavy case would not come within their purview. Their duty was to blacken the rebels to the utmost.

And if any doubt should remain as to the effects of their first endeavours to rouse the Scots of Ulster, there is no mistaking the attitude of the Lords Justices and Council in Dublin Castle, when we come to consider their Proclamation of 8th of February, 1641-2.* At the head of the long list of the proscribed we find the names of :—

> Sir Con Magenis, of Newcastle, in the County of Down, Knt.
> Patrick M'Cartan, of Loghnelan (Loughinisland), in the same county.
> Art Oge MacGlasny Magenis, of Ilanderry, in the same county.
> Ever M'Phelim Magenis, of Castlewellan, in the same county.
> Rory M'Brian oge Magenis, late of Edentecullagh, in the same county.

and about sixty more, in other counties of Ulster, as well as Leinster, all reputed leaders, who

> Instead of that loyalty which his Majesty's good and gracious Government might justly have wrought in them, have returned nothing but their fruits of treason and rebellion, to the disturbance of the public peace and happiness of this kingdom, and to the distruction (as much as in them lay) of this State and Government, and of the persons and estates of many thousands of his Majesty's good and faithful subjects therein, whereby they have showed themselves to be most ungrateful, detestable, vile, and unnatural Traytors and Rebells. WE, therefore, *according to the custom of this Council-Board* in cases of this nature (though no former rebellion can parallel this for acts of cruelty and horrid crimes), do, by this present Proclamation, in his Majesty's name and by his Majesty's authority, Declare, Publish, and Proclaim them, the said Sir Con Magennis, Patrick MacCartan, etc., etc., and every of them and *all their and every of their partakers, aiders, maintainers, comforters, confederates, complices and associates*, apparent, notorious, ungrateful, wicked, vile, and unnatural Traytors and Rebells, against our Most Gracious

* Borlase, App. vi. Also in Gilbert's *Affairs in Ireland in 1641*, vol. i.

Sovereign Lord, Charles, by the Grace of God, King of England, Scotland, France and Ireland, Defender of the Faith, etc., his royal crown and dignity of this realm, and malitious oppugners of his Majesty's Royal Sovereignty, Preheminences, and Prerogatives, *willing,* therefore, *requiring, warranting, and authorizing all his Majesty's good and loving subjects to pursue and plague with fire and sword, apprehend, destroy and kill,* BY ALL THE MEANS AND WAYS THEY MAY, *all the said persons, their partakers, aiders, etc.* (as before down to ' wicked, vile, detestable, and unnatural Traytors and Rebells.' ⟩

Now is not this, in the clearest and most emphatic terms, an incitement to, and *warrant* for, murder, assassi-nation, etc., " by all the means and ways they may " of any and every person whom they may choose to call "rebel " or rebel sympathiser ?   For " the State " Proclamation " requiring, warranting, and authorizing " such killing, etc., necessarily, though tacitly, concedes to " all his Majesty's good and loving subjects " the right to judge and decide for themselves who are rebels, their aiders, abettors, com-forters, and so forth.   The murderers of the Ballyday O'Gilmores, and the murderers of the Magees of Island Magee, might flatter themselves that in shedding the blood of their victims they were simply acting the part, and discharging a duty, of " good and loving subjects."   The atrocities just mentioned were, indeed, committed before the issue of this Proclamation ; but the " warrant " would be interpreted alike by " the State " and the " good and loving subjects" as retrospective to the extent of condoning in the past what it authorized in the future.   That issue of the 8th Ferbuary, 1641-2, was no surprise to anyone ; it merely gave formal expression to the views entertained by " the State," and well-known from the first to those who were on " that side."   It was very well understood, within a week of the outbreak, that the killing of " rebels " and their " complices " was not to be regarded as a crime, but as " acceptable service " to the State.

The Proclamation of 8th Feb., 1641-2, proceeds :

And We do hereby make known to all men, *as well good subjects as all others* that *whatsoever he or they be* that shall betwixt this and the five and twentieth day of March next, *kill and bring* or cause to be killed and brought, unto Us the Lord Justices, or other Chief Governour or Governours of this Kingdome for the time being, the head of the said Sir Phelim ôNeale or of the said Sir Con Magenis, or of the said Rory Maguire, or of the said Phillip Mac Hugh, MacShane ôRely, or of the said Collo MacBrian MacMahon, who were of the principal conspirators, and have been the first and principal actors in this present rebellion, *he or they shall have by way of reward,* for every of the said last-named persons so by him

to be killed and his or their head or heads brought to Us. . . . viz.,
for the head of the said Sir Phelim ôNeale *one thousand pounds,*
for the head of the said Sir Con Magenis *six hundred pounds* (the
same sum of £600 for each head of the remaining three.)

I am induced to follow the Proclamation beyond what
my theme would appear to require, because I look upon this
document as a more than ordinarily important State-paper
—as one which throws much light upon that " indiscriminate blackness " of which Carlyle speaks with so much self-
assurance. It will be seen that the highest price was set
upon the head of Sir Phelim O'Neill, although it is doubtful
enough whether his was the best head of the lot. There is
another scale fixed in the same Proclamation, of sums to be
paid *on proof of killing,* the head or heads not being brought
in, namely, £800 for killing Sir Phelim O'Neill ; £400 for
each of the remaining four.

And as " the good and loving subjects " were not likely
to have the same opportunities of earning the rewards so
offered, it was further provided in the Proclamation that

Whosoever under the degree of a knight, other than the said
Phillip MacShane ôRely, and Collo MacBrian Mahowne,* and
other than the said Luke Toole, and other than the children and
grandchildren of the late *traiterously-descended Traitor Feagh
MacHugh Birne,* and other than the said Rory *alias* Roger More,
(We not holding it fit that the most malignant conspirators should
obtain pardon for so high and heynous offences, and the causeless
destruction of so many thousands of innocents, upon the only service
of cutting off persons of no greater consideration) shall, betwixt
this and the five-and-twentieth day of March next, *kill or cause
to be killed* and brought to Us . . the head or heads of the said
Patrick MacCartan, Art Oge MacGlasny Magenis, Ever MacPhelim
Magenis, Rory MacBrian oge Magenis. . . Tirlogh Roe O'Neale. . .
Art Mac Tirlagh MacHenry O'Neal. . . . Tirlogh MacHenry
MacTirlagh ôNeale, Hugh Oge ôNeale, . . . Collo MacBrian
MacMahowne, Neal MacKenna, Collo MacEver MacMahowne. . . .
for each, four hundred pounds . . [£300 on proof of killing, but
not bringing in the head], and shall have pardon for all his or their
offences. . . .

Does anyone believe that the Proclamation foregoing
had no effect in stirring up " good and loving subjects " to
deeds of blood ? Before it was issued, we have seen that
such " acceptable services " were not neglected ; and are
we to conclude that this call, not so much to arms as to
outrage, was productive of peace and good will among men,
and nothing else ? The writers who hold that the insurgents
indulged in more crimes and cruelties as they grew stronger,

* *Sic* in this place, *in Borlase.*

would do well to consider whether, so far as the alleged growth of cruelty on that side is well-founded, the operation of this " State " warrant and incitement of the 8th February, 1641-2, was not the more influential, if not the only real cause. Yet that element, which I hold to be of no ordinary importance, in the development and progress of events, has been overlooked or ignored, and the place which by right belongs to it has been taken up by " causes " arising not so much out of the real facts as out of the imagination and ingenuity of the writers.

While some " historians " take their cue from Dr. Henry Jones and his brother commissioners, some, on the other hand, are generous enough to admit that " the rebels " had not a monopoly of crime or cruelty in those times ; but, as I contend, they contrive, while making such admission, to misrepresent matters. For instance, Borlase says :

I may admit that many things *contrary to the laws of arms and Christianity*, during the Rebellion were severely commited by the English,* in memory and anguish of former villainies commenced against their friends.—Page 57.

This statement appears to have commended itself to many modern writers, more especially those connected with the history of Ulster. I take extracts from Hill, Knox, and Reid for the purpose of examining the merits of such time-honoured allegations.

In Note to page 318 *Montgomery MSS.*, the Rev. George Hill says :

The soldiers and others *sometimes imitated* the atrocities of the Irish, as the following details now printed for the first time will show.

He prints two of the T. C. D. depositions, one being the statement of Katherine O'Gilmore, of Ballynahinch ; the other relates to the murder of a man named M'Gueer, at Ardglass. Elsewhere I give evidence relating to a much more atrocious proceeding on the part of the soldiery stationed in the same town of Ardglass. Mr. Hill has simply adopted the view set forth by Borlase ; and I don't for a moment assume that he was conscious of either plagiarism or misstatement. He gives expression, in few words, to a current and long standing prejudice—for prejudice it is, and nothing more. And at the best, it is but a sorry excuse for " good and loving subjects " to say that they merely " imitated the rebels ! " And how ludicrous when we find

---

* *British* would, perhaps, have been more in accordance with the fact.

H

the same defence made for the children of the Covenant—
"The meaning of the Scotch Covenant," Carlyle assures us,
"was, that God's divine Law of the Bible should be put in
practise in these Nations"* And how do the Covenanters
practise that divine Law when they come to Ireland? By
imitating those "apparent, notorious, ungrateful, wicked,
vile, and unnatural Traitors and Rebels," those benighted,
Bible-burning bondmen of Rome, the Irish Papists! What a
confession! Such apologists little know how ridiculous
they can make themselves and their clients. Might not
the "waves of blood" speeches and pamphlets be responsible
for some of this "imitation"? And might not the State
"warrant"—"to pursue with fire and sword, to plague,
to kill, by any means they may"—have something to do
with the matter? Well, none of these writers seem to
suspect that these things could have influence on "the
good and loving subjects." It was simply an affair of
"imitation"! So innocent and child-like!

Dr. Knox, the more recent historian of the County
Down, alluding to the expedition under Lord Conway and
General Monroe for the relief of Newry, mentions the
accounts left by Monroe, Turner, and Roger Pike as giving
"a revolting picture of the cruelties practised by the
successful soldiery:"

But the cruelties practised by the army were outdone by the
horrible atrocities committed on many of the unoffending people,
as vividly depicted in the pages of Froude

So Froude is the authority! And in the matter ot
Irish history, more especially the history of that period,
Froude is as untrustworthy a guide as he would be in an
Irish bog on a foggy night. This "vivid" historian takes
his pickings from "the faithful relation" of Sir John Temple†
and the Remonstrance of Dr. Henry Jones, in which he
found a store of wild tales taken "upon oath," it was said,
but taken without the slightest attempt being made to
substantiate or investigate them. Dr. Knox merely chimes
in with the old-time story, and he did not invent it; he is
a compiler, and of course, it was enough for him to take the
matter upon trust, and to hand it over to others just as he
found it himself—no better, no worse. Besides, he does not
appear to be aware, as Mr. Hill is, that atrocities were
committed against the Irish by others besides the soldiery.

Dr. Reid, a great favourite with Froude, has sometimes

* *Letters and Speeches of Oliver Cromwell*, ii, 154, edition 1857.

† And from Col. Audley Mervyn, whose 'waves of blood crowd up in
heaps.'

been spoken of as an impartial historian, as indeed he tries to be, and might have succeeded had not some of the long-standing inveterate prejudices proved too much for his judgment and sense of fair play. He admits and regrets—in regard of his excuses, I can hardly say he condemns—the atrocities on "the British side." He does not, as the learned and indefatigable Harris does, affect total ignorance of contemporary records from British hands, condemnatory of British misdeeds. Dr. Reid sets forth some evidence of wrong-doing on the part of those who were to make things right ; but he makes his admissions with so much reservation, and finds such a wealth of excuse —even justification—that he brings to my mind the parable of the cow that filled the pail and then kicked it over. I question whether Dr. Reid's great admirer, Froude, could in his palmiest day have succeeded in packing within the confines of half a page, more misrepresentation at once virulent and honeyed, more artful and dexterous phrasing, or more unctuous sophistry, than are to be found in the following :

These dreadful massacres were no doubt *retaliated, to a certain extent*, by the exasperated British. Suffering under the treachery and revenge of the Romanists, who declared they would be satisfied with nothing short of the utter extirpation of the heretics, it was scarcely possible for the Protestants to provide for their security without inflicting summary punishment on such perfidious and implacable enemies. The violence of the Protestant soldiery was *in some degree justified* as well by the authority of the State, as by the circumstances of the country, and a due regard to self-preservation. In many instances they doubtless exceeded their orders and acted with unnecessary and culpable cruelty. But their severities have been grossly exaggerated by Romanist and even by Protestant writers ; * who, not only shut their eyes to awful provocations previously received, but endeavour to fix upon the British the guilt of being foremost in the work of Blood.† Thus the murder of several Roman Catholic inhabitants of Island Magee, near Carrickfergus, in the beginning of the month of January, has not only been egregiously exaggerated, and attributed to parties wholly innocent of it, but it has been placed early in November and averred to have been the first blood shed in this unhappy contest.‡—*Reid*, i., 326.

And that is the way the Covenant was to work in Ireland !

* I wonder what Protestant writers have merited such censure. None of them, I think, go further than Turner and Pike, who were eye-witnesses to what they relate, and who allege no " provocations " or any other " necessity."

† This, perhaps, refers to Carte's *Ormond*.

‡ Reid fixes the date of the tragedy as 9th January, " by which not more than thirty individuals—though still too large a number—lost their lives." I can partly agree with him as to the use made of this dreadful occurrence, which was, after all, but one of many practised upon the native Irish.

This, " the divine Law of the Bible," as expounded by a
Minister of the Word—a professor of civil and ecclesiastical
history to boot! Friends and admirers of Dr. James
Seaton Reid! don't you think the passage a bit overdone,
at all events down to near the end ? Well I must tell you
what I think of it, and of the writer : So far from finding
here the hand of the impartial historian, I find—judging
mainly from this performance before us—but a more
sleek sort of Hugh Peters. Leaving out the Island Magee
matter, the rest is a tissue of assumptions and misrepresentations netted and entangled with a bold and dexterous
hand, so that the disentanglement could not be achieved
in a short time or with little labour. The first thing that
strikes me is the omission of any explanation applicable to
the Ballydavy case, or even to the case which he mentions
—that of Island Magee. Now what "treachery" or " revenge "
can be laid to the charge of those " exasperating Romanists,"
the Magees of the Island or the O'Gilmores of Ballydavy,
in the parish of Hollywood ? What excuse is it to allege
that " Romanists " *elsewhere* had done something of the
kind themselves ? Does such an excuse accord with that
" divine Law of the Bible " which the disciples of the
Covenant were so eager " to establish in these kingdoms " ?
Candidly, wouldn't it be bad enough for those same wicked
misguided Romanists to put forward so lame an excuse ?
How was the reign of righteousness to be set up, if " the
good and loving subjects," and the children of the Covenant,
instead of setting the good example, must, under plea of
" provocation," follow the ways of those sons of Belial, the
Irish Papists, rebels, and idolators ? Following up the
theme, and in the spirit of Dr. Reid's apology for " the
violence of the Protestant soldiery," we can imagine some
man of light and leading taking his stand in the market-
place of Bangor, and thus addressing his Scottish kinsmen
and neighbours :—" Men of the town and parish of Bangor !
Know ye not there is among you a remnant of that
Canaanitish nation which the Lord hath doomed to destruction for their iniquities ? Have ye not heard of all the
blood they have shed ? What mean ye then ? Is it meet
that such 'perfidious and implacable' enemies should live?
Have ye already forgotten the ' awful provocations ' ? Ye
will wait and afford them time to imbrue their hands in
your blood ! The duty of ' self-preservation,' and the
commands of ' the State' will be your justification if ye
smite the wicked, and cut them off in the day of their
evil-doing. Come then, and in the name of God, let's cut
their throats, before they have time to cut ours ! "

All this is very strange language, but no more strange than Dr. Reid's apology : it is the Rev. historian's doctrine applied in a particular instance. The same writer lays stress on the " Romanists " rather than on the " rebels," as if the movement had no object but extermination of Protestantism. Dr. Reid ought to have learnt something from his contemporary, Mr. W. C. Taylor, Trinity College, Dublin : that the war was rather about property than religion is more particularly true of Ulster ; and in other provinces, where the land was not the primary object, the war was defensive rather than offensive, although so many writers will contend that the Irish Catholics of that day had nothing to complain of. It is altogether untrue that the Catholics of Ireland, or any considerable portion of them " declared they would be satisfied with nothing short of the utter extirpation of the heretics." I don't say that Dr. Reid was the author of that calumny : it was not new even in his day : it was from the beginning of the outbreak, then and always since necessarily connected with the theory that the Catholics had no cause of complaint—that *they rebelled simply because they had too much liberty.**

It seems to me that the credit of " the British " and the " Protestants " stands none the higher of being so paraded in connection with this " imitation " business—that the British, hardly less than the Irish, suffer wrong by the same mode of dealing with the atrocities of that day. The Irish, " the British " and " the Protestants," are not " represented " by the evil-doers ; and it would, perhaps, be the wiser course to allow the evil-doers in each case to bear the blame of their own misdeeds. The line of offence and defence adopted by Dr. Reid, in the passage above-quoted is, I submit, radically and fundamentally both unsound and reprehensible. The distemper reaches the acute stage in the following :

The Irish women were so obnoxious to the English and Scots, on account of their *well-known cruelties* to the Protestants, who fell into the hands of the Rebels in the beginning of the insurrection that *the soldiers could scarcely be refrained from cutting them off whenever they met with them (!).* This was the case at Newry.— i., 355 *note.*

Surely this is the hardest saying of all ! The soldiers— elsewhere " the British," " the Protestants "—had heard before coming to Ireland that the Irishwomen were guilty

---

* See Froude, *The English in Ireland,* i., 98, *note* : " Of practical intolerance there was at this time none. The Catholics were indulged to the uttermost and *therefore rebelled.*"

of great cruelties, and *therefore* every woman in Irish garb must needs be taken to be the murderer, or torturer of unfortunate Protestants ! Is not the defence more damaging, more infamous, than the charge ? This maltreatment and "cutting off" of Irish women, let us say, comes from these "exasperated British, suffering under the treachery and revenge of the Romanists," and "it was scarcely possible for the Protestants to provide for their security without inflicting summary punishment on such perfidious and implacable enemies." Now would it not be in better taste to leave off speaking of the perpetrators of acts so disgraceful to religion and humanity, as "British" or "Protestants," and call them by their right name—blackguards? For they were blackguards first, and anything you like after that. At all events, call them, as Sir James Turner calls them— "godless rogues." The military men who recorded the outrages committed upon Irish women by the soldiery set up no such pretence of palliation as the ingenious Dr. Reid has discovered.

The history of Lord Conway and General Monroe's advance to Newry, as told by Pike, Turner, and Monroe himself, is an interesting study ; and it is best to allow the narrators to appear in person. *

Roger Pike's narrative is to be found in the second volume of the Thorpe Collection of Tracts illustrative of Irish history. It is in the form of a letter dated at Carrickfergus, the 30th of May, 1642, and addressed to Mr. Tobias Siedgwicke, living in London, and appears to have been printed " June 8, 1642," or perhaps the letter was received in London on that date (at top of title page).

On Thursday, 28 of April, 1600 of the Scottish army, 500 of the Lord Viscount Conway's Regiment, 500 of Col. Chichester's, 400 of the Lord of Ardes' Forces, and 400 of the Lord of Clandeboye's, 3 Troopes of Armed Horse, the Lord Conway's, Col. Chichester's and the Ld. Cromwell's, and part of the Lord Grandison's together with some 4 or 5 Troopes of Light Horse; all these forces met together and encamped at a place called Drum-Boe,† near Belfast, in the County of Antrim ; Sir John Clotworthy promised to come with 400 men, but he could not get so many men to make his regiment compleate ; all these Troopes made some 300 horses.

On Friday, the 29th April, the army marched " onwards all together towards the Nury." Beyond Lisburn (Lisne-garvey), at the woods of Kilwarlin, they encountered a

---

* A series of extracts from these narratives, by Mr. Wm. Pinkerton, appeared in the eighth volume of the *Ulster Journal of Archaeology* (1860), pp. 77-87.

† Drumbo is in County Down. It is famous for the great earthwork known as the "Giant's Ring," which contains a *cromleac*.

force of Rebels. Pike's account of the engagement is circumstantial and rather out of proportion to the magnitude
of the action. Dr. Reid's account is to be noticed :

After a short skirmish, the rebels were put to flight ; and the
British following the example which the Irish had too often set in
the previous encounters,* of refusing quarter, cruelly and unjustifiably put to death all who fell into their hands.

Turner's account is instructive for the view it gives of
violation of the laws of war and humanity by the British,
and not on this occasion alone. He makes no plea of
" imitation." :

My Lord Conway went along alsoe with neere 2,000 English.
In the woods of Kilwarlin we encountered some hundred rebells,
who after a short dispute fled. Those who were taken got but
bad quarter, being all shot dead. *This was too much used by both
English and Scots all along in that warre ;* a thing inhumane
and disfavourable, for *the crueltie of one enemy cannot excuse the
inhumanitie of* another. And herein the revenge over-mastered
their discretion which should have taught them to save the lives of
these they took that the rebells might do the like to their prisoners.†

A hard knock at the " imitation " plea. Turner knew
no reason for such severities, as he knew they were against
all reason, and against humanity.

General-Major (as he is styled) Robert Monroe, writing
to Leslie, describing the engagement at Kilwarlin Wood,
mentions, in strangely distorted forms, the names of some
of the Irish leaders who took part in that action :

The enemy were commanded by Lord Evack, Mackartane,
Sir Con Macginnische and Sir Rory Macginnische. . . . Sir Rory
Macginnische and Mackartanes two active men, brothers, were killed
with 150 more ; with the loss of two men on our side, and four
wounded.‡

Turner's account is silent about incidents of the march
from Kilwarlin to Newry, which make some figure in Roger
Pike's narrative. To some it may seem rather remarkable
that while Dromore and Loughbrickland come in for notice,
Banbridge, the town which in later times is more consider-

* " Imitation," of course. I should like to know what encounters Dr. Reid
relies on in justification of the charge. Refusing quarter, on the side of the
Irish, was, I believe, hardly known. Possibly Dr. Reid was here thinking of
those " fifteen " *he* hanged at Newry, or of the fate of Mr. Tudge and
companions.

† Clearly old " Dugald Dalgetty" did not look upon these Irish " rebels "
as so hopelessly " bloodthirsty." No wonder Dr. Reid tries to put Turner out
of court, by pointing to his own cruelties in Scotland.

‡ Gilbert, *Affairs in Ireland* in 1641, etc., i., p. 420.

able than either, and situated between them on the line of march, is not mentioned.*   Banbridge is of more recent origin.   Pike (after his long recital of the Kilwarlin engagement) proceeds :

> The next day being Saturday, the 30th of April, the army marched onward on their way to the Nury, through Drommore, which is so consumed with fire and ruinated, that there is not a house left standing, except the church.

The result of Sir Con Magennis's expedition against that old cathedral town about the end of the first week of the insurrection.   Pike's account of Loughbrickland, and of what occured there, is well worthy of attention :

> This night (30th April), we incampt at a place, some eight miles of the Nury, called Logh Brickland; in the middle of this Logh there is an Iland in which were some of them with divers English and Scots which were prisoners with them there, and a great deale of provision, there was a house upon this Iland, upon which one of our field pieces played, and we shot at them with muskets; sometimes they wd. shoot againe but hurt none of our men ; there came a bullet through Col. Chichester's hare, as he stood amongst his souldiers, but hurt him not : All that our army could doe could not make them yeeld, for our shot could not come to hurt them in regard that they had digged a cave underground where they did remaine ; so as that it was impossible to hurt them with shot, as to shoote down the Iland, this night there was a strict watch set round about the Iland least the Rogues should steal by night, the next morning being Sunday the first of May the boate which belonged to the Logh being ignorantly left afloat by the Rebels by the side of the Iland, it became the only means of their ruine, for six Hilanders undertook to swim for the Boate to fetch it over, whilst they were swimming our Army played so hard upon the Iland with Musket shot, that not a Rebel durst peep out of the Cave : Of these six Hilanders, two returned, not being able to swim over, two striving beyond their strength were drowned, and only two got over, who swimming with their swords in their hands cut the Boate loose, and brought it over, which was manned with musketeers, which took the Iland, releast the prisoners and cut off the Rebels.

So that " the rogues "—those " treacherous and implacable enemies "—in a neighbourhood made " for ever infamous (as Harris says) by " prodigious slaughters " and wholesale drownings, had kept alive their prisoners seven months in

* *Banbridge.*—This flourishing market town, and seat of the linen manufacture, anciently called Ballyvally, acquired its present name from the erection of a bridge over the Bann in 1712, on the formation of a new line of road from Dublin to Belfast. The old road passed a little to the north of it, and crossed the Bann at Huntley Glen by a ford, through which the army of William III. passed on 11 June, 1690, on its way to the Boyne. Population in 1891, 5,634. —John Vinycomb, M.R.I.A., in *Ulster Journal of Archaeology*, vol. iv., p. 31 (New Series).

a place where there were uncommon facilities for putting
them to death ; and in return they are themselves *cut off !*
In Monroe's account this " cutting off " and the hanging
of prisoners taken on the march are made to look like the
more glorious achievements :

> Saturday, the last of April, we marched in the former order
> through the wodes towards Lochbricklane, where being come on
> the plaine, our horsemen on the wings, *killed divers of them returning*
> and some taken prisoners were thereafter hanged. . . . (the boat
> on the lake being clamped up with salt hides) . . . took the isle,
> *the whole sixty therein put to the sword,* and our prisoners, which
> they had, released.

No pretence of " imitation " here. The slaughter is
paraded as a thing good and sufficient in itself ; no occasion
for excuse or apology. And the butcher's bill is not a slight
one, when, to the sixty cut off on the Island, we add the
hanging of the unresisting that came into the hands of the
victors and those that fell in the flight ; and it is pretty
certain that those so hanged, and those so cut down by the
troopers, were unarmed peasants or villagers, for there is
no word of arms except on the Island, where, indeed, they
must have been few.   Sir James Turner, the man who had
seen real service, was the only one, it appears, that was in
any way shocked by the cutting down of the unresisting
and the summary execution of those taken captive or those
that surrendered ; to the other commanders, every one in
Irish garb, or who had an Irish face, was a "treacherous and
implacable enemy" whose cutting off was "acceptable
service " to " the State "—perhaps to a higher power.

After beginning the Lord's Day so well, the army proceeded to Newry the same day.   We follow Roger Pike :

> After this was done, the army marched on to the Nury, the horse
> rid fast before, and when they came within sight of the towne they
> pursued the rogues flying out of the towne, and running as fast
> as their nimble feet could carry them away ; upon this a Troope
> of Light Horse were sent out which were under the command of
> Captaine Winsor, *and cut off about* 100 *of the Rogues as they*
> *fled,* the rest of the Troopes drew neare unto the towne, and making
> a stand on a little hill, about a quarter of a mile from the Towne, one
> Master Reading came riding out of the towne to them, who had
> been prisoner with them ever since the beginning of the Rebellion
> and hee brought us word that the Rogues were all fled out of the
> Towne, except some of the ancient towne dwellers, and that they
> willingly yielded the towne, but that the Castle stood out still, *in*
> *which were divers prisoners of the English,* among the rest Sir
> Edward Trevers, Sir Charles Poynes and his sonne came out to
> meet us, who were taken prisoners at the first surprisall of the
> Nury. Colonell Chichester's Troope drew nearer the towne and

stood close by the church within muskett shot of the Castle untill the foote came up, which was for the space of two houres, when the Generall-Major came, they sent away the troopes half-a-mile out of the Towne, and set a strict centrey at the townes end that none should come in but those whom he permitted ; what was gotten the horse got no share of, although they best deserved it, the Lord Maginnes's lady was now in the Nury.

And there were prisoners alive, although that "forward and wicked Rebel, the Countess of Evagh" (Iveagh) was in the town ! Roger Pike, it appears, felt aggrieved that the Horse got no share in the pillage of the town : it was hardly fair to send these meritorious troopers a good half mile away from the town while the foot were helping themselves to the best they could find. How gleefully he mentions the cutting off of the hundred persons—"Rogues," of course— who were trying to make their escape from the town. Yet Roger has some interesting things for us although he is a bit slow in his movement, and has a junior school-boy way of putting his sentences together. He proceeds to tell us how the Castle was given up :

The next day being Monday, the Generall-Major Mount-Roe (Monroe) and the Lord Conway and Collonel Chichester resolved to come to a parley with the Castle, not that they held it any difficultie to take it, but in regard of those prisoners which they had within the Castle, least if they had fallen upon it in the severest way, the Innocent had been destroyed with the Guilty. This made the Rogues to stand upon their tearmes, and to refuse any gratious proffers of mercy, and kept them all this day in dispense, refusing to yeeld, the next day being Tuesday, the third of May, Generall Mount Roe sent word unto the Captaine of the Castle,* that notwithstanding the prisoners he had of ours with him, if he would not yeeld, since there was no remedy, he would blow up the Castle, the Captaine of the Castle returned him answer that if he blew him up he would be forced to borrow some of his powder ; this peremptory answer made all to be prepared for to set upon the Castle, at last when the Captaine of the Castle saw that they were like to goe to it in good earnest, he yeelded upon quarter to himselfe and some more. After this Castle was surrendered, they found but half a barel of powder, sixty muskets, and of them not above a dozen fixed ; they had two murtherers which they put out only to make a shew, which were found without chambers, and so foule and rusty that nome of them durst have shot them off ; such little proof is commonly in great bragges when they come to the trial, what other things of worth were found in the Castle were altogether concealed from the English except some who had great friends.

Here, and in subsequent passages in his narrative, Pike has a shy at the rapacity of his Scottish auxiliaries in this

---

* Colonel Daniel [or Donnell] Magennis, younger brother of Sir Con, and uncle of the young Viscount Magennis of Iveagh.

expedition. He tells us that " on Monday the fift, ten out of every Troope were sent to Dundalk to the English army " under Sir Henry Tichbourne ; but there is an obvious error in the date—the fifth was Thursday—a misprint, no doubt ; the tract is a rough enough specimen of the printer's art.

On Thursday, the 5th of May, the Lord Conway's Troope, Colonell Chichesters, and the Lord Cromwell's, with part of the Lord Grandison's went out towards Armagh, and by the way they saw a thousand of the Rebels which stood in a Bogge, but durst not stir out . . ; nor the troops come at them . . , although the same would have charged them, therefore they returned back to the Newry, thinking to fall upon them the next morning, and bringing some foote with them, but they heard the next day that they were fled, and that Sir Phelim O'Neale was among them. Some of the prisoners that made an escape from them report that Armagh is burnt, and that the Rogues are fled from thence towards Charlimount (Charlemont).

This Armagh expedition, after every allowance is made for exaggeration on the part of hostile deponents, is certainly the most painful chapter in Sir Phelim's career as a rebel leader. We must see, however, what " the good and loving subjects " have done at Newry for *his* imitation.

The common souldiers without direction from the Generall-Major tooke some 18 of the Irish women of the towne, and stript them naked and threw them into the river, and drowned them, shooting some in the water ; more had suffered so, but that some of the common souldiers were made examples on and punished.

Readers of Prendergast's *Cromwellian Settlement of Ireland* are familiar with this recital, for which Roger Pike is the authority. Mr. Prendergast has found another such record :

For about the 4th of May, as I take it, we put near fourty of them to death upon the Bridge of the Newry, amongst which were two of the Popes pedlers, two seminary priests ; *in return of which* they slaughtered many prisoners in their custody.—*The Levites' Lamentation*, pp. 13, 14. (Cited in *Crom. Settl.*, p. 7, *n.*, 1st. ed.)

The " return " slaughter more strictly refers to Sir Phelim's performances on this occasion in and around Armagh. It has again and again been asserted that he, Sir Phelim, committed such atrocities in chagrin for the loss of Newry. But surely those who say so, if they do not assign the wrong cause, leave out an essential factor when they ignore the deeds that followed. and some that preceded, the recapture.

On Friday being the sixt of May, those of the Rebells that were in the Castle, which had not quarter and divers of the ill affected

Irish in the towne *were shot to death* on the bridge, some *three score or more ;* there was a great Iron Battering peece taken in the Nury, which was left in an old Turret in the towne, throwne off the carriages, which I forgot to name before.—*Pike.*

The shooting of so many in cold blood might have moved to retaliation a cooler and more competent commander than Sir Phelim.* And the outrages committed on the women (on which Dr Reid makes his over-ingenious gloss) would doubtless be even more "exasperating." It will be seen that Newry, the most important position in the north-east, had been left without means of defence—a severe commentary, indeed, on the qualifications of the commander-in-chief and his colleagues in the insurrectionary movement. The ninety barrels of powder and store of arms found in the Castle on 23rd October, 1641, have, in the beginning of May, 1642, dwindled down to half a barrel of gun-powder and not more than a dozen serviceable muskets ; while the three old things in the shape of cannon were altogether useless for any purpose of offence or defence. The powder and arms of the King's store must have been dissipated by supplying other places in the hands of the insurgents. The army of relief could not have suffered any loss at Newry, and there was none worth mention. The slaughter after the surrender was all the more unjustifiable ; and it need not be matter for wonder that the common soldiers took action on their own account, as Turner points out :

The fortifications of the town being but begunne, it came m-mediatelie in our hands, but the rebels that were in the Castle keepd it two days and then delivered it up, upon *a very ill-made accord, or a very ill-keepd one,* for *the nixt day most of them with many merchands and tradesmen of the towne,* who had not been in the Castle, were carried to the bridge, *and butchered to death,* some by shooting, *some by hanging and some by drowning,†* *without any legal process ;* and I was verily informed afterwards that *several innocent people suffered.* Monro did not at all excuse himself from having accession to that carnage, nor could he purge himself of it ; although my Lord Conway as Marshall of Ireland was the principall actor. Our sojors (*who sometimes are cruell for no other reason bot because man's wicked nature leads them to be so.* . . .) seeing such pranks playd by authoritie at the bridge, thought they might do as much any where els ; and so runne upon a hundre and fiftie women, or thereby, who had got together at a place below the bridge whom they resolved to massacre by killing and drowning ;

* When on his trial before the High Court of Justice in February, 1653, he assigned the cruelties of the British captors at Newry as the cause of his own crimes at Armagh.

† "Drawing" as printed by Gilbert, *Affairs in Ireland in 1641,* a misprint "drowning."

which villanie the sea seemed to favour, it being then flood. Just at
that time was I speaking with Monroe, bot seeing afar off what a
game these *godless rogues* intended to play, I got a-horseback and
gallopd to them with my pistoll in my hand ; bot before I got at
them they had despatchd about a dozen ; the rest I savd.

This execution had not the success which Conway and Monroe
had promised themselves ; for instead of terrifieing the rebels from
their wonted cruelties *it inraged them* and occasioned the murthering
of some hundreds of persons whom they had in their power. . . .

My Lord Conway and Monroe plunderd the Neurie, except
a very few houses ; most of the men that were left alive, Conway
forcd to carry arms under his own regiment. . . . *

That the slaughter committed by Conway and Monroe
at Newry, and the slaughters committed on the way to and
from Newry "enraged the rebels" and incited to further
crimes and cruelties can hardly be doubted. No more can
we doubt that many "innocent persons" were summarily
executed "without any process of law," as Turner relates.
Monroe must have been conscious of some excess on his
own part, for he makes nebulous mention of the pains he
took to separate the innocent from the guilty. That story
may do to tell ; not to examine too closely. His drum-head
inquiry, if it took place at all, could mean very little—
nothing, I fancy, beyond sorting out the men fit to enlist
and who would accept reprieve on such terms ; if he does not
really mean that he sorted the Papists into two lots—the
one for death, the other for banishment. This is what he
says :

Wednesday, 4th May, '42. This day I did write to Dundaake
to Sir Henry Tigburne to come to the Newrie to learn of him the
estate of the country beyond him, who came to us on Thursday,
5th May, of whom I could learn nothing, who being returned we
entered in examination of the townsmen, *if all were Papists ;* and the
indifferent being severed from the bad, whereof 60 *with two priests,*
were shot and hanged, the indifferent are banished.†

'Tis wonderful the readiness and certainty with which
he culled out the "bad." There was no difficulty about

---

* ' It is certain that at the taking of the Newry, a rebel being appointed to be
shot upon the bridge, and stripped stark-naked, notwithstanding, the
musketeer stood within two yards of him and shot him in the middle of the
back, yet the bullet entered not nor did him any more hurt than leave a little
black spot behind it. This many hundreds were eye-witnesses of, one of
which of good trust hath related it to me. Divers of the like have I been
confidently assured of, *who have been provided of diabolical charms.*'—Bernard,
Siege of Drogheda, p. 100. [Quoted in *Vindiciæ Hibernicæ* by M. Carey,
2nd Edition, 1823, page 57, *note.*
    The Irish rebels, it would appear, had more arts than their own ; they must
have been able to retain in their service all the spirits of mischief !

† Gilbert, *Affairs of Ireland in 1641,* etc., i., 421.

assigning the priests—"the Pope's pedlers," of another writer—to that class, for *they* were, of necessity, "bad"; and among Papists there could be no "good." "*We* entered in examination." Whoever may have made up the *We*, it is clear that Sir James Turner does not admit that there was anything deserving the name of examination or inquiry.

In Dublin the recapture of Newry was hailed as a great event, as it brought back the possession of other strong places on the shores of Down and Louth.

The fifth of May, news came from Dundalk to the Lords Justices by Captain Cadogan. . . . that the Newry was not only retaken by the Lord Conway and Munroe, the Scots commander, from the Rebels, but also that the town and castle of Carlingford was taken by a ship that came from Knockfergus. . . .

The Narrow-water Castle was likewise soon after taken, in which they found the old Viscountesse of Evagh, daughter of the old arch-rebel, Hugh, Earle of Tyrone,* Sir Edward Trevor, Sir Chas. Poynes, Captaine Henry Smith, and several others that were taken prisoners at the beginning of this insurrection, and close kept in the Castle of Newry, were all released, and are now going at their liberty.— (*Affairs in Ireland* i., 427–8.)

Turner says that in their march back from Newry they passed through Mourne ; not the barony of Mourne,† for in that case they should have to face the perils of the Ballaghonery Pass (or Dundrum Pass). I understand by the allusion to Mourne that their route was near, or within view of the Mourne mountains. I gather this more particularly from Pike's narrative (and Monro says the mountains were on his right) :

On Saturday the seventh of May they provided to march back again, leaving behind in garrison at the Nury about 300 men well armed under the command of Lieut. Colonel Sinkcleare, promising to send him some 500 more from Carrickfergus, with all the speede possibly could be made, being some of the rest of Lieut. Col. Sinkcleare's Regiment which came over since the army went abroad ; General-Major Mount-Roe left private direction (as I heard) with Lieut. Col. Sinkcleare to banish all the Irish out of the towne as soon as he was gone [We have practically the same from Monroe's own hand.]

* If so, there were two dowager Viscountesses Magennis then living. The old Viscountess, Tyrone's daughter, the wife of Arthur, first Viscount, and mother of Hugh (*b.* 1599, *d.* 1630), the second Viscount, might still be alive in 1642, thirteen years after the death of her husband. The younger dowager, the relict of Hugh, second Viscount, and mother of Arthur, the third Viscount, was the daughter of Sir John Bellew of Castleton : she is the "forward and cruel rebel" of the depositions ; but no instance of her cruelty is forthcoming, beyond the words which rumour attributed to her.

† Then called "Bagenal's country." Pike says they marched through Magennis's and M'Cartan's country.

The Army marched home through Magennis's and M'Cartan's country, and marched in three divisions, *burning all the houses and corn* before them, and brought away the spoyle of the country before them and cattle in great abundance, there was much goods left behinde and provision which they could neither destroy nor carry away, being hid under ground in the backside of every house, the division that Collonel Chichester commanded burnt M'Cartan's* and Ever Magennis's* own dwelling houses. Sunday at night was such stormy weather, that some thirty of the souldiers and others which followed the camp, perished with meere cold ; and no wonder, for it killed some fifteen horses which were found dead the next morning. Collonel Chichester's troope marching a pretty space before the army took divers prisoners and *killed divers of the Rebells* upon the march.

And in the Magennis and MacCartan territory they were all " Rebells "—men, women, and children.   Turner's account confirms Pike's, and shows that the march was all the way accompanied by slaughter as well as pillage.   He notes that the rebels let slip a fine opportunity during the prevalence of that terrible storm on the night of Sunday, the 8th of May, 1642.†   He says :

We took our march through the woodes and mountaines of Morne, *where severall rebells were killd* and many cows taken. I do remember that there we sufferd one of the most stormie and tempestuous nights for haile, raine, cold, and excessive wind (though it was in the beginning of May) that ever I yet saw.   All the tents were in a thrice bloune over.   It was not possible for any match to keep fire, or any sojor to handle his musket, or yet to stand.   Yea, severalls of them dyed that night of meere cold.   So that if the rebells whereof there were 500 not farre from us had offered to beat up our quarters . . .   They would undoubtedlie have had a cheap market of us.   Our sojors, and some of our officers too (who suppose that no thing which is more than ordinarie can be the product of nature) attributed this hurrikan *to the divilish skill of some Irish witches.*

As indeed the Irish were supposed to be capable of any other excess of wickedness.   Roger Pike is now our authority to the end of the return march.

On Tuesday, the 10th of May the army met together and incampt in the middle of M'Cartan's woods,† when they came altogether,

* Ever Magennis's house was at Castlewellan ; the Viscount Magennis's house was at Rathfriland (Castle Hill).   Between these towns was another Magennis family (at Islandmoyle and Cabra) ; another branch of the family was settled at Clanvaraghan, about three miles north-west of Castlewellan. MacCartan's place was at Loughinisland, about four miles west from Downpatrick.   Briansford and Newcastle were included in the Magennis's territory.

† Turner was on the return march.   He was to bring up from Carrickfergus the reinforcement for the garrisoning of Newry

* Loughinisland.

there were at least 800 baggage horses (as they call them), loaden
with the spoil of the countrey, and I think I speak within compasse,
if I say 3,000 cowes ; but, by the way, as they came this day through
the thickies (sic) of M'Cartan's Woods, the Ld. Conway's troope
Collonell Hill's and Captaine Mathewes', and some other troopes of
Light horse ; the Rogues shot at them from behinde trees, and killed
the Livetenant to the Lord Conway's troope, Livetenant Fishers'
ed horse and him that led him, and got in betwixt the troopes and
the baggage horses, and cut off some of the men that were along
with their horses, and had cut off more but that Captaine Trever's
rid back againe with some of his troope and relieved them.

On Wednesday, the army marched through the rest of M'Cartan's
woods with the aforesd. loaden horses and cowes, marching all
together, but spreading the foote abroad in the Woods *to burn the
Cabbins* which were built there, and to cleare the woods before them.
They found no opposition this day, at night they encamped at
Drumboe.

Roger had a keen eye to the " spoyle." He is much
displeased with the behaviour of his " canny " allies, who
appear to have been particularly active that night at the
Hill of Drumbo :

The next day when the cowes were to be divided, many of them
were stollen* away into t..e Ardes and Clandeboyes the last night,
and *the goods so sneakt away by the Scots* that the English troopes
got just nothing, and the English foote very little, which gave them
too just a cause to mutany, insomuch as I think it will be hard to
get them to march with the Scots againe, who will have both the
credit and the profit of whatever is done or had.

The " profit " was an important part of duty as understood by all from the " Castle " to the Covenanter, in their
dealings with the rebels. And Roger Pike would go almost
so far as to say that the last-mentioned were more
distinguished in pillage than in deeds of bravery. He gives
two instances :

In the absence of the army there were six score Musketeres less
to garrison at Malone,† which was set upon by the Irish and most
of it burnt ; *these valiant Scots*, set to keep the towne, *when it was
set upon, fled.*

The other affair is still more significant :

Some 800 of the Scots which lay in the trench some six mile of
Carrickfergus in the absence of the aforesaid army *went out to plunder,*

---

* Monro's account confirms this : "The next morning we divided our
cattell, such as remained unstolen by the horsemen and plunderers, being an
infinite number of poor, contemptible countrymen, which could not be reduced
to order." How, then, must they have acted towards the Irish peasantry ?

† Malone, in recent times, "Balmoral," two miles from Belfast, towards
Lisburn, was then an important industrial centre.

and being set upon by some horse and foote of the Rebells, not much
above their number, I will not say fled from them but *retreated
so fast,** as that they were forced to blow up a barrell of powder
they had with them, and blew up some eight of their men with it,
and, as I heare credibly, lost above a hundred Armes; *they carrv the
matter very privately here, but this is truth.*

 This was written at Carrickfergus " this 30th of May,
1642, by your humble servant to command, ROGER PIKE."
I have drawn so largely on his narrative, and upon Sir
James Turner's, because they let in so much light on the
proceedings of the Scots and English forces in the North
of Ireland in those days, and, at the same time, furnish
the best answer to the ingenious moderns who will have it
that the British "sometimes imitated" the excesses of the
Irish rebels—a theory wholly unknown to the writers who
were also witnesses of the transactions which they record.
The slaughter of unresisting, on the way to Newry, at
Newry, and on the return from Newry, in the course of a
fortnight, far exceeded anything which, on the strictest
examination, can be charged against the rebels of the County
Down during the six months or more of their holding the
greater part of the same county at their disposal. The
charges founded upon stories told by Dr. Robert Maxwell
while a prisoner, are simply ridiculous—there is not a particle
of trustworthy evidence in support of any one of those
charges, whether relating to the "for ever infamous"
Donaghmore, Killyleagh, or "the thousand and more " put
to death by the "inhuman" (because mythical) "butcher."
There may have been some foul play at Lough Kernan;
but the evidence† is wholly unsatisfactory and unreliable
as to the drowning, its superinduced horrors, and the
number of alleged victims. There were crimes which, no
matter what the example or the provocation, were still
crimes in the sight of Heaven ; but the number of such
committed by the insurgents of Down is insignificant in
comparison with that in the indictment. Yes, I say insignificant if compared with the "cutting off" of the
unresisting, during the fortnight we have deen reviewing.
And it is not to be forgotten that so far from alleging excuse

 * There is a touch of humour in the distinction made between "fled" and
"retreated so fast " equal to anything the modern war correspondent can
attain to.

 † I cannot meet that so confidently as I can dispose of the Donaghmore and
Scarva Bridge myths, but I must say that the story I once heard by the side of
the lake in Kernan even yet seems to me the strongest evidence existing for
such an occurrence. The old farmer, James MacInerney, could make a
deposition on the subject as well as Mr. Peter Hill—from hearsay.

of any kind, or any " provocation," the leaders virtually
certify to the contrary. Monroe says :

— in the whole march I had never an alarm given us, being
quartered in the fields untrenched.

The " cutting off," the shooting, the hanging and
drowning were simply massacre in cold blood, in open and
daring violation of humanity and religion, which is not
palliated or improved by setting up any allegation that others
have incurred " the guilt of being foremost in the work of
blood." Whether " foremost " or only next to foremost in
shedding blood, the conduct of—I don't say the British and
the Protestants, but—the authorities of the day, and of
those who acted on the express or implied mandate of those
in the highest place in the country, was in itself criminal,
and calculated to drive the others to the commission of
crime which, without such provocation, they would not
commit. The defence set up, more particularly by Dr.
Reid, assumes, tacitly but necessarily, that every " Romanist"
in Ireland at the time (if not at any time, and at all times)
was either an actual or prospective murderer of Protestants ;
and that in cutting off Romanists wherever met with or
wherever opportunity offered, the British and Protestants
(as *he* will have it) were simply showing " due regard for
self-preservation " ! Dr. Reid does not, of course, put the
matter in terms so blunt. Yet I should like to see in what
better form his suppressed premise can be put. If only
" murderers " met with " summary punishment " there
would be no matter of complaint. How does that apply to
the cases reviewed in this paper ? If we except (as we ought
not to except) Monroe's sham " examination " of the Newry
townsmen, all the rest was indiscriminate butchery, without
pretence of distinction between guilty and innocent, between
" bad " and " indifferent," and without knowing whether
anyone was guilty. There were no " awful provocations "
in any of these cases ; and no pretence of any is alleged.
Nor need the authors of such " summary punishment "
trouble themselves with inquiry. " The soldiery was *in
some degree* justified by the authority of the State." In
some degree ! Hadn't they the fullest and most unqualified
warrant that the chief power in the State could issue, in
that Proclamation of 8th February ? And the murderers
of the O'Gilmores of Ballydavy, had they waited only a
few days, could have stood on their legal right to cut off,
by any manner of means, those undoubted rebels whose
names begin with O. For such was the right and the duty
of all " true and loving subjects "—to pursue and plague

with fire and sword, apprehend, destroy, and kill, by all the means and ways they may, all the said persons, *their partakers, aiders,* and so forth. And I hold that the powers and requirements, if not the terms, of that Castle ukase, were well known, at all events in Ulster, almost from the beginning of the insurrection when the first attempt was made to rouse the Scots of that province against the rebels ; and in my next paper I can give some illustration, if not absolute proof, of this contention.

It is chiefly in respect of the action of " the State " that I look upon the controversy over the Island Magee massacre as but a side issue to the main question. Had there been an Island Magee or a Ballydavy affair in every barony in Ulster, the incitement held out on the part of those in power—not to speak of the exhortations of the Covenant teachers—were amply sufficient to account for so general a carnage.

It is also a mistake to attribute such disgraceful conduct to the people of Scotland or England. Monro's followers acted as they did, not because they were Scots or English, but because they were fanatics who went forth as on a holy crusade against the Irish Papists, even as God's Chosen People went forth against the Canaanites. And when, over and above the commands which *they* could produce from the Bible, they were fortified by the warrant and authority of " the State," we need not wonder that blood and rapine marked their course in Ireland

The " historians "—with a few honourable, but, unfortunately, little heeded exceptions—repeating one another as instinctively as one cuckoo follows another, insist that the British forces were justified in using all manner of barbarous practices against a " people who had themselves set the example." Self-satisfied ignorance and racial jealousy have conspired to keep up this calumnious assumption to the present hour. In a recently published work of great merit and ability, I find the following which, clearly and strongly, reflects some of the old-time prejudices :

The butchery that followed [Philiphaugh] is frightful to contemplate. In accordance with a decision formally made by the Parliaments of Scotland and England, *no quarter whatever was given to the Irish soldiers ;* and three hundred Irish women and some children were put to death. Such a decision can only be explained by the horror and indignation which was excited in the minds of the people of both countries at the danger of being exposed to the atrocities connected with *savage modes of warfare,* and perpetrated on such a large scale in the massacre of Protestants in Ireland. The resolution that no quarter should be given to Irish soldiers was therefore not an unmeaning piece of cruelty, though it seems to us at this distance of time very ruthless and unjust. . . . . Many modern writers, who are hostile to the Covenant and its defenders seem to gloat with a kind of grim satisfaction over this massacre of Philiphaugh, and consider that the execution of the women, probably as brutalized as the men, was an act of cruelty unparalleled in those times. Yet, unhappily, a similar deed of vengeance took place after the battle of Naseby.*

I have no doubt about the writer's good faith. He could, I am sure, cite an array of authorities. What he says has been said by a thousand others. But of the thousand and one, who has ever given a thought to the grounds upon which such charges of Irish barbarity and massacre are built up? Self-appraisement for higher civilization is cheap, and terms of disparagement admit of easy application to the down-trodden. The history of what occurred in the early hours of Sunday, 1st May, 1642, at Loughbrickland, furnishes refutation of such aspersions on the Irish people of that day. Very ignorant of the history of the seventeenth century must the writers be who take the massacre of Philiphaugh as unparalleled. Why, there was, as far as the opportunity was afforded, a Philiphaugh at Kilwarlin Wood, a Philiphaugh at Lough-brickland, a Philiphaugh at Newry—it was Philiphaugh all the way to and from Newry; there was many a Philiphaugh, enacted by Coote, by Cole, by St. Leger, and in some degree by every commander who then represented the superior civilization of the foreign masters. The people of Ireland had become well used to such evidence of " superior civilization " before Cromwell came to dower them with his " crowning mercies."

* *The Great Marquess :* Life and Times of Archibald 8th Earl and 1st (and only) Marquess of Argyll (1607:1661). By John Willcock, B.D.; Edin. 1903, pp. 184-5.

VI.

ACCEPTABLE SERVICE.

I HAVE elsewhere made use of this expression, although it is not mine. I owe it to Mr. Peter Hill, of Downpatrick, High Sheriff of the County Down in the earlier years of the civil war. As a deponent, Mr. Peter Hill has already been busy in these pages, and we have now to see what part he played in the exciting drama of those times. He claims to have rendered much " acceptable service " to the State ; and he had unquestionably a high opinion of himself. Yet until I read his somewhat voluminous contribution to the deposition books of T.C.D. I had scarcely a notion of the former existence of so important a person, owing to the culpable negligence of authors in altogether omitting to take due notice of him ; and had not Harris called him as a witness in the Lough Kernan case the world had lost all knowledge of the man. But even Harris gives us no information about the High Sheriff, or his great " service. *That* is to be found only in Hill's own deposition. A very remarkable one it is, remarkable for many things, but, to my mind, remarkable most of all for what it tells of the eagerness on the part of " the State " to " outlaw," at the very beginning, and so to drive into absolute rebellion, every man of Irish blood or Irish sympathies who was a mark for damages. I let the deponent tell his own story :

And as to this deponent's knowledge concerning the persons that are or were Acters in the same rebellion, and their bearing armes and comitting outrages and cruelties against his Ma'ty or his loyall Protestant subjects, he saith, That he, this deponent when the Rebellion began, being in Dublin *was directed,* sent and went in a barque *by the comand of the right honble., the Lords Justices and Counsell of Ireland, with* directions that if it were possible *there should bee a quarter Sessions sitten within the said Countie of Downe for indicting of the Rebells.* Whereon the deponent took such care,

* Peter Hill's deposition was sworn on the 29th of May, 1645 (three and a half years after the Commissioners to take such "evidence" were appointed), before Dr. Henry Jones and Mr. Henry Brereton.

and so farr did hazard himself that, first, a quarter Sessions was at
Killyleagh, before divers Justices, when and where, all the parties
Rebells hereafter named in Writts *were legally indicted*, before a
lawful Jurie, then and there impannelled and sworne, for rebellion.
And afterwards another Session of the peace was sitten alsoe within
the said Countie when and where *at least one hundred rebells more*
were also indicted.

He gives the names and addresses of all so indicted at
the Quarter Sessions held for that purpose, and one may
safely say that, if any man of means and substance in the
same county of Down, being a Catholic, was overlooked,
it was through no wilful omission or negligence on the part
of the High Sheriff, Peter Hill, Esquire. What more
effective steps could be taken to commit every man of
these, hopelessly and inevitably, to " the Rebellion " than by
so giving them to understand that, in any case, they were
booked for all the penalties of rebellion ?   And the beauty
of the thing is that all is " worked off in due course of law,"
as Dennis the hangman would say. The High Sheriff
of the county, being in Dublin—on the King's business,
he tells us in another place—is hurried home with instructions how to effect the outlawry of all whom he
pleases to fix on as rebels. The magistrates who then
meet in Quarter Sessions are, we may be sure, all deadly
enemies of " the rebells "; " the jurie legally impannelled "
is made up of their bitterest foes ; it is laid down by the
" Court of Chief Place " that common report is sufficient
evidence ; and in the smoothest and most regular fashion,
all and every of those whose names are so presented are
called upon to " bee and appeare in the said Corte of Cheefe
Place," or, " as he openly proclaimed,"

They would all be outlawed for want of appearance, and answer-
ing our Soveraigne Lord the King, of the treasons, and present
Rebellion of which they stood indicted, And this deponent made his
returns upon the same writts according to his due execučon of the same.

How heroically the High Sheriff acted in the discharge
of the duty so imposed on him by " the State," he himself
can best tell :

Howbeit, the deponent saith, That in and about the execučon
and proclaiming of those writts, he [did] run a great hazard and
danger not only of his owne liffe, but of the lives of all his souldiers
and servants which hee at his owne charges kept, and which attended
him therein, But this deponent is confident that none of the said
parties so indicted, or proclaimed, did appeare, *neither coud this
deponent apprehend any of them.*

The " hazards " had evidently a deterring effect, when,
always surrounded by his souldiers and servants, he

could not effect a single arrest, although, as he tells us further on, he did some terrible execution among "the rebells" Nevertheless he has the satisfaction of assuring all whom it may concern,

That by reason of their default they were, and are, and stand, all outlawed for their present rebellion.

And this deponent further saith, 'That the Rebellion in the said Countie of Downe by and amongst the irish papists was so generall that few or none of the gentrie, freeholders, or other of the irish papists, did exempt themselves for that action, nor were clere, but all, as this deponent is verily persuaded, highly guiltie, some of murthering, some of robbing, some of stripping the Protestants naked, and soe turning them away in frost, snow, or cold weather, and some all.

On the deposition a pen-stroke (by a later hand, I think), encloses so much and leaves out the concluding words of the paragraph, which are these :

Neither did any of those Irish papists *of value* within that countie, that he knoweth of (although he knoweth the countie well), *soe escape but that they were either indicted or outlawed* for their *rebellious*, or both. In the prosecucõn whereof *this deponent was noe weake nor unwilling instrument*, nor a man that any way sleighted his service either for favour or feare of danger, as by his service therein appeareth.

In "indicting" and "outlawing" "Papists *of value*," Peter was undeniably heroic ; although in matters of arrest, not a success :

The High Sheriff of the county cut a great figure on arriving home from Dublin :

And this deponent further saith. That when the Rebellion first broke out hee, this deponent [being as aforesaid] att the cittie of Dublin [about] his Matys affairs there by him to be done, And hearing as aforesaid of the generall Rebellion of the Irish papists there, and how the English and Scottish Protestants were all robbed and stript and many of them murthered, Hee, this deponent, at his own charges, bought and furnished himself with armes for four score and fourteene men, and hadd only powder, match, and shott out of his Matys store. And being so furnished, freighted a Barque with those armes and am̃unitions from Dublin and thence sayled thorow, and with drums and cullours which he had also bought, to Strangford where he landing with them, raised [and] armed, a company of men, vizt., some horse, some foote, and kept them *at his own charges* for above a year and a half, *all saving such provisions of corne and cattell* [which] he and they took from the rebells. And in that tyme this deponent and his souldiers *executed by martiall lawe, and slew above three score notorious Rebells* within the said Countie of Downe [and] other places adjacent, drove many other Rebells out of those parts, took divers preys of cattell, horses, sheep, and corne from them and DID OTHER ACCEPTABLE SERVICE, to the often hazarding of himself and souldiers ; and did till, plow, and sow within the territory of Lecale, a [good] quantity of corne and graine. And there contynued until about May last, 1644.

Mr. Peter Hill's munificence is as noteworthy as his valour. Having heard this statement about the great numbers outlawed—over a hundred at one of the five Quarter Sessions by him held for the purpose—and his inability to arrest an individual of them, we may well ask, Who were these "notorious rebells," whom he executed by martial law, or otherwise slew, not to speak of the many he drove out of the country—into the sea, perhaps ? One may almost surmise that he found the said "notorious rebels" at their spinning-wheels, or playing marbles at the cottage and cabin doors. And we have to remember that then, or about the same time, Sir James Montgomery's "tygers" were giving proof of their "spight" in Lecale and the country adjacent. Does anyone wonder that some cases of crime and outrage occurred on the other side ? There is indeed, room to wonder that "rebel atrocities" were so few while all this was going on against their families and friends.

Then comes a pretty quarrel. Sir James Montgomery, and all the Montgomerys were royalist. Hill, the high sheriff, would appear to be the fast friend of the Lords Justices and the Puritans. He complains to the State that Sir James doesn't make it hot enough for the rebels.* There is an outfall, which comes to a climax in manner as follows :

That this deponent and his family, his dwelling howse of Bally-hornan, within Lecale, aforesaid, with some part of his howsehold goods, corne, cattell, horses, mares, armes, amunition, apparell and other things [which were left him;] were forcibly surprised and taken by a pty of souldiers under the comand of Sir James Montgomery, Knight, Colonell of a Regt.; And a few days after by a pty of souldiers under the comand of Lord Lindsey, Scottish Colonell, which parties divided and shared among them the most of the deponents said goodes and chattells, and all his armes and amunition [which] he had there, and that done, expulsed [and drove] the deponent out

---

* So the deponent intimates, but he hardly goes to the beginning. The High Sheriff appears to have been honoured with a *Commission of Array*, and may have assumed direction of the army. Sir James would scarcely submit to being "bossed" by the " pragmatical jackdaw," having had his own commission direct from the king, as his son, Mr. William Montgomery tells us (p. 310) : the same messenger that carried to the King in Scotland the report of the "rising" brought back the royal warrant. Mr. Peter Hill's powers, though granted in the name of the King, were really derived from the State in Dublin. There was some rivalry, and, perhaps, not the best of feeling, between the Mont-gomerys and the Hills, as at a later period there was between the Hills and the Stewarts, owing to contests for the representation of the county.

of the said countie of Downe. Soe as he was forced to fly to Dublin
for succour, relefe, and safetie of his life. But, before he went away,
hee was putt to that distresse and danger, that one Maior John
Keithe, [under] Sr James Montgomery, inforced [this deponent]
by want and threats, to accept of 16ʰ for his Corne, which was worth
200ʰ, and to give him an acquittance for it; ffor otherwise the
said Keethe said, that hee would have the said Corne, and give nothing
at all to the deponent for the same. * And although the deponent
complained to the said Sr James Montgomery (who lived not above
3 or 4 myles frō this deponent's said house), of his said evill
entreaty, oppressions, and wrong, and desired to have his goodes,
meanes, armes, and amunition re-delivered unto him, yet the said
Sr James Montgomery would not nor did releeve, nor rectify this
deponent therein, Although, as this deponent is perswaded, he
might and could have done it if hee had soe pleased [but had con-
trariwise] sett the said Keith and his souldiers on work to stripp
and extirpate this deponent, for that this deponent had formerly
(as indeed there was too great cawse) complained against him, the
said Sr James for deserting of Downe, loosing the country to the
Irish, and for severall other fowle abuses.

Surely an ungrateful world, when a man, who at so
much sacrifice and hazard to his own life, had rendered
"the State" so much "acceptable service" is treated little
better than one of those notorious rebels whom the High
Sheriff had hunted out of the country!

And as to murthers and cruelties comĩtted by the cruell Irish
Rebells of the County of Down and province of Ulster, upon the
Protestants, this deponent thereunto saith, etc.

The deponent gives his account of the murder of Mr.
Tudge and others, at Ballaghonery (Bloody Bridge). Also
his first, and, further on, his second statement about the
Lough Kernan tragedy. I have elsewhere discussed these
matters with some minuteness, and do not resume the
subjects here. But once more I must remark how significant is Mr. Hill's silence not alone about Glenwood
(Donaghmore), Scarvagh-bridge, the "thousand and more"
slaughtered by Col. Bryan O'Neill (or by his traducers),
but also about the "big massacres" of his own immediate
neighbourhood—not a word about the Killyleagh, Castle
Island, or Downpatrick "massacres"!

Yet it is now certain, from Mr. Peter Hill's exploiting
of his own services, that there *were* massacres in the same
part of the county. But for these, or the worst of them,
Mr. Hill, and not the rebels, must be held responsible.
And there is reason to think he must also be held in some
degree responsible for the blood which some among the
rebels *did* shed.

* Sharp practice ! But, on his own showing, Mr. Peter Hill had himself
fixed the price of corn and other chattels at a still less generous rate.

In another place I have made allusion to Mr. Peter Hill's extraordinary credulity in respect of matters reflecting discredit on "the rebels," by which term he means the Irish Papists without exception. What is the hearsay evidence of a man worth who gravely assures us that, among the Irish of his county, cannibalism was so common and ordinary a thing, that when they had no opportunity of killing and devouring the English, "they would kill and divoure one another!"

I have also alluded to his execution of a woman on suspicion of cannibalism :

And about one yere now since there [was] brought to the deponent at his house, called Ballyhornan, an Irish woman, for wounding and attempting to kill another Irish woman and her child ; which woman soe accused and brought before him, upon her examinačon, confessed that she had hurt, but had an *intent* to have killed the other woman and her child, and to have eaten the child. Whereupon, and because *he was credibly informed* that such a lyke fatt woman had killed and devoured divers others, he this deponent cawsed her to be hanged, Before and at the tyme of which suffering she was soe graceles that she could not be perswaded soe much as once to cry or call upon God for mercy.

King Solomon was a simpleton in comparison with Peter Hill, Esquire. He can *swear* to the following, as he can swear to the Lough Kernan massacre and all its alleged accompaniments :

About the tyme aforesaid, vizt., a yere sinse, three troopes under the Lord Conway's comand, going out frō Lisnegarvie over the river into the County of Downe, with their horses, about two miles off, to fetch some grasse, were suddenly surprized by some of the Irish, together with their horses : which three troops were then and there murthered, and afterwards their flesh eaten and devowred by divers barbarous Irish women that lay in that wood. And the very bones of these men were afterwards fownd in the woodes cleene pickt, and the flesh (first [as was believed] boyled), eaten quite off the same.

Some one who had himself heard the story may have " confessed " all this to Peter Hill, Esquire. And the story served a purpose quite as well as if it had been proved by credible eye-witnesses. And so it stands part of the " sworn evidence," between the deponent's two stories about the Lough Kernan affair.

I submit, therefore, that the evidence of such a man about what he learnt from others is absolutely worthless. One of his capacity for the marvellous and incredible, would find story-tellers to suit his taste. And even when he certifies to what occurred in his presence he cannot

be always trusted. The woman whom he so inhumanely
executed, would not, in her last moments, avail herself of *his*
ministrations, and, for that reason, she was " graceless."

We owe a good deal after all to Mr. Peter Hill. His
self-revelation is not the least important feature of his
evidence. In so unwittingly airing his own importance,
he lets us see with much clearness why the Rebellion spread
so rapidly, and was kept up so long ; also why murders
were committed by some among the rebels. And about
these murders committed by the rebels, apart from charges
which rest on no kind of evidence, the number, however
much to be lamented, in the County Down is not surprising
when compared with the cold-blooded atrocities committed
by men in power. Putting aside the Lough Kernan case,
about which I cannot feel decided one way or the other,
I have a very strong conviction that the number of those
put to death by the rebels in cold blood would fall short
of what the High Sheriff takes credit to himself for execu-
ting and otherwise slaying. I do not forget that Mr. Hill
was, so far from being conscious of doing wrong, very
proud of his achievements. But the people against whom
he turned his military prowess and his judicial acumen,
would hardly look upon his doings as "acceptable services"—
to *them* the executions and slaying of the defenceless were
murders at once atrocious and perhaps calling for vengeance.
A deplorable state of affairs, but due in a much higher
degree to State policy, and to the action of those acting
on behalf of " the State," than to any in-born wickedness,
or preconceived design, on the part of the natives. The
rebels could commit murders and robberies, and be guilty
of numberless cruelties—were capable, if we believe all
we hear, of nothing better ; but Mr. Peter Hill and his
followers could do no wrong—the worst *they* could do
amounted only to " acceptable service " wholly (not " partly "
as Dr. Reid suggests) " justified," that is, " required,
authorised, and warranted " by " the State." And even
before the issue of that warrant of atrocity, its spirit was
abroad and actuated " good and loving subjects," those
of position and influence more particularly.

There is ample evidence of this spirit and of its workings,
in at least two places in the Lecale district—Ardglass and
Kilclief—which I mention in particular, because of the
figure they make in the later depositions.

The examination of John Mackdonnell of Lecale, being aged
about thirty-four years, taken the 7th of May, 1653 :

Who being swore, saith, that, in the second year of the Rebellion,
he was in Ardglasse, and on a Sabbath day, in the morning, being

lying in his bed, the drumer of that company of Sr. James
Montgomery's regt., whereof Captain Wooll was then lieutenant,
came into his, the examinant's house, and asked a loan of his foulling-
peece. This exant. desyred to know what he would doe with
it. The said drumer (whose name was Dunbar), replyed that he
had some use for itt, but knowing by this examinant's further
answer, that it was roosty and not fixed, he went out agayne without
it. This examinat further sayth, that about half an hour after the sd.
drumer went out, he, this examt, heard a cry, in the street, and as
he was rysing to putt on his clothes, Thomas Rischer, one of the
four men, who (as this examinat after heard) was killed there, came
unto this examinat's house, having a wound on his neck, from which
the blood did spring apace. That, the sayd Risher did say to this
examinat, that the soldrs were about to kill him, and desyred this
examinat to goe to Lieut. Wool to cause hinder (*sic*) the soldrs in
that action ; that this examt. said he knew not what good his
speaking could doe, yett began to putt on his cloathes, and being
come abroad, he found that foure men were killed, whose names
as this examinar remembers were Thomas Risher, Peter M'Lenan,
Richard McDyon, and Patrick M'Eley. But by whom they were
killed, he this examinat knoweth not. But he sayeth, that the
report was that Edward Jackson and Will Hamilton were the killers
of them ; and lykewise that the report was amongst the soldiers that
Lieut. Wool gave order for the killing of the foresayd foure men.*

Jurat.	his
G. BLUNDELL.	JOHN + M'DONNELL.
JA : TRAILL.	marke.

Had we no other statement on the subject we should
be justified in distrusting the report mentioned in the
last sentence of the deposition. But there are several
other depositions to the same effect, and among them
the explanations offered by the parties accused, this being
one of the cases fully gone into by the Commissioners
of the High Court sitting at Carrickfergus in 1653. The
Irish Government of the Commonwealth, with more sense
of Justice than that of Parsons and Borlase, had Captain
Wooll and others committed to prison on the charge of
murder. The Captain's own examination furnishes a
remarkable commentary on the ethics of men in power
in those days :

The examination of Captain John Woll, taken before us, ye
27 day of May, 1653 :
Who sayth, yᵗ in or about May, 1643, Maior Keith, having been
importuned by Mr. Patrick Savadge of Portaferry, to receive into

---

* This deposition has been printed by Rev. George Hill (*Mont. MSS.*), but he
makes Wode the name of the officer charged ; in the MS. depositions it occurs
in the forms Woll, Wool, and Wooll.

protection a ffriend of his, one * Shimcocke Savadge, then out with the Irish, who would bring in with him a considerable number of cattle, the said Maior Keith directed this examinat, then an officer under his command, to take a party of souldrs with him, and to march to Newcastle, neere Dundrum, to meete the sayd S—— Savadge, and to receive him with what goods and ffollowers he had to bring in, where meeting the sayd S—— Savadge, the sayd S—— took this examt. by the hand, saying, Welcome, Lieutenant Wooll, now I am sure I am saffe. You shalbe [saffe], said this examt, when I receive further orders from my superiour, and asked the sayd S—— how strong the Irish were in that part ; hee answered this examinat that there were of them aboute three score ; and being demanded who came to him with the sayd S—— hee sayth hee sawe only a boy with him ; and falling into further discourse the sayd S—— desired this examt. that he would allow of five or six of his followers to come in with him, for that the sayd S—— alleged that Mr. Savadge of Portaferry had prevayled with Maior Keith that soe many should come in with the sayd S—— ; unto which this examt replyed that unless he sawe the Major's orders to that purpose hee would not, and withall tould the sayd S—— that if any came in with him in that kinde without orders, hee would not secure them from the party or garrison, but they to stand to hazard themselves (*sic*).

The examt. beinge demanded whether he did know Patrick, O'Lenan, Thomas Reicher, Patrick M'Lee, and Richard M'Dohen, or any of them ; hee saith he did not know any such men soe called. And being demanded who or how many of S——'s followers did venture to come in with him from the Irish, hee saith, as hee remembers, the number of six. Whereas he saith, two of these persons [about 4 dayes after] went forth againe to the Irish. And whether the said Patrick O'Leenan, and the others above named were the 4 that stayed within, he knows not. This examt further saith, that the sayd 4 persons who did stay were going and coming about the town of Ardglas, till that hee heard they were kild by some soulders of his Maior's company there under this examinat's coñand in the garrison of Ardglas. And saytʰ that one Robert Merriman desired this examt. that they sayd 4 persons should help to burn wrack for Mr. Houston, wch. this examt would not doe, hee saying that hee would not have any medling with them one way or other, till he had received orders concerning them.

* The deposition is written in a loose, ill-formed hand, sprawling over three folios, in some places very indistinct, particularly in the matter of names. The Christian name of the Savage who was to be taken into protection I cannot fix with any satisfaction. Each time it turns up in a different shape. The more probable reading I take to be " Simcocke." The writer of the deposition evidently had but a vague and uncertain notion of the name : he uses " Shimcocke," " Shinicock," etc. In William Hamilton's examination (folio 139) it is almost clearly written " Ginnicocke." Instead of following these vagaries, I put down at first what seems to me the more probable form ; and, subsequently, where the Christian name ought to appear, I mark its place by " S——." Throughout these MSS. the proper names are often a source or perplexity. Iı 'Iigh Sheriff Hill's list of rebels outlawed in County Down, is the name ' Jennock Savage, of Ballidock, Gent.,' and this may be the Savage whom Capt. Wooll met at Newcastle by order from his superior officer, Major Keith.

This 'examt. confesseth and saith, that about five days after the said Robert Merriman would have those 4 men employed in burninge of wracke to make kelpe, hee, *this examt. gave order to the soulders then in garrison at Ardglass, and under his command, that they should goe and slay the sayd 4 persons and all other loose people in the towne and about it, that had no protections !* And sayth, that for S—— Savadge, he had allowance from Maior Keith to goe into the Ile of Man ; wch is the cause he was not cut off with the rest.

This examt denyeth that hee had any cowes from any of the sayd 4 persons slayne, nor that hee, this examt. ever promised to protect them.

This examt denyeth that hee ever protected Cormick Maguire, * but saith, that the sayd MaGuire did always contynue, goeing and coming to Ardglas till he was kild. This examt denyeth that he ever did send him with a boat to the Ile of Man, but sayth that hee heard that MaGuire was at sea in a boat, and turned back by a contrary wynde to Ardglas, and believeth that he was in the same boate that S—— Savadge was intendinge for the Ile of Man. Hee this examt. sayth, that the sayd Cormick was, after his return from sea, murdered in Ardglas, but by whom, hee knoweth not, nor by what direction. And further sayth not.

Taken before us,	his
GEO. RAWDON.	JOHN + WOLL.†
ROGER LYNDON.	mark.

An extraordinary story, that deposition of the Captain. Clear in only one part—the deponent thought himself empowered to kill, like rats, all to whom the stigma of re- bellion did at any time attach. And in spite of his parade of deference to the orders of his superior officer, he acted, first, at Newcastle, in defiance of the commands on which he went there, and, subsequently at Ardglass, he appears to have acted in complete independence of Major Keith, as if he felt he had powers from a higher quarter " to kill rebels, their comforters, aiders," etc., at any time and in any way he might think proper. What did he go to New- castle to do, if not to receive Savage into protection ? I suspect he declined to execute his orders, finding that there was to be no " prey " of cows, or that the prey fell short of expectation. On his own showing, he deceived Savage and his companions. What he told them at Newcastle and what he told Merriman at Ardglass, could not lead them to think that *he* would be their murderer

---

* Or M'Gueer, another victim of this officer's " general order," although he disclaims responsibility.

† Rather strange that a commanding officer, the absolute master of the people's lives, should sign by mark, or rather three marks, very childlike in execution.

if they ventured " in that kind " " to come in." In the Proclamation of 8th February, 1641–2, no power was reserved to officers of admitting such rebels to quarter or to protection ; but the power to cut them off was beyond doubt. Should anyone ask why the commander of the garrison did not have the men arrested when they came to Ardglass, and have them tried before some kind of tribunal, the answer is—The Proclamation saved all that trouble. Lieutenant Wooll did no more than he believed himself " required " as well as empowered to do. And as long as the same order of things stood at the Castle he was safe, in putting to death as many rebels as he might choose ; in doing so he was, in fact, making " favourable records " for himself. But what might be the effect of the murder of those men on their companions who were still " out. " ?

On folios 137, 138 of the Co. Down volume of depositions is a series of questions to which the statement of Capt. Wooll, as given above, would appear to furnish replies. On folio 139 is the examination of Edward Jackson, then a prisoner, who

Saith, hee, this examt. with sundry of the soldiers of the garrison of Ardglass were commanded by Captaine John Woll, then their Lieutenant *upon paine of death* (early in the morning), to goe unto the towne and kill the said four persons, and that examt. and the soulders went and killed the sayd four persons. And further sayth not.

Taken by ROGER LYNDON,

And on same folio, 139, the examination of William Hamilton, taken the 27th of May, 1653 :

Who saith that Captaine John Woll, then his Lieutenant, and comāanding the garrison of Ardglass, in Summer, 1643, comāanded, this examinat with more soldiers then in said garrison, one night, to rise early the next morning, to goe into the towne, and there or where els they could finde any that had no protections, *to kill, them ;* where they found four men in severall places of the towne, *and killed them,* but what their names were hee knows not. And saith that they did not find S—— Savadge then in towne, nor did they inquire after him.

Taken by ROGER LYNDON.

The examination of Katherine Bretnogh, taken the 9th of June, 1653, aged 40 years and upwards :

Being duly sworne, sayth : That in May, about 9 or 10 years since, her husband, Patrick M'Gilleigh,* having being out with the Irish in rebellion, was received into protection by Captain

* The name M'Glue occurs in County Down to the present time. But I take this to be the same as M'Ley or M'Eley (as in other examinations), a name which, as M'Leigh, still exists in East Down. Proper names sometimes undergo strange mutations in these old MSS.

Wooll, then comanding in Ardglasse, in the County of Downe, and served the said Captain Wooll for two or three days in leading out wracke to dounge (*sic.*) his lands ; that upon the Sabbath day three or foure of ye sd. Captain Wooll's souldiers came into the house and slew him, her said husdand then lying by her in their bed. The cause of her knowledge of her husband's protection, is, that her husband told her soe ; ffurther she saith, yt ye sd. Captain Wooll tooke from her after her husband's death two cowes, which was all her stock, and that her brother and a child then sucking at her breast thereby dyed for want of ffood, ffurther sayth not.

Taken before us.   [No Signature]

G. BLUNDELL, JA. TRAILL.

The examination of Robert Merriman of Lecale, aged about three score and ten years, taken the 7th May, 1653;

Who being sworne, sayth that in the second year of the Rebellion, he dwelt in Ardglasse, and that Captaine Wool (then Lieut. Wool), commanding there, went out with a party to get some prey from the Rebells. And the said partie brought in Cormick M'Gueer, who the year before went out of Lecale for fear of his life (as he alleadged) as others also that were then brought in did alleadge the same reason for their going out.

This examinant further sayth, that the said Cormick M'Gueer, after he had remayned about fourteene days in Ardglasse was killed (as he this examinat heard say) by one Thomas Dixon, now prisoner, then dwelling in Bishop's Court. The examt. being asked upon what score or by what order the said McGueer was killed, he sayth that he, this examt. heard say that the said Dixon came from Bishop's Court to Ardglasse of purpose to kill the said MackGueer (*sic*) because of some difference between the said McGueer and a brother of the said Dixon, And further sayth not.

Jurat :   ROBERT MERRIMAN.

G BLUNDELL, JA TRAILL.

Thomas Dixon was examined on 7th May, 1653. He states that " severals of them " were drinking in a house, when it was told that M'Gueer (or MacGuire) was in " the Rocks." Hearing which, Cornet Johnson and others went out and killed him there. On the back of the deposition made by M'Gueer's widow, the following names are noted :

CAPT. WOLL, in prison.
CORNETT JOHNSON.
THOMAS DIXON, in prison.
JOHN KELLY.
MANUS MAGERE.

The intention probably was to bring them up for examination. Capt. Wooll might, perhaps, plead ignorance, but some of his men were implicated, and he ought to have made some inquiry.

What would be thought in these days of the military
officer who could make it his standing jest, if not his boast,
that the first blood he drew with his sword was that of a
baby, and that the little head fell to the ground like a ball !

The examination of Mistresse Anne Fitzsimons, taken the 6th of
June, 1653 : *
Who being duly sworne sayth that about eight years ago, when
some of the Scotts Regiments quartered in Lecale, Captaine
Alexander Adaire who was one of the Captains in Col. John
Hamilton's Regiment had his company quartered in the house of
Kilcleef,† where this examt. hath her dwelling, and then also
had. That the sayd Alexander Adaire did often resort to this
examt.'s . house, by reason of his company being quartered in
the said towne, That this examt. heard the sayd Captaine Adaire
say that *the first blood that ever he shed of the Irish* was by the killing
of a young child [somewhere without the] Island Mackgee [but
hard by it]. And that it was by occasion of an Irishwoman her
flying away from him and *he following and striking att her his stroke
light upon the child* who was on the woman's back and the head of
it hanging over the bracken.‡ *That his blow did cause the head of
the childe fall to the ground lyke a ball.*

And this examinat further sayeth, that often times the sayd
Captain Adaire [did] speak of his killing of the sayd childe upon
occasion of his looking upon a young child of this examinat's who
the sayd Alexander Adaire used to say was very lyke one of the
same age with the child wch. he killed as aforesaid, and that he
was putt in mynd of the sayd act by looking upon this examinat's
childe. And this examinat further sayeth that she heard the sayd
Alexander Adayre [say] that the same day on which he killed the
child as aforesayd in the morning, he and many others *fell upon the
Irish and killed three score of them* without ever shotting a shot.
[But] that their swords went like flails. And that within three
nights after they alsoe went out (it being a very darke and rainye
night) and killed thirty familyes, and suffered not them yt were
in this bed (poynting at the beds by him) § to give warning to them
yt were in yt bed. ‖ And further she sayeth not. But yt when

K

the sayd Adaire was commending the service of killing the pre-sayd persons this examinat sayd unto him that it might come to passe that she would rise up in Judgment against him for it.

Taken before me

JA. TRAILL.   ANN FITZSIMONS.*

What a hero is pourtrayed here! We may imagine how delighted Mrs. Fitzsimons must have been with her visitor! None the less, he understood the kind of service most commended in high places. The murder of the little innocent was to Capt. Alexander Adair what the fall of Seringapatam was to a certain Colonel: every one had to listen to the story. And wasn't the killing of a rebel, six months old, as profitable as the killing of one twenty or thirty years older, and much less hazardous! At any rate the gallant Captain appears to have thought so.

The Examination of Nicholas Fitzsimons of Kilcliefe, taken before us the 3rd day of June, 1653† :—

Who being duly sworne and examined, saith that Alexander Adare of Ballemeanagh in the county of Antrim,‡ being sometyme Captayn under the command of Collonel John Hamilton, had his whole company quartered uppon the sayd Nicholas and his tenants, and uppon that score the sd. Captain did much resort the house of the sd. Nicholas, where *very often* he did use to bragg of his feates att the beginning of the Rebellion, and howe he himself with divers others went into Island McGee in the county of Antrim, and there killed a number of the Irish, nott sparing man, woman, or child, and spetially named one Ever McGee, an aged man, whom they had killed, and after they *had killed him in his bed, fired the house and soe consumed him* in that fire ; and further, that the Captayne tould this deponent and his wife that the first blood he shed was a little child, saying *he rid after an Irishwoman to kill her*, and she having the child on her back, he striking att the woman, he stroke the child on the neck and cutt off the child's head so that the head fell att the sd. Captayne's feet like a ball ; and many more things did the sd. Captayne say in the deponent's hearing wch. he, the deponent, now forgetteth.   And further sayeth not

Taken by

GEO. RAWDEN,

JA. TRAILL,   N: FITZSYMONS.

ROGER LYNDON.

The Examination of Bryan O'Kelly of Kilkleef, aged about six and thirty years, taken the 6th of June, 1653§ :—

* A fine signature.

† County Antrim depositions, folio 191.

‡ The reason, I suppose, why these depositions are included in the County Antrim book.

§ County Antrim depositions, folio 190.

The Examinat being duly sworne, sayeth that when Col. John Hamilton's Regt. was quartered in Lecale, Capt. Alex. Adayre's company was quartered in the towne of Kilkleef. That one day the sayd Capt. Adayre being in this examinat's house drinking with his lieutenant, Robert Gordon, and his own brother, his ensigne, this examt. heard the sayd Alex. Adayre relating unto the foresayd two officers how he killed in the first year of the Rebellion in a certayne place (the name whereof this examt. remembers not) neere to Island Mackghee, a young child on a woman's back yt was running into a bogg. And that having lighted of his horse he overtook the said woman as she was entering into the bogg, and struck att her, by wch. stroke the head of the child on her back fell to the ground; that thereupon the sayd lieut. [Gordon] replied to him, that *itt was not well done to kill a child or any of those that were not gone out into rebellion ;* whereunto the sayd Alex. Adayre answered, saying that *he, the sayd lieut., was a foolle,* for there was not one of them to be spared, that *they would all goe into rebellion,* when they had their opportunity

This examinat further sayeth that there was one of the sayd Capt. Adayre's soldiers called (as the examt. remembers) Sandy McDowell, who att that tyme sayd to his Captaine that he had been his servant before he was a soldier, and also since, and he expected to have the same fee from him which he had in the county of Antrim. And the Captain asking what fee yt was the soldier answered, " You know, Captain, I had a shilling for every person I killed of the Irish ; that the sayd Captain sayd " You shall have as much here." And the soldier demanded to have some earnest in hand, the Captain bad him to sit down, saying that he should have it. But this examinat sayeth that he knoweth not whether they thus spoke in jest or in earnest. And further he sayeth not.

Taken before me   BRYAN $\times$ ôKELLY,
   JA. TRAILL.   his marke.

The caitiff who could make the murder of the baby his standing jest was capable of practising all the foul deeds of which he made his " bragg," and could at the same time assure himself that his jest and his duty lay very close together.

The Examination of Phelomy Smith ot Ballycutter (Lecale) taken before us the ffirst day of June, 1653 :—

Phelomy Smith . . . sworne and examined before us, sayth that Redmond ffitzsimons one of his neighbours, being then aged sixty years or thereabouts went into Kinnalerty* for the preservation of his life, seeing his neighbours a-killing by the Scotts souldiers, and acting nothing against them ; and when some rule and settlement † came amongst them, Redmond ffitzsimons sent a woman to this deponent, in to Strangford where he was then souldier of the company of Captain Valentine Payne, signifying that the said Redmond durst not come home saffe with his liffe without a

---

* Kinelarty, the country of the M'Cartan's (MacArtaine's).

† This must mean the Cessation of 1643.

protection or a passe from the Lo. Viscount Clanneboyes, whereupon
this deponent tould his said Captaine of the said woman's message
unto him, who soon after went into Killyleagh and gott a protection,
relating unto the said Lo. of Clanneboyes the said Redmond's
honesty and conversaĉon and acting nothing prejudicial to their
government, wᶜʰ protection was delivered unto this deponent,
who sent it unto the said Redmond ffitzsimons by his own wiffe
[Ewny Smith] and when he came into the barony of Lecale, this
deponent went to meet him, fearing that any should doe him hurt or
pilladge him. And soe meeting [him, &] going towards the garrison
of Strangford aforesd. they were mett with one Thomas Dixon
and Jordy Worke, the [said Dixon] now prisoner before the High
Court of Justice for another murther, this deponent knowing his
wickednesse before that time, and to prevent his furie went before,
and tould the said Thomas Dixon that the said Redmond ffitzsimons
had my Lo. of Clanneboyes' protection, wch. protection the sd.
Redmond showed [the sd Dixon], notwithstanding, the said Thomas
[Dixon] drew his sword and *murdered the poore ould man*, cutting him
in pieces, and took away his money and left him there at Mullaghbane
neere Ballenary, where he is lying buried in the same place, and
except that this deponent had a horse to carry him away he had
been so served.

(Three lines struck out and defaced.)

The same Examinat Phelemy Smith [ffurther] saith that the
said Thomas Dixon and Jordy Worke did kill another man that
night (being in the evening late) the month of May, 1642 named One*
ôSterky, *(sic)* a poore ffisher who had this deponents Lieuts.
letter [namely, Lt. Abraham] to come to him to be his fisher.
And this deponent further sayth that he prayed the sayd
Thomas Dixon to carry the said Redmond ffitzsimons and
One ôSterky prisoners with them untill his Captain
or Lieutenant had come in place, yett he *(sic)* most cruelly did not,
but murthered both. His cawse of knowledge, for that hee, this
examminat, was present when the sayd Dixon kild the sayd
Redmond ffitzsimons, and that the sayd Dixon and Jordy Worke
kill *(sic)* the forementioned ôSterky, the cause of his beliefe thereof for
yt, this deponent when he fled from them at the killing of ffitzsimons,
hee then saw the said ôSterkey in their hands, who the next morning
was found dead in the same place where ffitzsimons was killed.

Taken before us,

SAM BONNELL,   PHELLYMY + SMITH.
OWEN WYNN.
ROGER LYNDON.   his mark.

The " protection " could but seldom be obtained, and
even when obtained, it sometimes, as in the foregoing case,
proved of no avail. The officers, or even the common
soldiers, who were pleased to treat it as a nullity might do
so, and keep still within the lines marked out for all " good
and loving subjects."

* Owen.

If they show nothing more, these "depositions" show, or help to show, the extent to which military licence was allowed to run. Nor was this state of things confined to one locality or one county.

The Examination of Andrew McOwen* of Cloghanduffe in the countie of Antrym, yeoman, adged 22 years or thereabouts, being sworne and examined, by virtue of his oath saith :—

That between Christmas and Candlemas in the year 1641, hee being in his this deponent's ffather's Barne att Cloghan duffe aforesd. hee did see two troopers entering into his said father's house, and then there being not any therein [as this examinate remembereth] but one William Magucane and Marie his wife who repayred thither about three or four days before for their preservation and saftie, as this examinate heard, from the furie and violence of the Scotts, who then were murthering many of ye Irish in those partes. And saith yt [att] the tyme the sd. troopers entered into the sd: house, the sd. William Magucane and Marie his wife were living ; and presently after their entrance there into, he heard a sobb or crie in the house att which tyme this examinate thought or feared that they were killing the sd. William and his wife, and not long after hee sawe the Corpes of the sd. William and Marie caryed out of the sd. house on a Barroe. And further this examinate saith that hee saw the sd. troopers lead away a working Gelding belonging to this examinate's ffather. And saith that he creddiblie heard that the said troopers were caled James Morrison and one Gordon, belonging to Capt. Lindsey his troope att that tyme. And further deposeth not.

Taken before us, 6 May, 1653.

PHIL. PINCHON.   A. McKOWEN.

SAM. BONNELL.

Elizabeth McOwen sworn and examined on same date corroborates the foregoing.

The son of the murdered William and Mary Magucane (M'Guckian), gives further information concerning the the murder :

The Examinačon and Deposition of William Macogen (*sic*) of Kilmacraed in the Parrish of Killfodd and County of Antrym, aged 35 years or thereabouts, taken before us this 19th of Aprill, 1653 :

Who sayth that in the first yeare of ye Rebellion William Magogan, ffather of this examinat, lived in the parish of Ballykooshen, neere Temple Pattricke, and that about twelve days before Candlemas in the year aforesd. Capt. Lindsey with a troope of horse came over the Bann and quartered att Donedrey Bridge where several Irish people were slaine by them, and that some of thattroope came to the house of this examinate's ffather the first night they came to their quarters as aforesayd and *kild this examinate's sister and wounded severall others*, at wch. tyme William Magogan, this

* County Antrim depositions, fol. 261.

examinate's ffather, being *wounded* runn to Castle Norton in Temple Pattricke for safety where this examinate was then a souldier under the command of Capt. Upton, whome he acquainted with his ffather's condičon, whereupon Captain Upton gave a charge to Alexander McOwen that hee should take this examinate's ffather and mother to his house and to keep them in safety. And that hee the sd. Alexander McOwen did accordingly take them to his house, and further this examinate sayth that about three nights after, James Morrison and Alexander Gourdon came to the said Alexander McOwen's house and with an axe murthered this examinate's ffather and mother, and that ye said James Morrison now liveth in or neare Carrickfergus and is by trade a saddler, and that ye sd. Allexander (*changed to* 'Roger') Gourdon, liveth about Maine Water. And further this examinate saith that the cause of his knowledge of this fact is that Alexander McOwen afterwards tould him that hee would testifie it to be true, also his son namely Andrew McOwen and Pattrick McBeagh who was then servant to the said Allexander McOwen who were present in the place when the murther was committed, and further sayth not.

Taken before us
(No Names).   WILLIAM McGUCKIAN.

The omission of the names of the justices is rare.* But the statements are fully borne out by those of other examinants. All these examinations testify to the audacity and impunity with which such murders of the Irish could be, and were, committed.

The murders in all these cases were by Scottish soldiers. I am not going to "imitate" Dr. Reid by attributing this bloody craze either to the "faith" or the nationality of those soldiers. Speaking of the various estimates of the number of "Protestants" who were "massacred" by the Irish, this writer says † :

Suffice it to say that the lowest probable computation presents an awful sacrifice of human life, and a fearful *proof* of the implacable spirit of the Romish *faith* in those days of ignorance and bigotry.‡

So 'twas the "Romish *Faith*" that murdered the Protestants ! That's the condensed essence of the statement, indeed, of a good deal of what Dr. Reid has written in connection with the same period. He did not of course suspect that in penning that well-turned sentence he was solemnly propounding nonsense, not to speak of the offensiveness of the allusion   I don't look to the "faith" of

---

* Probably a copy of the original deposition.

† Reid i., 339, 340.

‡ I daresay he found little improvement in the same *faith* in his more "enlightened" age.

the North Britons for the explanation of the murders and
other outrages committed by those soldiers while among
the Irish. An hypothesis analogous to Dr. Reid's I hold
to be uncharitable, unchristian, *and wholly unnecessary.*
I am sure that any troops or military forces which the
world has yet produced would be very dangerous neighbours if placed in similar circumstances and accorded
similar licence and impunity in the practice of outrages.
That the Presbyterian clergy of Ulster were at the time
uncommonly busy is amply testified. I am far from holding
or suggesting that they counselled to the commission of
crime. They, doubtless, felt, like their polished historian,
impelled by high sense of duty to make war upon Rome,
and to impress a similar sense of duty on their hearers
and followers ; but they stand charged with being over-
zealous in promoting turbulence. Their activity could
hardly fail to be productive of results not easily recon-
cilable with the Gospel of " peace on earth and to men
good will." Yet, I am satisfied that the crime and outrage,
to a very great extent were, in any case, the necessary
outcome of the order of things encouraged and " required "
by the State.

The period of the Cessation is pointed to by the
author of the " Montgomery MSS.," and his able editor,
the late Rev. George Hill, as the time when turbulence and
outrage were most freely indulged in by the Scottish
soldiery,—the time, too, when those who ought to have
been ministers of peace as well as of the Word were most
industriously bent on making peace and order impossible
or indefinitely remote.

To those who love to descant on the mischief-making
" the Romish " priests of Ireland—a topic on which, unfortunately, it is not necessary for the " historian " to be
well informed or to be very guarded in the use of language—
the following may prove of some interest. It is taken from
the " Montgomery MSS.," (p. 326) :

In *the fermentation raised by the Covenant teachers* (which were
imposed on parishes, and the legal incumbents ejected by the Scottish
army's violence) *against the peaceable Irish Papists*, in the Lower
Ardes, yet Sir James* procured the Lord Conway's order, dated
December, 1642, that only bonds should be taken of Henry Savage
of Ardkeen, esquire, for the delivery of his arms in his house at any
time when called for . . . There was need and reason . . .
because of *the unruly Scottish mobb and common soldiers* who would
make the pretence of searching for arms and ammunition an
opportunity to plunder.

* Montgomery.

And, alluding to the Scottish army,

Such was the factious humours of these men, and the country gentlemen *blown up by their teachers, who had so hooked them to their line* that they could pull the people on shore with a single hair.

On the latter passage, the Rev. George Hill has the following note :

The Presbyterian ministers were very actively engaged in the general excitement of the crisis, arousing the Scottish soldiers and settlers to resent and disregard the Cessation, and to some extent directing the movements of the army under Monroe.

The " Romish " priests, and the Old Irish leaders, have often been rated for not observing the Cessation ; which observance would mean that *they* should keep quiet and leave the Scottish army, and those who influenced that army, a free hand !

On page 327 Mr. Hill has this note :

Quarrel and Plunder.—It was taught and believed among the Scots in Ulster that the Roman Catholics intended to employ the year of Cessation in a grand attempt to expel them from the province, and under this impression the Scottish troops, *at the instigation of the Covenant teachers,* set forth in various directions to disarm all Papists in Ulster, *taking that opportunity of committing rapine and plunder.*   Outrages of this nature were carried on to such an extent as to attract the notice of certain leading Irishmen who had stood aloof from the several parties into which their countrymen were divided but now thought it necessary to set limits to the depredations and spoils committed by the Scottish Covenanters in Ulster. The Earls of Clanrickarde and Thomond, the Viscounts Dillon, Taafe, Fitzwilliam and Ranelagh, and Lord Howth addressed a letter to the King in which they depict their own unhappy condition ' exposed to the mercy of two powerful armies now in the field ; the one of the Confederate Catholics' party, if they were disposed to make any invasion upon us ; and the other of the Scotch Covenanters, and such as adhered to them, who *by burning, spoiling, and committing cruel and hostile acts, have broken the Cessation,* and cast off their obedience to your Majesty's government here.'

The Ormonde or royalist influence had risen somewhat in " the State," but " the true and loving subjects " had already got their charter of outrage, and they were not going to surrender it merely because a hollow compact had been made with " the rebels." The Cessation was, in any case, but of temporary character. The Proclamation of 8th February, 1641-2, was not so restricted, excepted as to the money prizes offered for killing the prescribed leaders ; and, in passing, it is worth observing that none

* Mr. Hill quotes from *Desiderata Curiosa Hybernuica*, 260-4.

of these tempting prizes appears to have been earned, a thing in itself not a little remarkable in so turbulent a time, and when there was so great inducement held out to treachery on the part of the disaffected. Other prizes might, however, be had in the shape of "preys" and pillagings which were not to be had if the Cessation were binding. The "profits" as well as the previous commands of "the State,"—even putting out of sight such matters as racial antipathy and "the implacable spirit of their *faith*,"—were motives powerful enough to keep up on the part of the Scots "the burning, spoiling, and committing cruel and hostile acts," of which Clanrickarde and his compeers so much complain ; but I don't know that it is altogether correct to charge them with having broken the Cessation, seeing that they did not recognise it.

Mr. William Montgomery, of Rosemount, and the Rev. George Hill appear to think that the Scots army in Ulster were particularly and unusually given to excesses during the Cessation. The commission of such outrages would be more felt and more complained of in a time of comparative peace ; and the pretence, or the practice, of searching the houses of Papists for arms, in itself an outrage, would produce a plentiful and varied crop of wickedness. Yet, I would submit there was nothing new in the conduct of those Scottish soldiers, nothing but what they had been doing from the beginning,—except that the marauders who might feel "justified by the State," would have more opportunity of making unwelcome visits to their neighbours' houses. I don't see what new inducement to the commission of atrocities against the rebels—the Irish Papists, of course —was necessary after the State warrant "to pursue and plague with Fire and Sword, apprehend, *destroy, and kill*, by all the ways and means they may," not only the rebels by name proscribed, but every one else who might, by their enemies, be supposed to have even a trace of "the poyson " * in their veins. Nor does it weaken the force of my contention to point to acts more or less atrocious committed within the time preceding the issue of the said Proclamation. Quite the contrary, for it will show that the spirit of the Proclamation was active, and everywhere felt, long before the publication of the more formal authorization, and that the Scots in the North were only following up, perhaps improving upon, the tactics already adopted by the English in Munster and Leinster acting under direction of those immediately connected with "the State."

* Colonel Audley Mervyn.

That the spirit and the very terms of the proclamation
of 8th February, 1641–2 had gone abroad—in Ulster, at
any rate, and not in Ulster alone—almost from the very
outbreak is, I submit, clear enough, from the following
which I take from Borlase (" The Execrable Irish Rebellion,"
folio 27); and it is well to bear in mind that the writer,
as an officer in the service of "the State," and the son of one
of the chief rulers, had special opportunities of knowing
thoroughly this particular subject :

About the 27th of October (1641) the Lords Justices and Council
sent Commissions to the Lords Viscounts of Clandeboys and of the
Ardes, to raise the Scots in the Northern parts ; they also writ to
Sir Wm. and Sir Robert Stewart, with other gentlemen of quality
in the North, giving them power to prosecute the rebels with Fire
and Sword ; yet so as to rescue such as should submit to his Majesties
Grace and Mercy ; signifying withal, that although by the said
Commission they gave them full power thereunto, yet they did then
let them know that for those who were chief among the Rebels and
Ringleaders of the rest to disobedience, that they adjudged them less
worthy of favour than the others whom they had misguided : And
therefore, for these principal persons, they required them to take care
not to be too forward (without first consulting the Council Board)
in proffering or promising mercy to those, unless they, the said
Commissioners, saw it of great and unavoidable necessity.   They
likewise writ to the Lords Presidents of Munster and Connaught
advising them to be upon their guard.

The plain meaning of which is, that the nobles and
gentlemen favoured with such commissions had unlimited
powers as to the use of fire and sword ; but as to the
exercise of mercy and clemency they were so restricted and
hampered by conditions that their safest and only practi-
cable course was to kill and slay wherever and whenever
they could. Between the lines they might read that a
rebel of *value* (as Mr. Peter Hill puts it), was not a fit subject
for pardon. They could err only on the side of humanity.
We have seen how Captain Valentine Payne of Strangford,
made complaint against Sir James Montgomery for pro-
tecting the wife and children of George Russell of
Rathmullan (p. 81, *note*).
Mr. Lecky calls attention to a case which in point of
atrocity and inhumanity, yields to nothing imputed to " the
rebels," and, unlike many things so imputed, this is well
attested, not by hearsay, but by eye-witnesses.   The account
is to be found in the *Memoirs of Castlehaven*, in a letter
to Lord Castlehaven from his brother Col. Mervyn Touchet.
The incident occurred at Rathcoole between Maddingstowne,
his lordship's place in the County Kildare, and the

City of Dublin. Col. Touchet's account is as follows :*

In a short time the Irish came and drove away a great part of your stock to a village near.   It being night, you desired me to take your servants and endeavour the recovery ; which I did bringing with me two or three of the chiefest conductors of that rabble.   This enraged the Irish so much that you conceived I was not safe there, and therefore sent me to Dublin to attend the Justices' orders, and assure them of your readiness to return on a call, they sending a convoy, which they promised to do as occasion required.

When I went from you, you thought it necessary that I should take with me all the poor English that were saved ; and to let them go with the carts which were loaded with wool for Dublin.   .   .   . In the passage near Rathcoll the rebels fell upon them, and barbarously killed some and wounded others, myself and one more escaping by the goodness of our horses.   But a servant of mine governing the carts being an Englishman, they took ; and whilst they were preparing to hang him, Sir John Dungan's eldest son, Walter Dungan, came forth from his father's house with a party, and rescued him with the rest of those that were left alive, and brought them safe to Dublin, where I was got.

Col. Touchet does not take much credit to himself for bravery, and it will be seen that he is no admirer of "the rebels."   The outrage committed would have justified extreme measures towards those who were guilty, and it would have been quite easy to identify the rebels who had part in that business.   Col. Touchet thus relates what followed :

In a few days after, the Marquis of Ormond sent out a party towards the place where this murder had been committed.   I went with them, and coming near we met Sir Arthur Loftus, Governor of the Nass, with a party of horse and dragoons, *having killed such of the Irish as they met.*

But the most considerable slaughter was in a great straight of furze seated on a hill where the people of several villages (taking the alarm) had sheltered themselves.   Now Sir Arthur having invested the hill *set the furze on fire* on all sides, where the people (being a considerable number), were all burnt or killed, men, women, and children !   *I saw the bodies and the furze still burning.*

An achievement worthy of the house of Loftus in Ireland ! It would, indeed, be wonderful if any of the Irish in that part of the country remained peaceful when they had such terrible proof that, in any event, they should suffer the pains and penalties of open rebellion.   Among those so cruelly put to death, there may not have been one who had act or part in the attack on the travelling party, while it is absolutely certain that there were young children

* I quote from the edition of the *Castlehaven Memoirs*, printed at Waterford, 1753, p. 29.

and old people, not to speak of women, consumed by the flames who had no share in the guilt. But what renders the crime of Loftus so particularly atrocious is the fact that the parties most forward in the attack were well known, and could probably have been apprehended by the force employed in putting the innocent to death in so shocking a manner. The following information was made very soon after the attack on the convoy :

The Examination of Richard Paget taken xxixth day of April 1642, before Sir Robert Meredith, Chancellor of the Court of Exchequer :—

Who being sworne and examined, saith that on Tuesday last hee, this examt. and others were coming into this Cittie with ffoure wain Loades of Wooll of the Earl of Castlehaven, and that within less than halfe a mile of Rathcoole, and on this side of the said Towne, they were sett upon by two of Scurlock of Racredon his sonnes, with the Hethringtons of Rathcoole to the number of thirtie or ffortie persons, there being above a hundred in all in the ffields thereabout who upon their coming unto this examt. and his companie kild an Englishman, his wife and child, one Irishman and besides three other Englishmen, and compelled this examt. and the rest to drive the said carriage (*sic*) after them into Kildrought, and from thence unto a common towards Sir John Dungan's houes. And the said Sir John, as this Examt. understood afterwards, having from the topp of his castle seene the said carriage and prisoners soe comeing, he sent out one of his servants to know what the matter was, and as soone as he had notice that the said Goodes and parties belonged to the Earl of Castlehaven, hee, the said Sir John and three or ffoure with him came out on horseback with his pistoll cockt and told the said Rebells that the said carriage and prisoners he would take and keepe for the said Earle of Castlehaven. And accordinglie the said Sir John rateing and railing on the sayd Rebells tooke the saide carriage and prisoners unto his owne house, by which meanes this Examinat conceives that the Goodes and the people's lives were preserved. But being demanded whether the said Sir John or anie of his companie did hurt or kill anie of the said Rebells saith that neither the said Sir John nor anie of his companie did kill or hurt anie of the said Rebells other than a sonne of the said Sir John stroke some of the said Rebells over the head and shoulders with a half pike or cudgell.

ROBERT MEREDITH.

Not so desperate a party of rebels after all. One cannot help contrasting the behaviour of the gallant Colonel with the front shown by Sir John Dungan and his son. Had Touchet shown any pluck, fewer, if any, had fallen. The attack at Rathcoole, I have no doubt, grew out of something connected with the recovery of the cattle and the arrest of the cattle-stealers or their leaders—something about which we are, indeed, left in the dark, although curious to know why the Colonel had all at once become so obnoxious that he had to leave Maddingstown, and why the prowess which enabled him to foil the rebels in the first instance should so suddenly desert him on the occasion when his honour as a soldier was more at stake. Although we have not been told so, it is hardly conceivable that so slender a force was able to recover the cows, and to effect arrests without some conflict ; and if there was conflict some one or more may have been killed on that night. This is only surmise ; but some such explanation—or assumption—seems necessary to reconcile matters. I don't say that either Lord Castlehaven or his brother would be guilty of " murder " ; but killing in conflict would, all the same, enrage the friends of the fallen. That, however, is not of so great importance as the action of Loftus, "governor of the Naas," inhuman and impolitic, but that it fitted in to a nicety with the policy then in vogue with the chief rulers and the local rulers of Ireland.

Governors and commanders were not all like Captain Wooll at Ardglass, or Sir Arthur Loftus at Rathcoole. But if any acted on different principles (when they could), they are deserving of praise all the more that the inducement was in the direction of the most extreme measures on every opportunity. And the best intended efforts of the more nobly disposed were sometimes unavailing.

Sir Charles Vavasor, after a well-regulated dispute (stoutly defended by the Rebells) took in Cloghleigh commanded by one Condon wherein was 20 men, 11 women and about 7 children, some of which the soldiers stripped, in readiness to kill them ; but Major Howell, drawing out his sword, defended them ; and whilst he went to Col. Vavasor (then at Ballyhinden, Mr. Roche's house where he was invited that day to dine) committed them to Capt. Wind, who leaving them to a guard of horse, *they stripped them again,* and afterwards *fell upon them with carbines, pistols and swords :* a cruelty so resented by Sir Charles Vavasor that he vowed to hang him who commanded the guard ; and had certainly done it had not next day's action prevented it, which was the most considerable loss the English ever received from the Rebells, a mischief they might have avoided had they been less confident and given greater credence to their intelligence.[*]

I cannot close this article without taking some notice of two other matters pertinent to the subject of it. Few who have read anything of the history of the period are unfamiliar with the names of Sir William Saint Leger,

[*] Borlase : *History of the Execrable Irish Rebellion,* folio, 1680, p. 117. The last sentence in extract alludes to a surprise on Sunday, 4th June, 1643, in which Vavasor, Wind, and other English officers were made prisoners, several officers killed, men killed estimated from 300 to 600, two pieces of ordnance seized, besides colours, etc.

Lord President of Munster in the earlier period of the civil war. That this personage is responsible for the rapid spread of the Rebellion in Munster is, I am satisfied, as well established as any fact recorded in history. In the postscript to a letter addressed to Ormonde, dated, "Downerayle, 8th November, 1641," the Lord President, says :

In these days, my Lord, *Magna Charta* must not be wholly insisted on.

A neat little sentence, seeming mild as mother's milk, don't it ! Looks altogether captivating in its simplicity and innocence ! No peace-loving subject of that day or of any other day, could quarrel with so moderate a departure in so stirring a time. But let us see the practical meaning, as interpreted by the Lord President himself and set forth in the following extract from an account drawn up by a Mr. Kearney, for the information of the Duke of Ormonde, then Lord Lieutenant of Ireland. This document (printed entire by Miss Hickson * for the first time from the Carte MSS., in the Bodleian Library), shows in the clearest light that the Catholic gentry of the County Tipperary were forced into rebellion by the savagery of St. Leger. That the writer of the paper was well informed on his subject is evident enough, and that he is not inclined to overstate in favour of the rebels is shown by the use which the advocates of " St. Bartholomew " make of his name. This " Catholic brother of a Catholic Bishop " (Froude) is paraded as one of the authorities for " the massacre," because he admits that, after St. Leger's atrocities were well begun, some murders were committed by the insurgents :

ı find that the first insurrection in the County of Tipperary was on the eve of the Presentation of the Virgin, being the 20th of November, 1641, when a great many of the common sort and many young idle fellows of the barony of Eliogarty, some of the barony of Middlethird, some of Kilnemanagh, gathered into a body and took away a great number of cows and sheep from Mr.Kingsmill, from Ballyowen, whereof notice being sent to Sir William St. Leger,

* *Ireland in Seventeenth Century*, ii., 240, etc. (1884). Mr. Kearney is one of a number of Catholics who are cited to uphold a view differing much from what was really theirs. " At the same time," says Miss Hickson, " it is evident that the Catholic writers, *in certain cases*, honestly relate what they have seen for themselves." With the help of so much generous patronage, the Catholic Church ought to be able to hold out a little longer, although it excommunicated Father Peter Walsh (as this writer tells us) " for his candour." The said Father Peter Walsh, O.S.F., afterwards sought and was granted reconciliation with his Church. Carte (i., 265), in his account of the origin of the rebellion in Munster, follows Kearney's narrative almost textually, so far as it concerns the exploits of St. Leger.

then Lord President of Munster, being brother-in-law to Mr Kingsmill, he within two or three days after came with two troops of horse to Ballyowen, and being informed that the cattle were driven into Eliogarty, he marched that way, and as he set forth *he killed three persons* at Ballyowen who were said to have stolen some mares of Mr. Kingsmill, and near it at Grange *he killed four innocent labourers*, and at Ballygalbert *he hanged eight persons and burned several houses there*, and with much importunity and intercession the life of Mr. Morris Magrath, a well-bred gentleman, being one of the grand-children to Archbishop Milerus, was saved, it being plainly proved that he had no hand in the prey. And from thence Capt. Peasley with some of the troops marched to Ardmaile (*sic*) and there *killed seven or eight poor men or women*, and thence marched to Clonulta and there *killed the chief farmer* of the place, being Philip Ryan, a very honest and able man, not at all concerned in that insurrection. And thence they marched to Gowlyn (*sic*) and there *killed and hanged seven or eight* of Dr. Fenning's tenants, and *burned many houses in that town*. And in all this march the Lord President and Peasley took up all the cattle of the inhabitants they met, being great numbers, and sent them to the County of Cork.

Then comes a highly significant item of information, showing what was then the attitude of the Irish gentry in Munster :

After this service the President about the 25th of November, went to Clonmell where Captain Peasley with his troop met him, and the prime nobility and gentry of the country being surprised at this rash and bloody proceeding of the Lord President, many of them flocked after him to Clonmell, as James Lord Dunboyne, Thomas Butler of Kilconnell, James Butler of Killslaugher, Theobald Butler of Ardmaile, Richard Butler of Ballynakill, Philip O'Dwyer, and divers others of good quality, and observed to the President how he had exasperated the people generally to run from house and home and that they were gathering in great numbers together, not knowing what to trust to. And that they the aforesaid gentlemen waited upon his lordship to be informed how affairs stood, and that they coveted nothing more than to serve his Majesty and preserve the peace, and desired that he would be pleased to qualify them with authority and arms, and that they would suppress the rabble and preserve the peace. But he in a furious manner *answered them that they were all rebels, and that he would not trust one soul of them but thought it more prudent to hang the best of them*, and in that extraordinary passion he continued while those and divers other persons of quality their neighbours waited on him. And they withdrawing returned to their several habitations much resenting his severity and *the uncertainty of their safety*. And then suddenly the President marched from Clonmell unto Waterford, hearing some of the Irish of Carlow, Kilkenny and Wexford went over the river into that county to plunder and prey some of the English. In which march *his soldiers killed many harmless poor people*, not at all concerned in the rebellion, *which also incensed the gentry of the county Waterford to betake themselves to their defence.*

Little wonder that in the rising murders were committed in Cashel and some elsewhere, about the end of December, some of them of parties who had taken part in St. Leger's forays. Kearney mentions 13 as the number killed in Cashel.

But all the rest of the English were saved by the inhabitants and by the Roman Catholic clergy of the Town, who, in the streets exposed themselves to rescue them. Some of those preserved were Dr. Pullein, his wife and children who were protected by the Jesuits (*illegible*) Darling, and one Banks by Richard Conroy, Rowland Lynch and his wife and children by William Kearney; etc.

I cannot here enter into the details of the Cashel murders. They are bad, indeed, but the circumstances are not those of general massacre. Mr. Kearney's evidence clearly shows where the " massacre " began.

" I do the wrong, and first begin to brawl," says Gloster. And after the same fashion we find the accusers of the insurgents very loud and vehement in charging the latter with such cruelties and atrocities as they were themselves practising under the name of "service" acceptable to the State. Nalson, who holds rather exaggerated views as to the excesses of the Irish rebels, hits off the pharisaical attitude of " the State " party in Ireland :

I think, and on all occasions shall endeavour to make it appear, that the Rebellion of the Irish was a most horrid and treasonable defection from their duty and loyalty, and carried on with *most* barbarous and unexampled cruelty. . . .
There is not any one particular which has been exaggerated with more vehemence than the cruelty of the Rebels, by Sir John Temple, Dr. Borlase and others ; and, doubtless, their cruelty was strange and barbarous ; but, then, *on the other side there is not the least mention of any cruelty exercised upon the Irish*, or of the hard measures they received from some of the Board in Ireland who were of the parliamentarian faction and Scottish religion ; *which rendered them desperate, and made the rebellion universal ;* they take no notice of the severities of the Provost Martials, nor of the barbarism of the soldiers to the Irish, which was such that I have heard a relation of my own, who was a captain in that service Relate, that *no manner of compassion or discrimination was shown* either to Age or Sex, but that the little children were promiscuously sufferers with the Guilty, and that if any who had some grains of compassion reprehended the soldiers for this unchristian inhumanity, they would scoffingly reply, *Why ? Nits will be lice*, and so would despatch them !

So that Captain Adair, the baby-killer, was by no means singular in his " first blood." What follows may be put against Froude's suggestion that the Irish exiles of the seventeenth century, in guilty silence, never attempted to deny *the fact* of " the massacre."

And certainly, as to acknowledge an undeniable truth, does in no manner excuse the barbarous cruelty of the Rebels ; so to deny or smother Matters of Fact so easily to be proved, even by many Protestants still alive, has given the Papists the advantage *to bring into question, especially in foreign courts,* the truth of all those inhuman cruelties which are charged upon them by such writers as are found guilty of such manifest partiality.

—Nalson, ii., Intro. pp. vi., vii.

One could make allowance for the glaring partiality of big pamphleteers, like Temple and Borlase, who were in the fray, but it is otherwise with writers of later times, who, instead of approaching the subject in the spirit of fair play, must needs have on one side nothing but demons and butchers, while on the other side they find only—"sheep ; " and these findings, we are supposed to accept as history ! It was not the King, but those most opposed to the King, who, in those days, could do no wrong.

Many writers have made allusion to the achievements of an officer in the North whom Borlase thus holds up as the model of his order :

That, *from Hercules his foot,* the success and courage of the English may be drawn, accept an abbreviate of Sir William Cole's services with his regiment, consisting of 500 foot and one troop of horse out of his garrison of Enniskillen, performed in the counties of Fermanagh, Tyrone, Monaghan, Cavan, Leitrim, Sligo, and Donegal, since the 23rd of October, 1641 : —

Swordsmen of the rebels killed in several fights and skirmishes, that account hath been taken of	2417
Starved and famished of the vulgar sort whose goods were seized on by this regiment	7000
English and Scotch Protestants rescued from bondage, and relieved by this regiment	5467
Colours taken from rebels in those fights	13
Drums (with some arms) taken from them	11
Boats taken from them in Lough Erne and Lough Melvin	27
Cots broken and sunk there	109
Islands taken and cleared in Lough Erne	365
,, ,, ,, ,, Melvin	6
Leather boats or curraghs taken from them by sea-service at Teelin Head, and Lough Erne	10
Boats gained by sea from them by this regiment	5
Castles taken from the rebels (Castles of Newport-town, Atkinson, Knockballymore and Hasset).*	4

Incidently, and unintentionally, some compliment is paid to the rebels, for isn't it a good deal to their credit that

---

* The particulars are of some interest, apart from the atrocities so revealed. Lough Erne is credited with " an island for every day in the year." The same claim is sometimes set up on behalf of Clew Bay.

L

they had reserved between five and six thousand Protestants from the " universal slaughter ! "

Now, in this "abbreviate" there may be an element of bluff, but all the same it shows the spirit which then actuated the English no less than the Scotch garrison commanders in Ireland. Borlase is not scrupulous in his statements regarding the Irish, but he has supplied us with a variety of contemporary documents which sometimes serve a better purpose than he intended. The figures here given he doubtless had on good authority, and, even if exaggerated, they amount to a terrible indictment of the policy then favoured by the Government, and, to my mind, they go a long way to show why it became necessary to cry out Massacre ! against the Irish. Himself an officer on active service against the rebels, the son of Lord Justice Borlase, he knew well what was expected from " good and loving subjects," and what " required " by " the State." For these reasons, if for no others, the views of Borlase regarding brother officers are of special importance when we come to estimate the horrors of that period ; for, it must not be forgotten he holds up Sir William Cole not as a solitary performer, but as a fair sample of the men who were then doing the work of Attila in Ireland. The 7,000 persons of " vulgar sort " starved and famished to death are as triumphantly paraded as if they had been so many foreign swordsmen worsted and slain in fair fight. Even though it be contended that the figures much exaggerate the devastation marked by Cole and his followers, the very fact that they are put forth as genuine by the man who was so connected with one of the chief rulers of the country as well as with the army, shows only too well what sort of " services " would in those days prove most " acceptable " to " the State." Perhaps they will help to show something more—that while the acts of some among the rebels are to be condemned and deplored, the greater " massacres " were committed by those who might plead warrant, real or implied, from the Lords Justices and Council of Ireland.

VII.

ALL SWORN!

PART FIRST.

"THIRTY-THREE volumes of depositions are preserved in the Library of Trinity College which tell the tale with perfect distinctness."

So says Froude, with an air of assurance rather pronounced for one who had not himself examined the depositions, and who could, at the time he wrote this, know them only from the garbled selections used by writers bitterly hostile to the religion and nationality of those responsible for the Insurrection of 1641. This certificate suggests that unless we take all the witnesses " as imaginary beings, forgers, liars, and calumniators," we are bound to accept " the Saint Bartholomew " of Ireland " as a fact " established on sworn testimony. In all this there is, indeed, nothing new, for the same statement had grown into a cuckoo cry among the calumniators of the Irish people more than two hundred years before Froude wrote, and has been kept up for purposes strangely supposed to be necessary to the predominant partner's interests in Ireland. The suggestion that " the massacre" (as understood by Temple and his numerous school) must be well established, because proved by witnesses on oath, has misled many generations into the belief that a regular judicial inquiry was held into all the circumstances of that unhappy movement. This view of the matter is simply a delusion ; and Froude's statement that " the most minute particulars were searched into with agonized curiosity " is but one more instance of the " agonized " extravagance with which he could write about Ireland. As I hope to show the evidence so called was collected by the earlier commissions not by way of legal inquiry, but in the way, perhaps, best calculated to serve the then political situation of " the Castle " and of the Parliament in England. The present generation can remember a sensational inquiry which may serve to show the character of that held under the warrants of Parsons and Borlase. We may well ask what would have been the result of the Parnell Commission if not only the great Russell but the alleged culprits and the Press had been shut out, and the matter left wholly in the hands of the judges, the attorney-general, the police, and *The Times*—to tell the "one consistent tale"! Yet the inquiries held in the earlier years of the rebellion were, in many respects, worse than this supposed case could be. The judges can hardly be accused of sympathy with Parnell and his supporters, but they were men not unused to legal inquiry and would, in any case, have some regard to judicial decorum. How was it in the actual case upon which such horrible fabrics of guilt and crime have been piled up?

The Commissioners appointed to take the examinations were certainly not chosen by reason of any particular qualification for judicial duty. Why the eight Commissioners were all taken from the clerical rank I cannot tell, except that they were then out of employment, and it was not the first or the last occasion on which men were chosen by the Castle on the same principle for public duty requiring better equipment than influence at head-quarters. Yet, I think it may be conceded that if the object was to rake together such matters as would serve to give not merely "the rebels" but the Irish nation and the Catholic religion a bad name, the Commissioners were worthy of the appointment, and it was through no fault of theirs if they failed to reach the high level of expectation. What sort of things they gathered into their nets I try to show further on.

Readers who are assured on the authority of a writer of Froude's celebrity that the books of depositions tell "one consistent tale" may well conclude that these papers all, or almost all, tell of deeds of blood, and that all the blood was shed by the *Irish* rebels. Many have been gulled into this notion, whose information and intelligence would seem to warrant better conclusion. Indeed, I think Froude has allowed himself to be gulled as much as any of his readers can be, for in respect of the Ireland of the seventeenth century, if not the Ireland of every century since the days of St. Patrick, his mental vision betrays infirmity analogous to colour-blindness. As regards the papers in question, the bulk of those, in a big majority of the books, have nothing to say about murder, and are concerned only with "spoil and robbery," things bad enough in their way, but not sufficient to uphold a charge of "universal massacre" or of any such massacre as the Temple-Froude school would have us entertain. Among the papers just alluded to are many which, while mainly devoted to details of " spoil," make incidental mention of murders, generally in some place of which this deponent knows little, but has been " credibly informed " or " verily thinketh and believeth " that such murders and such cruelties have been perpetrated.

The matter upon which I would most of all insist in this place is, that the depositions, so far from establishing the fact of a general massacre, or of anything approaching what Temple maintains and Froude insinuates, afford direct as well as indirect and implied proof that nothing of the kind either did take place or was ever intended to take place. I shall have occasion to mark some important differences between the depositions taken in the name of the King (who had nothing to do with the matter) and those taken in 1652-3 on behalf of the Commonwealth. In respect of these and some other aspects of the question I do not hold myself bound by the views already before the public, for I have formed my estimate, such as it is, not so much from what has appeared in print as from what I have seen in the MS. books about which Froude speaks with the freedom of one un-embarrassed by any particular acquaintance with his subject.

The writers who touch upon the stormy period to which these papers refer may in general be classed as (1) those who would set aside the depositions as *wholly* untrustworthy, and (2) those who would treat them as so many chapters of Holy Writ, not to be doubted, questioned, examined or analysed.

Froude would not, I dare say, *expressly* claim such authority for the depositions. But he writes about them as if he would have his readers put some such unquestioning faith in the " evidence," although careful, all the time to tell us nothing about what he really thinks of it himself. It seems to me that Froude's treatment of the question may, not unfairly, be put thus : " The question is—*St. Bartholo-mew* or *a dream?* I don't dictate, I leave you free to decide for yourself. You take your choice. But I can show you why you ought not to *dream*." And then he proceeds to fill his kit at Temple's shop. There is all through the performance much more of the pamphleteer's tricks of trade than of the honest historian's practice. He does not, in express terms, assure his readers that the depositions are equal in authority to the Bible, but he contrives none the less to go as far in that direction as may be necessary to set aside inquiry or doubt. To give any hint that all the big massacres—*e.g.*, Archdeacon Maxwell's "massacres"—are built upon hearsay, upon rumour that has travelled far, would only spoil the game.

It is a fault perhaps common to all—to writers of both classes above-mentioned—to treat of the depositions as of equal merit or demerit throughout. The fact is that—as I would appraise them—they are of every degree of merit from worthlessness upwards. Dr Curry has been severely criticised for describing the depositions as "a great heap of malignity and nonsense"; but he intended that description, of course, for the samples that had become known to him through the works of Jones, Temple, Borlase, Rushworth, Cox and others of that line. But keeping those selections to the front, had the doctor declared that the said samples show "heaps of malignity and nonsense," I should very heartily second the motion. All those excerpts are taken from the returns made by the first appointed commissioners, whose duty evidently was to make the rebels look as diabolical as hatred and terror could depict them; and anything and everything that might tell in that direction found ready place on the depositions without cross-examination or any embarrassing question. No wonder Curry pronounced a strong opinion as to the worthlessness of the entire collection; and, truly, it were paying to a great deal in the same selections an extravagant compliment to call them forgeries, when the absurdity is so glaring. His contemporary and opponent, Walter Harris, jeeringly asked him to examine the MSS. for himself; knowing very well that Curry was not likely to seek any favour in the same quarter. " It is not far to the College." It was not far for Harris, living in Clarendon street, and having access to the College Library. It was otherwise with the Catholic physician who had to go to a foreign land for his education and professional qualification, being shut out from the advantages offered by the Dublin University only to those who made no scruple about the " tests." Nor could he be blamed if he took, as a fair sample of the whole, what he could have without placing himself under disagreeable obligations to an institution which proscribed him because of his faith.

Considering the use to which these extracts had been put, one may feel safe in saying that Temple, Borlase, Harris —and we may pick up further examples a century and a half after Harris went to rest*—have proved more hostile to the credit of the depositions than even the " violent Nationalists like Curry and Carey." If all the papers were of the quality shown by the sample they would then tell

---

* 1761. Carey's work was published in Philadelphia in 1819. The time and the place show how inappropriate is Froude's descriptive phrase.

" one consistent tale," but it would be a very different tale from that intended in high places.

Carey's classification* of the depositions has been, of course, condemned by those who are satisfied with the " evidence " as it stands.   The only fault I can see in his treatment of the subject is that he assumes each particular examination to belong to some one class.   Now the fact is that many of them, the longer ones more especially, are of such character that one part of the statement may come under the head evidence, another part conveys only opinions, a third part may be about something that happened miles away from where the deponent was at the time, and a fourth part may be about something altogether out of the course of nature ; and all this without assuming that the deponent is consciously perjuring himself.   The statement may begin with a detail of the deponent's losses "through and by reason of the present rebellion," mentioning of how much he was " robbed, deprived, and dispoyled " by the rebels, with the values he would put on each description of goodes, chattels, etc., so taken from him by the said rebels. These are matters on which the deponent's statements may be regarded as evidence of more or less weight.   We have direct statements as to matters of fact within the knowledge of the deponent, and if we are satisfied of his veracity and judgment, we have evidence ; nor would that part of the statement be invalidated by a certain excess in the value he puts on the goods so taken.   In fact every man has a right to expect something above the market value when forced to part with what he wishes to keep.   So, also, if a man deposes to a crime which he saw committed, the matter is such as could be taken in evidence in open court.   But before the statement could be accepted as against the accused it must be corroborated, or the deponent's veracity must be above suspicion ; and in all cases there is an opening for doubt in the absence of cross-examination.   There were deponents who were certainly above forging, lying, or consciously calumniating.   Yet, how very different the general drift of their statements might have been, had they been brought under the search-light by a cross-examiner,— not   necessarily   a   Russell,   but   even   an ordinary   advocate.   One-sided   statements   taken   in camera may not be " inventions," but, all the same, they may give a strangely distorted view of what actually did occur, more especially when those conducting the examination   are   hostile   to   the   accused.   But   when   the

* It is given in Sir John Gilbert's Report in the Appendix to 8th Report of the Hist. MSS. Com.

deponent proceeds to relate what happened outside his own
knowledge, his assurance that he " has credibly heard " so,
or that he " verily believes so," he rules himself out of court.
But not out of Dean Henry Jones's court ; for it is on such
statements that the credit of " the massacre " rests. And
if, beyond all this, the deponent has some ghost stories
to reveal, we may doubt his judgment, and, whatever we
may think of his veracity we cannot put out of view that
we are asked to believe the statement of one who is in some
degree the victim of delusion.

The deposition of Dr Robert Maxwell I examine more
fully further on, and I mention it as affording examples of
all the four classes under which Carey would classify the
depositions in general. He gives long accounts of his own
personal experiences, and he speaks in high terms of Mrs.
Katherine Hovenden, the mother of Sir Phelim O'Neill.
He has his stories, too, of prodigies and apparitions. That
he is a man of strict veracity has been questioned ; but it
is hardly necessary to go so far for the present. He, poor
man ! has been made the medium of circulating more
baseless stories of massacre than any other deponent. To
him we owe the wild romances about Glynwood (Donaghmore), Killyleagh, and Brian O'Neill, which I have elsewhere dealt with, and about which I have something more
to say. Whether Dr. Maxwell did, or did not, invent the
stories, they are equally worthless as evidence. He gives
them " as the rebels did confess to this deponent." It would
not have required a Russell to dissect those " confessions,"
or to elicit how Dr. Maxwell, then a prisoner, got so far into
the confidence of the " murderers." One would think from
the wording of the deposition, that he heard all this from
some of the parties concerned in the alleged crimes. That
such baseless allegations were treated as " evidence " of a
massacre fit to " take place by the side of the Sicilian Vespers
or St. Bartholomew's Day in France " is sufficient indication
of the objects for which this " inquiry " was instituted. If
all this hearsay evidence were swept out of the depositions
" the St. Bartholomew " would go to the wall, even without
the services of the cross-examiner.

There is another feature of the depositions which alone
would distinguish them from good evidence. The deponents
are, in many cases, made to rehearse long conversations in
which " rebels" had a prominent, perhaps the chief part. The
conversation, I need hardly add, always in such cases turns
on the purpose of the rebellion, the aims and objects of its
authors and promoters. That in every case the conversation
bears out some portion of the theory favoured by " the

State " need not be wondered at when we consider that *the deposition is made in the absence of the party or parties so implicated,* that the witness, we may assume, is hostile and has " the ball at his own foot," the Commissioners being if possible, more hostile than he, towards " rebels, their comforters, aiders, and abettors." Moreover, the Commissioners have the duty or privilege of recording the evidence, and in doing so, of translating it into the phraseology of such instruments, a transformation which may possibly reach farther than the deponent is, for the moment, altogether sensible of.

It is wonderful what an amount of " information " has been collected in this way from friars and other ecclesiastics. In some cases names are given. I wish to say something more particular about Dean Henry Jones' celebrated interview with a Franciscan friar whose name we have not heard ; for the present, merely observing that, in reading those conversations so reported, I have often thought how different the version might be, had " the other side " been heard. Often have I wondered that these wily plotters of mischief (and the Commissioners and the deponents all knew that the friars could be nothing else) should, like prattling babes, be so ready to unbosom themselves and to disclose their plots and designs to any stranger who might come their way, or even to a known enemy. These friars were, as the country-folk in the North of Ireland would say, " good crack," that is, ready and entertaining in conversation ; I have no doubt they were all that ; but I have considerable doubt about many of the " sayings " with which they are credited by their reporters. I am not insensible of the shock some pious souls must experience at the bare idea of either deponents or Commissioners making any possible departure from the rigid veracity. I am aware that to some it were easier to believe that the friars were not merely the authors and " instigators " of the plot, but that, as a step to salvation, they " had one and all dyed their robes in Protestant blood." To believe all this were easy, for it is no more than one ought to expect from the agents of the Scarlet Woman ; but to suspect that there could be any tampering with the actual expressions of such friars were very wicked, indeed. And yet I have my doubts. The words and sayings attributed to these absent friars are just *too* like " what might be expected from them "—by their enemies. And it is the same also with the statements of other rebels who were not churchmen. In the depositions they are too often found to say—just what would be expected from rebels.

Of the distortion to which reported speech is, consciously or unconsciously, liable, we have an instance in the deposition of Roger Holland of Glaslough, in the County Monaghan, from which I have already drawn :

And the third day he (Friar Malone) went down to see us a-shipboard and the boatmen refused to goe along with us, pretending a leake in their vessell : Whereupon the said friar tooke a boate to goe to our boate and see whether there were a leake in it or not, and searching for the leake, he found some bibles and other prayer books, wch. said books he after cast into the fyre, and wished that he had *all the bibles in chrissendom*, and he would serve them all soe.

Now while Father Malone of Skerries (who had otherwise treated the poor fugitive Protestants with kindness and generosity) could very well have left them their Bibles and prayer-books, it is easy enough to see that his speech on the occasion is not correctly reported, although here put in a form likely enough to find acceptance ; and, as it happens another deponent who was present, supplies a version which, I have no doubt, makes a nearer approach to correctness.

The Rev. John Kerdiffe (or Cardiff) Minister of Desertcreaght, in the County Tyrone, a prisoner in the hands of Col. Richard Plunket, says :

Col. Richard Plunkett treated us with great humanitie, And in like manner did Friar Malone at Skerryes ; only this, (beside his rebellion, was condempnable in him) that he took our poor men's bibles which he found in the boate, and cutt them in pieces, cast them into the fyre, with these words that he wd. deal in like manner with *all Protestant and Puritan bibles*.

Now Roger Holland told the story as he recollected it ; but his recollection was swayed by the older impression that priests and friars are opposed to *The Bible* (not simply certain versions thereof). And when the same deponent, or the deponent's scribe, makes Father Malone say :

And hartily wished that the late Lord Lieutenant were alive ; for if he had lived, *they* had lived sure enough, and would have all the strength of the kingdom, and that *he knew very well of their plot.*

We may suspect that the version is coloured to suit the times. That the friar may have made some comparison between Strafford and the Puritan Lords Justices, much to the disadvantage of Parsons and Borlase, is not improbable. Under Strafford the Catholics had a better chance for redress of the grievances of which they complained, than under the rulers who replaced him. But how easy to give this a turn to make Strafford and the priests all rebels alike !

There has been a good deal of controversy over the question whether these depositions have all been duly sworn. I cannot think the matter of so much importance. Dr. Warner called attention to the circumstance that, as regards the attestation, he found that in "infinitely the greater number of cases," the words " duly sworn " have been scored out, the scoring being in the same ink as the writing. He also found that the matter was in many cases so much crossed out that little remained. He concludes that all those depositions are but parole evidence and of no authority. Dr. Reid, who had made a cursory examination of the MSS., pronounced Warner's opinion not well founded. Sir John Gilbert, who examined the collection, holds that Warner is right, at least as regards certain books. I should say that the word "infinitely" in Warner's statement, was not well chosen, but the crossing out of the " duly sworn " and of the substance of the deposition is very remarkable, especially in the books relating to the South. Gilbert mentions, in particular, the County Waterford book. Dr. Reid is, how- ever, right as regards the books, which he appears to have been more interested in—those relating to the North-East. In a certain way they are all right. Miss Hickson has very properly pointed out that, even where the words " duly sworn " are crossed out at the beginning, the *jurat* or *jurat coram nobis* over the Commissioners' signatures at the end, remains untouched ; and this I have observed for myself. I agree with the same able writer that the scoring out does not imply cancelling, but contraction by the omission of details. I am sure it is so, at any rate in most cases. In the Waterford book, mentioned by Sir John Gilbert, the deposition is, in a great number of cases, cut down to some- thing like this : " A B . of —— deposeth to losses by reason of the present rebellion, amounting to ——. *Jurat coram nobis* —— ——," although the original statement of particulars may fill a page, or pages, of foolscap. The usual preamble placed at the head of the deposition is cut down by the omission of the words of ceremony, leaving in general but the name and address of the deponent. These contractions are met with only (we may say) in the state- ment of losses, never in the accounts of alleged murders and cruelties ; and I believe it is correct to say that over the greater part of the South and East the depositions tell of pillage only, or of little else, the murders being few—although we have heard much of " universal massacre," and so forth.

And what does it all mean? Dr. Warner appears to imply that passages were crossed out because they were of no authority. He does not, indeed, say so, but that looks like his meaning. The fact is, that the wildest hearsay statements about massacre and cruelty, even when they go beyond all limits of reason or probability, are preserved, while the details of losses, matters within the deponent's knowledge, are swept out, as if the great object were to avoid, as far as possible, what might withdraw attention from " the waves of blood." Pillaging didn't look so wonderful in those days. They were not unfamiliar with it in England at the very same time. There was little or no use in dwelling at great length on details of pillage. To excite the people of England, the " universal massacre " was just the thing ; and to attain that object the " crimes and cruelties of the Irish could never be too much exaggerated."

To those who believe that, because the statements are made upon oath, they must therefore be accepted as reliable, it ought to be a great consolation to know that Dr. Warner's discovery has not the significance which he, perhaps, attached to it. I don't suppose there is any reason to regard the evidence as simply parole so long as the *jurat*,* attested by the commissioners, remains.   I can heartily accord them such comfort as they may find in the admission. The admission costs little, and, in my opinion, is worth little to anyone. What is the significance of the *jurat* appended to a document which carries absurdity or contradiction on the face of it ?   We are constantly reminded that these documents are " sworn." Say that they are. Does anyone pretend to believe all that is sworn in courts at the present day, where the accused are represented, and where the witnesses have to stand the fire of cross-examination ?   But it is suggested—or, rather, insisted on—that just because these depositions are " duly sworn " they are to be trusted ! Speaking of written testimony in general, I would say that while some documents may be the worse of wanting a *jurat*, others are not a whit the better of having one. There may be circumstances which justify reliance on the unsworn statement, as there may be circumstances which authorize, nay demand, the rejection of the sworn and more formal " deposition."   If only " sworn " matter were admissible, history would shrink within narrow bounds, and even then would not be all gospel. There are heaps of things in those

* In the earlier depositions this Latin style is affected, even in dating. The Commissioners appointed under the Commonwealth make use of the English equivalent ' Sworn before us,' or ' Taken before us,' even when the ' duly sworn ' appears at top. But at no period was the practice invariable.

depositions which the oath of an archangel would not render credible or possible. Sworn nonsense can be no better, and may be much worse, than any other nonsense. Is anyone prepared to hold up his right hand and declare that twelve hundred persons were put to death at Glynwood, by the Irish—that the statement must be true because it is found in the deposition of a man of position, and certified as duly sworn ? Will anyone nowadays declare his belief in the 152,000 murders sworn to by Sir Charles Coote at Lord Maguire's trial ? Or in the 154,000 put to death, as we read in Dr. Maxwell's sworn information ? And on what better authority did Clarendon (in his revised estimate) fix the number at 40,000, or Carte at 37,000—all "ridiculously impossible ? "

When all has been said, and all has been settled, about the *jurat*, only the fringe of the matter has been touched. Sir John Gilbert has been represented as making frivolous objections, but he marks the real shortcoming when he points out the large part that " hearsay " plays in all the evidence of massacre, and the unsatisfactory way in which the information was taken, no test, it is evident, being applied beyond the administration of an oath. Now I do not attach so great importance to his objection to the ability of the Commissioners and the social standing of the witnesses. No illiterate witness has come up to the Rev. Dr. Maxwell* in putting on record huge fables. That the clergymen appointed to collect the evidence were or were not of any eminence is, I should say, hardly worth considering. That the Chief of the Commission, Dr. Henry Jones,† was eminent in the art of getting on in the world is certain enough ; he was a member of an eminently prosperous family, and he was equal to any of them in making sure of the loaves and fishes. That Dr. Jones was an able as well

* Robert Maxwell, D.D., of the University of Dublin, Rector of Tynan and Archdeacon of Down ; consecrated Bishop of Kilmore in St. Patrick's, Dublin, 24 March, 1643-4 ; the See of Ardagh granted him by Charles II., 24 Feb., 1660-1 ; held both Sees till his death, 16th Nov., 1672.—*Ware's Bishops*, p. 243.

† Henry Jones, Dean of Kilmore, son of Louis Jones, Bishop of Killaloe ; consecrated Bishop of Clogher in Christ's Church, Dublin, 9 Nov., 1645, the King having appointed him, on the recommendation of the Marquis of Ormonde. 'Yet he was not so straight-laced in point of loyalty to his Prince and Benefactor but that he could accept of an employment under the usurper of his Crown. For we are told that he was Scout-Master General to Oliver Cromwell's army, a post not so decent for one of his function. . . . However, he afterwards appeared early in favour of the Restoration, which gave him interest enough to secure his promotion to the See of Meath, on the death of Bishop Leslie. . . . Two of his children, Ambrose and Alice, changed their religion, and died bigoted Papists.'—Harris's *Ware* (' *Bishops* '), p. 160.

as ambitious man, need not be questioned. The other Commissioners were, perhaps, able enough for the kind of work they were put to. Had it been intended to hold a regular judicial inquiry into the state of the country, I should then say that they were not the right men to conduct such an investigation. But for making out bills of indictment against not merely " the rebels " but against the Popish religion in general, and against the Irish nation in particular, it may well be doubted whether any more fitting instruments could then have been chosen or found.

The question of language has, I think, a wider import than Gilbert appears to give it. I would say that there were many deponents able perhaps to speak or understand the English of everyday life, and who, at the same time, would have but an imperfect understanding of the quasi-legal jargon in which their answers were taken down. And it is also rather likely that the Commissioners were just as far from understanding the English of people who, among themselves, used only the Gaelic. It is to be remembered that the deponents are not all English or British. And the English spoken by the British settlers was not the language in which these depositions have been written. If, as Macaulay assures us, in England, so late as 1685, "Country gentlemen spoke the dialect of clowns," what may have been the dialect of the rustic deponents who are supposed to speak in the terms handed down to us by the learned Commissioners ? Even without a disposition to turn matters to pre-arranged account, it would not be easy for the Commissioners, in many instances, to make faithful returns of what was put before them. The intercourse between Protestant clergymen and the peasantry must, in those days, have been of a very distant character. But the fact appears to be that pressure was put upon deponents to make statements which would fall in with State requirements. I am well aware how dreadful a thing it is to impute anything like irregular practices to those Rev. Commissioners—how much easier it would be to many to swallow " waves of blood "—ay, to ship whole " seas of blood "—than to hear a whisper against those gentlemen. But I am not speaking of them as clergymen, or as Protestants. I speak of them only as a particular class of " Removables," whose first duty was to make themselves well informed as to what was " wanted," and then to do their utmost to supply the want. One thing, at any rate, is beyond denial : the " witnesses " were encouraged to the wildest and most extravagant rehearsal of what they heard about what had occurred—or should have occurred—in parts of the country which were to them very much as " regions in Cathay." The very sort of thing which would be scouted out of a proper court of inquiry, in this became a matter of foremost importance, and received the utmost encouragement.

All this implies no imputation against the " veracity " of the deponents. They did not necessarily perjure themselves in putting forth fables founded on hearsay, when the Commissioners had an ear for such recitals, when, indeed, the Commissioners drew out the deponents as to what they had heard going the round of the neighbourhood. It is idle to talk of the *veracity* of those who deal in hearsay, and who feel bound to supply it to order. We may, in nearly all cases where numbers are mentioned, distrust the deponent's *arithmetic*, without reference to his or her veracity. Many deponents glibly mention thousands, when they have, we may suppose, about as much idea of a thousand as of the distance of the nearest fixed star. It is not the *witnesses* who stand in need of vindication, but the Commissioners, the more eminent members of " the State " who marked out the lines of inquiry, and, above all, the " historians " who have made such scandalous use of the things collected by that board of examination.

I do not mean that in such an " inquiry " hearsay ought to be wholly excluded. Hearsay might very properly be noted as *a basis of further inquiry and investigation*. But the hearsay that goes no further is a fraud, if put forth as *sworn testimony ;* and I submit that such is the testimony on which " the massacre "—Temple's massacre—Froude's massacre—mainly, or wholly, rests. Everyone of Archdeacon Maxwell's big massacres rests on that foundation, and on no other. The wild statement is taken as *the confession* of " the rebels " (not one of them named). There is no further investigation of the terrible allegations. The monstrous charges are sent forth as *testified on oath !* A judge of the High Court of Justice accepts the allegations as duly sworn. An eighteenth-century historian gives currency to the calumnies. And most extraordinary of all, a nineteenth century historian of reputation gives an assurance that all is regular and trustworthy !

It is a delusion to suppose that " the massacre " which " held a place of infamy by the side of the Sicilian Vespers and the Massacre of St. Bartholomew " rests on the statement of *witnesses*. We owe that massacre to the infamous use made of hearsay stories and rumours, dignified by the name of " sworn evidence."

" Historians " have done all they could to keep up that delusion. Some of them, I dare say, could hardly be aware of the extent of hearsay evidence at the bottom of the charge. And writers of better information sometimes seem unable to get on the straight course. Miss Hickson, who has devoted much time and labour to the depositions, writes :

> The unfortunate deponents in 1641–4, swore not only as to the murders which they had *seen* committed, but also swore as to the losses they had sustained.—*Ireland in 17th Century. Intro.*, p. 131.

Now that little word " seen ". has got into a strange situation there. Those who take that, served up on the authority of a writer whose means of information were so ample, may well suppose that " the massacre " is proved by *eye-witnesses*—some murders are ; but the number is insignificant when compared with the big hecatombs of which the deponents only " credibly heard."

Of the " big things " resting on " hearsay " I have given some striking examples in other papers. Did Peter Hill, Esquire, *see* the Lough Kernan tragedy of which he draws so lurid a picture ? Or did he see the Ballagh " murders," although he depicts a massacre there with so much vividness and harrowing particulars ? It does not appear that this important " witness " saw any murders committed, except those committed by himself under the name and style of " acceptable service." *The most extraordinary testimony* as to " St. Bartholomew " *comes from those who were in prison at the time the slaughters* should have been committed elsewhere. Captain Henry Smith who was kept prisoner for twenty-seven weeks—from 23rd October, 1641, till 3rd May, 1642—testifies *from common report* to the drowning of over a hundred people at Scarva-bridge, and to the murder of Mr. Tudge and his friends. These were small " services " compared with what Dr. Maxwell was able to render. He does not pretend to have seen any of the big massacres to which he bears testimony, " on the confession of the rebels themselves " ; he didn't see the 1,200 and more put to death ; although one might almost think that if this deponent hadn't, at least Walter Harris had, seen the " bloody Papists," " like ravenous wolves," fly at their 1,200 defenceless victims, and mercilessly put all to death ! And all this took place in the parish of a rev. deponent (Mr. Dunphine) who had heard of murders in various places, but evidently never heard of any within or near his own parish. Possibly some rising Froude may discover that the very prodigiousness of the slaughter had worked oblivion in the brain of the worthy parson. To pretend that such " massacres " are given " on the authority of the rebels themselves," or the authority of any but the

Commissioners themselves, is a wretched imposture. And the imposture has duped, and continues to dupe, able and fair-minded men till the present hour.

At the trial of Lord Muskerry, the President of the High Court, Sir Gerard Lowther, had the coolness to remind the prisoner of having borne a part in the massacre of 300,000 British and Protestants ! At the trial of Sir Phelim O'Neill, the same high judicial functionary accepted all the hearsay statements in the depositions as evidence ! This is, I think, clear enough from his notes of what was produced against the prisoner.* These notes, written in a rapid, almost illegible scrawl, are succinct and business-like in form. Under the several charges he ranges first the witnesses for the prosecution, then those for the defence, each set being separately numbered. The circumstance to which I attach particular importance is this : After the name of witness the word " present " † appears in some instances, *but not in all*. The meaning, as I take it, is this : the word " present " denotes that the " witness " was examined in Court ; the other " witnesses " were represented by their " depositions " taken, perhaps, ten or eleven years before, said depositions being read or filed in court. Among those marked " present " are, Michael Harrison, Mr. Simpson, Jane Beare, Joseph Traverse, Mr. John Kerdiffe, Mr. Dixon, etc. And among those *not* so marked is Dr. Robert Maxwell.‡ Now one might think that Dr. Robert Maxwell ought to have been there, whoever else was not—the man who could tell more than all the rest put together about the " massacres," who had been a prisoner at Kynard, where he had conversations with the accused Sir Phelim, and was able to see a good deal of what was going on. Would it be very shocking to suggest that

* *Stearne MSS.*, F. 4, 16, T.C.D.

† Miss Hickson expands ' present ' into ' present in Court and swears.'

‡ If for no other purpose, Dr. Maxwell ought to have been in court to verify the following, which stands part of his deposition : " And further saith that in March, 1641, Alexander Hovenden, by Sir Phelim's direction, sent from the Camp before Drogheda, a prophecy said to be found in the Abbey of Kells, importing that Tyrone, or Sir Phelim, (after the Conquest and Settlement of Ireland, should fight five Set Battles in England ; in the last whereof he should be killed upon Dunsmore Heath, but not before he had driven King Charles with his whole Posterity out of England, who should be afterwards *profugi in terra aliena in æternum*. The paper itself, with the deponent's whole Library, to the value of seven or eight hundred pounds, was lately *burnt by the Scots* under the Conduct of the Lord Viscount Montgomery ; Since that Prophecy the deponent saith he hath often seen Captain Tirlagh MacBrien ôNeil, a great man in the County Armagh, with many others, no mean commanders, drinking healths upon the knee to Sir Phelim ôNeil, Lord General of the Catholic Army in Ulster, Earl of Tyrone, and KING OF IRELAND ! But the deponent professeth (*in verbo Christiano*) he did never pledge that health ; although sometimes he fled it with hazard of his life, if he had been observed."

M

this "witness" of so many great "massacres" was kept
away, as it might not be altogether convenient to have him
brought face to face with the prisoner, his former jailer ?   Be
that as it may, the sworn deposition appeared to be none
the worse of the deponent's not being in court ; and this is
how it appears on the Lord President's notes :

> Dr. Robt. Maxwell (*) :
>   900 in County Antrim.
> 1,200 more there.
> 1,000 in County Down.
>   100 (*Remark scored out.*)
> 2,000 murdered in   (*illegible*):
> 1,200 in Glenwoods.
> 1,000 Portadown.
> As many more besides yt and in ye Logh of Mountjoy.
> 36 at Corbridge.
> 18 or 19, and 56 at severall places near the examts. house.
> 600 (about) died of famine, etc.
> 154,000 from ye beginning to ye March following.
> Apparations at Portadown. †

Now surely the witness who could prove to so many
dreadful massacres of innocents ought to have been present
in court, or the trial was but an idle ceremony—the accused
could have been found guilty without going to such rounds.
It might be that the Bishop was then ill or otherwise unable
to attend.   But to secure the attendance of a less important
witness, trials have been postponed.   I know that " reasons "
could be assigned for the non-attendance of the man who, for
his part, had undertaken to account for eight or nine thousand
murders ; but would the right reason be among them ?
I would say that something more than the " mere gnat of
a flaw " is discoverable here.

There is, in Mr. Attorney's speech, another and much
longer summary of particulars of charges against Sir Phelim
and his party, the items being numbered 1 to 20.   All the
foregoing are included.   I give the principal additional
charges :

>   4. 3,000 in ye parish of Loughgall, above 2 (*ie.*, not including
> those drowned at Portadown.)
>   6. 1,200 in Killaman.
> 13. 100 and 80, 60, 50, 60 at Scarvah bridge.
> 19. 4,000 drowned in ye County of Armagh.

Whether this 4,000 is to include the 3,000 for Loughgall
and those who perished at Portadown, doesn't much matter

---

* If the ' witness ' had appeared, the word ' present ' would be entered here.

† Miss Hickson has omitted the portion of Sir Phelim's trial from which this
abstract is taken (MS. notes, p. 69, in F. 4-16).

If anyone wishes to tot them up, there they are, as noted by the Lord President of the High Court of Justice. It seems to me just as easy to swallow them one way as another.

This Lord President of the High Court of Justice, under the Commonwealth, was himself a sufferer to a considerable amount by reason of the Rebellion. On 26 February, 1641-2 (being then Chief Justice of his Majesty's Court of Common Pleas) he made a deposition " *coram* Hen. Jones, John Sterne, Randall Adams and Henry Brereton," in which he proves to loss of rent £400 a year, in the Counties Fermanagh and Wexford, with debts and arrears amounting to £1100. And I believe all the members of the Privy Council had similar statements to make, their pecuniary losses, we may suppose, helping to sharpen their measures towards the rebels. Captain Michael Jones " of the Citty of Dublin," who at a later stage made his mark, proves to the loss of rents from lands in the Counties of Cavan and Monaghan, amounting to £249 yearly, besides debts due to him. I mention this, by the way, my object being to introduce his reverend brother, the Dean of Kilmore, in the capacity of deponent, he being at the time the Chief Commissioner for the taking such examinations * ; I can hardly call this article a " deposition " ; it seems to me to have been intended rather as a manifesto for the guidance of his colleagues, suggesting topics for particular attention in the management of the examinations. This pronounce-ment was sworn † before five of his colleagues in the commission, namely, " *coram* Roger Puttock, John Sterne, John Watson, Will. Aldrich, and Will. Hitchcock," the remaining two members of the commission, Henry Brereton and Randall Adams, being, perhaps, otherwise engaged. The preamble sets out the objects of the commission as first issued (23rd December, 1641) :

I, Henry Jones, Doctor in Divinity, in obedience to His Matys Comission requireing an accompt of the losses of his loyall subjects, wherein they suffered by the present Rebellion in Ireland, and requireing an accompt of *what traiterous wordes, proiects,* or *Actions were done, said, or plotted* by the actors or the Abettors in that Rebellion, Do make and give the following report of the premises to the best of my knowledge upon oath, vizt., etc.

* There are two volumes of depositions for Dublin. Dr. Henry Jones occupies the first place in the first volume, and he is followed by Dr. Robert Maxwell. Dr. Jones makes a second deposition, but I treat of the one con-taining his celebrated interview with the Franciscan friar.

† '*Jurat* iii., Maii 1641 ' (*sic.*). This apparently is the reading, but it cannot be right. Possibly the ' Maii ' ought to be ' Mar,' and then the year would be 1641-2.

The absence of all reference to " murder " or " massacre " in the commission, issued just two calendar months after the outbreak, is well worthy the attention of those who may be disposed to accept the current statement that within a week " the Irish rebellion had grown to be an Irish massacre." If such were true at any time between the 23rd October and the 23rd December, then the Lords Justices and Council must have been disposed to let murder work its way.

The instruction anent " traitorous words, projects, and actions," covers a vast scope of ground, and gives sufficient latitude for working up any amount desirable of second-hand matters, and the commissioners were not slow to take the hint.

Dr. Jones evidently drew up his own deposition, and went through the form of " deposing," while, in reality, he was giving his colleagues an object-lesson in the science of cultured vagueness, as well as in the high art of moulding solid charges out of fleeting rumours. On page 4 of his " deposed " manifesto he introduces the mysterious inform-ant in Franciscan habit :

The last Session of Parliament being prorogued, and the time drawing nere for putting their design in execution, There was a great meeting appointed of the heades of the Romish clergie and other (*sic*) laymen of their faction, *said to be* att the Abbey of Multifarnan, in the County of Westmeath, Where a convent of ffranciscan friers being openly and peaceably possessed of the monastery (the daie of their meeting being alsoe on their St. Francis day), *about* the beginning of October last ; but *the time and the place I cannot confidently affirme*, yet, *wheresoever*, their severall opinions and discussions are as follow, Like as I have received them from a friar, a ffranciscan, and present there, being a guardian of that order, Thereupon *a man and many others* there agitated. And the question was, what course should be taken with the English and all others that were found in the whole kingdom to be Protestants.

Now about all this there is something altogether nebulous, something artistically vague. We are left in uncertainty as to the reality of the informant, the time and the place of the interview, as we are of the particulars of the meeting. Did this conversation take place before or after the 23rd of December, 1641, the date on which the first commission of inquiry was appointed ? If before that date, it could not be so long ; and Dr. Jones ought to have been able to find the obliging " ffranciscan." If after the 23rd December, why didn't the Chief Commissioner take the information in regular form ? He had power to compel the attendance of witnesses who could give important information ; and who more fitting to be called than this " ffranciscan "—if he had

not already vanished into thin air ?   There was no such
delicacy about giving the names of other friars of whom we
hear a good deal in the depositions.   It is very lame to allege,
or to suppose, that the information was obtained under
promise of secrecy.   Apart from that, how comes it that we
have not heard the name of any of those " heads of the
Romish clergie " or the name of any layman alleged to be
present " wheresoever " the meeting was held ?   We can
imagine that Dr. Jones would have an " agonized curiosity "
to learn the names ; and if he got them, I don't believe his
tenderness would oblige him to keep them to himself.   But
with a modesty not exactly characteristic of the same active
divine, he does not assume any knowledge of the proposers
of the resolutions which, as he assures us, had so momentous
issue.   " *A man and many others there agitated ! *"   *That*
man surely was a rebel, if any man was ; yet he remains to
us " a man in buckram," and the " many others " are left
in impenetrable mystery.   There is much room—but it is
hardly necessary—to say that the " ffranciscan " was but
another sort of " Mrs. Harris."   It is enough to keep steadily
in view the one thing about which we can feel quite certain ;
the deposition sets before us the Dean's version of the
Friar's version of what was said by " a man and many
others " at a meeting of nameless people held at some uncertain place, some time before the insurrection broke forth.
The deposition had, none the less, the great merit of serving
its purpose to the full.   It proceeds :

The Council was therein divided.   *Some* were for the banishment
without attempting on their lives :   For this was given the Kinge
of Spaine's expellinge out of Granada and other parts of his dominions,
the Mores to the number of many hundreds of thousands ;   All
of them being dismissed with their lives, wives and children, with
some of their goods, if not the most part :   That this his way
of proceeding redownded much to the honour of Spaine, Whereas
the slaughters of many innocents would have laid an everlasting
blemish of cruelty on yt State.   That the usage of the English to
their neighbours, and to whom many there present owed (if noe
more) yet their education, would gain much to the cawse both in
England & other parts.   That their goodes and estates seazed upon
would be sufficient without medling with their persons.   That if
the contrary course were taken, and theire blood spilt, besides the
curse it would draw from heaven upon theire cawse, it might
with all incense and provoak the neighbour kingdom of England
to the takeing of a more severe revenge on them and theires,
even to extirpation (if it had the upr (?) hand).

On the other side was urged a contrary proceeding to the Utter
cutting off, them and theirs ; and to instance of the dismissed Moores.
Itt was answered,   That that was the sole Act of the King and
Queene of Spaine contrary to the advice of their Counsell, which,

howsoever, it might gain that Prince a name of mercie : yet, therein, the event showed him to be most unmerciefull, not only to his owne, but to all Chrissendome besides :   That this was evident in the great and excessive charge that Spaine hath bin sinse that time put unto by theis Moores and their posterity to this day.   All Chrissendome alsoe hath and doth still groane under the miseries it doth suffer by ye piracie of Algiers, Sally, and the like Denne of theeves :   That *all this might have been prevented in one hour by a generall massacre,* applying that *it was no less dangerous to expell the English,* that theis robbed and banished men might againe re-turne with their swordes in their handes. . . . *That therefore, a generall massacre were the saffest and readiest way* for freeing the kingdome of any such fears.

Now what privilege of secrecy could be claimed on behalf of the proposer of such a resolution ?   Why was not that man dragged into the light of day, while, at the very same time, other men were put on the rack with the object of extorting some revelation or other !   I submit that there is a lamentable lack of fair dealing about all this, although it may not be beyond the powers of the ingenious to *find* a reason.   We get no hint of how many may have been in favour of such a course.   It is left in such a way as to smirch the Irish Catholics—not merely the proposer, if it ever had a proposer.

In which diversity of opinion, howsoever, the first prevailed with some, for with the ffranciscans (saith this guardian), did stand, yet others *inclining to* the second, some again leaning to a middle way neither to dismiss nor kill.   And *according to this doe we find the event and course of their proceeding.*

The " ffranciscans " ought to be sensible of the high distinction of being so singled out from among the " Romish " clergy of Ireland, all the rest being, by implication, here committed to the " universal slaughter " !   The whole thing is calculated to take the attention of those *who knew,* all along, that when mischief was afoot the priests were at the root of it.   The core, when looked into, is rotten, but the rind maketh goodly show.   Even the best disposed writers have not escaped the seduction of that interview.   They have been too easily satisfied with Dean Jones's deductions, and have not, I fear, taken any trouble to examine the grounds for themselves.   The Dean continues, now speaking for himself :

In some places they are generally put to the sword and other miserable ends :   Some restrained their persons in durance, *knowing it to be in their hands to despatch them att their pleasure,* in the meantime they being preserved either for proffitt by their ransome or by exchange for prisoners, or gaining their owne pardons by the lives of their prisoners, &c.

And having developed his theory as to the origin and working out of the plot, he concludes with this short but pithy prayer :

All which their treacherous, vaine and angrie projects, God disappoint!

—a prayer which, without doubt, came from his heart. To those who believe that rebellion is the natural condition of the Irish people, and that the " Romanist " clergy find occupation in promoting ʻturbulence and violence, the statement of Dr. Henry Jones may be quite satisfactory. But let it be examined, and it will, I have some confidence, be found, in almost every particular, and from every point of view but the one just indicated, eminently *un*satisfactory.

Take, for instance, the conclusions which have been adopted by Warner, and substantially by some more recent historians who have adopted Warner's views concerning Temple and his followers. " In some places they are generally put to the sword and other miserable ends." Now in what place has anything of the kind happened—the whole or the principal part of the Protestant population put to death in cold blood ? If true of any part of Ireland it ought to be of Loughgall and neighbourhood in the County of Armagh ; and, although we have been confidently told—by deponents who are ' credibly informed and verily persuaded the same is true '—of thousands who perished miserably ; yet no one, I think, has ventured to say that the Protestants there or thereabouts were *generally* put to death. In fact, if we believe what we have been told of that locality, we need have no hesitation about accepting the 300,000 certified by Sir John Temple and Sir Gerard Lowther, or even the 600,000 which Milton* appeared to regard as a probable estimate—rather under than over the mark ! There is no instance of such a state of things as Dr. Jones alludes to ; he cannot be supposed to allude to Sir Phelim O'Neill's burst of passion on the 6th of May, 1642, (for the deposition is of earlier date), nor, bad as it was, would it in any case serve his purpose. It will be seen from the Dean's statement, he will have it that none of the Protestants were spared through motives of humanity or with any higher object than that those so excepted from immediate slaughter might be turned to account ; and if no advantage could be derived—why, then they could be killed at any time. Now I have no hesitation in pronouncing this allegation as vile and as baseless a calumny as the

* In second edition of *Iconoclastes*, ch. xii.

slaughter of the 300,000, or, if you like, the 600,000 !
How would Dean Jones, on this principle, account for the
crowds of Protestants who were escorted through his own
County of Cavan towards Dublin ?   That the head of the
commission of inquiry should thus set the example of
calumny is no bad earnest of the lines on which that inquiry
is to be conducted. It is well to remember that Dean Jones
included his own deposition in the " Romonstrance " which
he circulated in England, in the middle of 1642 ; and he
" deposed " just in time for that publication.

There is, however, another way of testing the Dean's
conclusions. We have to keep in view what his contention
is—that the plan of operations was settled at this mysterious
meeting, this meeting which must have been held in some
dark cellar, perhaps in one of these " vaults " excavated
under the Hill of Rockoll.* Now, even if we are to assume
the fact of the meeting and of the " diversity of opinion,"
as related, before we can accept the Dean's conclusions,
we must be shown, and ought to be shown, that the parties
who stood up for general massacre were men connected
with, or had influence in the localities or districts wherein
the murders were committed—where the Protestants were
" generally put to the sword and other miserable ends."
Failing this what becomes of the theory ?   The Dean—
wisely perhaps—makes no attempt to establish any such
connection. His unwillingness to afford any definite information on the points essential to his findings, stamps the
statement as untrustworthy. I don't say it is a fiction all
through ; but I do say that Dean Jones has gone to a great
deal of trouble to inform us how he discovered a mare's
nest. If we are not to take the whole thing as a fraud or a
hoax, we may, at any rate, regard it as a striking example
of the use which can be made of speech reported and re-
reported at second-hand, every particular which might
serve as a test being artfully suppressed. We are asked to
find here the clearest proof that the Roman Catholic clergy
and their people were implicated in all the blood and crime
—" as Mrs. Harris says."

That deposition—" manifesto," I still prefer to call it
—furnishes the key-note of the inquiry. The Dean's
colleagues would, indeed, be very dense if they failed to
learn the lesson here set before them. They were shown
how things which, to the common mind, were fit only to be
rejected, might be put together in such a way as to look
substantial ; how hearsay and wild rumour might be turned

* Vide, p. 75.

to good account in the interests of "the State"; how
charges preferred by nameless informants against nameless
criminals had, all the more on that account, the quality
of applying to rebels generally ; and how easy it was to
bring in the Romish clergy and the Romish land-owners
as ring-leaders of the evil-doers.

At this point I cannot refrain from bringing forward
what Warner has to say about this "Abbey" meeting as a
curious instance of the fascinating influence of Dean Jones
over minds otherwise having little in common with his
own :

It must be observed that Lord MacGuire takes no notice at all
in his narrative of this meeting at the Abbey of Multifarnham, and
we may presume, therefore, was neither present at it, nor had heard
anything of it ; nor does any determination appear to have been
made there of this important point.   There is no doubt but that
Dr. Jones had the above account, as he hath related, from a Franciscan
friar, one of the Guardians of the Order at this abbey, and present
at the consultation : but *it would weigh no more with me*, for a reason
given before, than many other parts of the Doctor's examination
relating to what had been said by some Popish priests before the
Rebellion, *if the event had not corresponded exactly with the account
and confirmed the truth of it.*   (*Irish Rebellion*, p. 71.)

As if a prophecy *published after the event* were any proof
of inspiration !   A prophecy brought to light just in time
to find place in that pamphlet (endorsed by the Lords
Justices and Council in Dublin) which Dr. Jones presented
to the English Parliament, and had from them the sole
right to print and publish the same.   In the opening of this
remonstrance or pamphlet, he represents the rebellion as
got up "by the instigation of Popish Priests, Friars, and
Jesuits, with other fire-brands . . . As also by reason
of *the surfeit of that freedom and indulgence* which, through
God's forbearance, for our Tryall, *they of the Popish faction
have hitherto enjoyed in this Kingdom.*" (*Vide* p. 117 *note*.)

Nor does Warner stand alone.   It is not a little remarkable
how the writers of "the things called histories," have followed,
almost as by instinct, the lines marked out by Dean Jones
for the guidance of his colleagues in the "inquiry," and for
the information of the people of England.   I am not sure
that any British writer has kept clear of the Dean's bird-lime,
while the number of those who, however unconsciously,
accept him on trust, is beyond reckoning.   But take the
"historians" of the more popular order, and, in dealing with
this period, don't they, as a rule, seem over-weighted with
the self-imposed duty of making war upon Rome ?   It is
not the rebels, but the "Romanists" and the priests that

trouble them most.   With zeal, well-intended we may suppose, but rather obtrusive than discreet, while trying to write history, they must needs be wrestling with the Pope, who by this time ought to be well used to bad falls.   This sort of thing is rather characteristic of Dr. Reid's great work,* and in a greater or less degree of works influenced by his.   Some otherwise valuable contributions to the history of that troublous time are vitiated by reliance on that "ffranciscan" revelation.   The dominant idea with some of our more distinguished writers—whether sensible or not of it themselves—is that the rebellion of 1641 was simply a Popish conspiracy against the Protestants, and that the whole thing was "contrived by the priests."   And although the name is legion, of writers who hold to the theory of "the State," as laid down by Dean Henry Jones and his reverend colleagues, yet it seems, in those all the more pronounced, or all the more disappointing, who make a show of liberality.   In going through certain books I have often been reminded of what an elder of the Kirk in a northern county once said to me of a person whom I didn't know :   "He's a Roman Catholic, *but he's a right dacent fellow.*"   To be a "Romanist" and, at the same time, "a dacent fellow" was surely worth noting ; and, in somewhat similar strain, our authors compliment a few individuals at the expense of their Church and nation.   I don't know how such compliments "take" with "Roman Catholics of any eminence."   I should think them nauseous and offensive (although I am sure nothing in the way of offence is intended). We are also reminded that even in those days there were *a few* priests who showed some humanity towards the suffering Protestants ; but they were very few, and in no way representative of the great body of their fellow-workers in the Church.   In fact there is a suggestion, almost as forcible as if expressed, that the Romish priests of that time, if not of every time, were not merely very wicked, but very foolish, and that their sole occupation was in designing and working out projects of iniquity.   Now the honest Presbyterian farmer was quite unconscious of the humour in his remark; and I am certain the same man never was guilty of deliberate offence.   And able writers sometimes as unwittingly get into comic situations, their intellects being so saturated with horror of that dreadful "Romanism" which appears to harass most unsparingly those farthest removed

---

* We are assured that Dr. Reid's candour has been acknowledged by "all Roman Catholics of any eminence."   Not having any claim to such a position, I take leave to dissent from such unqualified admission ; and I do so without disparagement of the literary merits of Dr. Reid's work.

from Rome. Isn't it time to let that nonsense drop out? Or, if it must be kept up, to let it find more fitting refuge in " Bird's Nest " literature, the tracts of certain " Societies," or in Sandy Row stump oratory? It has long enough disfigured works that ought to be historical, the writers of which are not ill-qualified for their undertaking, were it not that they are so afflicted, day and night, by that cruel nightmare of " Romanism."

The glee of some writers when they think they have caught a " Romish " priest in what they seem to regard as the real character, is remarkable, and sometimes there is reason to find fault with the way in which the matter is presented. In the records of the High Court of Justice which Miss Hickson prints from the *Stearne MSS.* (F. 4. 16) in Trinity College, Dublin, the following occurs (ii., 234-5) : [*]

September, 1653.

Edmund Reilly, a priest, for murders at the Black Castle, Wicklow, on December, 29, 1645.—GUILTY.

Edmund Beirne, for same.—GUILTY.

Now this differs in two particulars—one of them of vital importance—from the original MS. :

At ye private debate, *Sept* 7, 1653.
    Edm. duff Birne,
        for   } GUILTY.
    ye murder at ye Black Castle
        of Wickloe.

And after this :
    Edm : Rely (priest)
        for   } GUILTY:
    ye murder at ye Black Castle
        of Wickloe—*as Accessary.*

As Miss Hickson prints the record, it would seem as if the Priest were the principal in the crime (or crimes), the entries being transposed and the words in *Italic* omitted. Now while the MS. notes of the trials are most difficult to decipher, the findings " at ye private debate " are written large and fair. I don't complain of the spelling being modernized, but comparison of the printed copy with the original notes has a good deal surprised me. As Miss Hickson remarks, the " evidence " against Father O'Reilly was chiefly hearsay ; and she enters into a long explanation to account for the discharge of the prisoner. I think it would be more to the credit of the Government of the Commonwealth

[*] Also ii., 229, names in same order ; same omission of ' as accessary.'

(which Miss H. so much admires), as well as more consistent
with the facts of the trial, to say that Father (afterwards
Archbishop) O'Reilly was not executed for the reason that
he was found guilty, on hearsay evidence, of being only
" accessary " to the murder.*

And if Father O'Reilly, or any other priest or bishop,
had committed murder, or had been guilty of any other
crime, the sin was his—the guilt would be upon his own
head, and not upon his Church.   These writers who so gloat
over the misdeeds actual, or imputed, of individual "Romish"
priests, would appear to have got it into their heads that
it was in this or some such way the " Romanist " Church
kept itself alive !   That it has lived, and flourishes, in spite
of—not by reason of—the few who may depart from the
path of rectitude, is the one thing the said writers cannot
or will not understand.   Dr. Reid, I suppose, by way of
showing his " candour " and " impartiality," has a gathering-
up of vile things which may, perhaps, be agreeable to his
admirers and lead them to fancy they have in these irregularities proof of *what they already know*, namely, that *such*
is the " Romanist faith."   The " love of truth " which
impels " historians " to such courses is of a morbid and very

---

* On page 241 of her second volume, Miss Hickson writes :—

' Sir Charles Gavan Duffy draws a terribly sensational picture of the
slaughter at the taking of Cashel by Murrough O'Brien, Lord Inchiquin, but
omits what *the better informed Irish Catholic contemporary of Inchiquin* takes
care to mention that one at least of those who fell on the " Rock " was Tiege
O'Kennedy, who had been a chief actor in the cold-blooded massacre of the
thirty-two unarmed men, women, and children at the Silver Mines.   If all of
the murderous brood who committed that massacre had fallen by the swords of
Inchiquin and his soldiers, it would have been, *even in the judgment of not a
few of their better disposed Roman Catholic contemporaries,* too honourable a
death for them.'

That is certainly very strange comment.   It implies—if it has any meaning
—that while a suspected murderer was among them, the people of Cashel
deserved their fate, and Inchiquin is entitled to praise, not blame, for his dreadful
deeds on the Rock !   Miss H. rebukes Sir Gavan just as Froude censures the
historians who find fault with Cromwell's ' marvellous great mercy' at
Drogheda !

Kearney (who was steward to the Duke of Ormonde, *Carte* i., 265 *n.*)
appears to be the Catholic historian referred to.   He mentions the circumstance that " Teigue O'Kennedy, ' the sixth brother,' was killed at St. Patrick's
Rock when surrounded by Lord Inchiquin's forces."   His supposed guilt, or
his presence, had no influence on Inchiquin.   And, assume that it had, are we
to take it that, to get at one suspected criminal, it matters not how many innocent
persons are slaughtered ?   Kearney says that sixteen were put to death at
Silvermines. . Miss Hickson says thirty-two, and refers to the deposition of
Ann Sherring.   In the original MS. (Tipperary Depositions, p. 415) this
deponent says ' Soe that none of those 23 men, women, nor children escaped
death.'   The figures are written distinctly.

questionable character.   Be the intention what it may, the practice amounts to misrepresentation, dishonourable only to the author who adopts it.

In the depositions relating to the County of Down, there is very little mention of priests ; and some would therefore infer that the priests could be about no good when we don't hear of it.   It is certain that, had the " Romanist clergy " been employed as suggested, we should hear all about it—perhaps something more.   Because the Mayor at the time, a Catholic, doesn't mention the matter in his deposition, Miss Hickson would cast doubt on a statement alleging that in Cashel certain priests protected Protestants. Now to the Catholic Mayor it did not seem so wonderful as to Miss Hickson, that priests should be employed in charitable work ; and, unless the question were put to him, he would, likely enough, not think of the circumstance when examined eleven years after the event.   Catholics don't think it necessary to blow a horn when a priest does his duty, although some excessively generous people will have it that the good deed, being so extraordinary, ought to be trumpeted forth to the admiration of all time.   That the good deed is the rule, and the irregularity the exception—and that it was so then as now—is, I am well aware, a thing utterly incomprehensible to some of the " unco guid."

To fix the guilt of murdering in cold blood 300,000 or 600,000 (Milton) was at the time a foremost object with all " Papist-hating men," and so continues to the present day with their representatives, clerical and literary, who feel bound to take part in the everlasting war against "Rome." The Commissioners were merely doing their part in raking together anything and everything which might serve so worthy an end.   Nothing that might serve that end could, by any means, be regarded as absurd or incredible.   Take the following, which is one of the choice flowers in Temple's anthology.*   I am rather surprised to find that Mr. Lecky refers to the circumstance as if he considered it a possible occurrence :

Alexander Creighton of Glaslough in the county of Monaghan Gent, deposeth, That *he heard it credibly reported* among the rebels aforesaid of Glaslough, that Hugh Mac O'Degan, a priest, had done a most meritorious act in drawing betwixt 40 and 50 English and Scots, in the parish of Gonally, in the County of Fermanagh, to reconciliation with the Church of Rome, and after giving them the Sacrament, demanded of them whether Christ's body was really in the Sacrament or no ; and they said, yea.   And that he demanded of them further, Whether they held the Pope to be Supream Head

* So Carey terms Temple's selections from the depositions.

of the Church ; they likewise answered he was. And that thereupon
presently told them they were in a good faith, and for fear they should
fall from it, and turn Heretics, he and the rest that were with him
cut all their throats! (*Jurat*, Mar. 1, 1641-2.)

That a writer well-informed and well-disposed should,
at this time of day, assume that this story *could* be anything
but a ridiculous hoax, shows, as I have said, how hard it is
to find a great historian who has· not unwittingly come in
contact with the Dean Jones' birdlime. This piece of
" evidence " shows, in collected form, a good deal of the
rottenness that underlies the whole business. As usual the
deponent swears on hearsay, and, of course, the wretched
and dishonest subterfuge that it is the " confession " of the
rebels themselves, confronts anyone who may be disposed
to object. It is idle to ask who these rebels were who made
so " credible " a report. We get no names, and we needn't
expect to get any ; it were as reasonable to expect to find
" Mrs. Harris " at home. As is not unusual in the case of
the particularly heinous deeds, and big massacres, the
" evidence " is procured far away from the scene of action.
And where should this have occurred ? In the County of
Fermanagh, the county in which Sir William Cole had his
head-quarters, and where chiefly he earned the glory of
slaughtering or starving to death so many thousands of people.
(*v.* p. 61).   This distinguished officer, who claims to have
rescued nearly 6,000 English and Protestants from bondage
(if not from death), ought to be able to give some account
of these " conversions." And if he could find a real live Hugh
O'Degan in the flesh, and forthwith proceeded to hang the
monster high as Haman's gallows, he would deserve credit
for at least one meritorious act. But, like the big massacres
that were so much better known in distant parts and to
witnesses who were at the time in prison than to any belonging to the neighbourhood in which the atrocities were said
to be committed, so, in this alleged instance of atrocity of
more than ordinary magnitude, the testimony comes from
afar. Now, supposing that Alexander Creighton heard the
story as he tells it, what was the clear duty of the Commissioners ?   Ought they not to have got the names of the
parties who so *credibly* reported the matter to the deponent ?
And the deponent might have been called upon to give
" the cause of his knowledge " when certifying to the
credibility of the report. In sending forward a deposition
so destitute of all means of test, the Commissioners have
writ large the condemnation of all who were in any way
responsible for the inquiry. Had they " confessed," in so
many words, that they believed the story was more "credible"

when not closely looked into, they could not, with more certainty, have indicated their opinion of the merits of the case made by their deponent. None the less, the story was good enough for Temple, and for all who put their trust in his " faithful relation." Let it not be supposed that I am, in making these strictures, trying to impeach the deponent's veracity. Alexander Creighton's mind was, perhaps, no more saturated with grotesque misconception of the Catholic religion and its ministers than the minds of many in these later times, who, regarding themselves as specially favoured and enlightened, are ever ready to remind us that they are not as the rest of men—or women. And, if the said Alexander, consciously or otherwise, described a Romish priest as ready to commit murder in the supposed interests of his church, he doubtless believed that he had discovered the typical clergyman of that order ; and there may even yet be an "enlightened" few who fancy that without such ministers as O'Degan of the story, the "Romanist faith" could not exist.

Froude's attitude is not exactly that of a member of the "Bird's Nest" school of writers ; he is professedly more anti-Nationalist than anti-"Romanist" ; but he cannot help making some effort to involve the Catholic Church in the "massacre." In the preface which he contributes to Miss Hickson's work,* he says :

The barbarities of which the Irish were accused *and were said* to have been found guilty were published to the world, and involving as they did the character of a Catholic Nation, it might have been expected their publication would have drawn forth at once an indignant contradiction. Hundreds of exiles who had been in Ireland at the beginning of the insurrection were scattered over France, Spain and Italy, and might have repudiated, had they been able, the tremendous accusation against their countrymen. They did nothing of the kind.† Individuals among them here and there, after a lapse of years, asserted that they had no share in the massacres at Portadown, at Shrule, at Silver Mines, Portnaw, Macroome, and other places, but it never seems to have occurred to them to deny *the general fact.*

The exiles denied, each as far as his own knowledge went, the truth of the wild statements given to the world on State authority. What more could these poor exiles, scattered over many lands, have done ? Perhaps they ought to have called a public meeting to denounce the calumnies !

* *Ireland in the 17th Century*, 2 vols., 1884.
† Is this true ? Nalson, who wrote just two centuries earlier than Froude, points out (*v.* extract above, p. 161) how, in their representations to foreign Courts, the Catholics had the advantage.

And what does our historian suppose the Church might
have done ?   Send a commission of inquiry to collect evidence
in Ireland ?   Or send a protest to Barbone's Parliament ?
There were many " indignant contradictions," we may be
sure enough.   But what " repudiation " would have availed
against the Parliament in England, or " the State " in
Ireland ?   Or what would denial or repudiation count with
historians of the Froude type, who will hear only the avowed
enemies of the Irish people ?   There is, in the depositions
published between 1641 and the Restoration, enough to
satisfy any man who is not biassed by interest or prejudice,
that the " evidence," so called, is to a very great extent *a
fraud*—a fraud, not because the witnesses had conspired to
forge, or lie, or calumniate, but because those who ordered
the inquiry and those who conducted the inquiry had (to
use a phrase of later origin) " an axe to grind."   Interest
and passion made the authorities of that day, and all who
acted on their behalf, dead to any sense of justice towards
the nation known as " the rebels."   All Europe, indeed,
heard of the barbarities of which "the Irish *were said* to
have been found guilty " ; but it was not so easy for the
Irish to make all Europe acquainted with the barbarities
which had driven many to action which, while technically
rebellion, was really no more than defence against the law-
lessness of those invested with State authority.   " The
general fact " was the Civil War.   To insinuate that on the
part of the Irish there was general massacre is unwarranted,
and to insinuate that Castlehaven and Temple (and why
not Milton and his 600,000 ?) alike maintain the massacre
is a very wide departure from the truth. *

And no writer of credit, Catholic or Protestant who had lived
through the rebellion, had thought of denying *it*.

What does the " it " mean here ?   They did not deny
the rebellion ; but not even one of the Catholic writers
here named admitted anything like what is insinuated—
general massacre.

Not only Temple, Borlase, and Clarendon, but the Catholics,
Clanrickarde, and Castlehaven, Father Walshe, the Franciscan

---

* In treating of Irish affairs, Froude writes with so much independence of
history that one is frequently at a loss to know whether to take him seriously ;
one cannot easily get over the feeling that he is all the time poking fun at the
gullibility of his readers.   There is room for a further suspicion, that his violent
anti-Irish tirades may be but a pretence to cloak the real sentiments of the
man.   Perhaps when the cryptic art is developed, it will be found that these
things were not written by the late James Anthony Froude, but by the late
Charles Stewart Parnell or the late Joseph Gillis Biggar, in furtherance of the
Home Rule movement.   The one thing discoverable at present is an air of
unreality far removed from sincerity in this writer's views of Ireland.

friar, Philip O'Reilly of Crom Castle, Mr. Kearney, the Catholic brother of a Catholic Bishop, with other Irish Catholic writers of the 17th century. . . . *All admit that massacres were committed.*

Observe the shuffle. " Massacres " now. These Catholic writers admit some deplorable incidents connected with the insurrection, and *therefore* they are in the same lobby as Temple, Borlase, Clarendon (and Milton)! Castlehaven, who held really exaggerated views on the crimes committed in Ulster, in effect charges Temple with falsehood and imposture. And not one of them would admit such massacre as Temple, or Borlase, or Clarendon assumes. Mr. Kearney is a strong witness for the charge of massacre against " the State " and its representatives. That there were crimes committed by the insurgents is admitted by all. But were there no crimes but theirs ? The crimes of the insurgents were too many, but they were in reality few in comparison with the crimes committed upon the people by small Attilas like Coote, Cole, St. Leger, Monro, and others acting under the warrant and the general licence of the State. The massacres committed by such commanders would of themselves account for most, if not the whole, of the crimes chargeable against the insurgents. In what country would not the same tactics on the part of rulers and their representatives have produced crime—ay, more crime than was committed then by the Irish rebels ?*

It is nonsense, if nothing worse, to talk of " the confidence with which the innocence of the Irish of any such crimes is insisted on." Let the matter be treated of all round, and the wonder will be that the crimes were not ten times what they were, considering the atrocities from which the people

---

* The audacity of calling these ' Catholic witnesses ' in support of Temple is of a high order. Father Peter Walsh, the Franciscan Friar, in his pamphlet, *The Irish Colours Folded*, addressed to the Duke of Ormond (1662), p. 3, says ;

' Your Grace knows with what horrour the Irish Nation looks upon these Massacres and Murders *in the North*, committed in the beginning of the Rebellion by the Raskall Multitude upon their innocent, unarmed, and unprovided neighbours ; but the number of Two hundred thousand (although this writer comes short One hundred thousand in his accompt of what the Convention Commissioners gave up to his Majesty in their Answer to the Irish Agents) is so exorbitantly vast that a stranger, who finds the dimensions of Ireland in the map, and understands this certain truth that *there were then in Ireland One Hundred natives* for each person these men would pass under the notion of an Englishman, will readily conclude, that the whole Iland is but one city so thronged with inhabitants as men cannot walk in the streets unjostled.'

When cut off at the semi-colon this passage can be made, by force of straining, to favour ' the massacre' theory. But the remaining portion shows how far the friar goes with Temple.

In his reply to Orrery (1664), Father Walsh says, on p. 27 :—' I said that many thousand Protestants in the three kingdoms have been far more heinously criminal both against his Majesty and his father of ever-blessed

N

suffered during the earlier period of the rebellion. " The
faithful relation " of Temple has all the crime on one side,
a circumstance which ought to have discredited him, quite
irrespective of his stupenduous exaggeration and fathered
falsehoods.

There is a comic element in Froude's lamentation over
the wrong which has been done to the Irish people by their
own historians, who have hoaxed them into the belief that
they have been calumniated as well as robbed. Very
unfortunate for the same people that they cannot be brought
to see the good feeling of Temple and his faithful followers.
Of course they would come to relish these writers if their
" agitators " and their own historians would only let them.
But the really comic thing is that English historians have
been culpably lax in not keeping up " the massacre "—of
course, the massacre of Temple, Borlase, Milton, Clarendon,
Hume, and Mrs. Catherine Macaulay and Carlyle—and the
result is truly deplorable ; perhaps the most regrettable
thing the English have done, or have not done, towards
Ireland and the Irish people :

> Thus, in the absence of any clear rejoinder, judgment is going
> by default, and we are sliding into an acknowledgment that the
> Long Parliament and their officers in Ireland were the real criminals
> and successfully carried through a conspiracy so base and infamous
> that Sir Phelim O'Neill and his confederates seem innocent in
> comparison.

This was, of course, intended as a jelly-making blow to
all those faint-hearted historians who will not put their
trust in Temple and his following. In penning this sentence
the writer must have felt that if it did not blow them sky-
high, it would at least bring home to these milk-and-water

memory, and have contributed, or intended, as little for bringing home his
Majesty as the most wickedly principled of the Roman Catholic Confederates
of Ireland ; and yet that all these Protestants are not only pardoned (except a
few of the most immediate Regicides) but equalled in all capacities with his
Majesty's most faithful and approved subjects.'

And on p. 108 – ' Though I detest all kinds of Rebellion against lawful
power, as being condemned by the laws of God and Nature, yet I can tell this
gentleman that the Rebellion of Ireland was *not only paralleled but surpassea*
by many rebellions of other countries, even amongst Christians. For not to
speak of that of Catalonia in our own days, the Sicilian Vespers, and the
butchery of the Swisses, and *the murther of the Danes in England*, and a
hundred others which we read in history did surpass it, and surpass it so :
And all those did that by design, and in effect subverted the very fundamentals
of government, Civil and Religious. And I am sure that if none else did, that
this gentleman's clients and their partakers must have done so, who made *thei*
rebellion the most unparalleled indeed by the most execrable Parricide that ever
was ; not to mention so many other adjuncts to render it *incomparably worse
than that of the Irish*.'

Heartily I can wish Froude and his friends joy of their witness !

people a sense of the absurdity of their situation. Yet it is the one sentence in which he comes more nearly in touch with the actual facts. Let all be fairly taken into account, and at least the officers of the Long Parliament in Ireland will be found to be the more blame-worthy criminals, and that their guilt, in the matter of this rebellion, far exceeds that of Sir Phelim O'Neill and his confederates, even though these were to be held responsible for all that has been laid to their charge.

One class of alleged offences, which make a figure in the depositions, may be very briefly dismissed—offences of the Jack-the-Ripper order, charges never made in Ireland before or since that Commission sat. Although Dr. Robert Maxwell happens to be among those who "on credible report" retail such incredible charges, the fact of these monstrous tales having been put on the record without any further investigation reflects the deepest disgrace on the Commissioners, and on the higher officials who were content to accept the hearsay testimony as all-sufficient. These stories, as they have been handed down to us, tell more seriously against the parties who rehearsed them, and the parties who, without test or investigation, accepted them, than against the parties who were to be blackened by them.

Dr. Henry Jones was not called to give evidence at Sir Phelim's trial although in Dublin at the time. The Prosecutor sought to widen the charges so as to embrace the plotting and contriving of the rebellion—the very thing to which Dr. Jones had devoted his energies in his own deposition. Yet that deposition is ignored by Judge and Prosecutor alike, whereas Dr. Maxwell's is largely drawn upon. Why should Dr. Jones and his deposed relation be ignored, while the files of depositions were being ransacked for matter to swell the indictment?

Jones has left a second relation in which he points to another origin for his information. In his deposition (*see* extract p. 180 above) he states positively that he had the whole story from a "ffranciscan friar, a Guardian of that order," who was present at the meeting of clergy and others when the course of the rebellion was settled. In the other version, just mentioned, there is not a word about the "ffranciscan" or the abbey, although the report of the alleged debate is practically the same. This account is contained in the T.C.D. MS. F. 3.11 (Depositions and Letters, vol. xxxii.) under "No. 14": it is in Dr. Jones's handwriting and is signed by him, but whether a *jurat* was appended does not now appear, the paper being clipped close under the signature. The first paragraph is identical with the corresponding portion of the deposition (p. 179). Then follows this significant bit of self-revelation :

And, first, to beginne with ye present troubles in this Kingdom, with the grounds pretended by the chief Acters therein for ye colouring of theire Rebellion, & theire Intentions, for ordering all things, all being (which God forbid !) reduced to theire, power : *all wch I was given to understand by my dayly conversing & discoursing wth some of ye Popish Clergie, vnto whom for this purpose I had insinuated myselfe.*

The informers of '98 and more recent times might look up to Dean Jones with " admiring despair." After giving a much laboured account of an alleged Puritan plot which " they "—the Popish clergy, perhaps—had discovered, the " insinuating " narrator proceeds :

At theire meeting upon ye said pretended discovery of what, they say, was plotted against them, it was long debated betweene the chiefe heads among them, what course should bee taken with ye English, and all others y^t were found to be protestants. Theire Council was divided into these two parts (*All wch I heard from the popish clergie whom I yet forbeare to name.*)

In withholding names, Dr. Jones exercised a wise discretion. Nor does it appear that he ever got so far as to charge any particular individual with taking part in that academic debate about " the King of Spain's expelling of the Moors." The two accounts are supposed to cover the same ground, and to refer to the same incidents. But, for the first statement, a solitary " ffranciscan " is the authority, while, for the second, the Popish clergie—as many as you please—are made responsible for the information.

At the conclusion of the second statement, Dr. Jones gives the following :

As for my private sufferings by this rebellious route, I have lost—

	li.	s.	d.
in cows, sheep, swine, riding horses, & my stud of mares & colts	500	0	0
in corne, hay, and turffe	100	0	0
in plate, household goods, & books, [& buildings at Tigher]	1200	0	0
in debts, in rents in arreare, & now due	483	10	0
in annual rents	736	0	0

3019^li 10^s 0^d

VIII.

ALL SWORN!

———

Part Second.

In comparison with the fatal operation of hearsay, other vitiating causes are of little moment ; but they are so only by comparison. Some of these affect not merely particular depositions, but in some degree lessen the value of the whole, at any rate those taken under the earlier commissions; for, as I have yet to show, there are differences between the earlier and the later examinations rather to the advantage of those taken under the Commonwealth.

All writers who have commented upon the defects of the " evidence " dwell—and I would say, very properly dwell—upon the circumstance that statements regarding prodigies and apparitions, and allegations of occurrences contrary to the course of Nature, are received in the same way as the relations of crime and outrage. It is contended by Warner, Carey, and others that as things impossible or otherwise utterly incredible are maintained on the same kind of testimony as the " massacres "—certainly the over-whelming majority of them—we can no more accept the fact of the massacre than the reality of the Portadown ghosts. I hold that this applies at least to all the " big massacres " which figure on Sir Gerard Lowther's notes of evidence, not one of which has any better foundation than hearsay, as to the occurrence or as to the estimate. We have, indeed, better evidence for the Portadown ghosts than for Harris's " massacre " of Glynwood, or any of the many reported massacres at " Scarvagh " Bridge. There are witnesses (if we choose to believe them) who swear that they *saw* the ghosts and *heard* them also ; but no one can swear to having seen any of these horrible slaughters where hundreds were said to fall almost at a single stroke. About these the news always travels far before it is heard.

Once more I must stigmatise as dishonourable and dishonest the subterfuge of seeking to cast the responsibility of such things on the rebels or any but the parties who have adopted the fables as relations of fact ; and again, I would direct attention to the circumstances that on Sir Gerard Lowther's notes the apparitions have place—fitting place, I ought to say—beside the 1,200, 2,000, 4,000, etc.*

In the Introduction, p. 136, *Ireland in the Seventeenth Century*, Miss Hickson says :

It will be seen by anyone who reads the depositions with common care that *the stories of apparitions* haunting Portadown River and other places where terrible massacres were committed, *originated, not with the Protesant deponents, but with the Irish Roman Catholic people themselves.* Of the few deponents who repeat these Tales, only one lady, Mrs. Rose Price. . . . alleges that she saw a spectral figure late one winter evening wailing in the river where her five little children and friends had been drowned a few days before.

Now supposing all this to be correct (and it is by no means correct), how does it improve the credibility of the evidence ? I say nothing against the expression of sympathy with the bereaved mother, but that, while honourable in itself, it is altogether distinct from, and without bearing on, the general value of the testimony. There need be no question of Mrs. Price's *veracity ;* and if she did see in the twilight the gaunt figure of some other distressed mourner, the question as to the worth of the evidence stands where it did Nor would the circumstance of the apparition stories originating as alleged make the

* In Lady Fanshawe's Memoirs (addressed to her son) the following entertaining passage occurs :

'We went to the Lady Honor O'Brien's . . . youngest daughter of the Earl of Thomond. There we stayed three nights. The first of which I was surprised by being laid in a chamber, when about one o'clock I heard a voice that wakened me. I drew the curtain, and, in the casement of the window, I saw by the light of the moon a woman leaning into the window, through the casement, in white, with red hair and pale ghastly complexion : she spoke aloud and in a tone I had never heard, thrice, *A horse!* and then with a sigh more like the wind than breath she vanished, and to me her body looked more like a thick cloud than substance . . . I pulled and pinched your father, who never woke during the disorder I was in ; but at last was much surprised to see me in this fright, and more so when I related the story and showed him the window opened. Neither of us slept any more that night, but he entertained me with telling me *how much more these apparitions were usual in this country than in England,* and we concluded the cause to be the great superstition of the Irish, and the want of that knowing faith which should defend them from the power of the Devill, which he exercises amongst them very much !'—pp. 92-3.

The explanation is amusing. It was the Irish superstition and the Irish want of saving faith that enabled his satanic majesty so to trouble this enlightened English lady while in Ireland ! (The time is while Cromwell was in Ireland.)

hearsay evidence one whit better—whether the rumours had a Catholic or a Protestant origin, the hearsay is hearsay still ; and the denominational element may be eliminated without turning the scales one way or other. This the old story, the subterfuge of shifting the blame of all the wild statements received in " evidence " and laying that also to the account of " the rebels." Now, if there is anything foolish or unworthy in this practice it did not originate with Miss Hickson : she merely joins in the chorus, and is hardly conscious, I dare say, even of irrelevancy. But the irrelevancy is there.

When Miss Hickson, says, " Only one lady, Mrs. Rose Price, alleges that she saw a spectral figure," etc., I am not quite sure that she means " the only deponent " who so alleges. As a matter of fact there was at least one other lady, Mrs. Cooke, who " saw a vision or spirit in the shape of a man." It may be interesting to bring together the statements of these two lady deponents anent the apparitions at Portadown bridge :

Elizabeth, the wiffe of Captain Rise Price* late of the parish and County of Armagh, deposes (*inter alia*) how she became a prisoner in the hands of ' that most bloody and cursed rebel, Manus O'Cane,' and how she was liberated on the arrival of Owen Roe O'Neill. . .

The said Owen Roe ôNeill suffered them all (about 50 prisoners), to goe up and down the country at their pleasures. And they hearing of divers apparitions and visions that were ordinarily seen neere Port-a-downe bridg since the drowning of her children and the rest of the Protestantes there ; and they being tould that the said Owen Roe ôNeill and his troope were resolved to be at Portadowne bridge to inform themselves concerning these apparitions, Shee, this deponent and her child, and those other parties, her companions att the same tym cam to Port-a-downe bridg, afore said [which was] about Candlemas last, and then and there mett the said Owen Roe ôNeile and his troope : And being all together at the water-side, there, nere the said bridg, about twylight in the evening, then and there upon a sudden, there appeared unto them a *vision or spiritt assuming the shape of a woman, waste-high* [*upright*], *in the water with elevated and closed hands, her haire dishevelled, very white, her eye seeming to twinkle in her head, and her skin as white as snowe*, wch. spiritt or vision, seeming to stand straight upright in the water, divulged, and then repeated the word, *Revenge ! Revenge ! Revenge !* &c. Whereat this deponent and the rest being put into a strange amazement, and frighted, walked a little from the place. And then presently the said Owen Roe ôNeill sent a Romish priest and a friere to speak unto it. Whereupon they asked it questions, both in English and Latin, but it

* *Rise Price.*—So I would read the MS. Miss Hickson reads ' Rose.' Temple has in one place ' Rice,' in another ' Rue ' (an evident misprint). This, like many of the names, can hardly be fixed with certainty.

confessed them nothing. When a few days after, the said Owen Roe óNeile sent his drum to the English Army for a Protestant minister, whoe coming unto him, and being by him desired to inquire of that vision or spiritt what it would have, the same minister went one evening to the vsuall place on the water-side ; whereat, the like time of the evening, the same or like spiritt or vision appeared in the like posture and shape as formerly it had done. And the same minister saying : ' In the name of the Father, the Sonne, and the Holy Ghost, what wouldst thou have, or for what standest thou there ? ' It answered, *Revenge ! Revenge !* very many times iterating the word *Revenge !*   Thereat the same minister went to prayer privately, and after they all departed, and left the same vision standing and crying out as before. But after that night, of six weeks together it neither appeared nor cried any more, that either this deponent, or any of the rest (that came thither upon purpose severall times), could heare or observe.

An extraordinary story ! And seldom, if ever, has ghost been seen to so much advantage, or been described with so much minuteness of detail.

Yet after six weeks ended, it appeared againe and cried as before. Soe as the Irish that formerly were frighted away with it, and wch. were comen againe to dwell in the English howses thereabout, In hope it would never appeare nor crye more, were then so againe affrighted that they ran quite away and forsooke the place, the lyke or the same spiritt or vision since that time appearing and crying out Revenge ! alloud every night untill the deponent and her child and late fellow prisoners came away with their convoy to Dundalk.

That this " deponent " was able on " credible " report to make a long recital of outrage and crime, is to be inferred. She has also *heard* of apparitions at the bridge besides what she herself saw :

And further saith, that the first vision or apparition after the Protestants drowned, were inshore a great number of heades in the water, wch. cried all with a voice, *Revenge ! Revenge !* &c., *as this deponent hath been credibly told by the Rebels themselves* (Whoe also tould this deponent that these apparitions were English Divells, *as is most commonly believed and reported* by most of the Irish inhabitants thereabouts.   And the Rebells discharging some shott at these, those heades, *flashes of fire thereat suddenly appeared in the water*, as she was also credibly tould.   And that quickly afterwards that shape or spiritt in the likeness of a woman appeared and cried all and every night, biginning about twilight as aforesaid.

That stories of the kind may have been heard among silly old women is possible enough, and the occurrences are as strongly vouched for on oath as most of the crimes laid to the charge of the rebels. But while these things are alleged to rest on the " confessions " of the rebels— the Irish Roman Catholic people, Miss Hickson, says—

we get no names of credible informants.   It is "Mrs. Harris," all the time.   If any representative members of "the Roman Catholic people" had come forward—the Commissioners had powers to compel attendance—and deposed to these matters, *then* would there be some grounds for saying the stories *originated* with them.   The "informants" are "credible" when most involved in mystery.   Here lies the core of rottenness in the sworn evidence.   No blame to the deponents : they supplied what was wanted ; and they would, in general, have done better, had better things been required from them.   And to brazen out the imposture, when it grows palpably ridiculous, the dodge is, shift it on "the rebels," or on "the Roman Catholic people themselves," and then proclaim to all the world that the matter rests on sworn testimony !

Katherine, relict of William Cooke, late of Clanbrassell, in the County of Armagh, sworne.* . . .

And further saith, that a great number of Rebells of the said County of Armagh did about xxth of December, 1641, most barbarously drowne at one time one hundred and four score Protestants, men, women and children in the river at the bridge of Portadowne. And about nyne days afterwards [*she sawe*] a vision or spirit in the shape of a man [as she apprehended, that] appeared in that river in the place of the drowning, bolt upright breast-high, with elevated and closed handes, and stood in that posture there [at times, more or less], untill the latter end of Lent then next following, att wch: tyme some of the English Army (whereof her husband aforenamed was one), marching by that place, many of them, and amongst the rest her said husband, (as he [and they] confidently affirmed to her, this dep[t]) sawe, that spiritt or vision standing upright and in the posture aforementioned.   But after that tyme the said spiritt or vision vanished and appeared noe more that she knoweth of [And she heard, but saw not, that there were other persons and apparitions there, and much screeching and strainge noise in that river at tymes afterward.]

It is not going too far to lay down that the strongest evidence taken by the Parsons-Borlase Commissioners goes to the credit of the Portadown ghosts.   Two eye-witnesses and quite an array of "witnesses" who have "credible report" on their side" ought to be sufficient to satisfy anyone who talks of "sworn" testimony.   The deponents who swore from hearsay are no less confident than those who saw *and heard* the ghosts.

* The passages here quoted from Mrs. Price and Mrs. Cooke are, in the MSS., marked by a vertical scoring along the margin to call attention to the specially important statements.   This is found in many depositions.   The papers were originally folded and endorsed after the manner of legal documents, a 'hand' being added when the contents call for more than usual attention, and the index finger is abnormally extended as the matter is more exciting.

William Gore (or, Gower), the Castle-Island deponent, already known to us (p. 96), although living far from the County Armagh, is able to certify,—

And the Rebells in the County of Armagh drowned at the bridge of Portadowne at one tyme (*as this deponent hath credibly heard*), one hundred and four score Protestants. And further saith, that *it was reported by one of the Rebells, and seconded by divers others,* that one whom the Rebells had drowned at the bridge of Portadowne did afterwards appeare above the water there, and *urged for vengeance* against those that drowned ['him' *struck out*, 'it' *interlined*] and the rest. And that although the Rebells endeavoured severall tymes to hold [and keep that body] under water, and make ['it' in place of 'him'] sink, yet they could by noe means doe it, but [it] still kept ['above' *struck out*], and floated on the water, and *urged for vengeance*, as afore for a long tyme together [it] had done. (*Jurat*, July 1, 1643.)

The ghost that cried for vengeance was just the ghost to get a hearing at that time. The ghost that would give any other counsel would earn no credit for itself.

As the evidence in support of the Ghosts and Prodigies is so much stronger than that of the massacres—being direct, positive, and (we may say) corroborated—I will here introduce a matter which ought not to be overlooked :

A RIVER AND A LAKE OF BLOOD !

Katherine the wiffe of Patrick ôKorrie, late of Loghgall, in the County of Armagh, tanner, sworne and examined, saith :

That shee, this deponent was, about the beginning of lent was twelvemonth, being in company with Mr. Laurence Robinson, parson of Kilmore, and his wiffe, and William Robinson, his brother and others, at the howse of Edward Taylor in Loughgall aforesaid one of the servants of that howse then and there fetched and brought in some water from a current or streame that runeth from the loch there ; wch. water seemed to be bloudie before it was used. And saith that one John Darbishyre upon sight of the water went to the streame and found the water [thereof] to appeare bloudie all along to [and at] the head thereof in the logh [as he tould her] yet said *hee neither could fynd nor see any one [either man or beast] slaine or wounded in the same*, And alsoe saith that one Capt. Kelly, a Rebell and [many other Rebells] yt sawe that water were extreame afrayd to see it bear that cullour [thincking it to presage some mischief to themselves], And thereupon went to one Hugh Goodall. an ould English papist to ask his counsell and conceite of the same : Whereupon he tould them that the water presaged a great mischeefe and shedding of the English blood. And therefore incorraged the Irish to goe on against them, saying that the Irish cawse was a good one, and that they needed not to feare. And afterwards the Irish (whether in pursuite of his consell and to fulfill his presage, shee cannot tell) eagerly sett upon the protestants [that were left] thereabout and slaughtered and putt them to death. And further saith, That divers others that went up to see the streame or current aforesaid reported alsoe that it seemed to be bloudie.

Jur : 19 *Julij,* 1643.   Sig. pro✕Katherine.
JOH. WATSON.
HEN. BRERETON,
WILL. ALDRICH.

Francis Leiland of Drumadmore, in the parish and countie of Armagh, yeoman, sworne and examined, deposeth . . . . . .
And further saith, That because the deponents wiffe was of the name of the Neils (though born in Leicestershire in England, and nothing akin to the ôNeales of Ireland). And that for that this deponents brother, Tho. Leiland had been a workman to Sir Phelim ôNeale, Therefore as this deponent conceeveth he and his [sd.] wiffe and 7 children were not putt to death by them ; but suffered to live amongs the Rebells for half a yeare. Yet every day subject to unspeakable danger, and yett not daring all that time to goe away for fear of death. The torments, threats, and menaces wch. he this deponent and his wiffe and children were exposed unto, in that tyme were very greate, and the manner and ways of their deliverance as greate, but farr more rare, yet too long to expresse. But saith that while he the deponent [and his] remained in that misery amongst the Rebells in the parish of Armagh *he was credibly tould,* That a streame or brook running from a lough through the town of Loughgall was turned from pure water into the cullour of bloud. And because he desired to know the truth thereof, *Hee sent his wiffe in Irish habitt* to inquire of some of the English of Loughgall (in or about the beginning of Lent was twelvemonth), whether that report was true or noe. Whoe returned *with severall serious protestants from the English* [then alive] that that streame or river aforenamed did one day, *whilst the Papist Rebells were at Masse* at Loghgall, turne from clere water to the cullour of bloude ! And that divers went upp to see if any creature (man or beast) were killd or putt thereinto [bleeding] wch. might bring that cullour into the water. And that upon diligent search and view they found noe creature at all in the streame nor any bloud-shedding running into the same. But that yet the streame all along to the lough, and the very lough itself, were both of a bloudie cullour, and *soe contynued whilst the Rebells were at Masse,* and untill halfe of them as they returned from Masse were comen over the same streame, and that then the water of the streame reverted and came to its former purity and cullour.

To those interested in the subject of " evidence," the foregoing ought to prove particularly entertaining. What an opening for cross-examination at every point ! Living in such a state of misery and peril, the examinant can still send his wife abroad to gather news. There is an exquisite touch in that Irish habit ! This woman who, on the examinant's showing, was so well known in the neighbourhood, trying to pass for an Irishwoman, is a rather comical kind of deception. That the stream, and the lake from which it ran, should look " bloudie," *whilst the Papist rebels were at Mass* was, of course, no more than might be expected from the same people and the same religion. And this report does not come from the rebels themselves, but from " several serious Protestants among the English ! "

It may still further illustrate the character of the evidence given in these depositions, to hear a little more from the same deponent :

And further saith, that the Rebells within the County of Armagh inforced divers of the English men thereabouts to goe along and partake with them when they went to robb, and stripp their neighbours, nevertheless for all that they afterwards murthered and killed those that did soe goe along and partake with them.

Names are, of course, prudently withheld. How prodigious the slaughter was in that parish ! The executioners must have been a mighty host :

And further saith that he, this deponent hath lived within the parish and countie of Armagh for the space of thirty years together last past, and above, and by that means very well knew the country, and many of the country people thereabouts. And *is verily perswaded* that when the [present] Rebellion began, there were of the English and Scotts Protestants dwelling within the two parishes of Armagh and Loughgall the number of eight thousand at least of men, women and children [Protestants], *the most of wch.*, the deponent is verily persuaded, *were murthered and putt to death by the Rebells* by drowning, burning, hanging, starving, the sword, and by other cruell deaths and torments, and that *but very few escaped.* This deponent and his wiffe and children by God's providence, amongst those few, escaping away after the most of the other Protestants were putt to death. By whose destrucion, and the burning of the Church of Armagh and towne, and Castledillon, and other howses, castles and buildings, most of which this deponent saw on fyre by the Rebells, those brave Royall plantations there are quite demolished, wasted, and of all the [former] inhabitants (saving the base Irish) depopulated.

Jur. 19 July, 1643.   FRANCIS LEILAND.
WILL. ALDRICH, JOH : WATSON.

The Protestant population of the two country-parishes as here solemnly " deposed upon oath " cannot be much less than the entire population of the city of Dublin at the same time. According to Harris (*Hist. of Dublin*, p. 336), the citizens were numbered in August, 1644, and found to be

	Protestants.	Papists.
Men	2,565	1,202
Women	2,986	1,406
	5,551	2,608

In the three years since the outbreak, the Papists had probably become fewer in Dublin. But on the other hand, there was a considerable influx of Protestant refugees. Mr. Francis Leiland's estimate of the Protestants of the two parishes is absurd. What matter ? The circumstance that he was " verily persuaded " made good evidence and good arithmetic for the Parsons-Borlase Commissioners, their aiders, abettors, and comforters then and since.

Besides the main objection to the statement that the ghost stories " originated with the Irish Roman Catholic people themselves," there is the implied suggestion that only such deluded people could set such things afoot. Now, will anyone stand up and declare that any man, or woman, or child of the benighted race was more under the influence of superstitious nonsense than the Rev. Robert Maxwell, Doctor in Divinity of the University of Dublin, Rector of Tynan, Archdeacon of Down, and (soon after) Bishop of Kilmore ? A sample :

The deponent further saith, that the first three days and nights of this present Rebellion, vizt. : October 23, 24, 25, it was generally observed that no cock crew, or any dogg was heard to bark, noe not when the Rebells came in great multitudes into the Protestant houses by night to robb and murther them. About 3 or 4 nights before [the] 56 persons were taken out of the deponent's house and drowned, and amongst those, the deponent's brother, Lieutenant James Maxwell, in the dark of the moone,* about one of the clock at night, a light was observed in manner of a long pillar to shine for a long way through the aier, and re-fracted upon the North Gabell of the house, gave a great light about an hour together that divers of the watch read both letters and bookes of a very small character thereby. The former, the

* Dr. Maxwell appears to be right in mentioning ' the dark of the moon,' if he means that this occurred at the very beginning of the outbreak. Carey prints the following communication from the Vice-Provost of the University of Pennsylvania :

'January 6, 1819.

' Dear Sir,—I find it was New Moon at Dublin at about 2 o'clock in the morning of the 24th of October, 1641 (O.S.) Consequently, the moon must have been invisible on the whole night of the 22nd-23rd of that month.— Yours, &c., R. M. PATTERSON.

' Mr. M. Carey.'

—*Vindiciæ Hibernicæ*, p. 326 (first ed. 1819).

Some will perhaps say ' Just the time for a universal massacre ! '

Carey's really great work, *Vindiciæ Hibernicæ*, has earned some high praise —none higher, I should say, than from Reid and Froude. Reid mentions the work ' only on account of its flagrant demerits.' The real merit of the book was, perhaps, the most flagrant thing from his point of view. Although containing some views which the author would doubtless have modified had he been able to examine the depositions for himself, it is a work of learned research, containing a collection of quotations from earlier authors (Protestants, chiefly). The author invites full examination of his facts and inferences.

deponent knoweth to be most true. . . . The latter was seen by all those of the deponent's family, and besides by many of his Irish guard.

Now the light shining "on the northern gable" could be accounted for as an event within the natural order of things. But it is evident that the distinguished graduate of the Dublin University takes a different view, and regards it as an "event prodigious."

Carey, in his *Vindiciæ Hibernicæ*, finds in Dr. Maxwell's deposition so much reckless talk about alleged occurrences that he cannot look upon it as the production of a truthful man. There is much room for severe commentary, all the more so owing to the deponent's position in life. Could he for a moment have believed these statements which he gives on the report of parties not named ? Yet it is unnecessary to follow up that question. The Commissioners accepted his statements as if true, just as the judges of the High Court received the same allegations against Sir Phelim O'Neill and others. There is not the slightest indication that these officials made any effort to test the allegations, or that they sought either confirmation, or the contrary, in any other quarter. They had got the thing to serve their purpose or the purpose of those who sent them ; and they appear to have thought it prudent to let well-enough alone. I don't know that any severer condemnation could be passed on men employed in public duty. These Commissioners have brought discredit upon the whole business in which they were then concerned by their bare-facedly presuming to palm on the public and on posterity so outrageous a gather-up as the following :

And further saith that *the Rebells themselves tould him*, this deponent that they murthered 954 in one morning in the County of Antrim, and that besides them *they suppose* that they killed above 11 or 1200 more in the County. They tould him likewise, that Col. Brian O'Neile killed about 1,000 in the County Down, besides 300 neare Killyleagh, *and many hundreds*, both before and after in both these counties !

All that is "sworn," and no question raised. It is equally vain and equally fraudulent for the Commissioners, their comforters, partakers, aiders or abettors, to allege that "the rebels themselves," or "the Irish Roman Catholics themselves" gave the figures as they are. Let it be kept in view that we are discussing the merits of "evidence." And I say that the sample now before us is as gross a fraud as ever was practiced on human credulity. Why were

not the parties who made the report to Dr. Maxwell brought
forward to show how *they* came by such knowledge ?
Why has not one of them been named ? The accuracy
implied in the 954 is, in a way, amusing. None the less,
the man, or the men, who could account for the *four* as well
as the 950, ought not to have been permitted to retire into
obscurity when there was a " royal commission under the
broad seal of Ireland," appointed to inquire into such matters,
with powers to the Commissioners to call before them
all who could testify to the matter of inquiry. The attempt
to shift the responsibility is but piling up imposture to
hide imposture. Nor will it improve the position a whit
to allege that the Commissioners gave the evidence for
what it was worth. They did nothing of the kind when
they sent it forth as duly " sworn." See what it was worth
to Mr. Walter Harris when writing his history of Down !
And, through the same Harris, it has turned the heads
of many well informed people—even well-disposed people—
down to the present hour.

Another passage in Dr. Maxwell's famous (but in the
greater part *infamous*) deposition has played a part which
ought to convince anyone of the grand object of the
Commissioners :

And further saith, that *it was credibly tould him* that the Rebells,
least they should thereafter be charged with more murthers than
they had comitted, comanded their priests to bring in a true
Accompt of them, and that the persons so slaughtered (whether
in Ulster only or the whole kingdome the deponent durst not enquire) in March last, amounted unto one hundred ffiftie foure
thousand. (The figures 154,000 have been placed in the margin
opposite).

How very sensitive those rebels were about their reputation ! They could take credit for putting to death
154,000 unresisting Protestants, but if charged with killing
any more they should lose their character ! On the face
of it, the statement is ridiculous. None the less, it has been
found good enough to serve " the State ; " and it formed
the basis of Milton's estimate of 600,000 Protestants cruelly
put to death within a few months—more than twice the
Protestant population of Ireland when the rebellion broke
out ! With Dr. Maxwell's " sworn " figures in hand,
it was the easiest thing possible for the author of
Iconoclastes—to make the estimate—just a matter of simple
multiplication :—

The rebellion and horrid massacre of *English* Protestants in
Ireland to the amount of 154,000, in the province of Ulster only,

by their own computation ; which, added to the other three, makes up the total sum of that slaughter, in all likelihood, *four* times as great. *

It was not necessary to work out the sum. And it is suggested that, as the rebels' own computation is the basis, the 600,000 may be far *under* the mark. I must say there is an honesty about Milton's which is wanting to Temple's, Clarendon's, and even Petty's and Carte's way of making up the account. The great poet indicates the lines along which he moves. No one can tell how Temple, or Clarendon, or Carte ·comes to his conclusion— except " by guess," as Froude says ; and in the art of guessing they but mock one another.

And Froude himself can compete with any of them in saying the thing that's groundless or absurd. He is rather old in his art to tie himself to figures ; and without the figures, he can do the work of all the " computators " from Milton's day down to Carte's :

Of the numbers that perished, it is rash to offer so much as a conjecture. In the midst of excitement so terrible, extreme ex-aggeration was inevitable, and the accounts were more than usually hard to check, *because* the Catholics in their first triumph were as eager to make the most of their success, as Protestants to magnify the calamity. In the first horror it was said that 200,000 persons had perished in six months. *For these enormous figures the Catholic priests were responsible ! !* †

Here we have the art that takes the place of mendacity. How ingenious, and how audacious, the allegation that it was only in the heat of " the first horror " that ex-aggeration went so high as 200,000, when in " the faithful relation of Sir John Temple " published five years later on (1646) the estimate goes fifty per cent higher still ! And the crowning audacity that " for the enormous figures of 200,000 the Catholic priests were responsible ! " For which allegation there is not a particle of trustworthy evidence. This charge—for it is nothing less—against the priests is on a par with every other charge, wild, reckless, baseless, resting solely on the representations of their

---

* In the opening of the twelfth chapter of *Iconoclastes* (Milton's Prose Works, 5 vols., Bohn's Series, 1848, i. 407). In some editions it appears the clause ' which added to . . four times as great ' is omitted. Carey mentions the editions of 1738 and 1753, in the Philadelphia Library, as wanting this clause ; which had probably proved too much for some editors. I should very much regret the loss. I have not made particular search, but it might be of some interest to examine the principal editions in respect of this clause.

† *The English in Ireland,* i, 122.

bitterest enemies. What priest then in Ireland—or what Catholic layman has countenanced this imputation ? There were some priests who went far enough in the way of accusations against their brethren in the ministry There were Catholic laymen who could not in truth be accused of excessive charity towards their own clergy. But who, among the cleric or the lay, has said anything like what Froude says ? Evidence there is none. For the pretence of evidence it is necessary to bring up some priest-hating deponent who is perhaps " credibly informed," or " verily believeth " that the matter is so and so.

In the sixth volume of the Thorpe Tracts,* on the fly-leaf of a pamphlet, is printed the testimony on which rests this extraordinary assertion.† Dr. Maxwell's evidence on the matter is given very briefly, but the figures there attributed to him are 150,000. There is only one other witness called, and he, for the moment, would appear to bring the estimate home to the priests. But it won't do :

Deposed also by Mr. Hugh Cunningham, on the 21st of April, 1642, that *he was told by a priest*, that the priests of every parish in Ulster were commanded by Sir Phelim O'Neill to return an account of the British Protestants that were killed by the Irish in the severall parishes, the number of men, women and children, so murthered at that time came to One hundred Five thousand.

Has a business like air about it ! All are made to pass through the turnstile on the way to death ! But, the pity of it ! we have got here no idea of the time covered by the figures. And have we not a clear right to hear that informant Priest speak for himself ? At any rate we ought to get his name. " Mrs. Harris " still ! But wide of the mark as the printed statement is, the original from which it is supposed to be taken is still further from the purpose. I copy the following from the Armagh book of Depositions (folio 609) :

Hugh Cunningham, late of Downeburg in the County of Armagh, gent, sworne :
. . . . And further saith, that one John Maxwell of Ballehalbert, in the County of Down, gent, a brittish Protestant, and this deponent's father-in-lawe, whoe hath been a prisoner amongst the Rebells at the Newry, and exchanged for another prisoner, and soe delivered from them about the first of March last, *Tould him this deponent :* That a Popish priest that often came to visitt him told him that Sr Phellomy ôNeale, the gran Rebell, did comãand the preistes of every parrish within Ulster to returne ye number of ye brittish that were killed [by ye Irish] monthly within their

---

* In the National Library, Kildare Street, Dublin.
† Borlase reprints, with some additions, the pamphlet (1679).

o

severall parishes. Wch. being done, the number of the people soe killed consisting of men, women and children, came to one hundreth [thousand] (*sic*), and five thousand, or thereabouts (*Jurat*, xxi April 1642, *coram*, Rand. Adams, Wm. Hitchcock, Hen. Brereton, William Aldrich.)

As printed in 1679, the extract represents Hugh Cunningham as hearing the priest say what is alleged. It turns out that *he only heard the man who heard the man that has got no name.* He who accepts all this is not hard to satisfy with " evidences."

The question at present is not as to the truth of the figures ; even Froude himself is shocked by such estimates. What are the grounds for saying that the Priests are responsible for the enormity of the computation ? The whole thing appears to be embraced in the two contributions just cited. Had there been anything better it would, doubtless, have appeared with these in 1679, the date of the pamphlet above-mentioned.* And what does it all amount to ? A vile trick, a shabby subterfuge (not on the part of the deponents, but on the part of all who make use of them), to conceal the essential rottenness of that " inquiry."

In the footnote to page 69, I have made a short extract from the speech which Cooke prepared against the trial of Charles I. : " Concerning Ireland, where there were no less than 150,000 men, women, and children most barbarously and satanically murdered, in the first four months of the Rebellion, *as appeared by substantial proof* at the King's Bench at the trial of Maguire." The trial of Connor, Lord Maguire, for High Treason " for being concerned in the Irish Massacre," took place in 1645, and the "substantial proof " mentioned by Cooke is to be sought in the following :

Sir Charles Coote's Testimony concerning the generality of the Rebellion :

Sir Phelim O'Neale and Roger Moore were the actors in the massacre, and by public directions of some in place, *and of the titulary bishops*, for the sending of an exact account of what persons were murdered throughout all Ulster, a fourth part of the Kingdom, to the parish priests in every parish ; and they sent in a particular account of it ; and the account was 104,700 in one province in the first three months of the rebellion.— *Cobbett's State Trials*, iv. 679.

A Collection of Certain Horrid Massacres in several Counties of Ireland since the 23 October, 1641. London : Printed for Henry Brome, at the Gun, at the West-End of St. Paul's, 1679. It is rather remarkable that neither the compiler of this pamphlet, nor Borlase in his additions to it, takes any notice of Dr. Maxwell's Glynwood ' massacre of 1200.'

And that is the "substantial proof"! One need
hardly hold the thing to the light to discover what the substance of it is. How could Sir Charles Coote swear to all
this? What man "in place" among the rebels—what
titulary bishop—what priest—is shown to have had act or
part in making such return? By whom was the account
made up? And how did the "witness" come to know
anything about it? Coote merely re-echoes (with the
"titulary bishops" thrown in) the allegations of Dr. Robert
Maxwell and Mr. Hugh Cunningham, which had, we may
feel sure, become well circulated, before 1645, among the
Parliament party.

But Froude has yet another card to play. Out of the
very prodigiousness of the exaggeration he brings forth the
prodigiousness of the slaughter. This purple island of
" massacre " must be of vast extent, surrounded as it is
by so vast an ocean of fraud, falsehood, and deception!

Clarendon, on cooler reflection, reduced the number to 40,000,
Sir William Petty, followed by Carte, to 37,000. Even these figures
will seem too large, when it is remembered how appalling is the
impression created by the slaughter in cold blood of innocent, unresisting people, how little rage and terror can be depended on for
cool observation, and how inevitably the murdered were confounded
afterwards with the enormous multitudes which indisputably
perished in the civil war, which followed. The evidence proves
no more than that *atrocities had been committed on a scale too vast
to be exactly comprehended*, while the judgment was further confounded by *the fiendish malignity of the details.*—(i., 123.)

The "fiendish malignity" is not confined to details:
it gives character to the entire performance. I should
like to know with more certainty the application of the
term "atrocities" in the foregoing passage. Does the
writer mean atrocities committed by the rebels, or by their
opponents, or by all together? He leaves that to the reader
to settle for himself Now, this artistically slipshod style
of writing is not without its meaning. You take your
choice; but you will kindly bear in mind that the evidence
taken before the Parsons-Borlase Commissioners was *all
against the rebels*. Again, what may be the meaning
of "innocent blood" here? If it is meant to include the
blood of all the unresisting who were slaughtered by the
Coles, St. Legers, Monros, and their following, then, indeed,
is the spectacle appalling. And something rather appalling had occurred within the recollection of many thousands of people then living, when Mountjoy and the Carews
sought glory in the slaughter of the unresisting. The
memory of the horrors marking the progress of those

human fiends was perhaps the thing which in 1641 most
of all " appalled " the British Protestants then in Ireland.
They could not be ignorant of the work of clearance prior
to the plantations, and there was unquestionably a latent
fear of retribution, which, however quiescent for years,
asserted itself on the first commotion. The " rage and terror "
did not necessarily spring from any actual slaughter,
but from the apprehension that the time was come when
the disinherited Irish would practise against the settlers
all the inhumanity that the old race suffered at the hands
of Mountjoy and his soldiery.

We are told by the same writer that the accounts were
more than usually hard to check " *because* the Catholics
in their first triumph were as eager to make the most of
their triumph as the Protestants to magnify the calamity."
Now, in the first triumph, it is admitted all round that
murders were few. And where at any time lay the advantage of magnifying their alleged crimes ? This pretentious nonsense may delude the writer himself, and
may serve to withdraw attention from the culpability
of the Commissioners, their aiders and abettors. What
evidence is there that they made *any attempt* to check
the returns ? Did they suppose that Dr. Maxwell's figures
were beyond question ?   I have shown elsewhere that the
big massacres which that deponent refers to the County
Down are absolute myths, and that the Commissioners
knew them to be such ; and not only the Commissioners,
but all who were in any way responsible for the conduct
of the inquiry. And if the Commissioners had any confidence in the allegation, then were they guilty of monstrous
dereliction of duty in not following up the charges. I
submit they made no attempt to check the accounts, and
that they encouraged extravagance and falsehood by the
unrestricted latitude given to hearsay charges and all
manner of " idle, silly tales." Warner's phrase, which
has just been used, is a very mild description, not only of
most of the tales told by Dr. Maxwell, but of much of the
evidence (so called), sworn to by other deponents, even
those of education and position.

The Rev. Richard Parsons, " Minister of the Vicarage
of Dronge, in the Diocese of Kilmore, and County of Cavan,"
furnishes a very good instance of the scope of a single
deposition :

And as to murthers and cruelties, saith, That *he heard it credibly
reported*, that the Rebells in the Countie of ffermanagh, the very
first day that the Rebellion broke out, murthered and killed all the
English wch. the could meet withall, and many women and

children in the Countie. The like they did in the County of Monaghan. And the Rebells in the beginning of the Rebellion murthered great numbers of Protestants in the severall counties of Armagh, Tirone, Downe, Londonderry, Donegall, *and generally in all the province of Ulster*, (*except in the County of Cavan*, where they spared more lives than were spared in other counties, although they robbed all the Protestants of their goods). And that for many wch. they kept to be their workmen or slaves, *they afterwards murthered them also*. In so much as *great numbers were thereby slaughtered*, and the goodes of the Protestants seazed on, and taken by the Irish Papistes. (*Jur.*, 24 ffebr., 1644. *Coram*, Hen : Jones et Hen : Brereton.)

As a specimen of fearless and sweeping swearing, that " deposed " statement may be exhibited anywhere. Perhaps the most interesting feature of this piece of " evidence " is that, while in the county of which he had personal knowledge he has no hesitation in declaring the murders to be few, he is no less ready to affirm that, in the counties with which he had no connection, the murder of Protestants was the order of the day !

According to this reverend deponent, at that dreadful time, the English in Ulster were hardly better treated by the Scots than by the Irish rebels :

And this deponent *hath been credibly informed*, That soe great was the hatred of the Scottes in the county of ffermanagh *and in divers other counties*, to the English, that when any of thenglish (*sic*) fled unto them for refuge or succour from those that pursued them, That these Scottes delivered them into the handes of the Irish againe, Whoe slew as many of them as were English (*sic*) other than those that got into the Countie of Cavan, and were saved by the ôRelies. . . .

Another matter, not indeed peculiar to this deposition, is the vagueness of the information—enough to move the envy of Dr. Henry Jones himself. You may as well try with a two-foot rule to take the dimensions of Milton's fallen archangel where he lay extended " many a rood," as attempt to apply any standard of measurement to this deponent's evidence. And as much may be said of many others whose tales make up the worst of the horrors. The author of *Paradise Lost* has not more undeniably reached the sublime of vagueness in his description of Satan than has many a country parson and many a simple housewife in these statements made upon oath. In the quality of vagueness, " Captain John Perkins, aged three score and thirteene," shows himself an adept, when he says : " In ye parish [and in ye countie of Armagh], there were murthered moste parte of the Brittish inhabitants and Pro-

testants *to a number not to be related.*" A pretty safe way
of presenting the reckoning! It were much easier to grapple
with Mr. Francis Leiland's estimate (*v.* p. 204).

Again, I must protest against any supposed necessity
of vindicating the "witnesses." The witnesses did admirably—they did just what was required from them.
It doesn't appear that the Parson of Drung, in the County
Cavan, was called upon to show "the cause of his
knowledge" when asserting that "great numbers of
Protestants were murdered" after they had been
kept as workmen or slaves. The particular would,
in such cases, be of more value as evidence than the
general. But the general aspersion was more serviceable
for the purposes of this inquiry. It would be easier to
make a mistake about the particular case. The general
statement was pretty safe from attack, since it made no
reference to time, place, or number—except "great numbers."
It was a very prudent way to perpetrate a great massacre—
"great numbers," "hundreds and thousands" of nameless
people cruelly murthered *and* put to death, at nameless
places, at no particular time, all murthered—by "credible
report!" Dr. Henry Jones had already committed himself
to the statements that some Protestants had been reserved
from slaughter that they might be turned to serviceable
account, and because they could be put to death when
it would better suit. Is it likely that he would neglect
to record an authenticated instance if the deponent had
knowledge of one? And if the deponent had no such
particular knowledge, why was the unverified statement
returned as evidence? The account given by Parson Parsons
is indeed a hard one to check. Perhaps some admirer of
Froude will explain in what way the priests are responsible
for the difficulty here.

I have already (p. 92) cited from the deposition of
Margaret Bromley of Tanderagee, in the County Armagh,
an instance of the transfer to Scarva *bridge* of events which,
according to other deponents, ought to have gone to the
credit (or discredit) of Portadown and Kernan. That was
no loss, however, to either Portadown or Kernan. The
transfer of the events to Scarva only makes a new series
of outrages without in the least detracting from the fame
of any other place. I mention this again as a glaring
example of the multiplication of massacres, and, further,
as an example of the latitude allowed by the Commissioners
to deponents who could add to the heap. The same
deponent could without any risk of cross examination
depose :

And it was a common report amongst the Rebells, that the preistes and fryers were the cawse of their killing and putting to death the English and Scottish Protestants.

The Commissioners were not likely to spoil that by asking embarrassing questions. It does not appear that she was even asked to name anyone who said so. Common report was sufficient ; for in those days " common report " was raised to the dignity of public prosecutor. Thousands were indicted and outlawed on no other evidence. What comes next in Mrs. Bromley's statement appears to me to have passed through some of the transmutations of speech reported at second hand, perhaps at third or fourth hand.

And the Rebells also *usually* said, that the Protestants were worse than dogges, and were noe Christians, but those that *Christened at Masse (sic)* were Christians. And the Rebells alsoe said that they knew that if they themselves shold dy the next morning, their sowles shold goe to God : And they were very glad of the revenge wch. they had taken of the English.

It will be news to most Catholics that " the Mass " is an essential element in baptism. The story was, however, good enough for the depositions. It appears it was much easier for Mrs. Bromley to declare that such and such was " usually said " than to give any particular instance. She heard some sensible things, of course, about the doors, and in her version this became the usual talk " of the rebels." But I find she *does* bear witness to *one* specific saying :

And this deponent being a prisoner among the Rebells, heard one of them, vizt., Patrick M'Court of the parish of Tandragee, aforesd. say these wordes : If I had the King of England in the chamble (vizt., where he, the said Patrick then was), I would take off the King's head within half an hour !

That must have seemed very shocking to President Bradshaw and Colonel Hacker ! How the man in the shambles would find employment for half an hour in the way indicated is not so easy to get at.

No statements were too general,—*none too far beyond the deponents' own experience,*—so long as they fell in with certain theories favoured by the Parliament of England and their supporters in Dublin Castle. Here follows a very large order for one woman (a farmer's wife) to fill, being upon her oath. The deponent, Ann Sherring, is one of the witnessess for the murders at the Silver Mines in North Tipperary. What I quote is not intended to reflect upon her in any way, but to show the sort of thing that passed for evidence :

And further, saith, That all the Popish gentry in the country thereabouts, especially all of the Septs and names of the ôBrians, the Coghlans, and the Kenedys were *all acters* in the present Rebellion against his Maty, *and either acted, assisted, incyted or consented to all the murthers, robberies, cruelties and rebellious acts aforesaid.*

This passage is marked by an enclosing line on the MS. deposition, as if it had more than ordinary value. And as evidence, the value is simply *nil.* Mrs. Sherring, I have no doubt, believed all that she said. But her belief, or her opinion, in the matter was insufficient to set up the *fact.* What are such statements the better of being made upon oath ?

In the deposition of " Ellen the Relict of Daniel Matchett, late of Kilmore, in the County of Armagh," is a passage marked in the same way, as calling for particular attention :

And further saith, that little children of the Rebells, *if they could but speak and goe,* would hold their skeans against the English and say they wold kill them if they wold not give them their money.

Even the little Irish toddlers, armed with skeans of lath, capable of terrorising the English !   This too at a time when the Irish soldiery were not half armed !   The skeans that seemed so terrible were, we may be sure, as dangerous as lath and paste-board, in such hands, could be. But I fancy I hear some one say, " Hold ! There you have decided indication of the implacable spirit of the Romish *faith.* The children were only doing as they had seen their parents and friends do." How many of these terrorising babes were there ? It may be that next door to Mrs. Matchett's was a little urchin who performed some such antics ; and *that* would make a case against all the baby rebels in Ireland ! The gallant officer, Captain Adair, whose great achievement was the cutting off of a baby's head, would also say that the Irish were rebels before they could either " speak or goe." Mrs. Matchett further says :

And this deponent was credibly tould that one Manus ôCane, who lived nere Loghgall, begged for his breakfast, the heads of all the Protestants of Sir Phelim Roe O'Neile, and that his request was granted : and *she verily beleiveth the same to be true,* ffor that at that very time, great numbers of poor Protestants were by the Rebells driven like heardes of sheepe, and *some burned, some drowned, some hanged, and ye rest murthered and massacred* in most barbarous and inhuman manner, which calamities [sufferings of the poor Protestants] were so frequent that at length this deponent [as overfrighted and scared therewith] grew almost insensible thereof.

But somehow she contrived to live when all " the rest were murthered and massacred." It is necessary from time to time to assure oneself that he is reading extracts not from nursery stories, or romances, but from the MS. books of depositions, the same which Froude has in effect certified to be beyond reproach and beyond question.

Alluding to this passage, Miss Hickson says :

One poor ignorant Protestant woman swore that she was told by her neighbours, Irish Catholics and English Protestants, that Colonel Manus O'Cahane, a commander in the rebel army (unquestionably a cruel and fierce fanatic), was in the habit of breakfasting on the heads of murdered Protestants. Her Catholic neighbours told her this absurd tale to amuse themselves with her fear and horror, and to frighten her out of the little wits she ever possessed. (i. 135.)

And why was the " absurd tale " received as evidence, and put on record as "duly sworn" and "solemnly deposed " ? It does not appear that the Commissioners raised any question or made the slightest difficulty about the matter. Why should they ? The "evidence" of this rebel's cannibalism is of the same character as that on which he is held to be " unquestionably a cruel and fierce fanatic," or, as another lady deponent will have it, " a most bloody and cursed rebel." Mrs. Matchett is not a whit more absurd than Peter Hill, Esquire, High Sheriff of Co. Down (see p. 89 *n*), and many others as well.

I have again and again had occasion to remark that in every case of a big massacre *the wrong person is put forward* to prove the charge. We have the honour of becoming acquainted with the man (or the woman) who is " credibly informed " on the subject, or the one who " verily and truly believes " all that he tells us, but his credible informants are denied us ! Yet we are to take the " evidence "—and many more important people have so taken it—as inspired and above question ! Here is another passage specially marked on the original MS. :

Richard Newberry, Loughgall. . . . sworne. . . And saith, that the Rebells, vizt., first the said Manus ôCane took and imprisoned him, this depont. and divers others in ye Church of Loughgall and kept them there a few days. And then ye said Manus ôCane and ye rest of ye Rebells by warrant (as they said) from Sir Phelim ôNeile, and ye rest of their great rebellious commanders [tould] a great number of these poore persons that they should goe to England, they gladly went out with these Rebells, among wch. prisoners one Mr. ffullerton, parson of Loughgall, one Mr. Scott of Massarene, gent, and one Richard Gladdish, goeing along were murthered and slaine by ye Rebells in the way short

of Portadown : and the rest of ye poore Protestants prisoners being
like sheepe to the slaughter brought to Portadowne, were all then
and there forced or thrown off the bridge of Portadowne aforesd. by
the Rebells into the river, when and where most of them (they being
in all about fourscore persons) were instantly drowned, and some
few swyming to or nere the shoare were most barbarously knocked
on ye heades (*as divers that were eye witnesses have confidently
affirmed to him, this deponent.*)*

Confident affirmation at second-hand we have in abundance, while the supposed informants are neither seen nor
heard. Why were not these " eye-witnesses " sought out
and produced to tell what they saw ? To say the very
least of it, doesn't it look extremely suspicious on the part
of the Commissioners that at this point all their " agonized
curiosity " was fully satisfied, and, so far as appears, they
did not even ask for the name of any one who so " credibly "
informed the deponent ? Of the murders committed on
the way to Portadown the information is more definite.
These alleged atrocities at the bridge of Portadown are
by no means so well authenticated as the ghosts at the same
place. We have at least two witnesses who both *saw and
heard the ghosts,* and these apparitions have been handed
down to us familiar and undoubted as—Hamlet's Ghost.
There is, indeed, one deponent who professes to have seen
these people drowned at the bridge ; but how he *could*
have seen them while a prisoner requires more clearing
up than we are now to be favoured with.

Phillip Taylor of Portadowne, husbandman, sworne, saith,
That at the xxiiird of October last, he, this deponent was taken
prisoner at Portadowne aforesd., by Toole M'Can now of
Portadowne, gent, a notorious Rebell and comãander of a
great number of Rebells, together with those Rebells, his
souldiers to the number of 100 persons or thereabouts. Att
wch. tyme the Rebells first tooke the Castle and victualled the
same. Then they assaulted and pillaged the towne, and burned
all the houses on the further side of the water. And then the said
Rebells drowned a great number of English Protestants, men,
women and children *in this deponent's sight* [some with their hands
tyed on their back.] And saith that the number of them that
were soe then drowned amounted, *as this deponent was credibly
tould and beleeveth,* to the number of 196 persons. And the same
Rebells alsoe threatened to shoot to death one Mr. Tiffin, a zealous
Protestant Minister there, and discharged a piece at him accordingly,
but, as it pleased God, they missed him, and at length he escaped
from them. And further saith that the same Rebells kept this
deponent in prison at Portadowne aforesd., for the space of seven

---

* The same deponent mentions that two of his servants who had joined the
rebels told him that M'Cann regretted the drowning of so many Protestants.
But it does not appear that the informants themselves saw any drowned.

weeks, and sett a horse lock upon his legge : but at length he got a passe from the said Toole M'Can, and soe got away from them. But whilst he stayed there many poore Protestants were by the Rebells murthered in severall places about Loughgall aforesd. And they alsoe in that tyme stript of his clothes one Mr. Jones, a minister, at Seagoe, nere Portadowne, aforesd. whoe afterwards escaped from them to the Town of Lisnegarvey. And this deponent hath credibly heard that one Mr. ffullerton, a minister, and another in his company were alsoe murthered by the Rebells before the drowning of the Protestants aforesd. [Signs by mark.]

Jur : viii., ffebr., 1641.

WILLIAM ALDRICH. JOHN WATSON.

Now what a fine opening for the cross-examiner there is in that allegation about what " occurred " in the deponent's sight." Did this occur while he was a prisoner and in irons ? For it would appear that on getting his pass from Toole M'Cann he came to Newry, the head-quarters of the rebels of three or four counties. Curiosity, however agonized, must here go ungratified. The Commissioners have left it so.

Temple and Harris, on the authority of one " William Clarke of the County Armagh, tanner," will have it that " the bridge was broken down in the middle, and 100 men, women, and children, forced on with pikes and swords, were thrust down headlong and perished." If anything like this occurred in Taylor's " sight," he says nothing about it ; and he betrays no disposition to minimise the guilt of the rebels.

What is certain about this matter is that, if any such tragedy was there enacted, it has been first magnified and then multiplied. One person says four-score were drowned, another has a hundred, another a hundred and ninety-six ; and so on. And by way of reconciling matters, all these wild and varying estimates are gathered together as the returns of so many separate atrocities. And not only this, but by confusion of geographical ideas, we have the further multiplication due to transfer of the alleged occurrences to other places some miles off. All this may be regarded as the necessary outcome of the unlimited licence accorded to hearsay. The Commissioners, and not the priests, are responsible for the difficulty of checking these accounts. They took what came and made no doubt about it. Dr. Maxwell unwittingly approves this view of the matter :

The number of people drowned at the bridg of Portadowne, *are diversely reported according as men stayed among the Rebells.* This deponent who stayed as long as any, *and had better intelligence* than most of the English amongst them had best reason to know the truth, and saith that there were by their own report, 190 drowned with Mr. ffullerton.* At another time they threw 140 over the said bridg, at another time 36 or 37, and *so continued drowning every day more or fewer for 7 or 8 weeks.* So that the fewest that can be supposed there to have perished *must needs be* above a thousand ; besides, etc.

The cross-examiner was badly wanted here, to unfold Dr. Maxwell's superior " means of knowledge." How interesting it would be to know something about " the rebels " who are credited with being reporters. Yet we don't get the name of any to help us to judge for ourselves. Supposing the object were to practise a monstrous hoax, in what other or more effective way could the thing be done ?

Dr. Maxwell also mentions great numbers said to be drowned in the Lake of Mountjoy (Lough Neagh). Now, if there was any drowning at the bridge of Portadown, bodies would be carried down to the lough, and being cast up on the shore, would furnish evidence of another massacre—one body so found would give the start to wild rumour.

That some atrocity was perpetrated in that neighbourhood is rendered more likely by the achievements of the Montgomerys and their " tygers," the Conways, Chichesters, and others operating against such peaceable people as they might choose to call rebels. The evidence produced by the Commission will bear no handling. The bit of " testimony " which, in my opinion, goes farthest in the direction of establishing some part of the case is that incidentally furnished by the

Examination of Toole M'Rory M'Cann, aged about 50 years, taken 5th of May, 1653 :
. . . He sayeth that he never saw any drowned at Portadowne. *But he heard of it.* And that he lived five myle from Portadowne.

Taken before us.   TOOLE M'CANN.†
        JA : TRAILL,
        SOLO : FFRITH.

There is a little admission here which I take to be of much greater value than all the " information " on the subject supplied by Dr. Maxwell. Some act of retaliation is likely enough, and wicked enough ; but the use which has

---

* Newberry's account is that Mr. Fullerton was murdered on the way short of Portadown.

† A good signature.

been made of the matter is abominable. Had the Commissioners held a proper and properly conducted inquiry into the circumstances, had they even sought the names of those who might be able to bring home the crime to the perpetrators, they had done something to their credit. Instead of doing anything of the kind, they appear to have studied how they could most effectually suppress such details as might be tested. They certainly found in Dr. Maxwell a deponent to their liking. None of them would of course tell a lie—*that* were very shocking ; but they would palm on the world, and on posterity, what they must have known to be monstrous exaggeration—such exaggeration as differs but in name from monstrous falsehood. Nor does it one whit mend the matter to allege or to say " The Commissioners, their comforters, aiders and abettors are not responsible ; if you like not the security,— blame the rebels,—blame the priests." Again, I repeat— so long as neither rebel nor priest has been identified with anything of the kind—that this allegation is but a flimsy cover for a false position, a subterfuge, a pretence, a fraud.

I have shown that the outrages which some deponents connect with one place, are by other deponents referred to different situations, and one massacre soon counts many. This would not be possible had proper inquiry been held. The " Scarvagh " drownings are but the Portadown cases re-echoed. But there is another circumstance to be noticed— the similarity of names. In Sir Gerard Lowther's judgment against Sir Phelim O'Neill, he says to the prisoner : " You yourself confessed (*as is testified*), that you killed 600 at *Garvagh,* and left neither man, woman, nor child in the barony." Dr. Maxwell's deposition is the authority : Sir Phelim did confess to him that he killed 600 at Garvagh, etc. Now, at Garvagh, Sir Phelim worsted a detachment of the Coleraine garrison, and his account of the exploit comes out in this distorted form when reported by Dr. Maxwell and the Parsons-Borlase Commissioners. The same garrison soon after met with a still greater disaster near Ballymoney in the County Antrim—the incident, I have not the least doubt, which Dr. Maxwell represents as 954 killed (in cold blood, we are to suppose) in one morning by the Irish ! Of these actions there is an interesting account in the T.C.D. MS., F. 4, 16 (the volume which contains the High Court records, and some other papers). The writer is a clergyman of Coleraine or the vicinity.

A command of two or three hundred men being committed to the chardge of Edw. Rowley of Castle-Roe, esquire, a garrison was planted at Garvagh, a small village 7 miles distant from Coleraine

to repress the risinge of the Irish within it. This garrison being
twice assaulted, fought prosperously in the first encounter slaying
diverse of the enemy ; but in the latter very disastrously, to the loss
of neer two hundred men's lives, whereof divers were of note, and
remarkable in the country, and amongst them the said Edw.
Rowley, commander of the party. This defeate was given on the
13th December, 1641. . . .

A second defeate was given (but far greater) neer Ballymoney,
five miles from Colerane, by 'that bloody Highlander, Alex.
M'Donnell, on y[e] 13th day of February following, where and when
diverse of the eight companies of Colerane, many of them being
English, with as many of the Scotts, who ambitionated to have the
van, perished miserably by a womanish feare without any manly
reluctance (sic.) ; to the eminent and unavoidable loss of the
garrison, if the enemy had pursued y[e] fortune of the day by an
assault thereof. The loss is vulgarly numbered to seaven or eight
hundred, with the arms of the whole party, and may without
injury be imputed to the too much forwardness of the Scottish
companies under y[e] command of Archibald Ewart his hare-brained
kinsman of the same name.

Such engagements receive no attention in the depositions.
Nothing there but—Irish butchers and British " sheep."

I have more than once intimated my objection to
Froude's way of putting the case, as being independent
of the real history, and as being a seductive attempt to
raise a false issue. For a long time he handles the matter
as if he meant to plump for Temple—or perhaps for Milton ;
and when he has made our ears tingle with " massacre,"
—" massacre,"—" massacre,"—" St. Bartholomew," he dis-
covers exaggeration so wild, that only massacre and " the
priests " could account for it. His method is simply this :
" You are first to take it as a *general fact* that there was
a general massacre. That little preliminary arranged,
we will talk of the discount." It were idle to expect that
he would in even the feeblest manner blame Temple,
Borlase, Milton or any great godfather of exaggeration
when he has the " rebels " and the priests at command.

The audacity of this is equalled only by his certificate
in favour of " the depositions," he having never examined
them. " They tell one consistent story." Nonsense !
Nonsense almost as glaring and as stupid as anything in
Dr. Maxwell's colossal output of mare's nests.

I cannot bind myself to follow any of the distinguished
writers who have treated of these depositions. At this
stage, no one, I think, can suspect me of much leaning to
those who will persist in treating these documents as inspired writings. And I do not agree with those who would
reject the whole lot as worthless. I have also to mark
some divergence from the views of those who regard the

depositions taken in 1652–3 as even less reliable than those taken by the so-called " royal " commissions (and which I choose to call the " Parsons-Borlase " commissioners, but will have no quarrel with any one who may prefer to know them as the " Dr. Henry Jones " Commissions.)

It may not be amiss to repeat here the oft-told story about the purposes of the several commissions of inquiry issued :

The first was issued on 23rd December, 1641, by the Lords Justices Parsons and Borlase.

The objects are set out in the preamble to Dean Jones's deposition (cited p. 179).

In the course of a month the powers of the commissioners were extended to enquire into the seizure of lands, and murders committed *by the rebels*.

On 11th June, 1642, the Rev. Edward Pigott was added to the Commission.

These are the so-called " royal " commissions and their powers were directed against only one class of offenders described as rebels, Irish rebels, Papists, Romanists, Catholics, Roman Catholics, or mere Irish, according to the taste or manners of the writer.*

Lastly, the Commissions issued under the Commonwealth to collect evidence for the High Court of Justice. I have made some use of the depositions taken under these by Commissioners, who sat at Carrickfergus in the years 1652–53. Unlike those issued in the King's name in 1641–2, the Commonwealth Commissions were not restricted to action against criminals of one nationality or religion ; and, if in only this respect, were more equitable at the start.

That in the earlier depositions we have heaps of " idle silly tales " is perfectly clear. Some writers have, however, fallen into the error of setting down the later depositions as of still less value, because taken ten to twelve years further on, when the recollection of witnesses would be less distinct. So far as there is question of mere memory, this may have some application. But, on the other hand, there should be a corresponding advantage in being able to review matters with a cooler judgment. I do not, however, attach so much importance to the contention regarding these circumstances. It is, in my opinion, but another instance of misdirected fire on the part of the assailants.

* Froude has at any rate the good sense and good taste to avoid generally the use of the offensive or ill-mannered terms so much affected by Reid, and no by him alone.

The later Commissions were put into the hands of a
different set of men (although Dr. Henry Jones is still
among them), had a different object, and were conducted
with at least the semblance of judicial inquiry. The
main object being, at least ostensibly, to prepare evidence
for the High Court of Justice, it was necessary to do more
than gather up silly stories for which there was no definite
authority. There was no place at these investigations for
a Maxwell, or any other, who could glibly talk of a thousand
murdered in a morning. The deponents were called
upon to state "the cause of their knowledge." While the
object of the first commissions was to collect every wild
rumour that might serve to excite horror against the Irish
rebels, that of the latter was to find out what parties had
been implicated in actual crime or outrage. Crimes committed against the Irish were not overlooked, although
there was not then the same facilities for following up
such cases, owing to the attitude taken up by the first
"inquirers." That the massacres committed at Island
Magee and Ballydavy (near Holywood) should receive
no attention from the Borlase-Parsons Commissioners
is, without any further instance of culpable omission,
sufficient to show the moral worth of their inquiry. True,
such trifles were excluded from their cognizance by the
terms of the instrument of appointment ; and this again
is an index to the moral value of their labours. *Their*
business was not so much to investigate crime as to find
pretexts for indicting and outlawing the Catholic land-
owners throughout Ireland, and to get up a howl in England
against the people favoured, it was alleged, by the King.
For this purpose a mythical massacre, audaciously based
on the reports and "confessions" of mythical rebels and
mythical priests, was good enough. I do not say that they
neglected to bring home crime to "the rebels" *when they
could.* They have not done so,—*they have not even attempted
to do so*—in the case of those appallingly great massacres,
for which the nameless rebels and nameless priests are
made "responsible." A sworn inquiry based upon such
"common report" puts romance and evidence on the
same level. That some deponents confined themselves to
matters more or less within their own knowledge is no
warrant of trustworthiness so long as a fabulist like
Dr. Maxwell—I don't say he is a liar—gets a full hearing,
and his supposed informants are shut out of court, as not
worth mentioning.

Fabulists so encouraged by the example and the practice
of the chief of the Parsons-Borlase Commission, were shy

of appearing before the officers of later appointment whose duty was, presumably, to find out what show of bottom there was in the "common report." That, even then, all witnesses told the truth, need not be supposed ; but, although only evidence for prosecution was received, there is about the depositions then taken, or most of them, such definiteness as is signally wanting in those of earlier date—those particularly which are held up as evidence of the "universal massacre." In short, the depositions of 1652–3 are, incidentally, the very best indication of the infamous tactics pursued by the Parsons-Borlase Commissioners, in putting forth so many charges not intended for investigation.

At the same time it is not to be inferred that the Commissioners of the Commonwealth were able to dispense, or attempted to dispense, even-handed justice all round To say that they did better than their predecessors is but a faint kind of praise. They could easily do better while still falling far short of what they ought to do. Their object was, we are assured, to bring to justice, if possible, all the evil doers. That object could not be attained without bringing to the block or the halter many men in high place who were busying themselves urging prosecution against men at any rate no more stained with blood than they were themselves. Sir Phelim O'Neill,—and take him at the worst,—shed less innocent blood than Coote or Cole, or any of the commanders who were employed and authorised to destroy the peasantry wholesale. To those commanders, their comforters, partakers, aiders, abettors, we undoubtedly owe the worst crimes which stain the Irish movement of that day. What would be the consequences in any other land of such a manifesto from the chief rulers as that of the eighth of February, 1641–2, and put into the hands of such instruments as then professed to do "the King's business" in Ireland ? But, short of bringing to justice the great criminals in place and high estate, the Commonwealth Commissioners did all that, perhaps, they were enabled or permitted to do. They appear to have followed up the Island Magee and Ballydavy murders as closely as they followed those at Ballagh, (Newcastle), Ballee, and other places where the rebels had been guilty of shedding innocent blood—although by way of retaliation. It was hardly possible for these Commissioners to follow up such cases as that of Ballydavy and Island Magee with the same effect as the charges against the Irish, for the very good reason that the earlier Commissioners had done nothing to help that branch of the inquiry. And at any

P

rate the massacre at either Magee or Ballydavy was but a small matter compared with the cold-blooded atrocities perpetrated by Coote, or Cole, and men who claimed high reward for so much "acceptable service."

The depositions taken in 1652–53 form the great bulk of most of the books, I would say that in the book for County Down they form over three-fourths of the whole; and they form even a larger proportion of some other books. In these documents we find the charge of general massacre *dis*proved.* In dealing with the charges which Harris in his history of the County Down professes to base on the sworn depositions, I have shown (if I have not made but poor use of the materials), that the depositions furnish proof of the falsity of most of the charges, and the wild exaggeration with which others have been preferred. What can be the meaning—can there be any meaning but the one—of passing over in silence the appalling "massacre" mentioned by the Rev. Dr. Maxwell as occurring at Glynwood (parish of Donaghmore), while we find large batches of depositions relating to the "Pass of Dundrum" (as "the Ballagh," Newcastle, is more frequently called), Ballee, Ballydavy, Ardglass, as well as to the execution of the postman O'Rooney, and the nameless "dyer" at Newry? I have shown also that the big massacres alleged to have occurred at Downpatrick, Killyleagh, and Castle Island have no foundation beyond what, in time of civil war, would be ordinary occurrences in any land. It is not certain that at the three places named a dozen deaths, save in armed conflict, occurred, and how most of even those occurred no one appears to know exactly. Now, I am not to be understood as making light of a few lives. I should be well pleased to know that the perpetrators of crime had been brought to proper account. But I must protest against the atrocity—for it is nothing else—of making such charges as Harris, under pretence of writing history, has made in reference to these places. Unlike the historians who have taken him as guide, Harris had seen all the papers. He had, I feel quite sure, gone through them ; and, if so, he had in his hands ample means of showing the baselessness of Dr. Maxwell's "discoveries" in County Down. He could see in those documents that while the Commissioners follow up with tenacity such comparatively small matters,

---

* Temple, of course, makes use of only the Parsons-Borlase Commissions, his 'faithful narration' having appeared about seven years before the Commonwealth Commissioners took any examinations. Harris, although he had these before him, prefers to be guided by the Temple and Maxwell fables.

they altogether ignore the big affairs—Donaghmore, Scarva, even Lough-Kernan, and " Bryan O'Neill's thousand and more " ! While appreciating in my own way Harris's great services as an antiquarian, I had long been used to regard his accounts of the " massacres " as the outcome of the rancorous hatred of Popery which he so loves to flaunt before his readers ; but not until I examined the original depositions for myself, had I any idea of the base imposture underlying those charges, or of the still baser imposture of putting forward nameless rebels and nameless priests to bear the responsibility. No one had a better right to know all this than Mr. Walter Harris, the man whose days and nights were given up to the amassing of materials for history. That such a man should be imposed on by the reports of the nameless rebels and the nameless priests is out of the question, or is explicable only on the hypothesis, that having got hold of stories to suit his purpose in assailing the " bloody principles of Popery," he sought refuge in the fiction that he was using only *sworn* testimony. What a simple sort of people they all were to be so misled by those nameless rebels and nameless priests ! Such simple, unsophisticated souls as Temple, Dean Jones, Borlase, Harris, Reid, and Froude with the rest ! Froude does not appear to admit any obligation to Harris, although he is under much more than he was perhaps disposed to admit. He professes his admiration for Reid, and has passages almost copied from that author, who is himself a rather servile follower of Harris—the Harris of *The Ancient and Present State of the County Down*. While these and many others profess to base their accounts on the " thirty-three volumes " of sworn testimony, the truth is that in the same volumes there is abundant evidence both direct and implied that " the general fact" —an Irish St. Bartholomew—which these historians yearn to establish is, if not absolutely, to a very great extent a calumny.

The later depositions, in many cases, put a very different complexion on occurrences which in the earlier statements figure as cold-blooded massacre. The case which I have followed with considerable care, that of the Ballagh (New-castle), is to the purpose. The depositions first taken represent Sir Con Magennis as going to very strange and needless rounds in order to put to death a number of the prisoners then in his power, the number being estimated at various figures from 13 to 50 ; and Harris would fix the minimum at twenty-four or five. And the massacre is described with every detail calculated to move horror. At the very worst this was a small matter in comparison with Dr. Maxwell's massacre at " Glynwood," or even in comparison with Mr. Peter Hill's Lough-Kernan tragedy ; but unlike those and other cases resting on the same or similar authority, this Newcastle case is fully investigated and turns out to be one of retaliation ; and there is no evidence that more than nine or ten, if so many, were put to death.

The Cashel massacre of the 1st of January, 1641–2, has been held up as an instance of the wickedness of the rebels. It was wicked enough, but it appears to have been the outcome of private revenge for the murders committed by St. Leger and his lieutenant Peasley, and had no sanction from the rebel leaders. The chief of these was Philip O'Dwyer, one of the county gentlemen who had been so rudely repulsed by the Lord President of Munster when they came to him at Clonmel, a short time before, offering their services to maintain the peace of the county (*v.* p. 159).

John Hackett, then Mayor of Cashel, examined on the 24th August, 1652, gives an account of the attack and surrender of the town on the evening of 31st December. There was much pillage, and some Protestants were imprisoned. Very early in the following morning about sixteen of the Protestant inhabitants were murdered. The deponent was able to give the names of the principal murderers :

> And further saith, yt James Rock, aforesaid, bragd that he had revenged the death of his wife by killing of two [English] with his one (*sic*) hands. Phillip M'Shane being slaine by Capt. Peasley's troop, the sonne of the said Phillip M'Shane made his brags that he had revenged the death of his father for that hee had killed twice so many of the English in Cashell, yt hee had killed Thomas Charlton by name, for that he, the said Thomas Charlton was one of the troope being under the comand of Capt. Peasley, aforesd., and yt ye sd. Charlton was hee which killed his father.

All this does not justify the Cashel murders, but it points to the fact that private revenge was the instigation to these and doubtless to many other murders about the same time. It is indeed lamentable that such should have occurred. But turn loose in any civilized land a St. Leger and his worthy lieutenant, a Coote, a Cole, place such a board of governors at the head of affairs, and see whether private revenge and retaliatory crime will not stain the land with blood. Moreover, would the blame of such an order of things elsewhere be detached from the government, and wholly fixed upon the people ?   From other depositions it appears that Philip O'Dwyer committed some of the murderers to prison, but he ought to have dealt with them more severely. Against these wicked murders must be set the praiseworthy efforts of both priests and laymen to protect their Protestant townsmen. The Rev. Samuel Pullein, D.D., Dean of Clonfert (but resident in Cashel), afterwards Archbishop of Tuam, says in his deposition that he, his wife, and children were kept prisoners in the house of a Jesuit, which means, I think, that they were preserved by the Jesuit.

In accounting for the enormous exaggeration, Froude stumbles upon one circumstance which has some reality about it, when he points out " how inevitably the murdered were confounded afterwards with the enormous multitudes which indisputably perished in the civil war." And it is also indisputable that many of those deposed to as murdered were killed in skirmishes and in conflicts with the spoilers. We have many touching descriptions of multitudes of poor Protestants, men, women and children, driven " like sheep to the slaughter," while the little Irish children, " if they could but speak and go," would hold up their skeans to the terror of the English. Now as a native of Ulster, and resident therein most of my life, I take leave to express my doubts that the Protestants ever showed themselves such " sheep " as all this would come to. In many instances they were doubtless surprised and overpowered before they could offer resistance. I feel pretty sure, however, that where they possibly could, they did not surrender—and more credit to them for it—without a struggle. In such conflicts many must have fallen while defending their homes who (with the usual large additions) were returned as " cruelly murthered and massacred."

In the deposition of " Julian Johnson, the Relict of John Johnson, clerk, preacher of God's Word, Parson of Athenry and Donmoore (Dunmore), in the County of Galway," there is a passage which shows that many of the murders may be accounted for without any deliberate action against the lives of those who fell. Mr. Johnson, it appears, was a pluralist, for we have a statement of the heavy losses he sustained in the County Leitrim as well as in the County Galway :

And afterward her said husband and she forsaking both those counties for safety retyred to the Island called the Inch, in the King's County, to the house of Capt. Robert Smith, and stayed about five weeks. And then her said husband [and her eldest

sonn, and one Mr. Baxter, a minister], and ye sd. Captn Smith,
and 20 more protestants of their company, being *in a skermish*,
all slaine by the sept of the Molloys and their souldiers : shee, this
deponent afterwards was by the same rebels robbed at the sd.
Captain Smith's house of goodes and chattells, worth 240.[li] more.
And then and there the sd. Captain Smith's wiffe was alsoe robbed
of all her goodes, and she and the deponent after for severall days
restrained with those rebels and [were constrained to] eat and drinck
amongst them that *had murthered* their husbands. And that
Preste O'Moloy, a frier, was the principall man in that slaughter
and robbery. Whoe quickly after in a triumphing and rejoicing
manner sayd : It was a brave sport to see the yong men (meaning
some of the English), *defending themselves on every syde*, and their
twoe eyes burning in their heades ! . . . And then all the Protestants
there were turned out of the Island, stripped of all they had. . .
And although the deponent and the sd. Capt. Smith's wife
escaped away and lived, yet many of the rest (being in all about 140)
being turned out without their clothes, dyed of hunger and starving.

The Friar O'Molloy's version would, perhaps, be
different. Although there may be no reason to doubt Mrs.
Johnson's veracity, her recital would necessarily borrow
colour as well from preconceived notions as from the
hardships which she endured. One thing, however, is
certain : the lives were lost in a well-contested skirmish ;
and no life was taken after the conflict ended, although
(if we may trust to the deponent's arithmetic) about the
seven score persons remained absolutely at the mercy of
" the rebels." That many of these, later on, died of hardships
and destitution,—which is only too probable—is a very
sad affair, but, at the same time, not to be confounded
with " deliberate massacre."

It is only in a rare case that we find the distinction
between foul murder and the fatality of warfare so distinctly
marked. It does not follow that the distinction holds only
in this case, or only in cases where the resistance is admitted.
As a rule the Parsons-Borlase Commissioners accepted
without question the statement that such and such " and
divers others were cruelly and barbarously murthered
and put to death," when, had the matter been examined,
a very different return could have been made.

The Commonwealth Commissioners, within certain prescribed limits, endeavoured to investigate real charges. Had
their predecessors acted on the same principle, the world
had never heard of an Irish St. Bartholomew ; and had
the real cause of murder and outrage been fully and
honestly gone into (as the Confederate leaders, in 1643,
urged should be done), it was not the old natives of
Ireland, but the rulers of Ireland, that had stood charged
and convicted of " the *deliberate* shedding of innocent blood."

Dr. Reid complains that the outrages—"the severities," he calls them—committed against the Irish in the course of the civil war "have been grossly exaggerated by Romanist, and even by Protestant writers, who, not only shut their eyes to *the awful provocations* previously received but endeavour to fix upon the British the guilt of being foremost in the work of blood,"—a statement which for reckless disregard of the real history may vie with anything written by Froude himself. He wrote this with an eye to the Island Magee affair, seeming to assume that, in that single atrocity, was comprehended all that the Irish had to complain of. We may put that matter aside—it has been too exclusively dwelt upon by all parties—and it will be as the loss of a drop out of the full bucket. I have shown in a former paper that the pretence of awful provocations is an invention of certain historians. The principal Protestant writers on the subject who preceded Reid were Carte, Warner, Brooke, Leland and Burke, and not one of them could be said to be partial—not even Burke—to the Catholics of Ireland ; nor did they, or any of them, concede anything for which they had not warrant in the history of the country. So far from exaggerating the "severities" practised against the Irish, they have altogether understated them—Burke being perhaps the only one who had sufficient mental vision to penetrate the fogs of prejudice raised by Jones, Temple, and their following, and to form a tolerably adequate estimate of the situation.*

Reid's statement is almost the reverse of what it ought to be. In the guilt of the shedding of innocent blood "the British"—as our historian will call them—were not only the first in respect of time, but were the first in actual performance all through, if we do not choose to shut our eyes to the achievements of the commanders and others empowered to "kill, slay, and destroy by any means they may." Cole alone claims credit for destroying more people by starvation, not to speak of slaughter otherwise, than can, on any fair computation, have fallen in any form

* Even Mr. Lecky, clear-headed and fair-minded as he is, in his general views, is hardly consistent, when he says : " Irish writers have very often injured their cause by over-statement, either absurdly denying the misdeeds of their countrymen, or adopting *the dishonest and disingenuous method* of recounting only the crimes of their enemies."—*Ireland in 18th Century*, ch. i. To charge their enemies falsely were dishonest and disingenuous. Not so to recount the oppressions from which they suffered. And who denies that the insurgents committed crimes ? In the Island Magee case there has been over-statement. What Irish writer has made stronger charges against the enemies of the rebels than Nalson has made against the same parties ?

at the hands of the rebels, and certainly far exceeds the sum total of murders and casualties in petty conflicts for which the rebels were responsible.

With Reid and others, the overmastering idea is that the Irish people rose in rebellion and gave way to all manner of gratuitous wickedness—just because they were " Romanists." Now, the man who starts with that idea, or who harbours it in any corner of his mind, deceives himself if he thinks he can write Irish history : he has got " a bias to his bowl " which will take him far out of the course he professes to follow. That unfortunate bit of " Romanism " is the dead albatross that weighs down many to practices which otherwise would be rejected by their better nature. They could all do better if they would try to regard the matter as a struggle between a grasping faction in power and a whole people who should think themselves too well treated if tolerated.

I do not, however, mean that Dr. Reid or any recent writer originated this unfortunate view of the insurrection of 1641, for it was very sedulously propagated by " the State " in Ireland, by the Parsons-Borlase Commissioners of inquiry, and by all the writers who caught inspiration from " the Castle " in Dublin. One cannot go very far into the depositions without feeling how much the Commissioners were impressed by sense of duty to put the " Romish " Church into the dock.

Would the writers, who are so positive in associating the " Romish *faith* " with the rebellion and its worst performances, go just one step further and assure us that the opponents of the rebels did all that *they* did just because they were Protestants ? I don't think any one has gone so far as that ; and it would surely be a great mistake to impute religion as the motive with anyone of the lot then of " the State and the Council in Ireland." They acted as they did, not because they were Protestants— not because they were of this or that nationality—but because they were a lot of worldly, grasping, self-seeking adventurers ; and from this description I don't except even the courtly Ormond or Dean Henry Jones. Ormond, in the ordinary sense of the term, could not be called an adventurer, but in the end he showed himself a more consummate grabber than Parsons himself. It may seem irreverent to impute worldly motives to so distinguished a churchman as Dean Jones, who was much given to preaching. A very active apostle he was ; so active indeed. that the care of a diocese was far too little to use up all his apostolic zeal. He became bishop of Clogher towards the end of 1645, but did not cease to act as chief of the Commission for taking depositions. His signature as " Hen : Clogher " with that of " Hen : Brereton " is met with not unfrequently, particularly on certified copies of depositions taken in the earlier period.

I don't know whether many, or any, among his co-religionists would put forward Dr. Jones as a typical Protestant. In my view, he is typical rather of the faithful worshipper at the old Temple of Interest on Cork Hill—the thrifty husbandman who " ploughs the Half-Acre."

And this would be of less concern to us now but that we owe to the same Dr. Henry Jones, as the master-craftsman of the depositions, and author of the Remonstrance of 1642, all the distorted views of the Irish of that period which have ever since given zest to " the things called histories." He it was who showed how to work out the theory that the Irish and Anglo-Irish, the peer and the peasant, alike arose in rebellion, at the instigation of their clergy, having been so long indulged in " a surfeit of freedom" that they would be content with nothing short of the utter extermination of the English and Protestants. The corollary to this is—That to preserve the Protestant religion, the Government had no other course open to them but to act as they did. The zeal for the preservation of Protestantism was in the Castle circle but a cover for monopoly, and worldly aggrandizement. What troubled the great " Protestant " divines and territorialists was not any fear of being deprived of their right to the Kingdom of Heaven, but the natural fear of forfeiting their sole claim to place, and power, and fat livings in the Kingdom called Ireland.

To Temple has been accorded the credit, or the discredit, of making the " idle silly tales " and monstrous exaggerations current in history. Yet Temple was in reality but a counter in the game in comparison with Dean Jones, who was the brain of that campaign of calumny. Temple's so-called history is little more than an enlarged edition of his reverend friend's Remonstrance.

How able, and how unscrupulous was this Dr. Henry Jones, Dean of Kilmore, Vice-Chancellor for fifteen years of the Dublin University, Bishop of Clogher under Charles I., Scout Master-General under Oliver Cromwell, and Bishop of Meath under Charles II. is well shown by the pamphlet just named and by the use made of cullings from the depositions. One of the most absurd things put forward as duly " testified " is the alleged boiling to death of a child at Newtown or Castlecoole, in the County Fermanagh. It is possible that a child may, through accident have been scalded to death—such accidents have occurred in our own time. Two deponents are cited who *heard* that it was the rebels who so put the child to death!

Margaret Parkin, widow, deposeth: "That by the information of divers credible persons she understood that the rebels boyled a young child to death in a great kettle in the church at Newtown aforesaid." And another woman also heard the story from divers credible informants. But as usual we hear nothing from the "credible informants" themselves, and get no nearer the alleged fact, although of the 80 deponents cited in the "Remonstrance" over twenty hail from the County Fermanagh. Dr. Jones calls attention to the outrage in this artful fashion:

> But *how can that be forgotten*, or where shall it be believed, which we hear to have been done in the church of Newtown in the County of Fermanagh; where a child of Thomas Strettons was boyled alive in a Caldron: A thing which as one bare reports, we durst not so neither can we now with confidence enough, present it to that your honourable Assembly, nor can we averre it for true, *otherwise*, than as *by concurring examinations we find them solemnly deposed*, whereunto we desire to be referred.

Notwithstanding, he gives the reputed outrage a place in his recital of horrors,—that Remonstrance presented to the English Parliament for circulation in England— well assured that the story would be accepted without question; and lest there might be any misgiving, the reader is reminded that the matter has been "solemnly deposed" and rests upon "concurring examinations."

Solemnly deposed! And no attempt made to come nearer than hearsay! In the books of depositions we now and then come upon allegations of trampling upon and otherwise showing contempt for the Bible (or certain versions thereof). But, assuredly, the most contumelious treatment of the Bible was at the hands of those reverend Commissioners who took upon oath such wild improbable rumours and sent them forth as "solemnly deposed," without test or investigation, well knowing that the "credible" information would not bear the ordinary tests of evidence. We could all—as many of us as like the security—swear to the bulk of the matter "solemnly deposed," as lawfully as most of the examinants who called God to witness in presence of Dr. Jones and his colleagues. The blame lies not with those who made oath, if wild fables have been put forth as "evidence." Never did sworn examinants receive greater latitude, or more inducement to commit perjury.

In the T.C.D. MS., F. 3, 18, the following copy of an order by Ireton may relate to Dr. Henry Jones in his capacity of Scoutmaster-General :

I desire, That on sight hereof you would receive, and by all safe wayes and means endeavour to convey to the Lo: Bp: of Clogher at Dublin, or to myself, all such letters or papers as shall be brought to you for ye purpose from ye Lo: Marquesse of Antrim. And hereof I pray you fail not.

To the Governors of Trim, Droghedah, &   HE: IRETON.
other garrisons in Vlster or any of them
respectively

The copy is in "the Lord Bishop's" handwriting. The initial " H " is his to perfection.

In the same MS. (F. 3, 18), is the following, which testifies to the success of the said Lord Bishop under even the bishop-hating Puritans :

Die Jovis, December 5th, 1650.

RESOLVED by the Parliament, That the Commissioners for Ireland bee authorized upon a Survey upon Oath to sett out lands *of the Irish Rebells in Ireland* of the clear yearly vallow of Two hundred poundes, according to vallow ye same held in ye yeare 1640, to bee Settled upon Dr. Henry Jones, and his heires, reserving thereupon to the use of the Commonwealth of England a yearly rent not under ye proporcõns set down in ye Act touching Adventurers, and to certify their doings in the Premises to ye Parliament, to ye ende ye same may be approved and confirmed by Parliament.   HEN: SCOBELL, *cl Parlm.*

A True Copy of the entry of the
Originall in ye Surveyor-Generall's
Office in Dublin, and examined,
January, 1657, per D. A. WMS.

The Lord Bishop of Clogher was appropriately placed when put on the roll of Adventurers ; for whatever else he might be to the world outside, Dr. Henry Jones was essentially an adventurer in clerical garb.

Under King or Usurper, always to the front, Dr. Jones was actively engaged on several commissions under the Cromwellians. In August, 1652, he was appointed one of the Commissioners to take further evidence as to robberies and murders committed in the earlier years of the rebellion, for the use of the High Court of Justice. To show how this distinguished prelate could adapt himself to the times, he puts aside the episcopal title and style which he had used for a few years, and once more comes before us as plain " Hen. Jones." In this form his signature is appended to the deposition of John Hackett, Mayor of

Cashel (24th August, 1652), Wm. O'Dwyer (same date), Jane Cooper (12th Nov., 1652), "and divers others;" also to some of the Co. Armagh depositions taken for Sir Phelim O'Neill's trial ; and as " Hen. Jones " he signs Sir Phelim's own examination before the Council (23rd Feb., 1652–3).* Written in a large, firm and legible hand (only the " J." somewhat like a " Z "), which soon becomes familiar to the reader of the MS. depositions, the signature is one to recognise at a glance. And herein we have, I fancy, one of those minor traits which best show a man's real character. The strongest point in his creed appears to have been, that, at all hazards a man ought to endeavour to make the most of his opportunities in this world.

I conclude this sketch with an extract from the Dictionary of National Biography (1892) Vol. XXX. p. 108:

After the Restoration, Jones was elevated to the bishoprick of Meath (25 May, 1661). Owing, however, to the offices he had held under the Commonwealth, he was not allowed to lay on hands at the consecration of the twelve bishops. He took a prominent part in promoting the Parliamentary grant of £30,000 to the Duke of Ormonde on his appointment as Lord Lieutenant in 1662 ; but Ormonde's tolerant views in regard to the Irish found little favour with him.† He was deepy involved in the " No Popery " schemes of the Earl of Shaftesbury, and was particularly active in procuring evidence as to the existence of a Popish plot in Ireland, his intercepted letters, according to Carte, showing " something more zealous than honourable in his proceedings in that affair." *He was certainly the means of bringing one perfectly innocent person*, the titular Archbishop of Armagh, *Oliver Plunket, to the scaffold.*

The performance was indeed worthy of the presiding genius of " the depositions," and author of the " Remonstrance" of 1642. *Finis coronat opus.*

* See the fac-simile in Gilbert's *Affairs in Ireland in 1641*, opposite p. 367, vol. iii.

† ' In May. 1652, Dr. Henry Jones, then Bishop of Clogher and Scout-Master-General, appeared at the council of general and field officers of Ludlow's army, held at Kilkenny, and made the officers protest, through a dread of the Lord they trusted, against the general's too great aptness to mercy —so they termed it—and sparing those whom the Lord was pursuing with His great severity.'—*Cromwell in Ireland*, by the Rev. Denis Murphy, S.J. (p. 7, *note*).

THE SCOUTMASTER-GENERAL.

IN an inquiry into the merits of the depositions relating to 'the Rebellion of Forty-one,' it will be necessary to take into account the personal history and character of the man who had the principal part in getting up the 'evidence,' if he may not also claim the sole merit of originating that campaign of oaths against the native population of Ireland. I have in the course of my investigations come to the conclusion that the more we are able to learn of Dr. Henry Jones's public career the better we shall be able to appreciate the merits of the depositions.

I think it well, therefore, to append some extracts I have made from the T.C.D. MS., F. 3, 18 ('Letters and Dispatches'). A very large proportion of the papers in this folio volume are in the handwriting of Dr. Jones. These are, in general, rough draughts, much corrected and interlined. Though very few are signed, the handwriting, as well as the internal evidence, is sufficient to fix the authorship. Some despatches in same hand would appear to be drawn up for the bishop's brother, Michael Jones, Governor of Dublin after Ormonde's surrender of the city in 1647; addressed to 'Lt.-Gen. Cromwell' and the Parliament. The documents here reproduced were evidently written by Doctor Jones in his capacity of Scout-Master General (for which office he had put aside his mitre of Clogher, as long as the Parliament and Puritans were supreme in Ireland). While these letters serve to show the writer, they at the same time afford some clear glimpses of the tactics adopted to ferret out all movements in the direction of favouring the cause of royalty.

(1)

"For MR. SECRETARY.

Febr. 10, 1657 (?)

" Right Ho^ble

"Since my last to yor Ho : I have received information of a meeting of ye Irish Clergie [& others] in ye Co. of Letrim [in ye province of Connaught] . . . about 16 of wch number, at ye least, ye comittee doth consist being sometimes doubled as they find necessary. To this meeting (distinct from others of ye kind held elsewhere) is comitted, or by them is affirmed, ye management of ye great buisnes of ye Irish in way of correspondence wth others in Flanders & elsewhere. Theire last meeting was on ye 3^d instant, for wch by orders from ye Junto (?) was sumoned an Irish officer in ('the late' *erased*) Sr Walter Dongan's reg^t of Horse [for ye Rebells], who appearing, he was there told y^t [on letters and encouragm^ts from their friends & others] they had in like manner sent to others of like quality [wth him] in ye severall provinces, desireing that they be in readines [wth theire p^tyes] to answere ye first riseing, and that ye time prefixed by theire friends in Flanders was about Candlemas, or, at ye farthest, about ye first of March (wch first of March according to theire computation is ye 10th with us), And advised y^t He (as they said they had advised others) should [in ye meanetime] keep himself from being [seised on] by ye govm^t, wch might be probably attempted on some discoverys, or jealousies of them, [least thereby an obstruction be given to ye main buisnes]. This relation was given ye 5 instant by ye very p'son, & transmitted to me (he being one engaged . . . in my work). This day I received ye enclosed from another hand, & l^tres in another place, seeming to speake y same thing, both wch I referre to yor Ho: consideration, and remaine

' Y^or Ho:

'Faithfull & humble servant.'

(Not signed.)

Endorsed : 'For Secretary Thurloe.'

In Thurloe's fourth volume a few letters from Jones have been printed, but I cannot find that those here given are included. The foregoing is much corrected, and in some places the inter-lining is illegible or uncertain. The date is not clear. The right-hand figure may be ' 2 ' or ' 7 '—the latter I take to be the correct reading. Although at the time, Jones had been deprived of the remuneration formerly attaching to the office of Scout-Master-General, or director of the ' Intelligence ' department, yet such was his love for that duty that (as will appear from what follows) he volunteered to continue his services in that capacity, as he would have it, at his own expense.

(2)

"For ye L^d. BROGHILL

Dublin, *Jan.* 11, 1657

"' Righ Ho^ble and ever Ho^d Lord,

"In my worke for Intelligence I am directed to some correspondence (as to . . . with Mr Secretary, to whom I have nowe transmitted by my brother some papers, & I desired my brother y^t he would first show them to y^r Lo^p; in which are ye hopes both of Anab[aptists] and Irish for some suddene change. One of these papers, dated ye 1st instant, is onely for satisfying Mr Secretary of some newe Agents [engaged in way of Intelli-gence] ; *one* of *them a friar*, whereby I have hope of good & seasonable discovery, and in ye while I have now so ordered y^t affaire y^t nothing considerable shall passe me, of wch yor Lo^p shall be informed on all occasions by my brother [to whose hand] I shall commit all things in this kind, If I be not taken off *and discouraged by my condition at present,* being now under a second change, or reducem^t . The first was from Scout M^r gen^el to ye compiling a narrative of ye late warre in Ireland, wth ye salary of 340^li, w^ch , in ye new reducem^t, is totally cut off, without any further consideration [had of me]. (*Crossed out :* ' So as in effect *I am as altogether laid aside* . . . I fear I shall be altogether disenabled to act in y^t hitherto expected of me, for ye Intelligence, & indeed under any of ye wayes . . .') Hereby I shall be disenabled for any publique buisnes, & therefore must betake myself to retirem^t, I find my Ld Deputys thoughts troubled concerning me, & his Lo^p hath beene casting about, and proposeing many things, of wch there would be nothing of settlement, & without something of settlement, *I shall chuse withdrawing rather than to come under a third fall*. However, I shall [in my change of fortunes], ever remaine, my L^d

" Yo^r Lo'ps faithfull & obliged servant,

" H. J."

This draught shows much alteration and emendation, especially towards the conclusion. It is on the back of the half-sheet, containing copy or draught of letter to Thurloe, dated Jan. 11, 1657-8. In the estimation of Bishop Henry Jones, there was no ' blest retirement.' Like Wolsey, he would reckon it a crushing calamity to be sent to look after the concerns of his diocese. Henry Cromwell, it would appear, was the only Castle ruler who was able to take Dr. Jones's measure, or the only one who would take the risk of dispensing with his services. Possibly the Lord Henry may have discovered that Jones was already looking forward to another political change. At any rate, the Lord Bishop of Clogher whines over his 'reducement' like a discarded bum-bailiff. He is, however, quite circumspect in what he writes to Secretary Thurloe, as the matter might come under the eye of his Highness the Lord Protector.

(3)

"For MR SECRETARY

Jan. 11, 1657.

" Right Ho^{ble}

" I continue as formerly to present yor Ho : with ye digestts of what papers I receive [where they seeme to containe anything of matter]. There hath beene [ye last moneth a] meeting of ye Irish [wch had beene] in Conaught, not fare from Loughreagh, whither some repaired from Dublin, of wch and ye result of ye meeting yor Ho: may find something in those papers of ye 17 of December & ye 3 instant. In ye other papers of ye 31 December and 5 instant, is something (intermixt) concerning y^e [hopes of y^e] Anabaptists to ye same [with . . . y^t of ye Irish]. That Rich, in ye last-mentioned papers, is a cavalere who maried ye daughter of Col. Huncks, an Anab. Wth y^t Rich, I placed my Agent, for discovery of ye secrets of ye Anab, if any were comunicated to his said father. In ye enclosed, dated Jan. 1, yor Hon: may understand of my nowe engageing of newe Instrum^{ts} for Intelligence, *one of them is a friar*, by [whom] there may be hope of some discoverys above w^t I expect from other hands. And now is the way for Intelligence so ordered, y^t I presume nothing shall move of consequence [in any part, but I] shall have it."

(The latter portion of the letter is so much emended and the interlineations so crowded, as to be only partially legible.)

(Y^e salary of 340^{li} [under . . .] . . . assigned on my reducement from Scout-Mr Gen^{ll}, and notwithstanding I have ever since continued to act as formerly for Intelligence without any personall pay on y^t accompt, Yet did I make use of ye new salary (paid on another accompt) for both   to answere ye one and ye other. *Yet shall no discouragements take me off from my service to ye Intelligence,* so offered, and heereby I confesse myselff overcome by ('My Lo: Deputy's,' *erased*) . . tendernesse . . . of my condition I have on this occasion observed in my lord deputy, wch shall be to me sufficient & above anything y^t might be other waies offered, beside ye desire I have of searving yor Ho: to ye uttermost of my poor abilitys : So I shall take leave, and rest

'Yo^r Ho: faithfull & humble servant.'
(Not signed.)

The concluding sentences show the hand of the accomplished and time-serving sycophant.

On a half-sheet following the letter to Lord Broghill, is the following, which appears to be the revised and fair copy of the second part of the foregoing letter to Thurloe :

'I am in the new reducement heere cutt off from ye salary of 340^{li} wch was [assigned] under ye notion of & for compiling ye history of ye late warres in Ireland : wch salary of 340^{li} was setled on my reducem^t from Scout Mr Gen^{ll}. And notwithstanding my reducem^t from Scout-Mr Gen^{ll}, yet for obedience to my Ld Deputy's comands, I have ever since continued to act as formerly for Intelligence, without any personal pay, [being satisfied in ye makeing use of ye newe salary (given on another accompt) of what should in some sort enable me for both. Nor shall I looke upon my [state at present] as any discouragement so as to take me off from my service to ye publique (though in a private capacity) & heerein I must acknowledge myself overcome by ye tendernes of my condition wch I observed in my Ld Deputy, etc.

'For ye right Ho^{ble} Jo: Thurloe, Esq.
Principall Secretary of State, & one of his Highnes his most Honble Privy Council at Whitehall.'

On the same day he writes to Fleetwood also, and puts his hard case in still clearer terms, forgetting to say anything about that 'tenderness' which is so prominent in the letter to Mr. Secretary Thurloe.

(4)

"For ye Ld FLEETWOOD.'

"*Jan,* 11, 1657.

" Right Ho^{ble},

I begg yor L'ps pardon y^t I have not written so oft as I might have been expected, there being hitherto nothing of Intelligence of y^t weight as to be presented to yor Lo^p. At present there are great hopes among ye Irish (wch is given them from abroad) y^t, setl'ng ye Parlm^t, there will be a change; [this is given me] from many handes & severall wayes ; whereof although ye grounds appeare not to me, yet could I not but lay it before yor Lo^p [who can better judge of it]. I had now so ordered the way for Intelligence, y^t I dare presume nothing materiall should have passed unobserved ; in ye midst of wch I found myself unexpectedly cut off by reducement from y^t salary of 340^li per an^m, in wch yor Lo^p had placed me at parting, for my subsistence under ye action of observing ye passages of ye late warre heere ; & by wch salary I had also ye means for enabling me. to carry on ye worke of Intelligence [also ; in both w^ch], my handes are now weakened, besides y^e *discouragem^t of being layd aside :* Soe as now [I am enforced to withdrawe ; yet shall] never be wanting in searveing ye publique. and yor Lo^p particularly, as it shall be in my power. The goode Lord be yor greate director in all yor wayes, wch is the dayly prayer of, my L^d ; yor Lo^ps humble and most obedient servant.

(Not signed.)

In a letter which appears to have been written on his coming to Dublin, after his escape from the Cavan rebels, Dr. Jones urges his claims on the authorities in the style of one who will have no refusal (T.C.D. MS. F. 3, 11, under " No. 12 ") :

(5)

" As for mine owne particular, had I respected my private [& not entire to serve my prince and country] *I might at first have shifted away from ye county of Cavan* where I was resident and *have saved the best of my substance,* whereas now by my stay hitherto, I have lost all, and with ye rest my raym^t on the way hither, beeing stripped well nigh naked : So that I ame in great want, and shall be vnserviceable for his Maty's service in y^t respect, if not releeved. *I have a party in ye enemy's campe, of my friends.* Some also of my servants were pressed by them *who would store me with Intelligence fitting for ye State,* but beeing disenabled to continue a chargable entercourse betweene us, y^t must be loste. I did propound to ye L^ds that I might be alowed, as chaplaine-generall to ye Army, wth ye alowance but of one farthing ech weeke out of ech soldier's pay and one ob (?), theire pay being raised, wch is but 12, or at ye most 2^s p^r an^m from ech. Y^e answere given me was, y^t it was a place in ye Lo: Livetenant's disposall, whom they would not, in the disposall thereof, anticipate therein. Therefore I doe address myselfe to you, in that his Lo: would honour me with a dependance upon him as his chaplaine in Ordinary, and to admit me into this place for ye Army : ye place was by ye late Lo: Livetenant reserved to his chaplaines in time of peace, wch now would be more proper. Captaine [Theophilus] Jones, my brother, is a servant of my Lord's, to whom I have formerly written for my dependance on his Lo: as his Chaplaine, of whom hitherto I have heard nothing.

" Pardon this greate trouble I presse you withal, whereby you shall oblige unto you,

" S^r

" Dec. 14, 1641:"   Yo^u most thankful & ready servant."

(Not signed:)

Q

The letter is in the Dean's handwriting, and the internal evidence is conclusive. It will be seen that, from the start, he had marked himself out for the " Intelligence " department; and if " Blessed be the man who finds his work," Dr. Henry Jones ought to have been one of the happiest of mankind.

Nine days after the date of this letter the first commission was issued authorising Dean Jones and seven other clergymen to collect on oath statements about spoil (no word yet. about " massacre ") committed *by the rebels*. Could the matter be traced up, I consider it highly probable that the entire plan of operations was drawn up, and proposed for adoption, by him who was nominated the first among the Commissioners to that end appointed.

There is also in the same T.C.D. MS. [F. 3, 11,] a fragment signed, which appears to relate to Jones's mission to England in the behalf of the distressed ministers ; of which this is the conclusion :

(6)

" But lastlie, yet chiefly, let the glory of God, the enlarging of the Church and planting God's worship in that hitherto land of darknesse and superstition, kindle a godly zeale and forward-nesse [in all ye vndertakers & subscribers] to a work so pious, so profitable, so honorable . . .

" In the behalf, therefore, of that distressed country of Ireland, imploring yor ayde . . . tendred, By

" The meanest of her children, and
" Y^e humblest and readiest of Yo^r Ho^{rs} servants
HEN: JONES."

On a folding-sheet (MS. F. 3, 11), containing notes on the conduct of the war, is the following suggestive paragraph. The paper was probably drawn up at the instance of Michael Jones, but it is in the Dean's handwriting ; and the handwriting is not more characteristic than the style and the sentiment :

(7)

" The cutting off of the Ringleaders in this Rebellion will be a ready meanes for shortening ye worke, & bringing ye warre ye sooner to an ende. For doing whereof, & experience of former times hath taught us that, for pardons or rewards, it is usuall with y^t enemy to betray each other. It would therefore be considered whether it doth not much conduce to ye service, that a general comission be graunted to all Comanders of Forts & Garisons to treat with some of ye Rebells in this way, y^t promise of pardon, or offer of a reasonable reward answerable to ye service and befitting persons imployed [*illegible*] may be ratified, Provided alwaies ye persons attempted upon be considerable, and that *ye Actor be not a landed man, or if he be, y^c reward extend not to ye setting of him in his lands.*"

The personal appearance of one so able, so plausible, so " insinuating " (*v.* p. 195) may be realised from the description which the Rev. James Graves gives of the portrait preserved in the Clerical Rooms, Lakeview, Monaghan :

"Henry Jones (1644—Age, Dress, and Characteristics)—Middle age; sacerdotal gown and bands; full brown eyes; high brow; meditative and mild expression ; brown curled hair ; light moustache ; skull-cap."—*Kilkenny Archæological Journal* for 1862, p. 139.

IX.

SPOIL.

IT is hardly possible to overestimate the importance of the
circumstances that all the Parsons-Borlase Commissions of
Inquiry were directed against those who, for State reasons,
were described as the Irish rebels ; and that the first Commission, issued on 23rd December, 1641, made no allusion
to murder. The latter circumstance would be inconceivable
had there been any foundation for the wild rumours which
for over a month had been going the rounds of England
and Scotland, rumours for which the chief governors of
Ireland were themselves in a high degree responsible. Why
it became necessary, early in the year 1642, to extend the
scope of the inquiry, the Lords Justices very well understood ; and had all real cases of murder been looked into,
it would doubtless have been worse for many in higher
place than any among the rebels.

Even as it is, the "evidence" so-called, collected by the
Commissioners, notwithstanding the strenuous efforts to
put the worst possible construction upon the aims and
actions of the accused, amounts only to this : murder was
local, while pillage was general. Indeed a very considerable
portion of the books of deposition consists of statements of
losses "since the present rebellion began, and by reason
thereof." In many cases the statements also include what
the deponent has "credibly heard" of some alleged murder
or cruelty. But the number of complainants who have
confined themselves to their own affairs is rather remarkable
when we bear in mind how acceptable to the Commissioners
were the wildest and most improbable allegations of murder
on the part of the rebels. I have already given some speci-
mens of these returns of spoil, which I regard as a fair kind
of evidence, the subject-matter coming within the personal
knowledge and experience of the witness. One or two more
of these I give here ; and, first, the statement of Henry

Lesly, Bishop of Down,* subsequently of Meath, because of its interest from more than one point of view :

Henry, Lo. Byshopp of Downe, sworne and examined, deposeth that

Hee had improved his Byshoprick to more than a thousand pounds a yeere, and hee hadd two hundreth pounds a yeere out of his Parsonage of Mullabracke which he held in cõmendam ; hee hath allready lost full 2 yeare's fruits, being twoe thousand fower hundred pounds and is never likely in all his life to recepve the rente that shalbe due heereafter.

Item he hadd an estate of 200ᵘ per annum [rent-charge] of the Lo. Cromwell s estate, and land secured to him for the same [which] uppon the determining of a short lease, would have been worthe to him 300ᵘ a yeare wch. estate he would not have taken 2500ᵘ for before the rebellion.

Item he hadd a lease of the Parsonage of Termonmaguircke during Mr. Blythe's life, wch. did afford him† eighty pounds a yeare, and was worth 140ᵘ if he had sett it at a full rate ; this he esteemes to be worth 300ᵘ before the rebellion.

Item there was due unto him more than 800ᵘ by bonde, wch. is nowe lost, many of the persons being deade and the rest beggered.

Item that was due unto him of arrears of rent before the rebellion began out of his Byshoprick and Parsonage at least 900ᵘ.

Item he lost all his horses to the number of eighteene, all his cowes to the number of nine and forty, all his corne, there being with him much olde malt, and his haggerd for that harvest untoucht, and his winter beare all sowed, all his hay, his fuell of all sortes in greate store, the provision of his house of wine, beere, beefe, butter, bacon, meale, etc., and a great parte of his bookes and household stuff, to the value at least of 600ᵘ

Item. A greate parte of his horses were taken away by [the followers of] the Lo. of Ardes and Sir James Montgomery, and a greate parte of his corne and household provision destroyed by them, they lyinge there to the number of five hundreth for the space of five days. The reste of his corne, haye, fuell, and household pro- vision were employed for the use of the garrison of Lisnegarvey, especially the Lord Conway's troope.

His cowes [other than] sixe only that were stollen by his servant Patrick Magee were delivered to Mr. John Davis then Mayor of Carrickfergus, who promised to make the best of them for his use ; some parte of his goodes were taken upp by Arthur Hill, Esqre., Roger Lindon, Esqre. for their owne present use and the service of the Castle of Carrickfergus. Much more of his goodes were riffled by such as he is not able to name.

Item his sonne Robert Lesly had a living wch. he farmed at 160ᵘ a yeere and a good while before the Rebellion begun there was a whole yeare's rent due unto him which he never received, and since

* Co. Down depositions, folio 21. (Original number, 1286.)

† Reading doubtful. Seems to be ' the clere.'

he hath lost a yeare's profitts and is likely to lose it for ever. So that the said Bish^p and his sonne's losses cannot be computed to lesse than 8000^li.

Jur : 15 Junij, 1643.

JOH. WATSON,   HEN. DUNENSIS.
WILL ALDRICH,

The bishop's statement of losses shows how well a poor apostle of the Church Establishment in Ireland could live before that insurrection. I admire the way his lordship puts the case, so clear and so straightforward, no affectation of piety, no mock resignation. The bishop feels his losses like any other poor man, not only losses actual but losses prospective. The wicked and cruel rebels who figure in many another man's narrative are hardly heard of here except as parties " such as he is not able to name." The spoilers of his goods—those, at any rate, by whom he feels most aggrieved—are not the rebels, but the rebels' great enemies, the Montgomerys, Lord Conway, Arthur Hill and Roger Lyndon, esquires, who have discovered that the bishop's goods, chattels, and winter store of provision and fuel would be serviceable to their garrisons. And great must have been the store, when after maintaining Sir James Montgomery's forces for five days, there remained so much to carry away. A company of five hundred hungry guests, one may think, ought to be able, in five days, to eat out any bishop.

And not a word has the Bishop of Down to say about murder or massacre, although the rebels have confessed to the Archdeacon of Down (Dr. Robert Maxwell) that the diocese of Down is reddened with Protestant blood. The " thousand and more " barbarously put to death by the " inhuman butcher, Bryan O'Neill," must have been, almost to a man, a woman, or a child, the spiritual subjects of Bishop Lesly—at any rate, resident within his jurisdiction. Downpatrick, Killyleagh, and Castle Island are situate in the very heart of the diocese. Yet is the bishop strangely insensible to all the innocent blood of his flock, while he bemoans the loss of his income, his cows and horses, his household stuff and provision, his corn and hay and winter barley ! Surely never did live on this our planet a prelate so self-involved as the said Bishop Henry Lesly, *other accounts being true !* He surely must have heard through the Dean of Down, if from no other source, of the barbarous and inhuman cruelties which threatened the extinction of his people. Yet he treats the stories as old wives' tales, not worthy of a thought. And that parish which he

held *in commendam*—on the Census list there is but one
parish named Mullabrack—is one of the three said to have
been desolated and depopulated by Sir Phelim O'Neill.   In
the interests of humanity, as well as in his own interest,
the bishop ought to have made some effort to bring the
destroyer to justice.   It does not appear that he did anything
of the kind.   If the rebels were doing wrong they were not
the only wrong-doers, as Dr. Henry Lesly well knew.

In the County Armagh depositions (fol. 118) there is a
statement not unlike Bishop Henry Lesly's.   The deponent
is, I believe, a near relation of the celebrated rector of Tynan,
Dr. Robert Maxwell, but he gives no indication of having
heard of the 954, and the 1200 more, Protestants cruelly
butchered in the diocese of which he was an official :

Henry Maxwell, Chancellor of St. Saviour's of Connor, in the
Countie of Antrim, sworne and examined, deposeth and sayeth :

That since the beginning of the present Rebellion, and by meanes
thereof, Hee was, and still is, deprived, robbed, or otherwise dispoyled
of the possession and proffitts of his Church Liveing Leases : and of
other his goodes and chattells, consisting of bills, bondes, debts,
cattell, and other things of the value, and to his present losse of
one thousand eighte hundred twentie-three poundes.   And this
deponent is like to be deprived of, and loose this present yere's
proffitt's together with the future proffitts and values of his meanes
and Church Liveinge (440 li per ann.) untill a peace be established.
And further saith that the parties that he knoweth to be in rebellion
against his Ma'tie are theis that follow, vizt.—Teage Boy O'Hara,
Esquire, Coll. McManus O'Hara, gent., Hugh Oge McCormuck,
gent., John Stewart of Glenarne (*sic*), gent., and   Alester   Roe
Stewart, gent., all of the said County of Antrim.

Jur : vii Julii, 1643.   HENRY MAXWELL.

JOH. WATSON.
WILL. ALDRICH.

The case of "William Bulkley, Cleark, Archdeacon of
Dublin," was, we may suppose, by no means singular.
Deposeth, "That he hath owing him in the County of
Kilkenny for tyth there 29li, which he cannot receive by
reason his tennant writeth unto him that the said tyth was
to be paid to the Popish priest."

The accounts of "Spoil" committed by the rebels is, in
the main, a monotonous repetition of the same details, and
in the same set terms ; and such are the matters which are
crossed out in many of the books, as heretofore described.
Too often, indeed, we read of distress and privation which,
however exaggerated, is strongly attested by the sufferers
themselves, and is, I have no doubt, substantially true in

many cases. Yet we sometimes find the narration not
without some touches of humour, as in the following deposition, taken from the County Down book (folio 29) :

Serjt. Maior Willm Burley of Magherhylinn (Magheralin) one of his
Majesty's Justices of the Peace and Quorum within the Countie
of Downe, sworne and examined, deposeth and sayth :—

That when the Rebellion began this deponent was lawfully
possessed and interested [in an estate of 60 years lease from the
Bishopp of Dromore] in certain howses, towns, farmes, and tenements within the counties of [Downe] and Armagh, whereof the
demesnes were well-stocked with cattle, horses, [mares], sheepe
corne, and other thinges of great value, and the tenements and
farmes in the hands of tenᵗˢ were of the clere yearly value of
500ˡⁱ, and then this deponent was possessed of household goodes
plate, money, woll, provition, and other goodes and chattels. And,
being so possessed and interessed, was the xxiiird day of October,
1641, forcibly dispossessed, deprived, or otherwise dispoiled thereof,
to his loss and damage of eight thousand pounds at least, as he is
verely perswaded. And sayth that the parties Rebells that soe
robbed and dispoyled him within the said Countie of Down were
ffargus Magennis of (*blank*) nere Dromore, gent., Hugh ôLory,*
Moiraghe, gent [and his wife and their family], Donnell oge
McEdmund Boy Magennis of the parish of Macherhelin, gent., and
divers of the septs and names of Magennisse, the Lories and McCans
of the Countie Armagh] whose Chr'an names he cannot remember..
And further sayth that this deponent and his wiffe and children,
being gone away to shun the danger of that great multitude, severall
of his servants confidently told him that after he was gone away,
and that the Rebells had entered his howse, the wife of the said
Hugh O'Lory, taking upon her to order and dispose of the household
[goods], furniture, apparrell and provition, went up into this
deponent's wiffe's chamber, and seasing on the deponent's wiffes
apparell, attired and dressed herself in the best of that apparell,
and that [done] came down into the parlor, called for strong beare,
and made her servants fetch it and drunck a confusion to
the English doggs ; and being sett at the upper end of the
table, in a chaire, asked the people *whether that choice apparrell
did not become her as well as Mrs. Burley* (meaning the
deponent's wiffe) ; and shee and her base rebellious crew
contynued their rebelly carousing and drincking untill all
or most of them were drunck. And because they found
some of the hogsheads or barrells of strong beare a little mouldy
about the place where they were corcked up, they concluded
that [that] was ratsbane, and therefore they forced and burst open
those hogsheads and wasted and lett out the beare (wch. was both
wholesome and strong), and like savage or brute people, devoured
and spoyled the provition of viandes, and spoiled and defaced the
howse. And at length (upon the deponent's returne with a pty
of foote and horse against the Rebells) *and doing execũion upon*

* O'Lavery.

*them** the said Hugh òLory and his sept burned this deponent's dwelling-house, and all the rest of [the Towne of] Magherhelin aforesd.

Jurat 7 August, 1644

HEN JONES,   W. B. BURLEY.
HEN. BRERETON.

(To the endorsement is added the " hand,'' indicating that the contents are of particular interest.)

Although the house incidents are related at second-hand, we can hardly doubt their correctness. Mrs. O'Lory, in her new apparel, seated in a chair at the head of the table calling for strong beer, and trying to outshine Mrs. Burley, is a rather life-like picture. The redeeming feature of the story is that no violence appears to have been offered to any of the servants who remained in or about the house.

In breaking up the barrels and letting out the strong beer, the invaders doubtless did what was more " wholesome " for themselves. That such carousings were only too common is beyond doubt ; it would be too much to expect anything else from an undisciplined mob finding their way to such a cellar as Major Burley's—even in later times, soldiers under more regular military rule have been found to indulge in riot and excess when the opportunity offered. Carte says that Sir Con Magennis, on the retreat of Col. Mathews from Dromore, " entered the town with his forces, and used the few inhabitants that adventured to stay behind very cruelly, passing the night himself and his men (of whom scarce any were left sober) in such a revelling manner that they might have been easily cut to pieces."†

What kind of ill-usage the people received at the hands of Sir Con, our author does not specify. Neither does he cite any authority for the alleged revelling. I dare say, however, he is not far wrong in what he says about the carousing ; yet in a work so ample as the *Life of Ormonde* there was room to be more explicit about the alleged ill-treatment of the few people who remained after Mathews and his company had left. But assuming the carousal, one may see how misconduct might follow without direct authority from the commander. Such carousals, it is to be feared, were common enough among the insurgent forces, and it is by no means certain that similar breaches of dis-cipline were repressed with any firm hand by the com-manders who were said to be on the King's side. Almost

* In this neat little phrase there is matter which, I have no doubt, would connect with Portadown, had all been cleared up.

† *Life of Ormond*, i. 187. I have already shown how Dr. Reid improves on this text, for ' cruelly ' substituting ' with wanton and unprovoked cruelty.'

a hundred and sixty years later on, the same County Down
was again in the throes of rebellion ; and at an hour when
the fever had reached the crisis—the night preceding the
fateful battle of Ballynahinch—the British forces, who had
that day entered the town, gave way to indulgence and excess,
and escaped the consequences only through the chivalrous
refusal of the insurgent leader, Henry Munro, in opposition
to the counsel of his colleagues, to make a night attack on
the revelling soldiery.

If such a lapse of discipline could, at so late a period,
occur among the forces of the Crown, one need not be a
necromancer to figure to his own mind what may have been
the usual state of things among irregular, undisciplined
forces under command, in many cases rather nominal than
real, of leaders, for the most part ignorant of the merest
elements of military science. I treat of this phase of the
rebellion further on. To resume the question of spoil :

The rebels were not the only parties who had to furnish
their commissariat from spoil, as is well shown by Bishop
Lesly's deposition, and by Sir James Turner's account of
the Scotch garrison of Newry. And, had the insurgents
not gone beyond taking what was necessary to carry on a
regular campaign, they could have escaped much of the
reproach which, after every allowance is made, must be
admitted to cling to their movement. We have therefore
to consider " spoil " under two heads—what was taken,
presumably, for the maintenance of such forces as were in
any degree subject to command, and what was seized by
unauthorized mobs and by the idle and ill-disposed, who,
taking advantage of the upheaval, robbed where they could.
Although in the indiscriminate style of the depositions and
of the " histories " all are jumbled together as " rebels,"
there is room for a well-marked distinction ; and when the
matter is more fully inquired into, the reason for such
distinction will, I doubt not, assert itself.

All deponents who had been possessed of live stock
complain of the rebels having seized on, deprived and
despoiled the said deponents of horses, cows, sheep, corn,
hay and all manner of goods such as could be carried away ;
and we owe to Bishop Lesly of Down decisive testimony
to the fact that such " spoil " was by no means peculiar to
" the Irish Papists in rebellion." The complaint comes from
various parts of the country that tenants describing themselves as British Protestants were by their own landlords
deprived of horses, cattle, and farm produce. One case
from the County Down is perhaps typical of what occurred
in many places (folio 177) :

The Examination of Nicholas Ward of Cloughmagherycat,* in the County of Down, gent., taken on behalf of the Commonwealth at Carrickfergus, the 9th of June, 1653,

Who being deposed upon his oath, sayth : That at May before the Rebellion he took to lease from Patrick McCartan of Loghin Iland, in the County of Downe, Esqre, one quarter of the townland of Loghin Iland, where he, with his family and goods, were resident at the beginning of the Rebellion ; and [upon Sunday being] the next day after the Rebellion began, the deponent's cattell were all driven away ; and within a day or two after the depon*t* (not knowing of a general insurrection) hearing that his cattell were taken away by Patrick McCartan his men ; the deponent repaired to the said McCartan, to a place called Lisstudery,† some three or four miles distant from Loghin Island, where he found the said McCartan and Owen McCartan his brother ; and the deponent demanding of the said Patrick McCartan, by the name of Landlord, wherefore his cattell were taken before any rent was due, the said Owen McCartan replied, There is another matter in the wind ; and the said Patrick then sayd to his brother Owen, Let us be favourable to Mr. Ward in restoreing him his cattell. Whereupon, Owen sayd, Brother our souldiers must have meat. Upon hearing whereof, the deponent made all the haste he could to get into Lecale ; but at parting the said Owen McCartan called the deponent aside, and unbuttoning his [the deponent's] coat asked the deponent, What have you here ? Whereunto the deponent replying that he had nothing, ymediately tooke horse and rode away. And further sayth that passing from them into Lecale, the deponent did see in a mosse a great number of cattell, wch. he concluded could not be less than 5000 cowes and oxen, wch. were all taken from the Brittish by the sd. McCartan and his brother Owen, as the deponent was then tould by an Irish-man. And deponent further sayth not.

(Not signed by Deponent).

Taken before us,
   G. BLUNDELL,
   GEO. RAWDON.

Mr. Nicholas Ward's was not, after all, an extreme case. His cattle had been driven off ; but, as it appears, his horse had been left to him, and there is no mention of house pillage.

As Patrick M'Cartan of Loughinisland, Esquire, and his brother Owen were charged with having taken active part in that insurrection, I give here the examination which each made in 1653, when, as it appears, they were prisoners at Carrickfergus (T.C.D. Depositions, County Down, folios 169, 171) :

* The village of Clough on the mail-coach road between Downpatrick and Castlewellan. Sir Bernard Burke identifies Cloghmaghericatt with Castle-wellan, which is, however, but four miles from Clough.

† Listooder in the civil parish of Kilmore ; in it is a long-disused, graveyard called Killygartan. (Note supplied by Rev. James O'Laverty, M.R.I.A.)

The Examination of Owen McCartan of Kinelarty in the County
of Downe, aged about 58 years, taken at Carrickfergus, 9th of
June, 1653 :—
Being demanded where he was at the first breaking forth of the
Rebellion, saith he was at his own house, and remayned there for
the space of three or ffour moneths after, at which time he was
amongst others thrust out by the Scotsmen. And saith he did not
goe to the siege of Downe till about seaven days after the siege was
begun by the ôNeylls and Magneisses, and that he continued
there but one night, his business there being to save the goodes of
ye Ld. Cromwell from spoyling ; and also to enquire after a horse
and some cowes taken from him by the Irish party ; and then
returned three or foure nights as he remembers before his brother
came home. Sayth the chiefe in com̃and of the Irish at the siege
were Ld. Iveagh, Bryan McHugh boy and Con og ôNeyll, and
he hears Donell McBirne Magneise was there, but he saw him not.
ffurther saith not.   OWEN McARTAINE.*

Taken before us,
   G. BLUNDELL,
   GEO. RAWDON.

On folio 171 :

The Examination of Patrick McCartan of Loghin Island, in the
County of Down, aged about 63 years, taken at Carrickfergus,
9th June, 1653 :—
Being demanded if he tooke up armes at the beginning of the
Rebellion, sayth that he lived quietly at his own house till about
two or three months after the breaking forth of the Rebellion, and
then was forced out by the Scots. Being demanded if he pillaged
any Englishman's goodes at the beginning of ye sd. Rebellion,
denyeth that he ever did any such thing ; further sayth he had no
com̃and of any men before Downe and that the reason of his
being there at the time of the siege of Downe was to preserve the
Lord Cromwell's and other people's houses and goodes from spoyling,
and spake to those that com̃anded before Downe to preserve the
goodes of the people and not to burne ye Towne. Sayth that those
that [were the chief men] there were the Ld. of Iveagh, Donell
McBirne McMagneise (sic) now in prison, Bryan McHugh boy
ôNeile, and Con ôNeile, and severall others.   Being further
demanded if he sum̃oned any castles in Lecayle, Denyeth that he
ever sent any sum̃ons or order for the delivery of any into the hand
of the Irish ; being further demanded if he received any letters from
Coll. Chichester or Sr Arthur Tyringham to invite him to come
in unto the English, denyeth that he ever received any such lre.
                                     PA. McARTAIN.†

Taken before us,
   G. BLUNDELL,
   GEO. RAWDON.

* A good signature ; not many better on the books of depositions.
† Also a good signature.

The following deposition, of same date, shows that the
charge of murder at Downpatrick was not so well
founded as to call for any notice from the English gentry
of the immediate neighbourhood.

Down, fol. 179.

The Examinaĉon of Arthur Stoughton; of the Quoyle, in the
County of Downe, Esqre., taken at Carrickfergus, the 9th of June,
1653, in behalf of the Common Wealth :—

Who being duely sworn and examined sayth, That at the
beginning of the Rebellion at such tyme as the Rebells came to the
towne of Downepatrick, this examinat, lieving within a mile of the
said towne, received a l^{tre} from Patrick M'Cartan; of Loghin Iland,
Esqre.: the substance whereof was an intimaĉon unto this Exa'at,
that all his frendes within the barony of Lecale, and in particular
the house of Downe, meaning thereby the lord Cromwell's house,
have submitted themselves vnto them ; and if he this exam^t would
submit to them he should have as good or better quarter then
his said frendes had gotten ; to wch this Examinat having returned
a denyall in writeing ; he heard no more from the said M'Cartan.
And this Examinat further saythe that about the same time this
examinat received notice from Mr. Robert Kinaston, who then
lived in Saul neer this Examinat's house, that the said Patrick
M'Cartan had written to him likewise to the same purpose for the
yeilding of his Castle,   And this Examinat further sayth not.

Taken before vs,

G. BLUNDELL,

GEO. RAWDON.

There are many depositions relating to the siege of
Down[patrick], and I have already made use of some of
them.   All or nearly all go to show that no effort was spared
to implicate, as accessaries, the M'Cartans * and Magennises
and O'Neills in the few alleged murders at or after the
taking of the towne.† The subsequent course of proceedings
before the High Court of Justice are involved in obscurity.
It is beyond doubt that the Irish commanders before Down
faithfully observed the terms on which the castle or " strong
house " of the Lord Cromwell at Downpatrick was surrendered by Colonel Hamilton.   And if any were killed

---

* MacCartan, 12th of September, 1605; granted to Lord Cromwell the third
part of Kinelarty in consideration of a certain sum of money, and that Lord
Cromwell should educate in a gentlemanlike manner his son Patrick, who was
then about fourteen years of age.—O'Laverty, *Down and Connor*, i., 85. It
strikes me as rather remarkable how many of the leaders in the insurrection of
1641 received an *English* education.

† I have already suggested that non-combatants may have been killed by stray
shots from the defenders of Lord Cromwell's house, beside and overlooking
the town (*v.* p. 83).

subsequently in or about the town, the commanders were responsible only so far as laxity of discipline might contribute to the commission of such crimes. It is too bad that anything of the kind should occur, but the attempt to found thereon a charge of massacre such as figures in the pages of Harris is monstrous, and is no less monstrous on the part of later writers who, without examination, accept his conclusions.

The seizure of cattle could hardly be looked upon as more than a misdemeanor in those days. All parties made " preys " on their opponents when and where they could, and rather gloried in the performance. It may be remembered how Mr. Peter Hill of Downpatrick vaunts his munificence in maintaining a force of four score and fourteen men, some horse, some foot, " at his own charges," *saving what provisions in corn and cattle he and they took from the rebels,* that is from any and all whom he chose to regard as such. It was impossible to avoid taking sides in the combat : those who were not with Mr. Hill were against him, and he was against them. And how triumphantly Mr. William Montgomery, of Rosemount, chronicles the raids which his father, Sir James, made into the Irish quarters of Iveagh and Kinelarty, and thereby " galled them to the heart " by the preys of cattle he took from them. Nor did the said Sir James scruple to gall his own neighbours and friends, for he subsisted his men " by the help of the grain of substantial British inhabitants living next the Ardes." And the Bishop of Down could tell how loyalist commanders did not limit their acquisitions to what " rebelly " Papists could furnish. Again, it was not for nothing that General Monro, returning from the re-capture of the Newry, made that circuitous march through Iveagh and Kinelarty ; but then the rich prey of cattle so mysteriously disappearing from the hill of Drumbo, almost severed the bond of union between the two branches of the British forces, as we learn from Pike and Turner.

It will appear from the following explanation of one of the articles in the treaty or capitulation of Kilkenny, 12th May, 1652 (copied from T.C.D., MS. F. 3. 18), that the seizure of horses, cattle, corn, and food-supplies in general, was recognised as in the usual course of war :

Vppon explanations of the Articles touching personall estates, wee doe hereby declare, that noe officer, or sould^r comprehended in ye said Articles shall be Impleaded or tryed at Lawe for any horses, cattle, money, or other provisions, or free quarters, taken by them by order of their superiour officers, from any of the inhabitants of this country, nor for any matter or thing comitted

or done by them as sould^rs in ye orderly and Vsual course of
Warr, Provided, this extend not to free any of them from beinge
impleaded for due debts, according to due course of Lawe.

Dated at Kilkenny, this 12 May, 1652.

JO: REYNOLDS, HIER: SANKEY
HEN: JONES, WM ALLEN
JO VERNON.

It were easier to palliate the seizure of cattle and horses,
and other things which were to be found without entering
houses, than the breaking into and rifling of peaceful homes,
as was not uncommon. And the forcible seizure of " household stuff " was not the worst part of what the sufferers had
to endure. It is a common story, not from any one county,
but from almost every county, that the deponent and others
were stripped—some add " naked," a few " stark-naked "—
and so turned out to the world in the winter season.

We have to bear in mind, however, that all these statements are taken in chamber, where there is no representation of the accused—taken, mereover, by Commissioners
who have themselves suffered the loss of income and goods,
and who, bearing the bitterest feelings towards the rebels,
have an interest in encouraging witnesses to make the
most damaging statements. Few witnesses would come up
without some inkling of what sort of evidence was wanted.
Few would be deterred from exaggeration, while exaggeration was so acceptable ; the fear, if any, on the part of
witnesses, would be rather to fall short of expectation.
There is no indication, at all events in the earlier depositions
—none that I have been able to discover—of any witness
being rebuked for extravagance or in any way made to feel
that he was to confine himself or herself to such statements
as would bear to be re-opened. On the contrary, the wildest
and vaguest assertion is taken for fact, now and then
slightly qualified by the admission that the deponent is
going on " credible " information. Under such circumstances one would do well to cross-examine, in his own
mind, every deponent who makes strong charges of murder,
cruelty, or robbery. Often, in going through the " evidence "
of the fearless swearers, I have come upon chasms in the
very place where I could most of all wish for particulars,
or *some* definite information.

There is still current in the north-east (if not in other
districts) of Ireland a use of the term " strip," which I take
to be the sense in which it is used in these depositions : to
" strip " meaning no more than to put off the outer garment.
" Strip, and fall to work," simply means " Take off your

coat, and get to work." " I saw him stripped " is the same as " in his shirt-sleeves," that is, his coat or jacket being off. Our etymologists could learn something among the country people of Ireland, whose everyday speech preserves terms and usages long obselete in the more refined circle, or too hastily rejected as bad English, being really good English of the olden time.

I have often, while reading the depositions, been reminded of the restricted meaning of the term " strip." But I do not look upon the offence, even so qualified, as a venial one. And after every allowance is made, it appears to be only too well established that people were, in not a few cases, deprived of clothing needful at that inclement season, when either taken from or driven from their own homes. There is a good deal of positive assertion to the effect that, in some cases, the poor people were absolutely stripped, either before being turned out, or afterwards while on the way to a place of refuge. The general character of the evidence would justify the rejection of such statements, as well as the no less positive assertions about some other offences never since heard of in Ireland. If any cases of the kind did really occur, they were the acts of ruffianly individuals—of the " Raskell Multitude," mentioned by Father Peter Walsh —and without sanction from the leaders. It is also to be observed that such allegations stand out in contrast to the experience of nearly all the deponents who were detained as prisoners, and who were in daily and hourly contact with " the rebels " that were under command.

The fault lies not with the deponents so much as with those who took and recorded the statements, that we have so many things charged against the general body of the Irish people, when the matter rested perhaps with some individual, acting on his own account and in utter disregard of the common cause. A deponent says " And the rebels did so and so," or " *they* did," when by a little cross-examination it could have been brought out that the deponent had no real knowledge of the matter about which he seems so positive, and had no right to mention such a thing when on his oath ; or, supposing some such occurrence, it was, in reality, the doing of some corner-boy or member of that ilk. The crime of some worthless and nameless individual, or of a number of such individuals, could, in this way, be made to asperse the Irish nation ; and the Parsons-Borlase Commissioners knew how to turn vague and extravagant statements to particular purpose. Nor were those Commissioners so singular in this respect. They had no claim to originality in the art of indicting a certain

people and creed. The practice neither began with them
nor ended with them. Only a few days since, at the end
of the street in which I write these pages, a plate-glass
window was, in the morning, found broken.. A pious old
lady, of somewhat anti-Irish sympathies, mentioning the
matter to me, added, in sorrowful accents, " The people are
so wicked ! " She was, I think, not very well pleased with
me for replying : " The *people* were not consulted in the
matter, I am sure. Some corner-boy could do it without
making anyone the wiser." Her reading of current history
was, it will be seen, restricted to papers and periodicals in
which the act of a nameless individual becomes the indictment of the Irish race. With such object in view, it would
manifestly be inexpedient to inquire too closely into the
bona-fides of most of the statements put forth by deponents
whose imaginations had been fired by hatred and alarm, in
addition to a sense of loss. Had the Commissioners been
disposed to discriminate between the acts of those " in
rebellion " and of those who thought only of turning to
their own account the confusion of the time, we should, I
have no doubt, be able to form a truer estimate of the
situation. They have, instead, done their utmost, and with
only too much effect, to confound all things with the object
of attaching odium, not simply on the authors of crime, but
on the nationality and religion of the Irish people for all time.

But while I feel that one can never sufficiently stigmatise
the malignity and dishonesty which not only underlie, but
wrap in mystery much of that " inquiry," I am far from
approving of what was, in many instances, done by the
leaders of the insurrectionary movement.

The want of a head was the great   fault—the parent
fault of many of the crimes and disorders by which the cause
was discredited and in the end ruined. The blow struck
by the arrest of the two northern leaders on the eve of the
insurrection paralysed and disorganized the management
of affairs in Ulster, and not in Ulster alone. The man into
whose hand the chief control of the North fell was not the
man to carry any great movement to success. Sir Phelim
was not a cruel man—there is much to the contrary in the
depositions ; but he was not a competent leader, and, in
the situation in which he was placed, incompetency may
prove to be a worse fault than cruelty itself. It was perhaps
intended that he should be chief director in Ulster only till
the arrival of a greater O'Neill, the man of European fame ;
and, had that arrival taken place at the start, it is likely
enough that things would have found another course, not
merely in one province but in all Ireland.

As it was, the general reproach of the insurgents is not
"massacre" but "spoil." That "the rebels" and the
spoilers were only practising the lesson which they had
been taught by their rulers so impressively within the
memory of many people then living in every parish in
Ulster, is the simple fact ; but, none the less, a fact which
ought not to count, and would not count, with men worthy
the position of National leaders in a great crisis.

Assuming that they were justified in the attempt to
resume the lands of which—let legal fictions say what they
would—they believed they had been robbed, the obligation
still lay upon the leaders to treat the dispossessed with
more consideration than in many instances was shown
them.   It would not be true to say that the insurgent
chiefs were insensible to this demand of humanity ; and
some of them, like Philip O'Reilly of Cavan, have, by their
humane and considerate treatment of the ejected, earned
complimentary mention from their bitterest opponents.
Nor was the action of the Cavan gentry so exceptional.
That here and there a local " captain " may have encouraged
what a man of honour and Christian character would feel
it his duty to repress, can hardly be denied.   Yet it is much
more likely that negligence or inconsiderateness, rather
than malevolence, was the fault of many who had assumed
authority—and no slight fault either, at such a time.   The
want of a cool strong head in the chief place of command was
for all parties a very unfortunate circumstance.   It was clearly
the duty of the provincial chieftain and of those who shared
the responsibility of seizing on the homes of people that
had not deserved such deprivation by any fault of their own,
to take measures for preserving the unhappy sufferers from
being looted and spoiled by the ruffian element, which in
any part of the world would be sure to make itself felt in
such a crisis.   Had the principal men in a few places
followed the example of the "Ould Rebell,* the Lord
Mountgarret," who shot a prominent spoiler, their cause
had been less stained with crime.   It would be the affectation of ignorance to assume that, on so sudden a breaking
up of the ordinary course of events, there would not be
found many who thought only of the spoil, and who, if left
to their own election, would not hesitate to commit crime

* ' A little after Christmas, 1641, Whereas the Rebells had possessed them-
selves of all the considerable towns in the County of Tipperary, as Cashell,
Clonmell, and ffethard, they mett together, and chose for their Generall *the
ould Rebell*, the Lord Mountgarret, and for the Lieut.-Generall the Lord of
Ikerrin, as alsoe Colonells and other officers.'—*Deposition of Rev. Samuel
Pullein, D.D.*

R

or to be guilty of inhumanity for the sake of the spoil.*
Leave such parties free to take what they may wish to have,
and it would be in any land no better than it was then in
Ireland—probably much worse anywhere else. The sufferings entailed by depriving the dispossessed of their needful
clothing and provision when sent away, and by exposing
them, with insufficient or no escort, to further spoiling
while on their pilgrimage, seems to me the worst thing that
can be charged against any considerable proportion of the
rebel leaders. The Temple-Froude allegations of the
" general fact " of massacre in cold blood I hold to be an
imposture as against the rebels in general, but not without
reasonable application as regards the anti-rebels—these
latter the only real enemies the King had in Ireland. But
that there was lamentable loss of life arising from destitution and exposure at an inclement season, every one who
considers the matter at all must sorrowfully admit. There
were, on the other hand, many who acted in a chivalrous
spirit towards the ill-used people so suddenly deprived of
their all. Acts of kindness and fellow-fellow not unfrequently
brighten up the narrative, although the narrators were
not much encouraged to pay compliments to the rebels.

---

* The Rev. John Kerdiffe, Rector of the parish of Disertcreagh, in the
barony of Dongannon and Countie of Tyrone, deposeth : ' Att Armagh they
acted better than in other places : ffor elsewhere as at Dongannon: Loghegall,
Moneymore, and the places adiacent, all the English and Scotch (a very few
excepted) were robbed, stripped, and cast-out of their houses. But at Armagh some
of the English fared but somewhat better : ffor though all their beastes abroad
were taken from them, yett many of them enjoyed what they had within their
howses. And some of them had their howses filled with the distressed English.'
    It was bad enough for the Irish rabble to rob, as in some instances they did,
the poor dispossessed people on their way to places of refuge ; but it was
infinitely worse for anti-rebel forces that ought to be under discipline to so
treat the unfortunate refugees.
    Elizabeth Rise Price, County Armagh, deposeth : ' And further saith that
that the said Owen ôNeile gave unto this deponent and severall of the better
sort of people that came along with her, when they had a convoy, xviii^d apeece
in money, and a peck of oatmeal to every two of them, and some money and
meal to all of the rest. But afterwards when this deponent and the rest mett
with the Scotch army under the cõmand of Cõmander Lesley the younger,
*those Scotts forcibly robbed and despoiled them of all the money and meal they
had left*, and bad them goe to the Rebells and fetch more. And it is cõmonly
reported by many English that severall English [that is, about three score]
that escaped from the Rebells and fledd to the Scotts for favour at the Newry
were turned away by the Scotts without relief.'
    Ann, the wife of Captain Thomas Dutton, County Donegal, deposeth :
' . . . And what part of the howsehold stuff and goodes, the Irish did not
destroy, or dispoyle them off, some of the Scottish companies under the
cõmand of Capt. James Cunningham, Capt. John Stewart, and Capt. John
Cunningham, tooke and carried with them quite away, to these deponents'
damage of £240 more, and upwards, by the direcõn or consent of the said
captains, *they being then and there present*.

I here take leave to reproduce from the Galway book of depositions the statement of Mrs. Mary Hamond, relative to her experiences on the way from Tuam to Galway :

Mary Hamond, wyfe of Wm. Hamond, clerke, . . . sworne and examined, saith :—*

That about a week after Christmas, 1641, she sent from Tuam [towards Galway] 3 horse loades of goodes (the remainder of what was left her, and not taken away by the souldiers of Redmond Bourke, garrisoned in Tuam) wch. goodes were taken away by Riccard Bourke's souldiers, and conveyed to Riccard Bourke's house at Ballyn Derry, some 3 miles from Tuam aforesayd, and soe by them detained.

Afterwards upon fryday the 12the of January, all the English being, by the ill usage of the aforesayd garrison, driven from Tuam, she being then . . . (within 2 or 3 days of the tyme she expected to be delivered) went on horseback towards Galway ; and at Bellclare-Tuam many Irishmen mett her and putt her from her horse, and much feared her ; being gon a little way further, there met her one Patrick Hyggins of Lyskerry, with his skeyne naked in his hand (in which posture he road violently towards her so soone as he espyed her) wch. made her, not without danger, leap from her horse as soone as he came at her, but then hee, for her husband's sake (as he sayd), did her no other harme.

About 2 or 3 miles further, two men and a woman met her, and tooke from her her knife, sissers and other things in her pocket and took away her apron and were stripping her of her gowne, when two men of Galway (of the Joyces) came accidentally and released her.

A little further two other [Irish] men mett and violently puld her off her horse, saying they would carry her to their Archbp (Dr. Keally†) as a prisoner instead of one of theirs then in ye fort of Galway ; but they (as she conceives, and as the Joyces told her) meant only to draw her out of ye way and strip her ; with these two men she sate in ye rayne till wett to ye skinne before she was delivered from them by one James Lally (that knew her) accidentally coming that way.

Coming to Clare (4 miles from Galway) the two Joyces carryed her to an English house, and left her there. When ye woman of ye house (Herbert Crosse his wife) durst not let her stay, saying that the Irish would kill her husband for entertaining her. Whereupon (though in bad case to stirr) she went out into ye street to looke for some other place to rest in ; being come to ye further end of Clare neere ye Castle, some Irishmen that saw her in Crosse's house, overtook her and would have forct her back againe, and

---

* Her husband, William Hamond Clerk, Prebend of Killabegs, in the Diocese of Tuam, had preceded her to Galway. In his deposition he mentions his 'abode in his Majesty's fort of Galway from Christmas, 1641, till May, 1643.' This fort was erected by Mountjoy in 1602, destroyed by the Confederates in 1643 ; stood on the site of the former abbey of St. Augustine, where the old cemetery remains, about a bow-shot to the rear of the railway station. The depositions for Roscommon and Galway are bound in one volume,
† O'Queely.

when she durst not goe with them they puld her up and downe
the street (then very dirty) and one of them stroke her a very greate
blow on ye backe with his pike, and setting the head of the pike to
her breast, threatened her that he would dash her face against the
stones.   Whereupon being very neere ye Castle where the two
forenamed Joyces were, she screeched out aloud, and the sayd
Joyces came out to her, and after much parley were faine to give
the rogues worth (*sic*) a shilling in drink to let them carry her to
some place in the towne ; and goeing towards the Castle a woman
spake out of a window and bad them not bring her thither ; soe that
thus wet, dirty, weary and bruised she was forct to goe a good way
through the dirt to a poore Irish house, where the Joyces left her
and bad the ma^r of ye house take some care of her.   Within two
houres after she fell into violent Trav'll and could get none to goe
for a midwife but ye man of ye house in whose absence the rogue
that stroke her before in the strett came and took off her mantle
[which she received from her man] (of which she never stood in
more need) and putt it upon himself and sat down by her, mocking
and flowting at her.   When ye midwife came and affirmed she
was in Trav'll, yet that rogue with many more would not allow
her the privacy of that poor chamber without either bed or fire,
but stayed there by her y^t night and [the next day and night].
In this case she continued from Fryday night till Sunday night
about 8 or 9 of ye clock at which time she was delivered of a dead
child : wch she verily believes was kild by ye ill usage she had
received, and want of fireing, etc. . . . Being thus delivered,
the next day she was brought to Galway in a carr and kish.

 Jur : 16° Augusti, 1643.

HEN. JONES,   MARY HAMOND.
EDW. PIGOTT.

The story is not free of difficulty.   It looks strange that
she should be going alone at a time when, as she says, all
the English were thrust out of Tuam ; and the English
of that neighbourhood, or most of them, made for the Fort
of Galway.   One also feels at a loss for the Joyces at the time
she was relieved by James Lally.   The Joyces had relieved
her a short time before, and a little later on they are again
with her, entering Clare-Galway.   There are other points
which would require a little clearing up.   But the statement
appears, in the main, to be truthful ; and a pathetic one
it is, although not an " indiscriminate blackness."   In
reading it, one cannot help regretting that the " Ould
Rebell, the Lord Mountgarret," did not cross the path of
some of Mrs. Hamond's acquaintances in Tuam and Clare-
Galway.   The two captains, Redmond Bourke and Rickard
Bourke, who robbed her of her household goods, and allowed
her, alone and unprotected, to take the risk of the road in
her then condition, amply proved their fitness to ruin any
cause with which they might be identified—that is,
assuming her statement as correct.

Mrs. Hamond has nothing to say about murder. She hints at harsh treatment of some kind on the part of the insurgent commanders, but we get no particulars. The two Bourkes behaved vilely enough towards this poor lady. But at a time of "universal slaughter and massacre," as the historians will have it, there is some satisfaction in knowing that no such execution was attempted in Tuam.

There can be no question that pillage must have led to conflicts in which lives were lost. Had there been anything like fair and open inquiry under the Parsons-Borlase Commission, we should have found that instances of murder in cold blood were very few indeed in the earlier period of the insurrection—few, indeed, at any period, excepting the retaliatory measures set afoot by the bloody exploits of those acting under State warrant. In the County Armagh book of depositions (fol. 248) there is an unsigned deposition (but endorsed in the usual form) in which we find relation of an incident such as must have been by no means rare :

The examination of Andrew Hutchinson of Knockcarne in the County Antrim, aged about forty-two years, taken at Lisnegarvey, 19th April, 1653 :
Who saith that at ye beginning of the Rebellion he lived in y ^{e} County of Armagh, in ye parish of Loughgall, and in ye townland of Hockley where this examts. habitacõn was ; in ye said parish, as he was returning from the town of Armagh, having left there some goodes for safety, and was returning home againe to carry some more thither [he saw] a neighbour of his named Rob. Millenton *running out of his house with a pike staff in his hand to save some cattle* which [some of y^e] Irish were takeing, [*who*] *was kild amongst them.*

Notwithstanding the technical defect in the document (likely an unfinished copy of an examination before Sir George Rawdon), the testimony is such as might have been given in many other instances instead of the usual " And the Rebells did murder so and so." But had the Commissioners gone into the circumstances they should have largely defeated the object of their commissions.

The number of those British who were foully murdered was insignificant in comparison with the death roll of those who perished in battle or conflict, and these again were few when put by the side of those who were taken off by privations and diseases mainly due to the privations. And the loss to the Irish themselves was very much greater under all these heads. Such is the conclusion to which I have come on my own account. That all losses on one side were confounded with the " murdered " was " inevitable "

only from the way in which the examinations were taken,
and from the inducements held out to deponents to refer
every casualty to the "bloody acts of the rebels," and to
multiply the number at will.

Even among those who found their way to places of
refuge the mortality was dreadful, as will appear from the
contemporary records of Coleraine and Limerick, which I
presently cite.

> One James Redfern of Maherafelt, deposeth . . . And further
> saith, That he had been credibly told by some of the English in the
> towne of Coleraine that since the Rebellion began there dyed there,
> of Robbed and Stript people, of protestants, that thither had fledd
> for succour, the number of seven thousand or thereabouts, besides
> those of the towne that anciently dwelt there, and that the mor-
> talitie there was such and so great, That seven hundreth or eight
> hundreth dyed in 2 days there.

This is from the sworn deposition. I have, however, no
hesitation in placing that authority, in respect of trustworthiness, below the unsworn document from which I
extracted (pp. 221-2) the accounts of the engagements at
Garvagh and Ballymoney (T.C.D. MS., F. 4,516). The
writer gives so graphic a description of the town, as a place
of refuge, that I must quote from him at some length :

> This towne built by the City of London is the second in that
> then county of Londonderry, of reasonable capacity and handsome
> structure, and the only walled Towne between Derry and Carrick-
> fergus : by reason whereof, it was the common sanctuary and sole
> refuge of all the neighbouring places about it.   Neer Twenty
> Ministers of the Gospel (whereof myself was one preserved like one
> of Job's scapeling messengers to tell this story) for safety of their
> lives fled hither with a great presse and multitude of people ; so
> that when all possible harbouring in the Houses fayled, the church
> was fitted within and without her walls and round about the
> churchyard, with little Hutts pestred (sic.) and packed with poore
> people.

Dreadful must have been the privations of so great a
multitude of people—many of whom were used to the com-
forts of life—pent up and huddled together as above described.
The writer, it is satisfactory to find, knowing so much of
the country around, has nothing to say about massacres.
He makes no such charges against the rebels, although the
" rising " had naturally occasioned the utmost alarm and
terror.   He has, however, some bitter complaints against
the Scots forces quartered upon them.

> The Towne soon put themselves in a military posture, raising
> and maintaining eight foot companies at their own proper costs
> and chardges, neer a twelve months' space, even untill ye Lords

Justices of Ireland (by whose authority they were raised) disbanded them to surrender ye Towne and Garrison to Generall Lesly his regiment, which afterwards did quarter heer under the comander, a surly Mercenarie, now called Sir George Monroe, for the full tearme of ix* (sic.) years or thereabouts ; living for the greater space of that time uppon free quarter, to the utter depauperatinge of the formerly spoiled and exhausted Cittizens and inhabitants who remained altogether unsatisfied for their owne services.

In connection with the rout at Ballymoney, he writes :

On the eleventh of February, but two daies before the sore and sad blowe, God from Heaven Thundered at ye.roofe and steeple of ye Church in Colerane, renting ye gable like ye Vaile of ye Temple (in a manner) from the Top to the Bottom, firinge with Lightninge the shingles wherewith the Steeple (or at least blowinge them off) was covered, and striking diverse persons of both sexes and all ages, to the number of eight or ten, whose Hutts or Cabbins were made under ye wall of ye Church. This was, and may well be, taken for an ominous presage of the ensueinge disaster by the Gun, inasmuch as the sound of ye thunderclapp did so nearly resemble the sound of some great Cannon, that most of us all (if not all) did persuade ourselves that it was the roaring voice of a Cannon.

Alluding to the Ballymoney defeat and the pestilence, he proceeds :

This great overthrow (which was the death of our priorly dying Courage and Resolution) pent as within our Trenches, like so many sheepe for ye slaughter, whereupon for want of fresh ayre and wholesome food, a pestilentiall feaver attended, to take up the leavings or gleanings of the sword ; though the number of ye dying within ye walls in comparison with the slayne without and in ye fields, may justly stile them by ye name of ye Death's Harvest, rather than ye Gleanings. For in the space of four months (the mortalitie beginning with the Spring) *there dyed an hundred a weeke* constantly, *sometimes an hundred and fifty persons* by just account taken (but not till after ye rage of death grew notably) by Henry Beresford, Gent., who was one of the last which closed that black roll or bill of Mortalitie, soe that ye number of ye dead may well be computed to reach unto 2,000 people, old and young.

This reduces the mortality to one-fourth of that seemingly proved on oath. But in this case, as in many others, the unsworn testimony happens to be more reliable than the " solemnly deposed." And a dreadful record it is for a town then of less than a hundred houses (as the same writer tells us).

Not less interesting is the *Diary of the Siege of Limerick by the Irish in* 1642, another of the MS. records bound up in the T.C.D. volume " F. 4, 16." This Diary, consisting

* From what appears further on, this ought to be ' vi.' years.

of eight quarto pages, is written in a very small but neatly formed hand. The abstracts which follow will show how much more fatal want and pestilence were to the refugees and garrison than the assaults of the insurgent forces :

May, 18, 1642. After long and tedious watching in our severall houses, upon Wednesday, May 18, 1642, we came into the castle of Limerick, about one of y⁰ clock ; when within 3 howers after, the towne began to lay at us with their muskets, that none of the castle durst offer out after that. None of yᵉ castle hurt that day, but one poore old woman kild without yᵉ castle halfe an hower after our coming in.

19. The enemy laid at us more fearily, and from yᵉ adjoining castle kild John Skegge, a little girl and boy, and hurt some three women and children, *a bullet shot from the enemy rebounding from yᵉ wall was catcht in a boy's mouth without hurt*, the boy laughing.

20. They shot not altogether so much ; did us no hurt that day.

21. They took more stations, shot (as before) at us, and towards night accidently killd Tho. Yong.

22 . . . This day 6 or 7 great pieces were shot of from yᵉ castle which did some damage to yᵉ towne. We had no hurt of man, woman, or child with us.

23. They took more stations, and by times, shot at us from 15 severall places round about us, but none hurt with us . . . .

24. They continued as before against us ; one woman dangerously shot in yᵉ arme, and a boy in yᵉ hand, none more hurt that day.

25 . . . None killd that day or hurt.

26 . . . None killd or hurt of ours.

From the time we came in till this day, were buried amongst us of sick weak poore yᵗ dyed there 21, besides yᵉ 5 yᵗ were killd.

That is, the deaths from sickness and privations were more than four to one killed by the enemy's fire. After another week, on 2nd June, he reports :

There was small shooting of either side, none hurt of ours. This morning was yᵉ Moon at yᵉ full, but she was not fuller of light than our hearts were of heavinesse, feare, and sorrow, in yᵗ yᵉ tydes and yᵉ winds had been now 3 days full and faire for us, and noe ships appeared, noe help, noe comfort, noe news came to us ; hunger, sicknesse, and weaknesse increased ; and our enemyes still girt us round about more strictly ; from Thursday last to this Thursday night were buried 38, besides four yᵗ were killd with yᵉ great gun (bursting ?) * one woman by yᵉ enemy and a boy yᵗ was wounded yᵉ weeke before, in all 44 souls ; from May 19 to this 2nd June, were buried 70.

---

* He says that the gunner ‘ violently threw in yᵉ shot, fired it, killed himself and three others, in yᵉ place, and hurt 6 more.’

Of the 70 it will be seen that only 11 were killed, and 4 of these by mishap on their own side. After another week (June 9)—

From Thursday last to this evening dyed with ye 2 y^t were killed, 40 ; soe y^t in all there were buried 110.

The weekly bill of mortality went on increasing, although the casualties from active warfare remained few. The enemy having succeeded in running mines under the Castle walls, the garrison were obliged to capitulate.

22 (June). This day ther was noe shooting from either side, as if there had been a formal cessation. In ye afternoone ye Bp of Limerick dyed, and in ye evening, ye answer to our Captain that they would accept of the two aforenamed to treat with them ; and accordingly they went out, and after much debate got quarter for life and goodes ; we were to have accoõodation for houses and necessaries during our abode in ye towne, and horses and carriages to convey us to Corke, we paying for what we tooke. (Subsequently it was arranged that they should be taken to Cork in some ships that had come up the river).

23. This day we yielded ye castle, and carried the Bishop to his grave and buried him in St. Munchin's Church ; and then every one of us began to carry out our goods out of the castle to houses assigned us ; *we had civill usage from ye souldiers, and our former acquaintances in ye towne gave kindly visits.*

. . . There dyed of our company this small time we stayd in ye towne 57 : we did impute ye cause of this mortality to our change of dyet, etc. : soe that ye number of our dead did in that short time amount to 280.

The writers who put down the murders committed by " the rebels " at 4,000, and allow that twice as many of the dispossessed perished of destitution and pestilence, do not, I am satisfied, overrate the latter. I cannot, however, admit that even the half of four thousand suffered from violence save in hostile conflict. We may as well accept, without question, Temple's, or even Milton's estimate, as have anything to do with the figures sworn to by most of the deponents. Will anyone come forward and declare for Archdeacon Maxwell's figures, any more than for the 152,000 sworn to by Sir Charles Coote at Lord Maguire's trial ? English writers would make short work of such figures, and such testimonies, coming from any country but Ireland.

It is otherwise with the allegations as to " spoil." When a deponent gives particulars of his own losses, he has a right to be heard. The subject of his own losses is one of which he can give evidence. Far otherwise is it with the deponent who tells us " he is verily persuaded that the wicked and cruel rebels did murder and massacre multitudes of innocent Protestants, as he is credibly informed." There is everywhere evidence of pillage ; and, although there is exaggeration, there is only too much reason to believe that multitudes of the dispossessed died because of their being deprived of all their means, and so left exposed to cold, hunger, and pestilence. Had the declaimers against the Irish movement, instead of rioting in rhetorical bounce, been content to deal with actual occurrences, they had found in this matter of pillage a proper mark for criticism, and even for condemnation, although pillage was almost the only thing which had been taught the insurgents by the example of the foreign masters of their country, more emphatically at a time not so far removed from the period of " the execrable Irish rebellion of Forty-one."

[SUPPLEMENT TO IX.]

In some cases deponents put in business-like statements, regularly drawn up, giving details of the losses, " since the rebellion began, and by reason thereof "

(1) The following is the account of losses sustained " at severall tymes since 23rd October, 1641," by Christian Stanhawe of Clanbelew, Parish of Loughgall, in the County of Armagh :

li. ster.

In household stuffe and wearing apparrell to ye vallue of ..	200
Two swords, three fowling peeces, 3 pistolls at ye first beginning of ye rebellion	006
In corne of all graines to the vallue of	200
Seven travalying geldings and naggs worth	035
A stoude howse with twenty four mares, fillyes, other horses and colts, being all of English breede	053
Twenty English cowes	050
Ten faire oxen of English breedes	035
Six Irish fatted beeves, cost	006
Two bulls, with twenty-five heades of young cattle; some whereof were of 3 yeres olde, some of 2, and some of lesser ;· all being of English breede, well worth	030
ffiftie fower English sheepe with their woll	020
ffourteene swine	004
Her mansion house with other out-houses burnt by the Rebells, cost the building	300
Besides in Annuall Rents to the value of 380* li per annum —	
Whereof one year's value she accompteth to be lost ..	280

And plate worth xxx^{li}.

And other goods and chattells, as cattle, corne, horses, and other things worth 305^{li} 13^s 4^d.

Soe that her present losse amounts unto the full some of 1633^{li} 13^s 8^d†

And [henceforth's] like to be deprived of at least 280^{li} annuall Rents above menċoned till peace be established.

(From the joint deposition of Christian Stanhawe of Loughgall, in the County Armagh, and " Owen ffrankland of the Cittie of Dublin, gent."—*County Armagh Depositions,* folio 75).

* Changed here to 380 from 280.

† The figures here have been altered, and are not clearly legible. The tot-up ought to be different.

(2) Lievetenant Anthony Stratford of Castle-Caulfield, within the
parish of Donaghmore, in the County of Tyrone, Esqre, made
faith (*sic*) before us, that upon the three and twentieth day of October,
early in the morning, he, with his wife, children, and family, were
taken prisoners, in his owne house at Castle-Caulfield, by Patrick
Donnelly, his neare neighbour, who was captaine of a hundred
men or thereabouts, under Sir Phelim O'Neale [then in rebellion],
and was at the same tyme spoyled of all his estate to the value hereafter following ; *and kept prisoner* there under a strong guard by
Sir ffelimy's directions *for y* space of nyne moneths*, after which
tyme, upon y* Newes of y* Scotch Army coming thither, the said
Donelly with the rest, being affrighted, fired the Castle, and so he,
this deponent, with three score and fifteene soules, tooke y* woods
for their shelter, *being guided by a gentlewoman of the Donellyes*,
who forsook all to go with us, and after three or fower days skulking
where she ledd us, she brought us safe to y* Lord Viscount of
y* Ardes his forces. The particulars of his losses ensue, vizt :

	li	s.	d
Imprimis, in lynnen, pewter, brasse, bedding, house-hold stuffe, and utensils to the value of	60	0	0
Item in wearing apparrell of his owne, his wife and five children, worth	60	0	0
Item xvii milch cowes of ye largest English breede	51	0	0
Item eight heyfers incalfe	16	0	0
Item twelve young almost two years old apeece	12	0	0
Item eight plow horses	16	0	0
Item fower saddle horses	20	0	0
Item nyne oxen and a bull, all of English breede	30	0	0
Item my dwelling-house and other out-houses which were burnt by them and lately built by *his* meanes, cost	60	0	0
Item two hundred barrels of wheate, rye, barley, besides oates	120	0	0
Item in muttons for slaughter, worth	07	10	0
Item in swyne, old and young, xxiii, worth	10	0	0
Item in hay, worth	20	0	0
Item in waynes, carts, and all other materialls for husbandry	15	0	0
Item in bookes, worth	20	0	0
In money	80	0	0
In plate to the value of	13	14	0
In rings and jewells, worth	12	0	0
A lease for nineteene years to come, worth xx^li per annum of wch. he hath lost a years proffitt	20	0	0

And this deponent is like to be deprived of and loose
the futur proffits of his farme worth xx^li untill a
peace be established.

Totall 643^li 19^s 0^d

Jur. 7 ffebr., 1642.
RANDALL ADAMS
WILL. ALDRICH

ANTH. STRATFORD.

(*Co. Tyrone Depositions*, fol. 35.)

A CASTLE-MADE REBEL.

JAMES TOUCHET, Earl of Castlehaven and Baron Audley, Peer of England and of Ireland, is the most prominent of the Catholic witnesses who are usually, but unjustifiably, pressed into service to testify to the " general fact " of the " massacre of Forty-one."

The case of this nobleman furnishes an instructive chapter in the history of that mis-called rebellion. For, although with extreme reluctance he joined the rebels, was appointed member of the Supreme Council of the Confederate Catholics, and a general of their army, there was not in the King's dominions a heart more sincerely loyal than his ; nor was there among the cavaliers who clung to the fortunes of the monarch a follower who would more dutifully shed his blood in the service of his royal master than this peer of the realm who takes his place in history as a rebel leader. Before the rebellion he had been in the service of Charles I., and in attendance on his royal person. How he became a rebel he has himself related ; and Horace Walpole is cruel enough to insinuate that had he not taken the trouble to chronicle his own exploits the world had remembered little about Castlehaven-Audley—which may be more a skit at the general ignorance of Irish history than at the claims of the noble lord to recognition. But . . . " he made all the amends he could to the King's cause. A little before Clanrickarde's failure he dispatched Castlehaven to the young King at Paris, whose service, when he found desperate, he engaged with the Prince of Conde, then in rebellion ; attended that hero in most of his actions ; entered into the Spanish service in Flanders ; was witness to the unsuccessful dawn of William's glory ; and died in 1684." He had the cavalier's air and self-importance to the full ; and the extravagant notions he had about his own importance led him, however unconsciously, to disparage the native Irish leaders in the same movement, and to treat with glaring injustice the man who was incomparably his superior in the art of war. He speaks of Owen

Roe O'Neill as he might speak of an uppish and pretentious non-commissioned officer. And no solemn-faced Puritan ever was more absurdly contemptuous of the old Irish, those of the North more especially, than was this same Catholic purple-man, who was for a time their fellow-rebel. Nor was there a man then living who, had his services been accepted by " the State " when he made offer of them, would have more gleefully advanced to do execution upon those Northern rebels, whom, later on, he was chosen, over the head of Owen O'Neill, to lead against the Scots.

That a man of his leanings and views should have exaggerated ideas of the irregularities and crimes of the original rebels in Ulster was natural and inevitable. Yet no one has pronounced more emphatic condemnation of Temple's so-called history than this Lord Castlehaven, whom Froude and others unblushingly bracket with Temple as witnesses in the same behalf. As to the origin of the rebellion he thus sums up all the evidence he was able to collect :

That whatever the primary grand design, whatever the source of this rebellion was or might have been, it is, notwithstanding, in all appearance, beyond dispute that (as I have said before) the unexpected success of the Scotch, and the daily misunderstandings, between the King and the Parliament in England was what gave it birth and life at this time, viz., on 23rd October, 1641.

And as to what followed :

As for the massacre that ensued, it was certainly very barbarous and inhuman tho' I cannot believe the tenth part of the *British* natives (reported by Sir John Temple and others of the same kidney to have been murdered by the Irish) lived then in that Kingdom, out of cities and walled towns, where no such massacre was committed. I am certain in Sir John Temple's muster-rolls, of whom the subsequent scribblers borrowed their catalogues, there are not 15,000 persons to be found, tho' it is manifest that in divers places he repeats the same circumstance twice or thrice over, and mentions hundreds as then murdered that lived many yeares after, . . . Nevertheless it is certain that there have been great cruelties committed upon the English, tho' I believe not the twentieth part of what is reported. But the truth is, *they were very bloody on both sides ;* and tho' some will throw all upon the Irish, yet 'tis well known who they were that used to give *orders* to their parties sent into enemies' quarters *to spare neither man, woman, nor child.* And the leading men among the Irish have this to say for themselves, that they were all along so far from favouring any of the murders that not only by their agents (soon after the King's restoration) but even in their remonstrance presented by the Lord Viscount Gormanstown and Sir Robert Talbot* on the 17 March, 1642 [-3], the nobility and gentry of the nation desired, That *the murders*

* Borlase, folio 58, gives a full copy.

on both sides committed should be strictly examined, and the authors of them punished according to the utmost severity of the law, which proposal certainly their adversaries could never have rejected but that they were conscious to themselves of being deeper in the mire than they would have the world believe.*

There is much matter for reflection in these remarks, particularly in the last sentence. Why should the Puritan Government in Ireland—for Puritan it was, even while using the King's name—first or last, have restricted inquiry to one side ? Many reasons may, perhaps, be assigned, but there is one reason worth a thousand others—the Lords Justices and members of their council could not, for their own sakes, venture on such an inquiry. A full and impartial investigation would inevitably have brought out that the sanguinary edicts issued by the State, and the sanguinary action taken on them, were the real instigators of most of the murders chargeable against the Irish. If people would only imagine for a moment a similar order of things in any other land, they could have little hesitation in fixing the responsibility for the crime and bloodshed.

And the Irish Government of Charles II., consisting of the same set, if not the self-same individuals, had still the same reason for refusing full inquiry. The Council urged Ormonde, then Lord Lieutenant of Ireland, to agree to the exclusion from " innocency " of every Irish Catholic whose name appeared in " depositions " ; but he, knowing too much about the way those documents were got up, would not be a party to giving them so much sanction.

There are some further passages in the Castlehaven Memoirs upon which, perhaps, the " massacre " authors, may rely. In continuation of last extract, he says :

This is plain matter of fact, and the consequences of it so obvious that, notwithstanding all the groundless clamours of some *who loudly cry out against the Irish, but speak not a word of their own rebellion,* I must do that Kingdom so much justice as to declare that I can no more believe that the leading part of the nation did ever design, much less encourage, the barbarous cruelties there committed, than I can be persuaded that the Lords and Commons who first made war against the late King in England did, from the beginning, intend to imbrue their hands in his sacred blood. Yet still I think them inexcusable, because I see no great difference whether a man kills another himself or unchains a fierce mastiff that will tear him to pieces.

This supposes murder to be *intended.* He has professed his disbelief in any such *design* on the part of the Irish nation.

---

* *Castlehaven's Memoirs*, pp. 18-20, Waterford edition, 1753.

I cannot therefore but believe the contrivers and abettors of the Irish rebellion guilty of the massacre that ensued, tho' committed by the rude rabble ; no less than *those that raised the late rebellion in England are guilty of their Prince's blood* as if they had been regicides. (*Memoirs*, p. 20.)

He shows his animus towards the Northern leaders, and attempts to make a distinction between them and the rest of the nation. But then weren't these Anglo-Irish lords " abettors " when they joined in common cause with the " authors " of the rebellion ? And, on his own showing, Lord Castlehaven-Audley shares the guilt of the " massacre " he describes—as John Hampden has his share in the execution of his sacred majesty. In his eagerness to heap reproach on " the Northerns," he sometimes cuts the sod from under his own foot, and lays himself open to unfair attack, as Lord Anglesey brought home to him, in his caustic reply to the Memoirs.*

As for the generality of the nation . . . 'tis manifest they knew nothing of the design before, nor favoured it after it was discovered ; as appears by their solemn protestation in Parliament, on Nov. 16, 1641, when meeting according to the prorogation, in the Castle of Dublin, and this rebellion being laid before them by the Lords Justices, Sir Wm. Parsons and Sir John Borlase . . . . both houses immediately declared their abhorrence to the rebellion: and agreed *nem. con.* to the following protestation.†

Thus both Houses of Parliament (the true representative of the nation's loyalty) unanimously declared *their readiness to prosecute and suppress the rebels*, and in order to bring them speedily to condign punishment, having with all possible zeal and alacrity offered their lives and fortunes to the Lords Justices, they fell immediately to consider of the most effectual means to do the work. But this way of proceeding did not, it seems, square with the Lords Justices' designs, who were often heard to say *That the more were in rebellion the more lands should be forfeited to them ;* and therefore in the very heat of business they resolved upon a prorogation. Which the Parliament understanding, the Lord Viscount Costelloe and myself were sent from the Lords' House and others from the Commons to the Lords Justices to desire the continuance of the Parliament at least till the rebels (then few in number) were reduced. But our address was slighted, and the Parliament the next day prorogued, to the great surprise of both houses, and the general dislike of all knowing and honest men.—(*Id.*, pp. 22-3).

To prorogue Parliament so abruptly, when the services of all who were willing to help was so much required, looks like madness ; but there was method in the madness. The rebels multiplied, and at once became a formidable body,

* This reply, written about 1680, is printed at length in the 1812 edition of the *Castlehaven Memoirs*.

† The protestation is also given by Borlase, p. 33.

Drogheda, about a day's march from Dublin, was besieged. Major Roper, marching to the relief with about 700 men, was, in a great mist near Gillianstown, set upon by the rebels and defeated. The rebels levied a weekly contri- bution on the adjoining portions of the Pale, as the Scotch had done the year before in the North of England. The reluctant compliance of the Palesmen brought them within the clause for " aiding and abetting."

The members of Parliament in this disorder retired to their several habitations in the country ; so did I to mine, but had not been long at home when I received a letter signed by the Viscounts Gormanstown and Netterville, and by the Barons of Slane, Louth, and Dunsany, with an enclosed one to the Lords Justices, which these noblemen desired me to send, and, if possible, get their lordships' answer. The letter was very humble and submissive, *desiring only they might have permission to send their petitions into England to represent their grievances to the King.* Wherefore, I sent it enclosed to the Lords Justices, who were silent as to theirs, yet answered mine, tho' little more than a cover ; in which they said, These were rebels and traitors, and advised me to receive no more letters from them. I readily submitted, nor do I know to this hour how that letter came to my hands.—(*Id.*, p. 24. *See* Appendix, p. 290.)

The petitioning lords had made themselves " rebels and traitors " by yielding to the contributions exacted by the northern army.

All this while parties were sent by the Lords Justices and Council from Dublin and most garrisons throughout the Kingdom *to kill and destroy the rebells ;* but the officers and soldiers took little or no care to distinguish between rebels and subjects, but *killed* in many cases *promiscuously men, women and children.* Which proceeding not only *exasperated the rebels, and induced them to commit the like cruelties upon the English,* but frightened the nobility and gentry about, who, seeing *the harmless country people, without respect to age or sex, thus barbarously murdered, and themselves openly threatened* as favourers of the rebellion, for paying the contribution they could not possibly refuse, resolved to stand upon their guard.

It is well, at intervals, to pause, and try to remember that this is the testimony of one of the witnesses called to support " the faithful relation of Sir John Temple." If the Catholic Lords of the Pale were not goaded to rebellion, no people were ever forced by rulers to act on their own defence.

Nevertheless before they would attempt anything against the Government *they sought several ways to get their petition conveyed to the King*, and at length prevailed with Sir John Read, a Scotchman, and one of his Majesty's servants (then going to England) to under- take it ; who, coming to the Marquis of Ormond upon his march towards Drogheda, was (on what suspicion I know not) by him sent to the Lords Justices and, not concealing what he carried, by them imprisoned, and soon after *put to the rack !*

S

Castlehaven had too much faith in Ormond to suspect him capable of any treachery to the King, or of any coquetting at this time with the Parliament faction. Yet, the many-sided sphinx scruples not to send, under guard, the King's servant to the two bitterest enemies the King had in Ireland ; and *they* show what they mean, by *racking* the King's domestic in the hope of extracting something which may implicate his Majesty in this new Popish rebellion. Lord Anglesey, commenting on the foregoing passage, can tell the reason why Sir John Read was sent by Ormond to " the State " :

> Concerning Sir John Read's treatment . . . though I will by no means allow of racking any man, as being contrary to the law of England, yet I must observe *it was a very jealous time* . . . and Sir John Read, being one of the King's servants, and a *designing Papist*, being there so unseasonably, without being able to give a good account of himself . . . might make them exceed the strict bounds of law in his examination.

A jealous time surely, when the men who were (or ought to be) themselves the King's servants, would, without any legal sanction, and without the knowledge of their royal master, assume the right to torture another servant of the King, with the object of discrediting the King ! And all because the suspected servant was a Papist ! The circumstances that the Papist was trusted by the King, and was not over-ready to gratify the curious, constituted proof sufficient to convict him of wicked designs ! Nor was Read the only Papist gentleman put to the rack in that " jealous time."

> Much about this time [Castlehaven continues] was the like done to Patrick Barnewall of Kilbrew, a man of 66 years of age, but upon what account I cannot tell ; only I have been told his crime was, that he ' came in ' upon the Lords Justices' proclamation of pardon to those of the Pale that would in ten days submit themselves ; and was so wise as not to consider that *freeholders* (as being more criminal than the rest, because of their estates) *were by the Lords Justices expressly exempt out of that proclamation.* As to Read, several questions were put to him ; and, among the rest, he was much pressed to tell how far the late King and Queen were privy to, or concerned in, the Irish rebellion. This is notoriously known, but I have it more particularly from my brother Colonel Mervin Touchet, who heard it from Sir John Read himself as he was brought out of the room where he was racked.
> This did not a little inflame the reckoning ; and it was a great addition to their discontent, that the King referred the whole business of Ireland (whereby, they thought he deserted the protection of his people) to the Parliament of England ; who thereupon passed such wild votes and ordinances as tended to the utter extirpation of the natives of that Kingdom ; not only declaring, on

Dec. 8, 1641, that *they would never give consent to any toleration of the Popish religion in Ireland*, or in any other his Majesty's dominions ; but enacting further, in February following, that 2,500,000 acres of profitable land *in Ireland*, besides bogs, woods, and barren mountains, should be assigned for small proportions of money (which was afterwards employed to raise armies against the King in England to reduce the rebels in that Kingdom.—(*Id.*, pp. 25-6.)

Froude, with his usual contempt of fact, says* : "*On the recovery* of the country the estates of the insurgent Irish gentry were confiscated by the Long Parliament, and were sold to pay the cost of the re-conquest." A very large proportion of the best land was sold *in advance*—more than ten years prior to " the recovery "—and the proceeds, for the most part, used against the King in England. How the Irish gentry became insurgent is no mystery. Far less atrocity of administration would have made rebellion inevitable in any State. And the confiscation, in the very beginning, of their best lands, made settlement impossible ; for, in that event, how were the Adventurers' bonds to be met ? Was ever rebellion more clearly and certainly provoked for the sake of the confiscation ?

But the greatest discontent of all was about the Lords Justices proroguing the Parliament (the only way the nation had to express their loyalty, and prevent their being misrepresented to their Sovereign, which, had it been permitted to sit for any reasonable time, would, in all likelihood, without any great charge or trouble, have brought the rebels to justice. For the war that afterwards ensued was headed and carried on principally by members that then sat in Parliament.

Yet Castlehaven-Audley stood aloof from his brethren of the Pale. He sought employment from the Government, and was contemptuously told to " go home and make fair weather." For reasons not hard to guess, he was refused leave to pass into England—doubtless to have a chat with the King. He went to Maddingstown, his seat in County Kildare, where his brother, Colonel Mervin Touchet, had already afforded shelter and protection to the refugee English of the district.

The contagion spread itself over the whole kingdom ; and now there's no more looking back, for all were in arms and full of indignation : there was fighting almost in every corner, and unfortunately for me, one encounter happened in the sight of my house at Maddingstown between the Marquis of Ormond, commanding the English, and the Lord Viscount Mountgarret, commanding the Irish forces, where the latter were defeated. This encounter goes by the name of the battle of Kilrush, fought the 15th of April, 1642.—(*Id.*, p. 27.)

* Preface to Miss Hickson's *Ireland in the 17th Century* (1884).

The English forces had the advantage in respect of discipline and equipment. It is not likely that the "Ould rebel" Mountgarret was altogether earnest in opposing his accomplished and captivating kinsman Ormond, who was not a whit more royalist at heart than he, the rebel leader, himself was.

The "rebellion" is now almost six months in progress, and Castlehaven-Audley still stands aloof, or looks towards "the State." But the time has come when he must, at any rate, accept the fate and fortunes of the rebel :

> After this defeat, my lord of Ormond being to pass with his army just by my gate, some of his officers of my acquaintance came gallop-ing before, assuring me his lordship would be with me in half an hour. Hereupon I bestirred myself, and having two or three cooks, a good barn-door and plenty of wines (besides my own family I had with me the Duchess of Buckingham, the Marquess of Antrim, her husband, and the Lady Rose, Mr. Daniel's sister) we patched up a dinner ready to be set upon the table at my lord's coming in ; but some that came with him turned this another way, magnifying the entertainment beyond what it was, and published through the army that it was a mighty feast prepared for my Lord Mountgarrett and the rebels. This, through the English army, passed for current, and I believe did me no small prejudice with the Lords Justices.

It did not require even so much to prejudice him in the same quarter. Much, indeed, has been made of his having then as guests the Marquis of Antrim and his wife, Katherine the widow of Villiers, duke of Buchingham ; and on that circumstance alone it was easy, in that "jealous time," when Catholic landowners were being indicted by the thousand,* to found a charge of complicity in rebellion. As Anglesey reminded our author, his guests were "*both* Papists, and afterwards deeply engaged in the rebellion"; that is, they took part in thwarting the designs of the party of which Anglesey himself was then a prominent member.

Without, as it appears, any intimation of what was coming upon him, Castlehaven was indicted, and then, on going to Dublin, was committed to the house of Mr.

---

* ' I am the more inclined to suspect *there was a good deal of corruption and iniquity in the method of gaining indictments*, because I find a very remarkable memorandum made by the Marquis of Ormonde, in his own handwriting, of a passage in the Council, on April 23rd, 1643. There was then a letter read at the Board from a person who claimed a great merit to himself in *getting some hundreds of gentlemen indicted*, and the rather for that he laid out sums of money to procure witnesses to give evidence to a jury for the finding those indictments. This was an intimate friend of Sir William Parsons, and might very well know that such methods would be approved by him.'—Carte, *Life of Ormonde*, i., 423, folio. It is worth while to read this in connection with what Mr. Peter Hill of Downpatrick says of his ' acceptable services ' in secur-ing the indictment of every Catholic landowner in the County Down (p. 133).

Woodcock, one of the sheriffs of Dublin. After being so detained for twenty weeks he was to be removed to the Castle. He says :

This startled me a little, and brought into my thoughts the proceedings against the Earl of Strafford. . . . I heard nothing almost whilst I was in prison, but rejoicings at the King's misfortunes and the ill-success of his armes, then engaged in actual war with his rebellious subjects *in England*. The Lords Justices and most of the Council were too plainly of the Parliament faction, and the Marquess of Ormond, who I knew most faithful to the King, fell desperately sick of a fever, not without some suspicion of poison, and was then given over by his physicians. Hereupon I weighed well my own circumstances, and concluding that innocence was a scurvy plea in an angry time, I resolved to attempt an escape, and save myself in the Irish quarters.

With the help of a common soldier he effected escape. Forthwith the Lords Justices sent out a party of horse in pursuit, and these coming to Maddingstown,*

In the night they invested it, but not finding me (after they possessed themselves of what they could find) *they killed many of my servants, and burnt my house.* This I saw as I passed by and had notice by the way that Castlehaven also was seized by the English, and all I had there pillaged and destroyed.—(*Id.*, p. 35.)

He went to Kilkenny, where the Supreme Council of the Confederate Catholics was just formed.

I was sent for to this Council to tell my story, where I gave them a particular account of all my adventures ; and being asked what I

---

* Castlehaven's account of what followed the 'dinner,' of his going up to Dublin, and of his 'escape' from Dublin, is far from satisfactory, and he leaves himself open to some caustic criticism by the Earl of Anglesey. There is more than one hiatus in the narration. At the very point where he ought to answer for himself he drops out, and leaves to his brother, Colonel Mervin Touchet, the duty of supplying information which could better be supplied by the principal himself. Whatever may be said against the author of the *Aphorismical Discovery*, he is undoubtedly an acute observer, and has had ample means of informing himself of what was going on at the time. There is in his remarks touching Castlehaven's relations with Ormond something which appears to me necessary to fill up the blanks above alluded to ; he says, in the first place, that Castlehaven was carried to Dublin by Ormonde and Coote after the dinner :

' The Earle of Castlehaven, in restraint in Dublin, enformed how the Irish behaved themselves in Kilkenny that his friends beared great sway there, the Butlers, left Dublin, arrived in Kilkenny, presented himself before Viscount Mountgarrett and his son and heir, Edmond Roe Butler. This Edmond was formerly married to a sister of the extant Castlehaven. By those Butlers it was publickly given out that he made an escape from Dublin. . . . We have had from very authentic hands that the aforesaid *Castlehaven was sent by Ormond* from Dublin, a verrie fit instrument to draw and worke private understanding between Ormond and his kindred and friends abroad. This I conceive to be more true as his actions will in the sequell of this storie give large testimonies.'—*Aph. Disc.*, ch. ix. (70).

intended to do, I answered, To get into France, and from thence to England. Hereupon they told me their condition and what they were doing for their preservation and natural defence, seeing no distinction made, or safety but in arms ; persuading them, as I was believed in the country, and had three sisters married amongst them; was persecuted on the same score they were, and ruined so that we had no more to lose but our lives. I took two or three days to think of this proposition, and to examine the model of government they had prepared against the meeting of the general assembly, and most particularly their oath of association.

(He sets out the terms on pp. 36-8.)

Having spent some time in these thoughts and at last taken my resolution, I returned to the Supreme Council, thanked them for their good opinion of me, and engaged myself to run a partner with them. *Whether anger and revenge did not incline me to it as much as anything else, I cannot certainly resolve.* This I well remember, that I considered how I had been used, and seen my house burning as I passed by ; besides that I was a light man with no charge, and without any hopes of redress from the King, who was then engaged in the intestine war. Now being thus a Confederate, and having taken the oath of association, they made me one of the Council and general of the horse under Preston.

These proceedings are well summed up by Mr. W. C. Taylor,* but much as I admire his treatment generally, I cannot entirely accept the following :

Though disappointed by Clanrickarde, *the Confederates obtained a valuable assistant* in Lord Castlehaven, whom the Lords Justices had forced into their ranks.

If Parsons and Borlase had granted Lord Castlehaven the Commission he so yearned for, they would not, I am sure, have inflicted more real misfortune on the cause of the Confederate Catholics than, however unwittingly, they were the means of bringing on it when they forced the baffled suitor to find refuge in Kilkenny. It would have been a great deal better for the Catholic cause if the Catholic peer had been encouraged to proceed on his way to France, with the object of joining the King in England. For even as a " rebel " leader he was but a courtier out of place.† His heart never was, never could be, in a movement which he regarded as beneath him and unworthy of " his nobility." The late Mr. J. F. Taylor,‡ in saying the " poor babbling

* *Civil Wars in Ireland,* i. 288 (Edinburgh : Constable, 2 vols., 1831).

† In officering their army, the Confederate Catholics were guided too much, or altogether, by heraldic distinctions. It was an unfortunate thing for the cause which they professed to have at heart ; but the weakness of preferring a lord to a man of real capacity was not peculiar to the country or to the age. History will take notice of something of the kind clinging to a ' superior race ' at the dawn of the twentieth century.

‡ In his classical little work, *Owen Roe O'Neill,* p. 176.

narrator " who was placed in command of Owen Roe " had
not sufficient military skill to lead a corporal's guard,"
perhaps does Castlehaven-Audley some injustice ; but not
much. His lordship is careful to point out that up to the time
of the first Cessation no military advantages had been
gained on the side of the Confederates, but what he himself
had gained. But, whatever advantages he had gained, he
nullified all by the dry rot he introduced into the Confederation when he took upon himself to champion the
Ormond intrigue called the Cessation. From Ormond's
standpoint the Cessation was an altogether brilliant achievement : it accomplished what all the force and material
resources at his command would, in all likelihood, have
failed to accomplish ; if it did not at once subject the Irish
Catholics to his control, it went a long way in that direction,
and put an end to anything like effective action in
furtherance of the cause for which they had taken up
arms.* The Nuncio has been much abused—by none
more than by Castlehaven-Audley—as being a fanatical
disturber, and what not. That he showed much lack of
discretion, and of the tact that smoothes the troubled waters,
his admirers, if any, must admit. But in the main he was
right, or the Confederates were all wrong from the beginning.

* Mr. W. C. Taylor, one of the very few writers who have formed anything
like an adequate notion of the intriguing character of Ormond, has the following observations on the Cessation negociations in which Castlehaven acted as
go-between :
'These negociations proved the ruin of the Confederates and the destruction
of the King. *This was principally owing to the conduct of the Earl of Ormond,*
who was far more bitterly opposed to the Catholic lords than to the English
Parliament. His hatred of Popery and his love of wealth were too powerful
for his loyalty, and, in the hope of some favourable circumstance arising, he
craftily protracted the negociations until his insincerity was manifest to all,
and his royal master ruined. Unquestionably, in the situation of affairs at the
time, the wisest plan would have been to assemble a new Parliament ; which
instantly would have superseded the Council at Kilkenny, and to have united
the Royalists and Confederates in one body. The Lords of the Pale eagerly
desired such a consummation ; they knew the secret of their own weakness.
Dissensions had already appeared in the Supreme Council. Some violent
ecclesiastics had insisted on the establishment of the Roman Catholic religion
in all its splendour, and denounced their more moderate brethren as traitors to
the cause of religion. The jealousies between the new and the old Irish had
manifested themselves on more than one occasion, and the Confederates at
once envied and dreaded the power and popularity of O'Neill. Ormond knew
all these circumstances, and hoping at once to crush Popery, and hoping to
reap some share of the future harvest of confiscations, he basely sacrified to
these unworthy motives the happiness of his country and the life of his
sovereign.'—*Civil Wars in Ireland,* i., 291.
Ormond's self-interested motives were well exposed by Lord Anglesey in
reply to *Castlehaven's Memoir.* Castlehaven was not an intriguer ; he was
sincere after a fashion ; but he was such a thing as the intriguer requires to
have at hand.

What, in reality, was the attitude of Castlehaven-Audley and the Ormond family party in the Confederation in and after 1643 ? Simply that Faith, Hope, and Charity were centred in the fair promise of his sacred Majesty, King Charles the First, and that Ormond's placid smile was ample security for the fulfilment. At the mere nod of the wily head of the Butlers, the Palesmen would lay down their arms (while their opponents in the North would agree to nothing of the kind) and supplicate for fair consideration of their claims ! It was self-condemnation as well as self-abasement. And no wonder that those who saw the fatuity of such a course were goaded into some overheated and unseemly display. The Confederates at the beginning professed to follow the example set by the Scots, who, with hostile front, entered the North of England. But the Scots were wise enough in their generation to make sure of what they wanted before they would lay down their arms. It is noteworthy that the people who most loudly proclaim the faithlessness of Charles Stuart are loudest in their denunciation of those who, as opponents of the so-called Cessation, distrusted Charles and his (not unworthy) representative in Ireland.

The poor "babbling narrator" gives a circumstantial account of his election at Kilkenny to the chief command of the force which was to reduce to submission the Scots in Ulster. Of this election Castlehaven says :

Now contrary to Owen O'Neill's expectation, who had designed this generalship for himself, by which he would be generalissimo, I happened to be chosen, which Owen Roe took extremely to heart, as I have reason to believe. However *he carried it fairly*, and came to congratulate and wish me success ; giving withal great assurances of his performance, and readiness to serve me to the utmost of his power.—(*Id.*, p. 54.)

It was indeed a spectacle at which angels might stare amazed—Lord Castlehaven-Audley placed in command of the defender of Arras ! And seldom in the world's history has anything so heroic been recorded as the self-conquest achieved by the brave Owen Roe in so promptly coming forward to offer congratulations and assurance of co-operation to his elected superior officer. Castlehaven devotes seven or eight pages to the account of his idle parade in Ulster. He indulges in some cheap sneers at the want of pluck in the Ulstermen, and accounts for his failure in these characteristic terms :

Thus ended the Ulster expedition, like to be so fatal to the Confederate Catholics of Ireland *through the failing or something else of General Owen Roe O'Neill* (! !) But, after all, the three provinces had no reason to complain of this campaign, for this army they sent kept them from being troubled either with Scots *or Ulster people* that year.*—(*Id.*, p. 61-2.)

Of Benburb, this is all Castlehaven-Audley can afford to say :

General Roe O'Neill *being proud of a late victory he had gained over the Scots in Ulster,* declared also for the Pope's nuncio.—(*Id.*, p. 77.)

On one or two other occasions he goes out of his way to disparage the Ulster forces ; and he has, to all appearance, never heard that Owen Roe's nephew, Hugh Duff O'Neill, and his sixteen hundred Ulstermen, gallantly defended Clonmel against the main force of the Cromwellians commanded by Oliver in person.

Macaulay has assured us that Boswell was one of the smallest men that ever lived. He certainly was no smaller than Lord Castlehaven-Audley, Peer of England and of Ireland !

One or two other traits of the same noble lord may not be overlooked even in so hurried a sketch.

Castlehaven and Ormond, in the course of a parade through Munster, coming near Cashel, had a bit of alarming intelligence :

As we came near the town, and made some halt, his Excellency received advice, I think from my Lord Dillon, residing at Athlone, that O'Neill was marching against him, with all the force he could make ; whereupon my lord was pleased to call me to him, and telling

---

* In his southern campaigns Castlehaven made some successful moves ; and, in his narrative, the least of these is a brilliant affair compared with Benburb, which is not mentioned by name. In the extract from Borlase (p. 157 and Note) allusion is made to an action on the Munster Blackwater, in which Sir Charles Vavasor suffered ' the most considerable loss' the English had sustained at the hands of the rebels. Of this encounter, Castlehaven (*Memoirs*, p. 47) gives the following account :

"Sir Charles Vavasor, tho' he had taken the Castle, remained still in his camp, till seeing me, on the top of the mountain above him, come to succour mine that were skirmishing, he drew to arms ; but being amongst hedges and ditches, and the Castle between us, I could not come at him, till he marched towards Castle-Lyons ; where in a large plain he drew up his : but I going by the advantage of a great valley, came into the plain unseen, almost as soon as he ; and having ordered three or four squadrons of boys on horseback to possess the ground from whence I came I lost no time in the charge, and quickly defeated his horse, who, to save themselves, broke in on the foot, and put them into disorder : their cannons were useless, being past the Blackwater. This (with God's blessing) and a great shower of rain, gave me the victory with little or no loss. Sir Charles that commanded with several other officers, remained prisoners ; their cannon and baggage taken, and all their foot defeated ; but their horse for the most part escaped. This happened on Sunday, 4th of June, 1643."

me his intelligence, asked what was best to be done! I gave it
quickly, that he should immediately march back the shortest way,
and endeavour to gain Leighlinbridge. This he did accordingly . . .
Having gained this point, *we lost no time in our march to Dublin*,
where coming near, I think the whole people of the city came forth to
meet his Excellency, with as much joy as ever man was received,
having for several days judged *him and his party lost*. As we came
into the suburbs *his Excellency honoured me* with the carrying of the
sword before him through the city, for which I can give no other
reason (besides his own goodness), but that I had always been a
promoter of the peace and the only man of the Confederate Catholics
that came with him, and never left him in these, his adventures.—
(*Id.*, pp. 79-80.)

Precisely! His Excellency—Ormond was then Lord
Lieutenant—knew his man ; knew him to be a serviceable
tool ; and knew that the leading part in a court pageant
best suited the genius of Lord Castlehaven-Audley.

Pageantry will not deter the approach of the soldier.
And there were two brave commanders now approaching
Dublin—both O'Neill and Preston. His Excellency once
more seeks counsel, and the counsel is not withheld.
Castlehaven advises to lay waste the country within eight
miles of Dublin. The upshot is that the city so isolated is
threatened with famine. His Excellency must treat either
with the Irish rebels, or with the Puritan rebels who had
blocked up the harbour. With the approval of the great Confederate Catholic, Lord Castlehaven-Audley, his Excellency
chooses to surrender the city and sword of State to the
King's mortal enemies.

Now all being agreed for the delivery of the places under the
Marquess's command to the Parliament Commissioners, of which
Mr. Annesley (since made earl of Annesley)* was chief ; I took
my leave of his Excellency, resolving to go to France, though *with
much grief of heart to leave this noble lord*, who had showed
so much loyalty, justice, and steadiness in his proceedings during
these transactions, even from the meeting in Suganstown to the
conclusion of the peace made with the Confederates ; and now, again

---

* *Sic.*, perhaps a misprint for Anglesey (edition of 1753). Arthur, 1st Earl
of Anglesey and 2nd Viscount Valentia, who was enrolled among the Peers fo
England, 20 April, 1661, as *Baron Annesley of Newport Pagnell* and *Earl of
Anglesey*. This nobleman was treasurer of the Navy in 1667 and lord privy
seal in 1673 ; *suc.* his father in 1660. (His father, Sir Francis Annesley,
was the second person upon whom the dignity of baronet was conferred,
7 Aug., 1620, in the following year he received reversionary grant of the Irish
Viscounty of Valentia but was in the meantime created *Baron Mountnorris,
Co. Armagh*, 8 Feb., 1628. Under the title of Lord Mountnorris he was
(1635) one of the victims of Strafford's all-round tyranny. The present Earl
of Annesley is the descendant of Francis, the fourth son of Sir Francis Annesley
aforesaid ; *b.* 23 Jan., 1628 ; *m.* 29 Dec., 1662, Deborah, dau. of Bp.
Henry Jones of Meath.—Burke's *Peerage*.

to the giving up of his Government to the Parliament, *for which I doubt not he shall remain in story, as he deserves, a fixt star, by whose light others may walk in his steps.—(Id.,* p. 78.)

Even Borlase admits that the surrender of Dublin to the Puritans was an unspeakable calamity to the King's cause, but he will have it that the Catholic Confederates were to blame, although only one of them had any hand in the business. The fiction is that the King himself was an assenting party, whereas at the time his assent or dissent meant so many idle words. The allegation that it was safer to trust the English than the Irish rebels is well met by the course of subsequent events. Michael Jones, the new governor of Dublin, told another story at Dungan's Hill and Rathmines, two of the bloodiest and most disastrous encounters of the civil war—the latter particularly, for which Ormond himself was responsible, being as ignominious a smash as ever befel any commander—and from the hand of the very man to whom he had given up the capital of Ireland. Ormond has been praised by Carlyle, Mr. John Morley, and others, for the tact and patience he evinced in bringing under the royal standard so many conflicting parties, when the Puritans had come to be triumphant. These writers choose to overlook the part Ormond had taken from 1643 in creating disunion and animosity among the Irish Catholics, the very parties who could, *at any time*, have been marshalled against the King's real enemies ; and the time when that could have been done with best effect—the time when, at all events, the attempt ought to have been made—was before he began to treat with the Parliament. But as Anglesey points out in his reply to Castlehaven, Ormond was working out another problem in which the King's interest had no place.

In a postscript to his memoir Castlehaven complains of

Having been extremely ill treated in a long letter from the Earl of Anglesey, then lord privy seal . . . but my good fortune was that his lordship, by an unnecessary digression, fell foul on the Duke of Ormond and others, for which being questioned, his lordship suffered in a high degree.

This Lord Anglesey is the Mr. Annesley already mentioned as chief of the Parliament commissioners for the taking over of Dublin in 1647. It was, as it appears, at his instance that Castlehaven wrote the Memoirs ; and there is room to suspect that so trenchant a penman as Anglesey was, merely wanted such opportunity to put the royalist-rebel to the torture. And unutterable must have been the bitterness of the poor man's soul when the triumphant

Parliamentary Commissioner, now Lord Privy Seal of Ireland under Charles II., upbraided him with rebellion, and mockingly advised him to get to his knees before his sovereign and implore pardon and protection ! And Castlehaven did actually sue for a royal pardon, and obtained it.

Of nothing in which he took part was Castlehaven vainer than of the Cessations. This is what Anglesey has to tell him on the subject :

Both [peaces of '46 and '48] were of advantage only to the Irish, and highly dishonourable to the Crown of England, and destructive to the English and Protestants.

Castlehaven says " The general assembly of 24 October, 1642, differed nothing from a parliament but that the Lords and Commons sat together." Anglesey replies ·

That assembly differed also from a parliament in this, that it was called by a *packed party of bloody papists* in rebellion and confederacy, and had neither legal nor regal sanction.

Poor Castlehaven, ever bent on disparaging the old natives, left himself open to a thrust, which was sent home with effect :

So improbable was what your lordship asserts ' that if a letter came to them written in Irish it would be wondered at, and hardly could one be found to read it,' unless you would confess that those skilled in reading the Irish language are extinct, for the meerest Irish of that kingdom and all the Popish clergy, who (if any) are likeliest to be skilled in it, were engaged in that rebellion, and constant promoters of it.

These passages are characteristic of the Lord Privy Seal's caustic style, but unluckily for himself, he introduced the *real* Ormond *:

---

* Plowden says :—' The Marquis of Ormond was a man of personal intrepidity, some military knowledge, and very extensive ambition ; imperious, haughty, vindictive, and impatient of control ; he was so implacable to the Catholics that, in his hatred to them, he not only contravened the commands and wishes of his royal master, but basely descended to execute the sanguinary orders of his determined enemies.'—*Historical Review of the State of Ireland* (1803), i., 142.

Carlyle's estimate is far from correct : ' The Marquis of Ormond, a man of distinguished integrity, patience, activity, and talent, had done his utmost *for the King* in Ireland as long as there remained any shadow of hope there.'— *Letters and Speeches of O. C.*, i., 237.

Mr. John Morley appears also to miss a point or two in forming his opinion. ' Ormonde represented in varied forms the English interest, one of the most admirably steadfast, patient, clear-sighted, and honourable names in the list of British statesmen.'—*O. C.*, p. 283.

It is apparent that now by the forfeiture and punishment of the Irish *his lordship* (Ormond) *and family are the greatest gainers in the Kingdom* and have added to their inheritance vast scopes of land and *a revenue three times greater than what his paternal estate was before the rebellion,* and most of his increase is out of their estates who adhered to the peaces ['46 and '48] or served under his Majesty's enemies abroad ; which shows that, whatsoever of compassion or natural affection, or otherwise might incline him to make those peaces, he is, in judgment and conscience, against them, and *so hath since appeared,* and hath advantage by their laying aside. The like may be said of the Duke of York, the Earl of Arlington, Lord Lanesborough, and others who have great estates of the Irish, freely given them upon the same foundation.

Seldom has such a blurt of reality and plain fact come from a Privy Councillor. No wonder, indeed, that the placid Lord Lieutenant, for once in his life, was furious to find himself so thrust upon the public without visor or disguise, and that he had the Lord Privy Seal removed from office. But if Anglesey allowed his anti-Irish zeal to betray him into indiscreet admissions, it by no means follows that history should ignore his view of what went on behind the scenes, he having every opportunity of forming a correct estimate of the situation.*

There is yet something worthy of even more particular attention, although " historians " are almost unanimous in overlooking it :

* Carte (*Life of Ormonde,* ii., 521) gives a particularly lop-sided and unsatisfactory account of the Anglesey affair in 1682, as if Ormond would not have noticed the matter but that the King was the first to take action regarding it. We are gravely assured that 'it was on account of certain passages' (in the Letter to Castlehaven) 'which the King conceived cast a reflection on the memory of his father' that Anglesey was dismissed.

Mr. W. C. Taylor has some incisive remarks on Ormond's administration which may be cited here : ' The conduct of the Duke of Ormonde . . . has been the theme of unmeasured praise and equally unmeasured censure. Yet is there no point of fact at issue between his advocates and his opponents. If, for the sake of establishing a Protestant interest in Ireland, it was lawful, and even praiseworthy, to commit treachery, fraud, and universal robbery, then may we join in all the eulogiums that have been heaped upon him ; but if the best ends cannot sanctify the worst means, if Mammon and Moloch be unworthy allies to the cause of pure religion—then must we condemn him as one who sacrificed upright principle to questionable policy, and was guilty of atrocious evil to effect a doubtful good. The most instructive commentary on his conduct is the simple fact that, before the Civil War, his estates only yielded him about £7,000 per annum, after the final settlement his annual income was upwards of £80,000, more than ten times the former amount. He felt to the last hour of his life, a lurking consciousness that the part he had acted would not bear a close examination ; and writhed under the attacks made on him in pamphlets by men he had betrayed and undone. One of these named *The Unkind Deserter* is distinguished by its superior ability and deep pathos. . . . Ormonde attempted no reply ; he suppressed the book and threw the printer into prison, but he was afraid to give the matter additional publicity by bringing the question into a Court of Justice.—*Civil Wars in Ireland* (1831), ii., 96-8.

And let this rebellion be compared to all before it, there will not appear, since the English title to Ireland, so just and clear grounds of forfeiture *and extirpating a nation* as have done upon this ; but the King hath mingled mercy with justice, and though by a providence from heaven, the Marquesses of Ormond and Clanrickard, his Majesty's chief governors, *encouraged the Irish to keep up a war against the English,* wherein they were so much hardened to their ruin that they were at length entirely subdued without condition to any save for life, and left to be as miserable as they had made others in all other respects ; yet multitudes of them have been restored. . : The wisdom of God thus punishing one sin of theirs with another till they are scarce a people ; and the English and Protestant interest never more flourishing in that Kingdom.

Here we have the true key of Ormond's policy. On the " estates " question, Parsons, Borlase, Temple, Annesley, Ormond, and Clanrickarde were all of the same kidney. Castlehaven, no doubt, gives us what he conceives to be a faithful sketch of " his Excellency." None the less, he pourtrays but a stage Ormond. The real James Butler, divested of the showman garb, stands forth in the rude but life-like pencilling of him who was Lord Privy Seal. What floods of denunciation and sarcasm have been poured upon the people who would not agree with Castlehaven-Audley in putting unbounded trust in the fascinating Ormond-Ossory ! The Irish were, forsooth ! prejudiced against him because he was a Protestant. And it is meet that they who adopt this hypothesis should be angry with the same people for thinking no better of the Catholic Clanrickard. The real reason of their unpopularity is to be found in the last cited passage from Anglesey. But it is fashionable among historians to affect blank ignorance of such a trait in the character of Ormond.

That a creature like Lord Castlehaven-Audley—a creature that would have esteemed it a never-to-be-forgotten honour to be permitted to lick the soles of any semblance of royalty—should thus find himself in rebel ranks, shows the trend of State policy when the rebellion broke out. Dr. Warner considered Carte unjust towards the Irish ministry, but Carte shows sufficient cause for any unfavourable opinion he expresses regarding the men who, nominally the ministers of the King, were, in reality, the ministers of the party in the Long Parliament who were about to make war upon the King. Froude would have us to infer that these Irish ministers of State could not have any hand in fomenting or extending the rebellion in Ireland : they were men of little influence ; they were unpopular ; and their letters to London breathe of terror rather than determination. I would say that the reasons are rather in favour of the hypotheses they are intended to disprove. A Wellington or a Canning at the helm of State would never have laid themselves open to the charge of fomenting civil war. Far otherwise was it with the grasping unprincipled adventurer who domineered at the Council-table in Dublin Castle, and ruled them all to his purpose. The ex-soldier Borlase was " the slight unmeritable man " of the co-partnery ; he was content to let Parsons have his way, which was indeed the way they were all inclined to take when there was confiscation in the air. " They were not popular." No more were any other self-seeking servants of the Crown, who have, at any time, goaded the people to revolt. " They had no influence in the country." Unfortunately they had, owing to their position, much influence for evil. That their correspondence tells of anxiety and alarm was due to the slowness with which the English Parliament set about the expected succour. They may have felt for the moment —and good reason they had to feel—that they had themselves moved too rapidly in anticipation of support from England. But men who have extension of territory in the mind's eye are very prone to underrate the cost, when they commit themselves to the project of acquisition.*

There was no period at which the rebellion might not

* In the earlier volumes of *Thorpe Tracts* we find some curious information as to the game then played in Ireland by the Lords Justices and Council : ' That regiment which went from thence under Sir Simon Harcourt hath done much good ; for he and Sir Charles issued out of Dublin with two thousand, and set upon a town called Swords, some eight miles from Dublin, which the enemies had taken and were there encamped, about five thousand of them ; our men set on them and slew three hundred with the loss of three men, and put the rest to flight, and took, as the report is, spoil worth six thousand pound, and set fire of the Town.—(*Good and True News from Ireland in a Letter sent to Mr. Francis Clay of Lumber Street and by him received, January 24*, 1641-2).

' From Dublin, Jan. 1641-2.

' As Swords, Finglas, Santry, and other towns thereabouts were lately burnt, *to take away from the Rebels the benefit of housing and to punish the Inhabitants who concurred with them*, so now Rathcoole and Tasagard are burnt by 200 of our horse sent out for that purpose. (*The Present State of Ireland—London, Printed for Joseph Hunscot,* 1642.)

' (*Feb.* 9, 1641-2. This day Grand Juries are summoned to appear for the Counties of Kildare, Wicklo, Meath, and other places, and I believe the Lords of the Pale, and most of the prime men who are active in the business will be indicted of Treason,'—*Id.*

' (*Feb* 24). Here is nothing but spoil and destruction on both sides, and when there will be an end of it God only knoweth, so many of all sorts in all places are involved in this fatall businesse, which will be the destruction of most of the ancient families of this Kingdom ; many whereof were never toucht with the least touch or blemish of disloyaltie before these uuhappie times. In the County of Kildare we have neer 300 indicted of Treason in the King's Bench, and the Bills found, among whom are most of our prime gentlemen.'—*Id.*

have been brought to a close, almost, or altogether without force, by a government really desirous of promoting peace. It is utter nonsense to allege that the Anglo-Irish were ready to rebel at the first. They were only *too* loyal for the then Government. Nor were the Ulster Irish in any degree hostile to the King. There were some wild expressions, not a little improved on in the reporting ; but they had not the significance attached to them by the King's undoubted enemies. The general feeling was one of indifference rather than of hostility to the English connection. The Ulster rebels of 1641 did not take up the same attitude as the Ulster rebels of 1798. The men of Forty-one are represented as aiming at nothing less than the utter extirpation of the settlers. And it looked so at the beginning. It is certain, however, that the leaders would gladly have closed, even then, with any reasonable compromise which would have carried assurance of protection in the future from such persecutions as had of late menaced them on account of their religion. Nor would it have been so difficult to satisfy their claims on the land question supposing that they had been met in the spirit of conciliation. But conciliation was then the thing most foreign to " the State " in Ireland. It is hardly going beyond the mark to say that there was not a principle of sound statesmanship which was not insolently trodden under foot by the Lords Justices and Council.

Parsons and Borlase did by their authority command many things which did not only exasperate, but render the Irish desperate, as will appear by several of their own letters and public acts of State ; and that, in the first eruption of the rebellion, *they had a greater eye to the forfeitures of the rebels' estates,* than to use such means as might, by the hopes of pardon, induce the better sort of the nobility, gentry and freeholders to hear reason and to come in and submit themselves to his Majesty's mercy, *though they had express directions* from the King and the two houses so to do : and it is no less notorious that *Sir John Temple in writing his history was bound by confederacy* to assert the proceedings of the Lords Justices.—*Nalson,* ii, 7.

The Lords Justices certainly acted all through as no sane governors would act, unless with an eye to extensive confiscation. Can there be any doubt as to the object of the instructions and orders from " the State " to the Commander of the Forces in Ireland ?

The mode in which these precious governors chose to conduct the war may be best learnt from their instructions to the Earl of Ormond, the Commander in chief of the royal army. He was directed not only ' to kill and destroy rebels and their adherents and relievers,' but also ' to burn, waste, consume, and demolish all the places, towns, and houses,' where they had been relieved and harboured with all the corn and hay there and also to kill and destroy all the male inhabitants capable of bearing arms. *

And similar orders and instructions to all other commanders. Need we wonder that people, themselves so exposed to massacre, would be goaded into crimes ? It is idle to plead that the Lords Justices were authorized in the King's proclamation to follow such courses. The King's name was used, but the King himself had little to say in the matter. And they could not plead the sanction of the King's name for refusing the submissions of the nobility and gentry. Ormonde was enjoined to make prisoners of any of the Lords of the Pale who might offer to come in, and he was not to receive them into his presence. A likely way to encourage submission, was it ? There is an outward flourish of impartiality in the order to make " no distinction between gentle and simple " ; but it is here only such " impartiality " as Surajah Dowla also was capable of showing.

Neither is it a bit unlikely that the same governors were capable of spreading a flame in which they might have perished themselves. That possible eventuality seldom if ever enters into the calculations of the unscrupulous and avaricious. The passions which blind men to all sense of justice and fair play will also blind the actors to a sense of their own peril. Rebellion-promoting in Ireland had long been almost a branch of State-craft ; it certainly had, for centuries, been looked upon, by needy adventurers, as a very promising kind of enterprise. And none ever had more inducement to play the old game than Parsons and not a few of his colleagues in the misgovernment of the country.

That the Catholics of Ireland had at least as good a right as the Scots to resort to force is certain enough. Yet is it a delusion to look upon the civil war that ensued as a war between religious sects. It was not because they were Protestants that " the State " followed such courses—not that they were men of religious principle, but men worldly of the worldly. The religion which inspired their policy and prompted their course of action was never preached from the Mount, but is every day preached on 'Change and in the gambling hells.

* W. C. Taylor, *Civil Wars*, i., 281.

T

APPENDIX TO X.

LORD CASTLEHAVEN, "THE UNITED LORDS," AND THE LORDS JUSTICES.

THE triangular correspondence to which Lord Castlehaven makes rather brief allusion (*Memoirs*, p. 24; cited on p. 273 of this work) I consider well worth reproducing in full, as setting forth more forcibly than in the *Memoirs* the attitude of all parties concerned. Certified copies of the letters are contained in the T.C.D. MS. F. 3.11 ("Depositions and Letters," vol. xxxii.) in which this set of papers is headed " No, 14."

(1)

Endorsed : "*Coppy*, 16 March 1641-[2] : L^re from Vnited Lo^s to ye EARLE OF CASTLEHAVEN. * "

" Right Honble our very good Lo.

" Vnderstanding of a Proclàmacõn (wch Wee never could come to the sight of) sett forth by his Maj^tie cõmanding vs to lay downe our Armes. *In obedience thereunto Wee performed accordingly*, and thereupon imployed Lt Coll. Read vnto the Lords Justices, that Cessation of Armes might be of all sides vntill Wee were informed uppon what grounds and conditions, Wee should be received; *Since wch time, the Army came forth from Dublin, pillaged and burned both our owne howses and our Tenants'*, not having once received answere. Wherefore our humble request vnto your Lo^p is (soe it may bee without inconvenience to yor Person) that you will be pleased to moove vnto the State in the behalfe of us the Vnited Lords, to bee licensed to meete by a certain time to bee in some convenient place, where Wee may drawe upp our grievances to bee presented to his Maj^tie, and in the meantime a Cessation of Armes to bee continued, and noe hostile act perpetrated ; wch by theis presents Wee fully authorize yor Lo^p to doe, and doe undertake that the Vnited Lords will approove the same ; for wch favour you will oblige us to bee

" Yo^r Lo^ps most humble servants
" GORMANSTOWN, SLANE,
" NETTERVILLE."

Ex. p^r MA. BARRY

(2)

From Lord CASTLEHAVEN to the LORDS JUSTICES.

Endorsed : " Coppy. 22 Mar., 1641—L^re from the Earle of Castle-haven to the L^ds Justices."

" May it please yor Lpps

" More than ten dayes sithence, I sent an expresse with a Letter, by the wch I would have desired from yor Lpps, a pass for my goeing into England, but that Letter being intercepted by some

---

* This letter is in Carte i., 297-8. Nos. 1, 2, 3 are printed at the end of the first volume of Gilbert's *History of the Irish Confederation*. But as printed now, all are taken direct from the certified MS. copies in T.C.D.

of the Irish Army, I resolved to send my brother, who should present my requests by word of mouth. His journey I thought fitt to quicken, haveing just now receaved a Letter from the Vnited Lords [as they stile themselves], wch I have, according to my duty, sent yor Lpps. A present Answere I perceive they expect, w^ch, if yor Lpps will, shall bee returned by mee. I beseech you give mee particular Instrucõns, wch I shall punctually observe, as in beeing ready to bee commanded, as yor Lpps real

"humble servant

" Madingstown,   " CASTLEHAVEN AUDLEY."
    the 22 of March, 1641."

" For the right hon^ble the
   . . . Parsons and ye Lo: Bourlacy,   *Ex p^r* MA. BARRY.
   Lords Justices of Ireland."

Lord Castlehaven-Audley could not have counted on such a reception as awaited this letter at the Castle of Dublin, or he would scarcely have undertaken the duty of intermediary between the ' Vnited Lords ' and the then chief governors of Ireland. That his own request for " licence " to proceed to England should be refused he, perhaps, understood ; but it is not so likely that one of his courtly views could, for the time, realise the attitude of the King's representatives towards the old nobility of the Pale. That Castlehaven's correspondents sincerely sought reconciliation is clear enough from their application ; and it is no less clear that Castlehaven, in acting on their request, believed he was discharging his duty as a Christian and as a subject. That the Lord Justices and Council were determined there should be no reconciliation for the " Vnited Lords," and that they were bent on picking a quarrel with Castlehaven himself, could not be made clearer than in the terms of their reply :

(3)

From the LORDS JUSTICES and COUNCELL to the Earl of
CASTLEHAVEN.

" After our very harty com̃endacons to your Lpp. your L^tres of the 22th and the other L^tres therewith sent, directed to yor Lpp., came to the hands of us the Lord Justices, on the 23 of this month, wch Wee communicated with the Councell, and have joyntly thought fitt to returne you this answere :
" ffirst, for those who, it seems, ten dayes since intercepted your former L^tres to us although yor Lpp, in yor L^tres due, stile them the Irish Army, yett Wee may not forbeare to minde yor Lpp that they might more justly bee called (as indeed they have declared themselves) Rebells.
" Secondly, Wee judge it not fitt in theis times, as now affaires stand heere, to License yor Lpp to repaire into England ; and, therefore, we pray *and Require* yor Lpp not to depart this kingdom without our speciall Licence.
" Thirdly, Wee hould it strange that yor Lpp should receave the other L^res directed to you which you sent to us togeather with

yor owne L^{res} *without causeing the person presumeing to bring you those to be apprehended and brought before us,* in regard that the persons from whom these letters came are rebells and traytors against his Matie, and their bould assumptions, as in all things els, soe even in these L^{tres}, doe declare theire Actions to bee still continued Disloayllty and Rebellion.

"Lastly, Wee observe by yor Lpps L^{res} that those persons expect to receave a present Answere, which as it is not mençoned in theire L^{res} to you, Soe wee cannot imagine how yor Lpp should know theire minds in that particular, vnlesse you had (it) from their Messenger, that brought theire L^{tres}, *who if he stayed to declare that to yor Lpp might well have beene Laid hould on* when hee Delivered you that Message.

"Considering the Condiçon wherein these persons stand it will benefitt for yor Lpp to beeware that you hould not any correspondence with them, or joine in theire Councells or Actions, least thereby inconvenience arise to you.   And so wee bid yor Lpp vere hartily farewell.

" From his Maj^{ties} Castle of Dublin, 24 Martch, 1641,

" Your Lpps very loveing friends,

" To our very good Lord,   " Wm PARSONS, JO: BORLASE,
the Earle of Castlehaven."   " ORMOND-OSSORY, R. DILLON,

                      "CHAS. LAMBERT, AD. LOFTUS, J. TEMPLE,

" Del^{vr} to Mr. Tutchett   " CHA: COOTE, FFR. WILLOUGHBY,
     25 Martch, 1642,"   " S. HARCOURT, R. MEREDITH."

   " *Ex. p^r* MA. BARRY."

And among them his Lordship's "loving friend" Ormond Ossory! Could anything in words be better framed to goad the recipient into some course which might be construed into disloyalty and rebellion? Yet Castlehaven, as he says, readily submitted ; although he joins this with the somewhat puzzling statement, " Nor do I know to this hour how that letter came to my hands." If he means the letter from the Lords Justices and Council, he ought to have received that by the hands of his brother, Colonel Mervin Touchet.

The most remarkable thing in the Lord Justices' letter is, perhaps, the reprimand to Castlehaven for neglecting to apprehend the United Lords' messenger, and send him to the Castle, so that the far-seeing people there might put him to the question—on the rack.   Something might have been got from the man in that way ; and in any case, it would have been an impressive lesson to him and others to carry no more messages from " those persons."

How those " Rebells and Traytors," the United Lords, were disposed towards his Majesty, may be easily gathered from the communication which so roused the ire of the distinguished persons then making such extraordinary use of the King's name.   Yet I must not overlook two other letters which show, if possible, still more clearly how earnest the Lords and Gentry of the Pale yearned for reconciliation, even after they had taken up arms, and how little they were to blame in the first instance for standing on their own defence.

(4)

"May it please yor Lo^{ps},

"Wee received this day a letter wherein yor Lo^{ps} desire to knowe the cause of this our Assembly, and in obedience to yor com̃ands Wee humbly certifie that Wee were thereunto constrained for ye safetie of o^r lives, wch Wee conceeved to bee in noe small danger, beeing all of us forced to forsake o^r howses on Tuesday at night last, by ye riseing out of such troopes of horse and foote as did on ye said night most cruelly murder fowre Catholicks, for noe other reason (as Wee are credibly informed) than bearing the names of that religion; an act wee conceive noe way justifiable, and of itselfe apt to strike feare and terror into all of that profession, a treaty being then entertained by the army, beneath wch Wee expected might have produced a happy conclusion; during wch treatie, Wee conceive noe act of that nature nor any such cause of distraction ought to have been given, Wee being before dayly putt into many feares by certain intelligence given of unexpected attempts against our lives, Wee therefore thought fitt to signifie this much vnto yor Lo^{ps}, desireing ardently to bee some certaine way assured of yor Lo^{ps} of ye safetie of o^r lives before wee runn the hazard thereof wch is the only motive that hinders vs from manifesting ye obedience Wee acknowledge to bee due unto yor Lo^{ps} com̃ands. The 10th of December, 1641.

" LUKE NETTERVILL, THO. RUSSELL,

CHRISTOPHER RUSSELL.

" To the right hon^{ble}   " GEORGE BLACKNEY, PATRICK CADDELL.
  the Lo^s Justices and   " GEORGE KING, WILLM. TRAVERS.
  Councell."   " JOHN TALBOTT, RICHARD BARNEWALL.

" RICHARD GOULDING, LAURENCE BEALLINGS

" *Concordat cum originali. Ex p^r*

MA. BARRY."

(5)

To the *Council Board* from the LORDS of the PALE.

" Right Honble o^r very good Lords,

"There came vnto ye L Viscount Gormanstownes hands some Proclamaçons sent by Fa. Cahell, ye 15 of this present, wherein yor Lo^{ps} doe take notice of ye distrust Wee have of o^r safeties, grounded upon some words mençoñed in o^r former Letters w^{ch}, wee were informed, Sr Charles Coote should have spoken att Councell Board; of wch yor Lo^{ps} doe, by y^t Proclamaçon free ye said Sr Charles, and did further require us to appeare, the 17th of this month, adding assurance of o^r safetie, the ingadgments of the publique faith, Whereunto wee would humbly ere this have made answere had ye remotenes of o^r habitaçons permitted a sooner meeting. There came likewise to o^r hands a Proclamaçon sum̃on-ing of Mr Luke Nettervill, Mr King of Clontarf, and others, to

appear before yor Lo^{ps}, ye 18 of this present, wth ye like caution
for theire safetie, And although Wee sincerely beleeve
yor Lo^{ps} heard not ye said Sr Charles speake any such words, Wee
humbly beseech yor Lo^{ps} likewise to believe, Wee never entertained
a thought to the dishonour of ye authority wherewith yor Lo^{ps} are
intrusted : Yett the bitter effects y^t followed are a cleere proofe
of Sr Charles his intentions against ye proffessors of o^r Religion and
a further motive to confirm vs in ye Assurance y^t such words
Issued from him, wch Wee are now confident yor Lo^{ps} did not heare.
"Wee beheld wth no small affright ye Inhumane Acts perpetrated
uppon ye Inhabitants of the County Wicklow . . . (*A line
clipped at foot of page*) . . . whereof dependants of
yor Lo^{ps}. *The late massacre of Santry, and also Mr King's house
and whole substance burnt by Sr Charles Coote, the 15th of this
present,* though by ye Proclamacõn, wth ye like assurance given
us of his safetie to appeare ye 18th. This Wee beleeve an Act
independant of yor comãnds, and therefore doe humbly pray
yor hon^{rs} would bee pleased to take into serious consideration how
just grounds Wee have to feare ye power of him who Comãnds
ye City wherein Wee were to appeare, Since he presumes to venture in
yor eyes on such hostile Acts against a Gent, (who for aught
Wee know) hath obeied yor comãnds. This, my Lords, makes us
unwilling to lay our Lives att his mercie who preferres ye execucõn
of his owne designs before ye publique faith ; wherein Wee are
confident he hath not attended yor Lo^{ps} directions.* Wee, therefore, humbly crave at yor Lo^{ps} hands y^t noe sinister constructions
may bee made of our stay, beeing ready to attend such Com^{rs} as
yor Lo^{ps} shall appoint, at such time as yor Lo^{ps} shall prefix: And at
such place and in convenient distance from ye comãnds and power
of ye said Sr Charles, as yor hon^{rs} will please to direct; whereby
Wee may stand assured, nott to bee made by him further examples
of ye breach of yor Lo^{ps} words. And Wee humbly pray
y^t ye Com^{rs} to bee named bee such of ye Lords of the Councell as are
best estated, and interested in ye Comõn Wealth of this Kingdom,
wth whome, when wee shall meete, Wee shall be ready to contribute
the uttermost of our endeavours, and the best of our Advices, for
the Advancem^t of his Maj^{ties} Service and the Comõn peace of this
Kingdome; And doe beseech yor Lo^{ps} to stand assured, y^t o^r Lives
and Estates are not so deare vnto vs as o^r Loyaltie and faith to
his Maj^{tie}. The least breach whereof was never harboured in
o^r thoughts, Thus humbly takeing leave, Wee rest,

" Yo^r Lo^{ps} to be comãnded

" FINGALL, GORMANSTOWN,
" From Taragh,   " SLANE, TRIMLESTOWNE,
     22 December,   " DUNSANY, OLIVER LOWTH,
     1641."   " NETTERVILL."

" Directed to the Lo^s Justices
     and Councell in a Cover."

" *Concordat cum originali—Ex p^r* MA. BARRY."[1]

* This confidence may have been misplaced.

That the Lords of the Pale, even after they had stood on their defence, wished to be reconciled to the Government, is clear from the foregoing correspondence. That the Lords Justices and Council would have no reconciliation, aspiring to the general confiscation of all the lands held by the Catholics ("Rebels," of course) is proved to demonstration under their own hands :

In a letter of March 19, 1642, the Lords Justices signify to the Lord Lieutenant (Leicester) that "some gentlemen " had rendered themselves to the King's justice ; that " many others had desired protections, and that very many, " even of the best rank, had endeavoured to make sub- " missions ; but they (the Lords Justices) thought it " necessary to observe that the State of England had been " too indulgent to the Irish in former ages since the conquest " of the Kingdom, and had too easily received submissions, " and granted pardon to Rebels, whereas if the Government " of Ireland had been careful to improve the frequent " opportunities offered them by those Rebellions, they " might have made such a full reformation in that Kingdom " as would have prevented the present general destruction " fallen upon the British there ; that none of the former " Rebellions could parallel the present either in the dangerous " original thereof, or in the unexampled cruelty and extreme " hatred to the British Nation showed in the progress thereof, " or in the fearful and terrible consequences finally aimed " at therein, being no less than to wrest out of his Majesty's " hands his Royal Sceptre and Sovereignty there, to destroy " and root out all the British and Protestants and every " species of English out of the Kingdom, to suppress for " ever God's truth and true Religion, and instead thereof " to set up the idolatries of the Church of Rome, and finally " to pour in forces into England to disturb that blessed " peace which by the mercy of God that Kingdom then " enjoyed . . . that if after such a series of rapine, " cruelty and bloodshed, to the enriching of themselves and " the ruin and destruction of the British Protestants, the " Rebels could wipe out their crimes by making submissions " they would be emboldened to attempt the like again, to " the continual unsettlement, if not destruction, of the " Kingdom, the English would be discouraged from settling " there, and the few British yet left undestroyed would " remove thence, and so the settlement of religion and " civility there would be prevented ; and the natives con- " tinuing without the mixture of English, would be " unserviceable either to the King or themselves, having no " trades among them, being generally idle, and for the

" most part barbarous ; and upon considering these par-
" ticulars, they hoped, his Majesty would have the glory of
" *perfecting the great work which his Father had begun*, and
" make the like settlement and reformation *all over the
* Kingdom*, as King James had done in Ulster."

Carte, Life of Ormonde, 1., 292.

———————